100 THINGS BATMAN FANS SHOULD KNOW & DO BEFORE THEY DIE

Joseph McCabe

Library of Congress Cataloging-in-Publication Data is available upon request.

This book is available in quantity at special discounts for your group or organization. For further information, contact:

Triumph Books LLC
814 North Franklin Street
Chicago, Illinois 60610
(312) 337-0747
www.triumphbooks.com

Printed in U.S.A.
ISBN: 978-1-62937-398-0
Design by Patricia Frey

For my brothers, Jim and John McCabe,
who love Batman as much as anyone.

For my nephews, Jude, Trystn, Lane,
and Nicolas—Boy Wonders all.

And for anyone who fights injustice.
No matter the scale, no matter the odds.

Contents

Foreword

At some point in his or her life, everyone has wanted to be Batman.

It might be the four-year-old kid with a dishtowel around his neck, bouncing on the sofa. It might be the father stuck in the evening commute, wishing for a Batmobile to blast through traffic. It might be the single person trying to work up the courage to tell the partygoers in the next apartment to keep it down, please. Situation after situation in which the abilities of normal humans fall short in the face of conflict, we all wish we could be as strong, as confident, and, should the need arise, as imposing as Batman. Or the Flash, or Black Canary, or whomever your favorite do-gooder happens to be. But for the sake of this book, it's Batman.

And why Batman? Well, he's the one hero an ordinary person could theoretically become. You don't need to have been rocketed to Earth from a planet of super men, or born with magic powers, or bitten by a radioactive whatever. Given the inspiration and determination, you could study, train, and push yourself to the pinnacles of intelligence and physical perfection. True, the money helps. But only in that it facilitates the training. Okay, yes, and helps fund the car, the cave, the costumes, gadgets, weapons, mansion, and Alfred's 401k.

For those of us without caves, butlers, inheritances, and the same threshold for physical punishment, there is this book, *100 Things Batman Fans Should Know & Do Before They Die*. Within these pages, fledgling Caped Crusaders will learn the secrets of the Dark Knight from Bat Masters past and present. This titanic alliance of actors, artists, writers, and filmmakers pull back the curtain on the world of Batman, providing essential knowledge for midnight avengers ready to strike at crime from the shadows, or fans simply wanting to know everything about their favorite hero.

Read it, live it, and I'll see you in the Batcave.

Paul Dini is a writer and producer best known among Batfans for his work on Batman: The Animated Series *(for which he co-created the popular character Harley Quinn),* The New Batman/Superman Adventures*, and* Batman Beyond*. He also wrote* Batman: Mask of the Phantasm, Batman Beyond: Return of the Joker*, and the* Batman: Arkham *video games, as well as* Dark Night: A True Batman Story *and the Eisner Award–winning* Mad Love.

Introduction

"I'm whatever Gotham needs me to be."

Of all the lines in Christopher Nolan's *The Dark Knight* that resonate, it's that simple statement of purpose in the film's final scene that cuts to the hearts of fans.

For no fictional character—not even Superman—has played as many roles, has served as many needs, has lived as many lives as Gotham City's savior. From the pulp adventurer of the 1930s to the camp crusader of the 1960s to the dour avenger of the 1980s and beyond, Batman has managed to be the hero the world needs and deserves time and time again.

It's not always easy reconciling these disparate incarnations with one another. But at their core, they share one idea that's remained unchanged since the character's first appearance in 1939: that loss, suffering, and loneliness can be conquered, harnessed, and used as a force for positive change in the world. It's a notion that never gets old.

My hope is that this book will offer evidence as to why so many interpretations of the Dark Knight are valid, regardless of the audiences at which they're aimed. And that the book's interviews with film, television, and comic creators will entertain novice Batfans as well as those who hold PhDs in criminology from Gotham University.

For it's the human brain and heart that propel someone from the depths of Crime Alley to the topmost spires of Gotham City.

He's whatever we need him to be, because he's already in each of us.

Introduction

1 Bill Finger and Bob Kane

The Caped Crusader has always stood as a pillar of virtue and justice. But the tale of his creation was long one of hypocrisy and cultural deceit.

Superman's debut in 1938 introduced the superhero genre to comic books, and the Man of Steel's publisher, National Comics Publications (as DC Comics was then known), was all too eager to capitalize on its success—which editor Vin Sullivan mentioned to a budding young cartoonist named Bob Kane. Born in New York City on October 24, 1915 (as Robert Kahn), Kane had worked for Will Eisner, creator of the Spirit, and his partner, Jerry Iger, before opening a studio of his own. A graduate of DeWitt Clinton High School in the Bronx, Kane had recruited fellow alum Milton "Bill" Finger to join his shop.

Born February 8, 1914, in Denver, Colorado, Finger too had grown up in New York, and, like Kane, had fallen in love with comic strips. But where Kane's personality was outgoing and dominant, hell-bent on making the kind of money Superman's creators Jerry Siegel and Joe Shuster were pulling in every week, Finger's was thoughtful and submissive. On paper, he was an employee of Kane's, and wrote Kane's *Rusty and His Pals* (a knockoff of cartoonist Milt Caniff's newspaper strip *Terry and the Pirates*) for no credit. But *Rusty* generated little fanfare, and Bill maintained his day job as a shoe salesman.

When Kane spoke with Sullivan one Friday afternoon to discuss the possibility of a "Bat-Man," he promised he'd be back on Monday with a design for the character. Fond of swiping panels from other artists in his work, Kane's own skills were limited. He drafted a costume, but was unhappy with it. He met Finger that weekend at his apartment and showed him what he'd come up with. His champion's colors were the inverse of Superman's—he was blond and wore a bright red union suit with blue boots and briefs, a yellow belt, a domino mask (taken from Lee Falk's newspaper strip hero the Phantom), and a pair of rigid wings. Kane would later claim the wings were inspired by Leonardo da Vinci's famed ornithopter drawing.

Finger disapproved, and said the Bat-Man's colors should be dark, like that of his namesake. Moreover, his face should be covered by a cowl, from which should extend bat-like ears. And instead of the stiff wings, he should wear a cape, scalloped, so it resembled wings when he soared through the air—which he would do on a rope, requiring gloves.

Kane revised his design per Finger's descriptions, took it to National the following Monday, and the Bat-Man was born. Taking his cue from Johnston McCulley's pulp superstar the Shadow (one story of whose Finger would swipe for Bat-Man's first adventure), Finger made his urban crimefighter's secret identity that of a wealthy playboy, Bruce Wayne—whom the writer named after Scottish king Robert the Bruce and American Revolutionary War general "Mad" Anthony Wayne.

March 1939 saw the Bat-Man swing to life on the cover of *Detective Comics* #27. Dated May 1939, the cover (which historian Arlen Schumer discovered was a swiped image from Alex Raymond's *Flash Gordon* strip) referred to him as "The Batman." His first story, "The Case of the Chemical Syndicate"—written by an uncredited Finger with art by Kane—also introduced Wayne's close friend Commissioner Gordon, another creation of the writer. Six months later, in *Detective Comics* #31, Finger gave his hero an origin: he was once a small boy whose parents were shot to death by a mugger trying to snatch his mother's pearl necklace.

The following year, Finger gave a name to Batman's city—Gotham—and conceived of the Batmobile, Hugo Strange, Wayne Manor, Robin, Clayface, Catwoman, the Joker, and a nickname for his hero, "The Dark Knight." In 1941, he co-created the Penguin and the Scarecrow, followed by Two-Face, the Batcave, the Riddler, and the Mad Hatter. He received credit for none of it, since Kane secured a contract that stipulated his name alone be printed as the creator of Batman comics in perpetuity. The lie was underlined in June 1940's *Batman* #1, which included a brief biography of Kane, written by editor Whitney Ellsworth, that stated he did all of the work on the character himself.

Enamored of trivia and research, clippings from which he would frequently send along with his scripts to the artists who illustrated them, Finger also co-created the Golden Age hero the Green Lantern and Superboy's girlfriend Lana Lang, and wrote tales of National's other characters (eventually commissioned directly by the company instead of via Kane). His Batman stories, however—weird, whimsical, and chock full of oversized props across which his heroes and villains would battle—are his masterpieces. He wrote approximately 1,500 over the course of 25 years, during which time Kane moved to Los Angeles, and schmoozed his way through Hollywood with the arrival of the 1966 *Batman* TV show. Every episode featured his name as the character's sole creator. Finger wrote one two-part episode—"The Clock King's Crazy Crimes" / "The Clock King Gets Crowned"—introducing yet another long-running supervillain. But by then DC Comics had stopped calling him, turning its attention toward a new generation of comic creators.

Finger found some extra work outside of comics, scripting, for example, the 1968 cult film *The Green Slime*. He also found time to marry twice, and had a son, Fred, with his first wife, Portia. By 1974, Finger had suffered three heart attacks, and his second marriage, to Lyn Simmons, had dissolved. On January 18, 1974, he was found alone in his Manhattan apartment, dead of arteriosclerosis at the age of 59.

Bob Kane died at the age of 83 in Los Angeles on November 3, 1998, after attending the Hollywood premieres of four Batman films. He liked to wear a scalloped cape when he walked the red carpet—a white one, to match his tuxedo. The plaque on his gravestone in the Hollywood Hills is adorned with the Bat-Signal and bears a lengthy memorial that begins, GOD bestowed a dream upon Bob Kane. Blessed with divine inspiration and a rich imagination, Bob created a legacy known as BATMAN.

As revealed in writer Marc Tyler Nobleman's 2012 book *Bill the Boy Wonder: The Secret Co-Creator of Batman* (as essential for fans as the 2017 documentary it spawned—directors Don Argott and Sheena M. Joyce's *Batman & Bill*), Finger was cremated, and his ashes collected by Fred, who spread them on a beach in the shape of a bat and let the tide wash them away.

Though Fred died in 1992 of complications from AIDS, he left behind a daughter, Athena, who, with the help of Nobleman, worked tirelessly to get Warner Brothers to give her grandfather the credit he so deserved. Their efforts were rewarded on September 18, 2015. Today, Finger is named as Batman's co-creator in most every form of media in which his Dark Knight appears. The Bill Finger Award for Excellence in Comic Book Writing is awarded every year at Comic-Con International in San Diego.

2 The Batsuit

Despite the many changes Batman has undergone throughout his history, his suit remains close to its original depiction, found in May 1939's *Detective Comics* #27 (in which it was first drawn by Bob Kane, after substantial input from Batman co-creator Bill Finger). Here was established the gray outfit's chest emblem, scalloped cape, black-blue briefs and boots, and bat-eared cowl. In this first incarnation, the ears extended from the sides of the cowl at 30-degree angles and Batman's gloves were short and purple, while his yellow utility belt featured a large round buckle.

Within a few months, the gloves' color was changed to match the boots and briefs, and the ears were extended and straightened; both the gloves and the boots were made longer. By the end of the 1940s, the ears were again shortened, eyebrows were added to make the cowl more expressive, and the gloves received their now-familiar fins (after those of the pulp hero the Black Bat). A brighter shade of blue was also employed, though whether the suit was *intended* to be blue is debatable.

"Because of the way comic book coloring traditionally was," says comic artist Alex Ross, "if you didn't have a version of black to light or color, you wound up using blue as the best indicator of black, and you got people thinking after a while, 'Is Superman's hair blue?' Spider-Man, for example, was a character who was clearly designed to be wearing red and black. But blue won out over time."

When the low-budget 1943 *Batman* film serial debuted, the screen's first Dark Knight (played by Lewis Wilson) had an ill-fitting cowl with an oversized snout and conical ears that resembled a devil's horns.

When Batman comic sales slumped in the early 1960s, editor Julius Schwartz had artist Carmine Infantino add a yellow oval behind the chest emblem, making it the most recognizable logo in comics next to Superman's S-shield. This "New Look" Batman premiered in May 1964's *Detective Comics* #327 ("The Mystery of the Menacing Mask!"). It was this suit that Adam West wore in the 1966 *Batman* TV show, albeit to comedic effect. If it looked like West's chest decal could get accidentally peeled off his shirt in the midst of a fight, well, that only made him look more like a life-size action figure to the series' legion of young fans.

Infantino's suit would be synonymous with the World's Greatest Detective throughout the 1960s, 1970s, and early 1980s—when he appeared on TV's *The Adventures of Batman* and *Super Friends*—though it was modified by artist Neal Adams during his run on the character in the late 1960s and early 1970s. Adams made the cape longer and the scallops more pronounced, suiting his vision of Batman as an imposing nocturnal avenger.

Midway through 1986's *The Dark Knight Returns*, Frank Miller removed the yellow oval, reestablishing Batman's early look. Though it retained Miller's attitude, Tim Burton's 1989 *Batman* movie used the oval, heralding the biggest marketing campaign in film history. Played by the slight-of-build Michael Keaton, this Batman's suit was comprised of body armor, and its gloves were true gauntlets.

In 1992's *Batman Returns*, the Keaton suit was streamlined to look less muscular. There's no more representative image for director Joel Schumacher's two garish sequels—1995's *Batman Forever* and 1997's *Batman & Robin*—than their suits' infamous nipples. But at least 1990s Batfans had *Batman: The Animated Series*, in which the Dark Knight returned to his iconic spandex look.

When Bruce Wayne's back was broken in 1993's "Knightfall" storyline, the bloodthirsty Azrael replaced him, wearing a suit of armor and razors. Bruce reclaimed the mantle of the Bat, and donned a black suit sans briefs in 1995's "Troika" storyline. When it premiered in 1999, *Batman Beyond* also featured a black suit, with a red emblem, outfitted with all the technology of the future.

The comics' Batman returned to his blue-and-gray suit for 1999's popular "No Man's Land" storyline and 2002's bestselling

The Batsuit has remained largely consistent throughout the Caped Crusader's history, including this version worn by Christian Bale in Christopher Nolan's The Dark Knight. (Nick Setchfield)

"Hush," as well as TV's *The Batman* in 2004 and 2009's *Batman: The Brave and the Bold.* But Christian Bale's Caped Crusader opted for all-black armor in Christopher Nolan's Dark Knight trilogy. A happy medium was found in the color scheme of the *Batman: Arkham* video games' suit—black and gray, with a design utilizing briefs and Kevlar—and in 2016's *Batman v Superman: Dawn of Justice*'s. A similar design was also used for 2010's *Batman Incorporated,* but once more adding the yellow oval, to distinguish its Dark Knight from the titular team's other Batmen. DC's 2011 "New 52" and 2016 "Rebirth" initiatives modified the ever controversial element by reducing it to a mere halo around the Bat emblem.

There was once a time when change came slowly to Batman's world. But with the Dark Knight's life now a never-ending series of emotional upheavals, he redefines himself regularly. Thankfully, he knows better than to mess too much with the most stylish suit in comics.

3 Batman's Origin

The engine at the heart of the Dark Knight's war on crime is his origin—the purest, most elemental ever given to a superhero.

So pure, in fact, that when the origin was first revealed, in November 1939's *Detective Comics* #33 ("The Legend of the Batman—Who He Is and How He Came to Be!" by creators Bill Finger and Bob Kane), it occupied a scant two pages of the magazine.

"One night some fifteen years ago," we're told, "Thomas Wayne, his wife and his son were walking home from a movie..."

"W-what is this?" says a crudely drawn, square-jawed man in a suit and hat, standing alongside an elegantly dressed woman and a small boy. "A stickup, buddy!" says a gun-toting hoodlum in a brown cap. "I'll take that necklace you're wearin', lady!"

"Leave her alone, you!" cries the man—and takes a bullet to the stomach. (One of several of the story's panels swiped by Bob Kane from a 1937 Big Little Book illustrated by Henry Valley, *Junior G-Men and the Counterfeiters.*) "Thomas!" screams his wife. "You've killed him. Help! Police...Help!" "This'll shut you up!" says the thug, and fires another shot.

"The boy's eyes are wide with terror and shock," reads the next caption, "as the horrible scene is spread before him." "Father... Mother!" cries the boy. "...dead! They're d...dead."

"Days later," we learn, "a curious and strange scene takes place." "And I swear," says the boy, kneeling by his bed, his hands folded, a single candle illuminating the scene—"by the spirits of my parents to avenge their deaths by spending the rest of my life warring on all criminals."

In the next two panels, we see the boy, named Bruce Wayne, is now a man: "He becomes a master scientist. Trains his body to physical perfection until he is able to perform amazing athletic feats."

"Dad's estate left me wealthy," he muses in his study. "I am ready. But first I must have a disguise." Then, in the most oft-quoted panel in comics: "Criminals are a superstitious cowardly lot. So my disguise must be able to strike terror into their hearts. I must be a creature of the night, black, terrible...a...a..."

"As if in answer," says the penultimate caption, "a huge bat flies in the open window!" The startled Bruce exclaims, "A bat! That's it! It's an omen...I shall become a BAT!"

"And thus is born," writes Bill Finger, "this weird figure of the dark...This avenger of evil. The BATMAN."

Though the image in the tale's final panel, a costumed Batman crouched beneath a bat-enshrouded moon, is a swipe from Hal Foster's *Tarzan* comic strip, it, like Finger's prose, is nonetheless supremely effective in establishing Batman's motivation and psyche.

The origin was expanded in June 1948's *Batman* #47 ("The Origin of the Batman!" again by Finger and Kane). Here, it's explained that Bruce's mother's name is Martha, and that she died of a heart attack upon seeing her husband murdered. It's also revealed that the murderer is named Joe Chill. Batman tracks him down, reveals he's the son of the murdered couple, and warns Chill he will always be watching him. The panic-stricken crook runs off and tells his gang he "created" Batman, which prompts them to shoot him dead. (The story is adapted to great effect in the 2010 *Batman: The Brave and the Bold* episode "Chill of the Night!")

The Wayne murder case was reopened in September 1956's *Detective Comics* #235 ("The First Batman," written by Bill Finger and penciled by Sheldon Moldoff). This tale explained that Dr. Thomas Wayne had once worn a Batman-like outfit to a masquerade party, at which he ran afoul of gangster Lew Moxon, and that Moxon had hired Chill as a hitman. In his father's old costume, Batman finds Moxon. Terrified, the criminal runs into the path of an oncoming truck.

In his retelling of the origin in *Batman* #232 ("Daughter of the Demon"), artist Neal Adams restored the original version of Martha's death, in keeping with his and writer Denny O'Neil's desire to return Batman to his violent roots.

The Dark Knight's origin was later explored in memorable stories such as March 1976's *Detective Comics* #457 ("There is No Hope in Crime Alley!" written by O'Neil and penciled by Dick Giordano) and March 1981's *Detective Comics* #500 ("To Kill a Legend," written by Alan Brennert with art by Giordano). It was further refined in 1980's *The Untold Legend of the Batman* limited series (written by Len Wein with art by John Byrne and Jim Aparo), 1987's *Batman: Year One* (written by Frank Miller with art by David Mazzucchelli), May 1987's *Detective Comics* #574 ("My Beginning...and My Probable End," by writer Mike W. Barr and penciler Alan Davis), and 1989's *Secret Origins of the World's Greatest Super-Heroes* ("The Man Who Falls," by O'Neil and Giordano)—like *Year One*, an inspiration for the origin presented in 2005's *Batman Begins*. (That film reestablished Chill as the Waynes' killer after Tim Burton's 1989 *Batman* made their murderer the Joker.) *Year One* also established young Bruce as having a fear of bats, which he channels into his crimefighting. Bruce's adolescence is depicted in depth in TV's *Gotham*, which functions as one long origin story for both Bruce and his ally at the GCPD, James Gordon. A more mature pre-Batman Bruce, experiencing the pangs of first love, is offered in the excellent 1993 animated film *Batman: Mask of the Phantasm*.

But everything that made Batman who he is was present in the story's first telling. A crucible of horror that launched a crusade of righteousness.

4 The Joker

Call it the balance of nature. Action and reaction. Or order and chaos. But nothing has so tested the Dark Knight as his greatest foe: the Joker.

The Clown Prince of Crime was borne out of a desire on the part of Batman artist Jerry Robinson to give the Caped Crusader a villain worthy of his awesome abilities; a Professor Moriarty to Batman's Sherlock Holmes. Robinson thought that a character with a sense of humor would provide a sharp contrast with Bill Finger and Bob Kane's earnest detective, and found the perfect visual representation in the Joker playing card. He brought the idea, and a sketch of the card, to Finger, who was reminded of a silent film he'd seen, the 1928 thriller *The Man Who Laughs*. Based on the 1869 novel of the same name by Victor Hugo, it tells the story of a man (played by German actor Conrad Veidt) whose face was mutilated when he was a child, and so must forever wear a rictus grin.

Thus was born the Joker. His first appearance, in Spring 1939's *Batman* #1 (in an unnamed story now called "The Joker," written by Finger and penciled by Bob Kane), opens with a splash page, in which the villain peers over his shoulder at the reader, brandishing three playing cards, with the faces of Batman and Robin and his own. The caption promises, "A battle of wits…with swift death the only compromise!!!"

The Joker is first heard on the radio, announcing his intention to kill millionaire Henry Claridge and steal the Claridge diamond. On the next page, he makes good on his promise. His victim dies with a smile on his face, the first of many to be killed by Joker's poisonous solution, Venom. Leaving his playing card at the scene of the crime, the Joker is introduced in his trademark purple suit, sitting in a black throne-like chair beneath an oversized comedy mask. Musing aloud that he injected Claridge with Venom before he even announced his crime, the criminal remarks, "If the police expect to play against the Joker, they had best be prepared to be dealt from the bottom of the deck."

The Batman meets the villain face-to-face when he flees another murder scene and the Dark Knight hops atop his car. Here, the Joker poses a physical threat to Batman, kicking him off a bridge. "It seems I've at last met a foe who can give me a good fight!" says Batman. The Dynamic Duo finally catch the Joker after he kills a judge who sent him to prison. Behind bars, the grinning clown swears, "They can't keep me here! I know of a way out—the Joker will yet have the *last laugh*!"

Clowns and bats aren't natural enemies, but the image of Batman's gloved fist landing on the Joker's chalk-white chin resonated. Yet the Joker's reign of homicide would only last until June 1942's *Detective Comics* #64 ("The Joker Walks the Last Mile"), by

One of the most famous villains in all of literature, the Joker has been Batman's nemesis for more than 75 years. Heath Ledger, pictured here, won a posthumous Academy Award for his portrayal of the Clown Prince of Crime in Christopher Nolan's 2008 The Dark Knight. (AP Images)

which time the Batman comics had become more kid-friendly, and the Clown Prince of Crime was content to merely match wits with Batman in a series of increasingly silly capers. In October 1946's *Batman* #37 ("The Joker Follows Suit"), he acquires a Jokermobile, Joker Signal, and Jokergyro helicopter. October 1952's *Batman* #73 introduced readers to the Joker's utility belt, a story faithfully adapted in the character's introductory episode in the 1966 *Batman* TV series ("The Joker Is Wild"). A gleeful Cesar Romero played the Joker in this, the character's screen debut, and refused to shave his mustache (to which he attributed his success as an actor), demanding the show's makeup artists simply paint over it. It was a move as enjoyably absurd as any of his character's. After the live-action show's cancellation, the Joker made his first appearance in animated form in 1968's *The Batman/Superman Hour*.

Writer Denny O'Neil and penciler Neal Adams gave the Joker back his homicidal urges in their classic "The Joker's Five-Way Revenge" (in September 1973's *Batman* #251), which saw him escape from a mental hospital and hunt down the sole member of his gang who sold him out—by killing five suspects.

Always the most popular of Batman's adversaries, the Joker earned his first comic book series with the arrival of May 1975's *Joker* #1 ("The Joker's Double Jeopardy!" written by O'Neil and penciled by Irv Novick), though it ran for only nine issues.

The new-old Joker's personality was cemented by writer Steve Englehart and penciler Marshall Rogers in February 1978's *Batman* #251 ("The Laughing Fish") and #252 ("The Sign of the Joker"), a two-part story that emphasized the random nature of the Joker's killings, and established his co-dependent relationship with Batman. Englehart's take on the character was so popular he was asked to write the first drafts of what became Tim Burton's 1989 *Batman* movie, using his version of the Joker.

In Frank Miller's 1986 *The Dark Knight Returns*, that co-dependency morphed into a kind of courtship, with its androgynous Joker admitting his entire raison d'etre is to win Batman's attention. In the limited series' third issue, they have their final confrontation, which ends with the Joker killing himself in order to frame Batman for his murder.

An origin story had been given to the Joker in February 1951's *Detective Comics* #168 ("The Man Behind the Red Hood!" written by Bill Finger and penciled by Lewis Sayre Schwartz and Win Mortimer). In it, readers learned the Joker was once the Red Hood, a criminal who escaped Batman and Robin by diving into a vat of chemicals at the Ace Playing Card Company. Though his hood saved his life, it allowed the chemicals to bleach his skin and dye his hair green and his lips bright red. In his retelling of the origin in 1988's *The Killing Joke*, writer Alan Moore and artist Brian Bolland expanded the tale to explain how the Joker was originally an employee of the Ace Chemical Company who tries, unsuccessfully, to become a standup comedian. Turning to thievery to placate his pregnant wife—in a gang that requires he wear a red hood—he goes mad after his wife is killed in a random accident and dives into a chemical waste stream to escape Batman. Another retelling of the Joker's early days came in the 2005 graphic novel *The Man Who Laughs*, by writer Ed Brubaker and artist Doug Mahnke. The grungy, naturalistic *Joker*, by writer Brian Azzarello and penciler Lee Bermejo, is another worthwhile graphic novel focusing on the Clown Prince of Crime. Almost as darkly compelling are writer Scott Snyder and penciler Greg Capullo's "New 52" Joker story arcs, "Death of the Family" and "Endgame."

Though Cesar Romero was the first actor to play the Joker on the silver screen—in 1966's *Batman* movie—Jack Nicholson, with his leering, fixed-grin and non-sequitur-slinging take on the character, wholly dominated Tim Burton's blockbuster *Batman*. When *Batman: The Animated Series* arrived in 1992, however, *Star Wars* star Mark Hamill became the Joker of choice for millennials, helped in no small measure by the popularity of the clown's long-suffering girlfriend, Harley Quinn. Hamill also performed the role in the *Batman: Arkham* video games, the 1993 film *Batman: Mask of the Phantasm*, the 2016 film adaptation of *The Killing Joke*, and 2000's *Batman Beyond: Return of the Joker*. The last is based on the TV series of the same name, in which the Joker's reputation outlives him to plague Neo-Gotham via the "Jokerz" street gang. (With Mark Hamill's very name holding the word "Arkham," the actor's true destiny lay not with the Force, but with "Mister J.")

The Batman, from 2004, introduced a visually outlandish, anime-flavored Joker, voiced by Kevin Michael Richardson. The first African American cast in the role, he won an Emmy for his performance. Other significant animated Jokers include those in 2009's *Batman: The Brave and the Bold* (voiced by Jeff Bennett), the 2010 comic adaptation *Batman: Under the Red Hood* (John DiMaggio), the 2012 adaptation of *The Dark Knight Returns* (Michael Emerson), and the 2011 TV show *Young Justice* (Brent Spiner). *The LEGO Batman Movie* (in which the character is voiced by Zach Galifianakis) poked good-naturedly at the Joker's obsession with Batman in 2017.

Oscar winner Jared Leto performed the role on screen most recently, in 2017's *Suicide Squad*. Next to Hamill's Joker, however, the ne plus ultra of screen Jokers, the version that takes the most chances and reaps the greatest rewards, is Heath Ledger's interpretation of the character in 2008's *The Dark Knight*—a smoldering volcano of sulfur and insanity that earned the late actor a posthumously awarded Academy Award.

Few roles in popular fiction have come to be so coveted by actors as that of the Clown Prince of Crime. He is the force of chaos to Batman's order, an archetype in the tradition of every culture/mythology's trickster figure. But one that feels as new as a freshly printed comic page.

Gotham Gazette Exclusive

Jerry Robinson

The inker/finisher for Batman co-creator and penciler Bob Kane on both *Detective Comics* and *Batman*, Jerry Robinson himself co-created two enduring legends: Robin the Boy Wonder and the Joker. The first truly great Batman artist—whose covers came to define the character during the Golden Age—Robinson passed away in 2011 at the age of 89, though his legacy will endure as long as the medium he loved. The following interview was conducted in 2008.

How did you first get involved with Batman?

I had graduated from high school at 17, and that summer—this is in 1939, believe it or not—I sold ice cream on a bicycle with a cart behind it. It was the custom in those days. We didn't have automobiles for ice cream. [Laughs.] So, being the newest man they hired for the summer, I was given the outmost part of the suburbs of Trenton as my area where I could sell. I had to do a lot of pedaling just to get there. This went on all summer, back and forth. I was on the 98-pound track team, and by the end of the summer I was about 78 pounds. My mother persuaded me to take $25 of that hard-earned summer money—when I think of how many ice creams we had to sell for that, I think we got a cent or something per cone—and go to the mountains and fatten up. Because she thought I'd never last my first semester at college. So I did. This was in the Poconos. Danny Kaye was on staff that summer...One of my lifelong passions has been tennis, and I was on the tennis team at the time. The first chance I got I ran out to the tennis court to find a match, and I put on a jacket.

I grew up in Trenton, New Jersey, and nearby was Princeton University. So we looked up to the college kids then, in high school, and the fad at the college was to wear a white linen painter's jacket, with lots of pockets in them. So we took up the fad and we decorated the jacket with drawings and what today you'd call graffiti. So I used that as a warmup jacket, and I ran out with the jacket on, looking to see who was playing, getting the lay of the land. Someone tapped me on my shoulder and said, "Who did those drawings?" I thought I was gonna be arrested or something. I turned around and said, "I did." He introduced himself. It was Bob Kane.

He said he just started a new feature called Batman. The first issue was on the stand, [but] I never heard of it. So we went down to the local candy store and he got a copy to show me. Bob was about six years older than me, he was in his early twenties. So it ended up that we hung out together that week. He said, "Well, if you come to

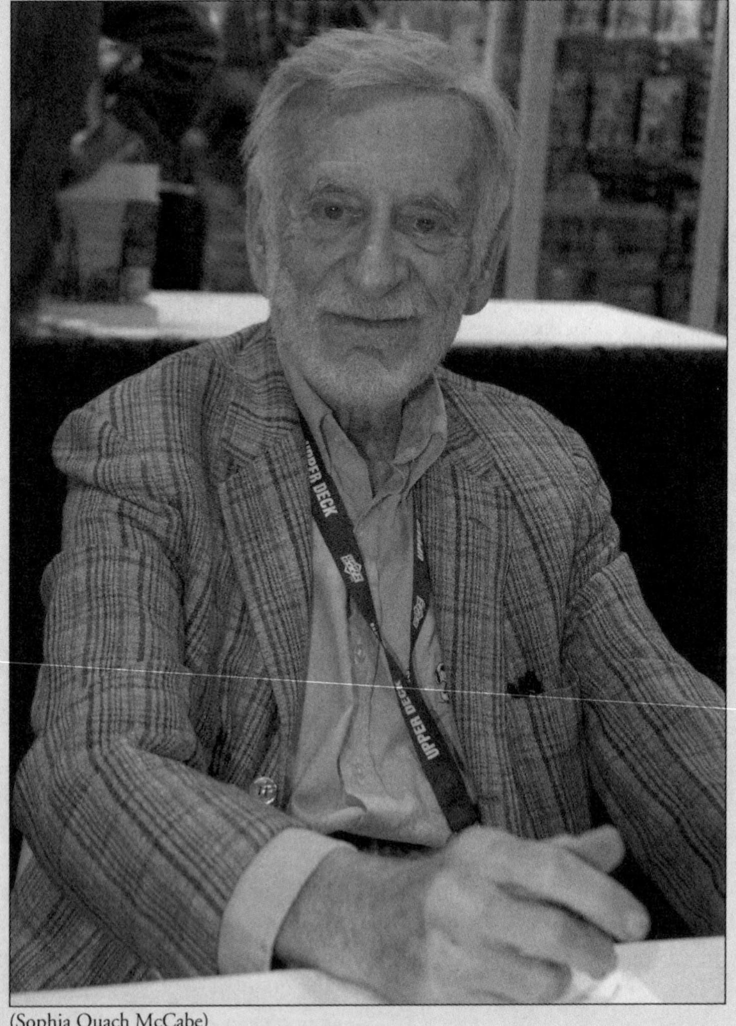

(Sophia Quach McCabe)

New York I can offer you a job to join the Batman team." It was just the writer and [him]. The writer was Bill Finger, who was really the co-creator of Batman.

I intended to be a journalist and a writer, which I guess I have been in my life. That was my goal. So I applied to Syracuse, Columbia, and Penn—the best schools in the East for journalism. I had been accepted and I decided to go to Syracuse, only because it sounded more like a college town to me. I don't know if it is. I've never been there. [Laughs.] So [Bob] said, "Well, it's too bad. If you came to New York you could start on Batman." So I called Columbia, right from the mountains to see if my application was still good. They said it was. I called Syracuse and told them I was not coming. I called home and said, "I'm going to New York and starting at Columbia and then starting work on this new cartoon." [Laughs.] Which I did. That was the beginning. I went to Columbia, and I took my writing classes, and was moonlighting for a couple of years when I first started Batman.

In those early years you developed Batman's first partner, Robin. Can you describe his genesis?
Well, Bill had the idea of adding a boy to the strip. There were not any sidekicks at that time. That was part of Bill's genius—he really was great at character creation and he knew what made good stories, the tension in a story. A kid was great because it expanded the parameters of the story, and also the demographics. The youngest kids could identify with Robin, and the older ones could identify with Batman as a role model. So it was good on both of those counts. But the story content was greater, and Bill had a great story sense. He was by far the best writer of comics during that so-called Golden Age. He named Gotham City, Bruce Wayne. He created all the other bizarre characters and the Dynamic Duo and the banter between Robin and Batman—that was Bill's contribution.

Names are very important in comics. I can still remember vividly the day we were working on the concept of the kid. We came up with a list of maybe 30 names, of all kinds. Biblical names, mythological names, everything. None of us were satisfied with any…The relationship between Batman and Superman was that Superman was the one with all the superpowers, he was invulnerable, and Batman was not. Batman was an ordinary human being. So I felt that the name should conjure up that same sensibility. So I came up with the name Robin. It's been written in a number of places that I named him after myself, or from my name, Robinson, which is entirely untrue, and embarrassing. [Laughs.] Because I was 17, 18 by that time maybe, and that would have been very presumptuous for me to name him after myself. It came from *Robin Hood*, which was one of the tales that I loved to read. I had been given a book in my early days, as a birthday gift or something—a beautiful edition of *Robin Hood* that was illustrated by N.C. Wyeth, the granddaddy of the [American painter] Wyeths. Those illustrations intrigued me. I used to pore over them.

I suggested Robin, and I had to maybe make my case with Bob and Bill for a while, but they came around and they finally agreed. They thought Robin was the best. So I had that image. I didn't have the book with me, but I had seen it so many times that when we sat down to design the costume I remembered the little vest and [chain] mail pants and so forth. So basically some of the elements of the costume were patterned after what I recalled of the N.C. Wyeth illustration of Robin Hood. That was it.

A little later, Bill tagged him "The Boy Wonder." At that time I was the youngest of the group. I started so young. So they used to kid me that I was "Robinson the Boy Wonder." They said that derogatorily. Now it sounds good, but at that time I was mortified. I wanted to look older. I didn't want to be thought of as Robin the kid, but Robin Hood. So I didn't like that at all. Now you can call me Robin the Boy Wonder and I don't mind. [Laughs.]

You were also responsible for the Batman's greatest villain, the Joker. What led to his creation?

It was very early on with the Batman [strip], which appeared just in *Detective Comics* once a month at that time. Its popularity was growing, so the publisher decided to put out *Batman* #1, a quarterly of four stories of Batman. There were three 13-page stories and one 12-page story as I recall. So all of a sudden we had to do five stories to meet the deadline for the first quarterly and the next issue of *Detective*. Bill, as good a writer as he was, was not fast, because he plotted his stories. He was a craftsman, and it didn't come easy. With some writers it flows and with some it didn't, and Bill used to work really hard on the stories. It seemed like it was gonna be impossible for him to write those five stories we needed all at once. So I volunteered to do one.

This, I thought, was a great opportunity because I wanted to write. Still, at that time, I had no idea of continuing as a cartoonist. This was just to earn my way through college. So I thought, "Well, I can write a story for Batman and get paid for that, hopefully, and it'll also do double duty as a credit for creative writing class." So I volunteered and they said, "Great."

I went back that night to my little room which I was renting at the time, and started to think of what I was gonna do. From the very start, I wanted a story about some antagonist for Batman that was stronger than what we were doing. At that time, we had just come out of, or were even still in, the era of Dillinger and Pretty Boy Floyd. Gangsters, embezzlers, hijackers—those were the run-of-the-mill villains. So I thought, from my literature, that all the great heroes had some antagonist that tested their skills and bravery and wits and so forth. Everything from the Bible—David and Goliath—right up to Sherlock Holmes and Moriarty. So that was my first thought.

Again, in my writing, I had written quite a bit in high school too. I loved short stories. I was doing a lot of short stories for the high school paper. I even submitted one, boldly, to the *Saturday Evening Post* at that time. I got a wonderful letter of rejection that I was very proud of—that they acknowledged my presence—and carried it around. [Laughs.] So I liked short stories with a little twist, and somehow combining that with that I wanted Batman to fight someone…I really didn't think of it in terms of a supervillain, but a major villain. I wanted somebody bizarre that would be memorable in the line of the great villains in literature.

A lot of what I had written was humorous short stories. So I guess I naturally thought of the next step, which was that I wanted to endow my character with a sense of humor, which I thought would be an interesting contradiction in terms—a villain with a sense of humor. That was the original thought. Once I thought of the sense of humor, I proceeded to come up with a name. It was a short leap to coming up with the name of "The Joker" for a villain with a sense of humor.

It's funny how everything in your life ties in somehow. Card playing was very popular in my family. One of my elder brothers was a contract bridge champion; he had master points and everything. And my mother was quite a contract bridge player also. I played, but not nearly as well as them. But I was familiar with cards, and when I thought of the name Joker, I thought of the playing card, the joker. I remember searching frantically in my room for a deck of cards, and luckily I found one and it had that plastic image of the joker on the playing card. Which was kind of a lucky association, because that image goes back in history—with the court jesters, the traveling storytellers, and so forth. I really didn't think of that at the time. I was just thinking of the image. It was endowed with all those associations, which I think added to the longevity of it.

That was it. As it turned out, Bill was so enamored of the idea that he wanted to write that story. And I, almost with tears in my eyes, handed over my baby to him the next day when we had a meeting, and I was gonna tell him what my story was gonna be. Because he had doubt I was the best writer. I had never written one before. I would have taken longer even than he would. I was just gonna relieve him of one of the stories, but that was it. He took my concept and the idea of having the playing card as a calling card, that he was gonna test the wits of Batman, and the image of the Joker—which Bob and I fleshed out visually. But he actually wrote that first Joker story, which everybody loved so much—and the character—that they slated him for the opening story of that first Batman quarterly, *Batman* #1.

Then we had a plan that finally Batman was gonna overcome the Joker. But he was too good to kill off. So we decided to keep him, and I guess the rest is history.

Bill Finger apparently further developed the character when he was inspired by the film *The Man Who Laughs*.

Well, yes. The story's been misinterpreted in some versions, saying that's where the idea came from—the Conrad Veidt film. Bill was an inveterate moviegoer. He knew all the classic movies and the foreign films, which he immediately took me to. He was kind of my cultural mentor. I was a raw kid from out of town. At 17 I'd never seen the Museum of Modern Art or the Met or foreign films. So he took me. In any event, he knew that film, *The Man Who Laughs*, because he had seen foreign films at the Museum of Modern Art. So that immediately reminded him of that. He said, "I'm gonna bring in a picture of him," which he did. Of course he bore an astounding resemblance. If you look at any version of a Joker playing card, you'll see the resemblance. That was after the fact, but that helped Bill and us kind of visualize him as a real person. So that's how it was fleshed out.

Bill often did this with his scripts. He'd attach all sorts of references to the story that he was writing. It would help the artist, if he was doing a story about a ship or a plane or the police department or some odd invention, he would attach some reference that inspired him to help the artist. In effect, that's what he did for the Joker.

Who developed the purple suit?
That came as we drew the first story. We began to do sketches and color sketches and combinations. We knew we were starting out with a white clown face and the green hair. So the purple contrast was good with the existing color scheme of the Joker.

There's been a number of actors who've played him. What are your thoughts on them?
Well, curiously on my very first trip to California, in about '40 or '41...I flew out to California for the making of the *Batman* serial, and I met Cesar Romero then. But that was before he did the Joker on the TV series. He was very good for the part in that he fit it physically. He was tall, slim, and had kind of an elongated face, and the makeup was pretty good. Of course Jack Nicholson gave a tour de force performance [in Tim Burton's *Batman*]. I wasn't crazy about the script for that film, but he was very good. But I think Heath Ledger might have paved new ground for the Joker. I was over in England for part of it, where they filmed the last weeks of it. But I didn't see much of Ledger there. He had filmed most of his scenes and flew back to New York. It was a tragedy what happened to him, of course. He gives a bravura performance. It's just a tragedy he's not here to enjoy it. But his portrayal will live on.

You served as a consultant on *The Dark Knight*. What were your responsibilities?
Basically to see that they were able to adapt our original concept of the Joker, and use as much of my original visual of him as possible, and the concept of the character himself. That was the Joker and the Batman that they were most influenced by.

What were some of Bill Finger's other inventions?
Bill was great at coming up with—and of course they became so identified with our strip—these interesting and bizarre villains like the Catwoman and, later on, the Riddler. And these other gimmicks which he created. He was a fan of the pulps. A lot of the gimmicks in the pulps he adapted to comics, like the Batmobile and the Bat-Signal and all these other things. He was also influenced by the early German Expressionist films. Bill was a year or two older than Bob. He really awakened me to a lot of influences, which I think influenced his vision of Batman and my awareness.

Of all the Batman artists who followed you, were there any that you were especially impressed with?
Well, you know, I guess the last comic book work I did was in the late '50s or early '60s. So it was a long time ago. Some of the very good ones who succeeded me in recent years, I wasn't familiar with them until I started getting invited to some of these Comic-Cons. They'd show me the updated versions of the characters. Of those, I'm very impressed with Frank Miller. I think he's a very creative guy. And Neal Adams of course did brilliant work, artistically. I think Dick Sprang did good work. He more or less succeeded me. But I don't know…A lot of them drew beautifully, like Neal and others. But we deliberately didn't—or maybe we were incapable of it—draw realistically at the time. In fact, I remember specifically we weren't enamored of the work that got too realistic or photographic. Artists who actually used models and photographs, it was limiting, and too realistic. It lost the magic. That was our view.

You felt that since it was a comic book, it should appear different from reality?

Yeah, yeah. Of course we tried to have good drawings, but not to that degree. We felt it was limiting in the storytelling and whatnot. But later, of course...For a while I drew right next to Jack Kirby, who was at the next table with his drawing board. He was fabulous. He was not realistic in the true sense of realistic illustration, and he was influential. We certainly admired him. He was a fabulous artist and creator. He really expanded the parameters of the dimensionally two-plane drawing. His stuff exploded all over the place.

My greatest influence though was Mort Meskin. Morton was my best friend. We shared an apartment and a studio together. We later became partners on several features. And Mort was great because he was the only one of us who really was a schooled artist. He graduated from Pratt Institute, a very fine art school in New York, one of the best. So he knew drapery, perspective, anatomy, what have you. But he wasn't limited by it. His figures flowed and so forth. So I was influenced by him. We did Vigilante and Johnny Quick—which he had created, and then when we became partners we did them together. We did several other features, "Black Terror" and "Fighting Yank" and a lot of individual stories. We worked with Simon and Kirby when they had their own studio.

How do you feel comics have changed over the last century?

Well, the new direction I guess—it's not new, it's an expanded version of the story—is the so-called graphic novel. But they are more in the form of novels, and have attracted some accomplished writers to the medium. I would have loved to have done that in my day, if we had that space to create some great stories. That's been one of the major things...And it became more of a medium for adult readers than when I was young. The age demographics have really enlarged from my time. Most adults looked down on the comics. As the kids grew up and they loved comics and appreciated them then they became the older readers. [Laughs.] Now they're fathers and grandfathers and great-grandfathers, I guess.

5 Robin I: Dick Grayson (aka Nightwing)

Comrade and companion, partner and pal, without Robin, the Dark Knight's darkness would have long ago devoured Bruce Wayne. Numerous young men (and women) have worn Robin's cape, tunic, and domino mask. But the most widely recognized remains the first—Richard "Dick" Grayson.

After Batman's successful debut in May 1939's *Detective Comics* #27, creators Bill Finger and Bob Kane began considering ways to expand their character's dramatic potential. They felt a sidekick would give their hero someone through whom he could share information with readers, conveying deductions as Sherlock Holmes had through Watson. Since their readership was comprised predominantly of children, it was decided a young boy would give fans someone with whom they could identify. Kane's new hire, artist Jerry Robinson, suggested the character be named after Robin Hood, and gave him the legendary outlaw's chain mail pants and red vest, as rendered by fabled illustrator N.C. Wyeth.

The first kid sidekick in comics, Dick Grayson introduced himself to readers by literally jumping out of the cover of April 1940's *Detective Comics* #38 (written by Finger and penciled by Kane), heralded as "The Sensational Character Find of 1940: Robin the Boy Wonder." His debut story's splash page describes him as "...an exciting new figure whose incredible gymnastic and athletic feats will astound you...A laughing, fighting, young daredevil who scoffs at danger like the legendary Robin Hood whose name and spirit he has adopted..."

In his debut story, Dick is the son of trapeze artists John and Mary Grayson (billed as "The Flying Graysons"), circus performers in the employ of a Mr. Haly, who are killed in the middle of their "death-defying act...the Triple Spin" by a gang of racketeers extorting money from their boss. He's given a home by Bruce Wayne, after Bruce witnesses the Graysons' murder and is instantly reminded of his own parents' deaths. "That night," reads a caption panel, "two grim figures take an undying oath!"

The panel depicts Batman and Dick—their left hands placed upon each other's, their right hands raised—standing in a room illuminated by a single burning candle. "—And swear that we two will fight together against crime and corruption and never to swerve from the path of righteousness!" says the Dark Knight. "I swear it!" replies his new partner. After a period of training, abbreviated due to his trapeze experience, Dick dons his costume for the first time and helps end the criminal career of the gang's leader, Boss Zucco. The Boy Wonder was born, and Batman was alone no more. (An effective modern retelling of Robin's origin came in November 1997's *Batman: Legends of the Dark Knight* #100, courtesy of writer Denny O'Neil and artist Dave Taylor.)

Dick soon reached high school age, at which he remained for most of his first three decades. In February 1947's *Star Spangled Comics* #65, Robin received his first solo strip, which ran 65 issues through July 1952's #130. He also had the honor of making regular appearances alongside Batman and Superman in the long-running *World's Finest* comic, starting with its first issue in March 1941.

Dick first showed up on screen played by 16-year-old Douglas Croft in the 1943 *Batman* film serial, and on the radio in *The Adventures of Superman* serial of the 1940s, performed by Ronald Liss. The Dick Grayson best known to post–World War II baby boomers—one with a penchant for shouting "Holy...!"—was played by actor Burt Ward, who became as big a celebrity as Adam West in the 1966 *Batman* TV series.

But there comes a time when every Robin must leave the nest. So in December 1969's *Batman* #217 ("One Bullet Too Many!" by writer Frank Robbins and penciler Irv Novick), Dick Grayson at long last graduated from high school and left Wayne Manor for Hudson University. For the rest of his career as Robin, he was referred to as "The Teen Wonder."

Dick had teamed up with fellow sidekicks Kid Flash and Aqualad in the pages of July 1964's *The Brave and the Bold* #54 ("The Thousand-and-One Dooms of Mr. Twister," by writer Bob Haney and penciler Bruno Premiani). The three joined Wonder Girl in forming the Teen Titans in *The Brave and the Bold* #60 and earned their own series with February 1966's *Teen Titans* #1. With Dick as their leader, the Titans' comic ran 53 issues through February 1978, and was succeeded by *The New Teen Titans* in 1980. Written by Marv Wolfman and penciled by George Perez—who infused it with all the adolescent angst and soap opera drama the notorious Comics Code Authority would allow—*The New Teen Titans* emerged as one of DC's most popular titles, outselling Batman's own books in the first half of the decade.

After years of living in the Dark Knight's shadow, including a run in 1975's *Batman Family*, Dick finally decided to resign from his role as Robin in February 1984's *The New Teen Titans* #39 ("Crossroads"), following Wally West's resignation as Kid Flash. "Robin," said Dick, "will always be the back half of Batman and—" Taking off the red-green-and-yellow costume he'd worn since he was a child, he told his startled teammates, "I keep playing a role I'd long ago outgrown. What I am now is a person with responsibilities, not a happy-go-lucky kid partner."

"Today that happens all the time," said Wolfman years later. "Characters live, characters die—all the time. Back then that didn't happen. So this was a pretty unique item, to let Dick quit being Robin."

After giving his costume to the next Robin, Jason Todd, and taking some time to find himself, Dick reemerged as his own man in issue #44 of the book, then retitled *Tales of the Teen Titans*, again written and drawn by Wolfman and Perez. Now operating as

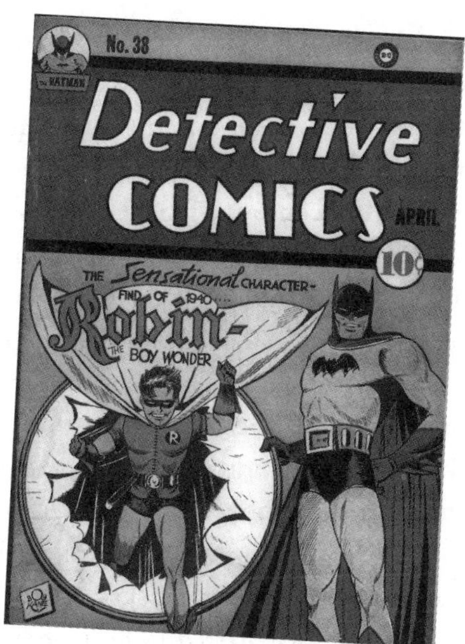

Robin, Batman's longtime sidekick, debuted in 1940's Detective Comics *#38.* (Cover art by Bob Kane)

Nightwing, he took his name from an alternate identity Superman had once assumed, based on a Kryptonian bird. He wore a uniform that nodded to his tutelage under Batman and his origins as a circus acrobat: pale and dark blue, trimmed in a gold-feathered design, with a birdlike mask and stand-up disco collar, and a shirt that revealed—to the delight of his "Wingnut" fans—a generous amount of chest.

"Nightwing is a great name. There is no better name. But I would have much rather come up with my own completely," admits Wolfman.

Nightwing's first mission saw him face down Deathstroke the Terminator alongside his fellow Titans in the team's most celebrated story arc, "The Judas Contract." His creators wasted no time in celebrating his grown-up status. In the first issue of the following storyline, issue #1 of *The New Teen Titans*' second volume, he's seen naked in bed alongside his long-term girlfriend and teammate, Starfire.

As Nightwing, Dick has protected Gotham's neighboring town of Blüdhaven, and his relationship with Batman has continued to evolve, with the two men often at odds over their different approaches to crimefighting. His costume has changed too, streamlining over time into the tougher, black-and-blue version he wears in DC's "Rebirth" continuity. Unfortunately, along the way, he's been saddled with some of the less savory hairstyles in superhero comics. (The less said about his mullet days, the better.)

From time to time, Dick has worn the mantle of the Bat, even as Jason Todd has briefly played the role of Nightwing. As Batman, Dick was paired with Bruce Wayne's son, Damian Wayne, in Grant Morrison's celebrated run on *Batman and Robin*. Far more often, however, he's answered the call to fight alongside his former teacher, mirroring him in his skills if not his degree of brooding.

Nightwing first starred in his own solo title in the July 1995 one-shot *Nightwing: Alfred's Return* #1 ("The Britannia Coup," written by Alan Grant with art by Dick Giordano), followed that same year by a four-issue *Nightwing* limited series. In 1996, he starred in his first monthly series, in which he acquired his signature weapon, a pair of escrima sticks that can join together to form a staff.

Nightwing first appeared on screen in a 1997 episode of *The New Batman Adventures*, "You Scratch My Back," in which he's voiced by Loren Lester (who'd played the younger Dick Grayson/Robin in the preceding *Batman: The Animated Series*). Jerry O'Connell provides the voice of the character in 2004's *The Batman*, and Neil Patrick Harris in the 2010 animated movie *Batman: Under the Red Hood*. *Firefly* star Sean Maher voices him in the animated film trilogy *Son of Batman / Batman vs. Robin / Batman: Bad Blood*.

Though Nightwing inspired the design of the Dick Grayson Robin as played by Chris O'Donnell in director Joel Schumacher's 1997 misfire *Batman & Robin*, audiences should soon have the opportunity to watch the swashbuckling sex symbol in all his glory. At the time of this writing, he's slated to make his live-action debut in his first solo feature film. Directed by Chris McKay, who helmed *The LEGO Batman Movie* (in which Michael Cera voiced an amusingly innocent Dick), the greenlighting of a Nightwing movie cemented the mainstream's hard-won acceptance of Dick Grayson as a character, a hero, and a man in his own right.

Gotham Gazette Exclusive

Marv Wolfman

The New Teen Titans co-creator Marv Wolfman was responsible for ushering one Boy Wonder into manhood when he made Dick Grayson Nightwing, and for creating an entirely new Robin in Tim Drake in the 1989 Batman story arc "A Lonely Place of Dying."

What prompted the creation of Nightwing?
From the moment I started *The New Teen Titans* with George Perez, our goal was to make Dick Grayson the real leader, not just a leader in name. At that time, with Batman, he was still the guy who made a lot of puns and jokes. He was still Robin the Boy Hostage. We aged him immediately, because of the way George drew him.

As this went on, as he kept getting more mature in the writing, it became very important to change him in other ways. We couldn't get him not to be Robin. He still was wearing those stupid short pants, and at 18 that doesn't work. We really needed to make a change. Coincidentally, just as we were trying to figure out what to do with him, Denny O'Neil, editor of the Batman books, said they would like Robin back.

I didn't care about Robin at all. I only cared about Dick Grayson. So I gave it some thought and I said, "Tell you what, why don't you take Robin back, but let us keep Dick Grayson. You can make a big publicity thing about the fact that you're getting a new Robin. Meanwhile, we can keep Dick Grayson." They said yes. They loved the idea. So we had him quit being Robin, and then we turned him into Nightwing.

Since that was the first time one of the junior heroes graduated into a major role, we took the time to develop him as a real character, make him his own person. So the character physically became what we were emotionally doing for a couple of years before that.

Initially, Nightwing's name and colors were said to have been influenced by the Kandorian Nightwing, from the Superman comic stories.

I went through a million names trying to come up with a good name. We ignored "Nightwing," or at least I did, for the longest time. It was the best name, but I ignored it because of the Kandorian. Finally, I think it was Tony Tollin, who was the colorist on *Titans*, who said, "You should really go with the Nightwing name." Because it was coming to the point where I had to have a name, and no name was working at all. It needed to be a name that almost gave the feel of Batman—the dark bat, and now you're going to a "night wing"—but be his own man at the same time. They weren't using Nightwing and Flamebird anymore anyway.

I hated doing it. But it was the best name we were able to come up with. Therefore I made it part of the story, that he was also honoring Superman; who was the second person who taught him how to be a hero. So at least I was able to incorporate it. But it wasn't the solution that I was looking for.

Around the time you created Nightwing you also created Deathstroke, the Teen Titans' enemy who eventually fought Batman.

Deathstroke was a mercenary, who was approached by a villainous group called H.I.V.E. to do a job. He turned it down. They approached his son and fed him a version of the chemicals that turned Slade Wilson into Deathstroke, and the son died. Deathstroke was sort of obligated to finish his son's assigned job. If his son had either succeeded or never taken on that job in the first place, because he took it behind Deathstroke's back, there would be no reason for Deathstroke ever to have attacked the Titans. They were not on his radar. He's not an assassin; he's a mercenary. There's a big difference between a mercenary and an assassin. He doesn't go out and kill people for no reason. He fights wars essentially. So it wasn't Dick Grayson, and it wasn't Cyborg, Starfire, Raven, or any of the other characters that made any difference to him. He now had to fulfill his son's assignment and kill the Titans, or capture them and bring them to H.I.V.E. George did a beautiful job creating a guy who looked older and looked like he could kill you. [Laughs.]

How about the third Robin, Tim Drake, in "A Lonely Place of Dying"? What led to his creation?
When I say I didn't care about Robin, I didn't care who that character was. I didn't care if he went back to Batman and Batman had a new Robin. I only cared about the human being. What costume he wears is irrelevant. But it was important to get him out of that costume as a physical sign of growing older. He was separating from his father the way all kids at that age separate from their parents. That was what was important.

As far as "A Lonely Place of Dying"...Jason Todd was the Robin who followed Dick Grayson, and they weren't quite sure what to do with him. I think there was an idea upfront, but they weren't quite sure how to handle him. The fans didn't like him for whatever reason. They decided to kill him off, and they approached me about creating a new Robin. That was Tim Drake. I was brought in because I had already proven successful at creating teenage characters with the Titans. That's the only reason.

When you were asked to create a new Robin, what traits did you want the character to possess?
It was important to me that Tim first be smart. I wanted Tim also to have a family. I didn't want him to be a character that felt he would take over for Batman when Batman died. He was happy with where he was, and he wanted to prove to Batman he was good. With the death of Jason, he saw—since he knew who Batman was, having figured out all this other stuff—that Batman was starting to fall apart; and he really wanted to help Bruce Wayne and Batman stop being a mindless vigilante, because Batman's anger was taking control. This was a way for Tim to make him go back to what he was.

6 The Batmobile

The word "Batmobile" resonates beyond the streets of Gotham City. Beyond even the Bat mythos itself. In three syllables, it captures everything people love about cars.

The first Batmobile—an elegant red convertible—made its debut as Bruce Wayne's car when Batman first appeared in May 1939's *Detective Comics* #27 ("The Case of the Chemical Syndicate"). It was given its name in February 1941's *Detective Comics* #48 ("The Secret Cavern," by Batman creators Bill Finger and Bob Kane). Based on the 1936 Cord 810, it featured a small, gold, bat-shaped ornament atop a reinforced hood capable of smashing into every criminal gang hideout in Gotham.

In March 1941's *Batman* #5 ("The Riddle of the Missing Card," by Finger and Kane), the first distinct Batmobile debuted. Stored in a barn on Bruce Wayne's estate, this "super-charged car" featured fender skirts over its tires, armored panels, a fin in back, and an enormous Bat head on the front of its hood that could serve as a battering ram. Its size, its shape, its features, and the color of its highlights would change from issue to issue, depending on who was drawing it. With *Batman* #20, the car first appeared on a cover. Unfortunately, when the Batmobile made its screen debut in the 1943 *Batman* serial, it was an unremarkable black Cadillac convertible.

The comics' Batmobile was destroyed in a bridge explosion in February 1950's *Detective Comics* #156 ("The Batmobile of 1950," written by Joe Samachson and penciled by Dick Sprang), but a sleeker car took its place. As detailed on the issue's cover, this new model had a "plastic bubble," "a knife-edge steel nose for cutting through barriers," "a radar antennae inside [its] tail fin," rear "rocket tubes," and a "laboratory with built-in cabinets, work bench, [and] stool." The whole thing was topped with a searchlight that "throws [the] Bat symbol as well as light beam when desired."

After Batman's Batsuit was given its "New Look" in May 1964's *Detective Comics* #327, the Batmobile was upgraded the following month, in *Batman* #164 ("Two-Way Gem Caper!" written by Ed Herron and penciled by Sheldon Moldoff). The swinging 1960s Batmobile was a sporty two-seat convertible roadster with Bat-head detailing on its hood.

Two years later, the most iconic Batmobile of all made its debut. In 1965, Hollywood's custom car king George Barris and Bill Cushenberry took a 1955 Lincoln Futura concept car from the Italian automotive company Ghia—that Barris had purchased from the Ford Motor Company for the supposed sum of just one dollar—and in three weeks turned it into the Dynamic Duo's ride in the 1966 *Batman* TV series. It was the first "real" Batmobile, a full-size car capable of doing much of what it did on screen.

Few vehicles have become as iconic as the Batmobile designed by George Barris for the 1966 Batman *television series.* (Sophia Quach McCabe)

Gotham Gazette Exclusive

George Barris

The Dark Knight has driven dozens of Batmobiles throughout the course of his career. The most recognizable, however, is that of the 1966 *Batman* TV show: a 1955 Lincoln Futura concept car customized by George Barris, Hollywood's "King of the Kustomizers." The following interview was conducted with Barris in May of 2012, three years before his death at the age of 89.

How did you come to create the Batmobile?
I was called in by [*Batman* executive producer William] Dozier over at the TV studio, and I reviewed the script. I noticed that he had "Pow! Bang! Whee!" in the middle of the script as they were filming. That meant he had actors doing things every time he put in a "Pow!" So I had the Batmobile do the same. I wanted to make it a part of the show, and I made it become a star. When the script went "Pow!" I sent out a rocket. "Bang!"—a chain-slicer. "Boom!"—an oil spray.

How long did it take to customize?
We only had 15 days and $15,000. The [job] was able to be done with the Futura, because of the fact that it was that shape…I had twin Bat-chutes, so that when we wanted to stop and make turns we popped the Bat-chutes, which were real parachutes used on race cars. I had the Batphone, I had Bat turn signals, I had the Bat recorders, Bat TVs—everything I incorporated in the car was related to a bat.

You traveled the country in the Batmobile. You must have had quite a few interesting experiences.
I was in Fargo, North Dakota, for the TV news, and I got pulled over. "This car is illegal," they said. "You do not have windshield wipers, license plates, headlights…" They arrested me and they put the Batmobile away. I got in front of the judge, and the judge said to the officer, "Wilbur, come over here. I want you to know you arrested George Barris and the Batmobile, and I'm demoting you from the

sheriff's department to a dogcatcher." That was kind of interesting. The judge knew all about the Batmobile. But the sheriff's guy, he didn't.

What did you think of the screen Batmobiles that followed yours?
In '89 there was the [Michael] Keaton Batmobile, and the second Keaton film was three years later. In '95, [Val] Kilmer, he had a Batmobile. In '97, [George] Clooney had a big Batmobile. Now, of course, the Dark Knight, he has the Tumbler. But the other Batmobiles had big funny-looking faces and great big huge fins, and each made people think, "This is not a real car." Whereas mine had great design characteristics—and I outlined all of them with an orange, glowing stripe—and people just seemed to feel more comfortable that it did things.

What are some of the car's other features of which you're proudest?
There were oil squirters that came out of the back—the little faucets they use for spraying lawns. It had the rocket tube, a five-gallon paint can that made it into a jet aircraft. It had three tubes in the back that shot bombs up in the air. Then we had the radar center, an electronic unit that came up. We had a sound system with amplifiers. We had Bat emergency fire extinguishers. We had twin Bat red lights in the middle [roll bar], with an emergency light that flashed around and around.

And you managed to make the front of the car look like the head of a bat.
The headlights went up and a pair of ears went out, that kind of followed in the front. The nose came down, and it had a right and left hand side [to] the mouth...In the comic book which Bob Kane did, the Batmobile was just a plain stock car with a bat face cut out and stuck on the front. There was no character. Bob Kane came over here, greeted me and shook my hand, and said, "Well, you finally got a real, great-looking Batmobile."

The ultimate in midcentury automotive design, the 1966 Batmobile housed beneath its hood an atomic-powered, jet turbine engine, and featured—among other necessities—a Batscope on its dash, Bat symbols on its hubcaps, an Emergency Bat-Turn Lever, twin rear parachutes (that could be retrieved by a dedicated Batmobile Parachute Pickup Service van), and a Bat-Beam laser.

When artist Neal Adams got hold of Batman in the late 1960s, he brought a healthy helping of realism to his world. Reasoning that a Masked Manhunter wouldn't want to attract unnecessary attention, he made the Batmobile a simple sport coupe—albeit with armor plating and a stylized Bat mask emblazoned on the hood.

But while Adams was getting real, the Barris Batmobile lived on, inspiring the version seen on TV's *Super Friends* in the 1970s and early 1980s—a blue two-seat convertible with bubble windows and a Bat logo on its doors. By 1978, the comics used a version that combined the *Super Friends* car with Adams' hood design.

In his 1986 opus *The Dark Knight Returns*, Frank Miller gave his Batman the biggest Batmobile in comics history, a rocket-launching tank he uses to combat the Mutant punks overrunning Gotham. Almost as gigantic was the Batmobile in director Tim Burton's 1989 *Batman* movie. The most popular since the Barris model, this dark, seductive beauty, designed by Anton Furst, featured twin side fins, grappling hook launchers, a plated cocoon shield, and decidedly un-Batman-like machine guns and bomb dispensers. Using a Chevrolet Impala chassis and V-8 engine, the Burton Batmobile was converted from the body of a 1970 Corvette. Retaining the 1966 model's rear afterburner and jet turbine engine, it was the first in a long line of Batmobiles with enormous hoods. In 1992's *Batman Returns*, the car could shed its shell in an emergency, and launch a slim Batmissile escape vehicle.

Batman: The Animated Series offered a simpler version of the 1989 Batmobile. More efficient and less ornate, it resembled a locomotive, with a hood that stretched on for days. Its origin was revealed in 1993's *Batman: Mask of the Phantasm*, as a concept car a pre-Batman Bruce Wayne sees at the Gotham World's Fair. *The New Batman Adventures* used a more curvilinear version, if less iconic. The futuristic spinoff *Batman Beyond* gave its hero Terry McGinnis a flying Batmobile, as state-of-the-art as his high-tech Batsuit. But 2004's *The Batman* opted for an earthbound Lamborghini-like model.

When Joel Schumacher followed Burton as the film franchise's director, he gave 1995's *Batman Forever* a Gigeresque biomechanical-looking Batmobile, with a shorter front than the 1989 car, a massive tail fin, and an undercarriage lit neon blue like a robotic lung. Schumacher's 1997 follow-up *Batman & Robin* introduced a one-seat, 30-foot-long roadster, capable in real life of reaching speeds up to 140 mph.

High speeds (up to 110 mph) were also attainable for the "Tumbler" of 2005's *Batman Begins*. Built by Wayne Enterprises for the U.S. military, this all-terrain stealth vehicle was shown to contain the next generation of Batcycle, the Bat-pod, in 2008's *The Dark Knight*.

The comics of the 1990s featured a host of different Batmobiles, changing, along with the books' artists, from issue to issue. The standouts, however, were artist Norm Breyfogle's "spaceship" Batmobiles. So named for their ultra-sleek, wedge-shaped designs and wraparound windows, they looked as capable of traveling the cosmos as they did Gotham's highways. In 2003, in the midst of his "Hush" storyline, artist Jim Lee paid tribute to the multitude of past Batmobiles, showing them safely stored in the recesses of the Batcave in July 2003's *Batman* #615.

The *Batman: Arkham* video games boasted an intimidating muscle car, mounted with missile launchers that referenced both Burton's and Nolan's vehicles, and preceded the Batmobile driven by Ben Affleck's just-as-muscular Dark Knight in 2016's *Batman v Superman: Dawn of Justice*.

As faithful as any knight's steed, the Batmobile charges ever onward, taking any form necessary in its relentless pursuit of justice.

7 Catwoman

With all due respect to Talia al Ghul, Silver St. Cloud, Vicki Vale, Julie Madison, Linda Page, Andrea Beaumont, Wonder Woman, and Kathy Kane, the most important woman in Batman's life was, is, and always shall be the Catwoman.

Her criminal career began in Spring 1940's *Batman* #1, in a story now referred to as "The Cat"—the name by which she was then known—by Batman creators Bill Finger and Bob Kane. Introduced as a young jewel thief disguised as an elderly socialite on a yacht trip, the Cat immediately wins the affection of Batman, who lets her escape at story's end.

In her second appearance, in Summer 1940's *Batman* #2 ("The Joker Meets the Cat-Woman," by Finger and Kane), she first demonstrated her usefulness as an ally to the Dark Knight, when she saved Robin from the Clown Prince of Crime. In the magazine's third issue, she first donned a cape and mask—an unnervingly realistic cat head—when she matched wits with the Caped Crusader in "The Batman vs. The Cat-Woman" (again by Finger and Kane). While she was still addressed as "The Cat" in this story, her next appearance, in April 1942's *Batman* #10 ("The Princess of Plunder," by writer Jack Schiff and penciler Jerry Robinson) saw her officially referred to by the name she's used ever since, "Catwoman." Several appearances later, in June 1946's *Batman* #35 ("Nine Lives Has the

Catwoman," by Finger and Kane), she first sports the green cape and purple dress, boots, gloves, and cowl she would wear until the mid-1960s. By the end of the 1940s, Catwoman's crimes would become cat-themed and she acquired a Kitty Car.

When the 1950s arrived, Catwoman's real name—Selina Kyle—and backstory were revealed at last, in December 1950's *Batman* #62 ("The Secret Life of the Catwoman!" written by Bill Finger and penciled by Bob Kane and Lew Sayre Schwartz). It turned out that Selina was an airline stewardess who fell from a crashing plane, struck her head, developed amnesia, and began a life of crime. Her love of cats was acquired from her father, who'd owned a pet shop when she was a child. In this story, she received a second blow to the head saving Batman from some falling debris, restoring her memory, after which she helped him catch a gang leader by pretending to remain a crook.

Selina then opened a pet shop of her own and continued aiding Batman, even against her own brother, Karl Kyle, the "King of the Cats," in *Batman* #69. But she resumed her criminal career in January 1954's *Detective Comics* #203. Alas, with the formation of the Comics Code Authority in 1954, DC's titles were sanitized and a whip-wielding Catwoman was deemed verboten. September 1954's *Detective Comics* #211 ("The Jungle Cat Queen!") would be Selina's last appearance until 1966, with the squeaky-clean Batwoman replacing her as Batman's costumed romantic interest.

When Catwoman did return, she returned in high style, embodied by a catsuit-clad Julie Newmar in the first season of the 1966 *Batman* TV series. Though she appeared in just one two-part story in the show's first season ("The Purr-fect Crime" / "Better Luck Next Time"), the character proved popular enough to make her silver-screen debut in the 1966 *Batman* movie, played by Lee Meriwether. Newmar returned to the role for the show's second season; and Catwoman returned to comics in November 1966's *Superman's Girlfriend, Lois Lane* #70. When both Newmar and

Meriwether were unable to play the role in *Batman*'s third season, Eartha Kitt became the first African American Catwoman.

With Batman comic sales skyrocketing due to the show's popularity, Selina was given a new costume in 1967, a green variant on her TV outfit, which she wore when she made her animated debut in 1968's *The Batman/Superman Hour* (in which she was voiced by Jane Webb). She earned an unremarkable black-and-blue costume with buccaneer boots and a red mask in 1969, a look on which her 1974 Mego action figure was based. Selina's role in Batman's life lessened in the 1970s, with the introduction of femme fatale Talia al Ghul. But with the arrival of the 1980s, she stepped back into the spotlight in her classic purple outfit. By this time it was established that the Golden Age Catwoman and Batman (who'd since been said to live on Earth-Two) had married and raised a daughter, Helena Kyle, aka the Huntress. The story of their union was told in April 1983's *The Brave and the Bold* #197 ("The Autobiography of Bruce Wayne!"). Sadly, this version of Selina was unable to escape her past, and she was blackmailed into performing one last robbery, resulting in her death. On Earth-One, Selina also forsook her criminal ways for Batman, though there fate again conspired to keep them apart.

After the DC Universe was rebooted with 1985's *Crisis on Infinite Earths*, Selina was given a new history and a sidekick, Holly Madison, in 1987's *Batman: Year One*. A street prostitute, this Selina is inspired by Batman to find a new line of work and don a costume, one more catlike than those she'd previously worn, complete with tail and whiskers. She earned her first comic title with 1989's *Catwoman* limited series, which introduced her sister, Maggie, a nun who tries unsuccessfully to turn Selina away from crime.

Catwoman was reborn on the big screen in the form of Michelle Pfeiffer in Tim Burton's 1992 *Batman Returns,* which gave her a new origin. An abused secretary, this Selina is shoved

Catwoman has had a long and complicated relationship with the Dark Knight. Michelle Pfeiffer gave a memorable performance as Selina Kyle in Tim Burton's Batman Returns. (Newscom)

out a window by her boss and somehow revived and given catlike agility by a clowder of cats. A version of this origin was also used in 2004's *Catwoman* movie, which won an ignominious Golden Raspberry Award for star Halle Berry.

With Catwoman again in the public eye thanks to *Batman Returns* and 1992's *Batman: The Animated Series* (in which she was given a gray catsuit and voiced by Adrienne Barbeau), Catwoman received her first ongoing comic book in 1993 (running until 2001)—in which her catsuit was made purple and she wore thigh-high black boots. The animated Catwoman was given a new look, similar to Pfeiffer's Catwoman, in 1997's *The New Batman Adventures*, the character's most nimble onscreen incarnation.

Writer Ed Brubaker and artist Darwyn Cooke gave the comics' Selina a short haircut and a practical jumpsuit inspired by Emma Peel's catsuit in the 1960s *Avengers* TV show, topped with a pair of infrared goggles, when they kicked off a new ongoing series for her with January 2002's *Catwoman* #1. Here, Selina explains why she believes she and Batman can never be together: "Because my world is all just shades of gray, Batman. That's why you'll never really understand me. It's about good people being forced into bad situations. That's my territory…in between right and wrong. Which is a place you can never go. And we both know it."

Later that year, Cooke wrote and illustrated a graphic novel prequel to the series, *Selina's Big Score*. Like all his work, it's cartooning of the highest order. Though Cooke passed away in 2016, Catwoman continues, with slight alterations, to wear the costume he designed. It was recalled by Anne Hathaway's Selina Kyle in 2012's *The Dark Knight Rises*; Hathaway based her performance on the sultry 1940s film star Hedy Lamarr, whom Bob Kane claimed was an inspiration for the character.

When DC again rebooted its continuity with 2011's "New 52," Catwoman and Batman at last consummated their relationship. After the company's 2016 "Rebirth" relaunch, the Dark Knight finally proposed marriage to the Princess of Plunder.

On screen, the Catwoman has also starred in the 2000 flash-animated web series *Gotham Girls* (again voiced by Barbeau), the 2011 animated short *DC Showcase: Catwoman* (voiced by Eliza Dushku), and *The LEGO Batman Movie* (voiced by Zoe Kravitz). A young Selina, dubbed "Cat," appears in TV's *Gotham*, played by Camren Bicondova. In the *Batman: Arkham* video games, she's voiced by Gray DeLisle. Selina's set to return to theaters in the live-action film adaptation of *Gotham City Sirens*, the 2009 comic series in which she partnered with Poison Ivy and Harley Quinn.

So rich is Selina Kyle's history that entire books have been and will continue to be written about her. Feminist and femme fatale, antihero and heroine, sinner and saint…though a cat has but nine lives, Catwoman's are countless.

8 Commissioner James Gordon

Before Robin, before Alfred, even before Batman himself embarked on his first mission, there was James Gordon. There in the first panel of the first page of the first Batman story, "The Case of the Chemical Syndicate" (by Batman creators Bill Finger and Bob Kane in May 1939's *Detective Comics* #27). There, lighting a cigarette whilst entertaining his socialite friend Bruce Wayne, sat the gray-haired and bespectacled police commissioner, sporting a thin black mustache. At first distrustful of the shadowy vigilante, Gordon came to depend on him to nab the criminals who evaded his men. He eventually deputized the Dark Knight, making him an honorary member of the police department in November 1941's *Batman* #7.

Little, however, was known about the commissioner until August-September 1951's *World's Finest* #53 ("The Private Life of Commissioner Gordon!" by writer David Vern Reed and penciler Dick Sprang), which introduced his wife and teenage son, Tony. Gordon's family was seen infrequently before the introduction of his adult daughter, Barbara, in January 1967's *Detective Comics* #359 ("The Million Dollar Debut of Batgirl!"), by which point Gordon was said to be a widower. The commissioner's physical appearance also changed over time, his mustache having grown fuller by the 1960s and gray by the 1970s.

Gordon's life grew more complicated with the addition of Lieutenant Harvey Bullock to the Gotham City Police Department. Briefly introduced in July 1974's *Detective Comics* #441, Bullock became Gordon's assistant in July 1983's *Batman* #361. Though he was assigned by the corrupt mayor Hamilton Hill—in an attempt to sabotage Gordon's work, resulting in the commissioner suffering a heart attack—the slovenly Bullock eventually reformed and became Gordon's loyal if cynical ally. (A second heart attack in 1991 prompted DC Comics and the American Heart Association to use Gordon in a public-service ad that ran throughout the publisher's titles.)

Writer Frank Miller and artist David Mazzucchelli's reboot of the Dark Knight's origin in 1987's *Batman: Year One* is as much a story about Gordon's early days as it is Batman's. Here, Gordon arrives in Gotham City from Chicago, where he served for years on the force. The city's last honest cop, he attains the rank of captain. But, in the tradition of noir detectives, he's not without weaknesses of his own, and has an affair with a colleague, detective Sarah Essen. This later led to a divorce from his wife, Barbara Kean-Gordon, who took his son. Gordon would marry Essen years later. Before the divorce, Gordon and his first wife adopted their niece Barbara.

Despite the Joker's attempt in 1988's *The Killing Joke* to drive Gordon mad by shooting and crippling his daughter, the commissioner's sanity remained intact. But the Clown Prince of Crime caused Gordon more suffering when he killed Sarah while she saved an infant from him at the end of 1999's "No Man's Land" storyline. Still more horror occurred when Gordon's son James grew up to become a murderous sociopath. James Jr. matched wits with Gordon and Dick Grayson's Batman in the 2011 *Detective Comics* story arc "The Black Mirror," by writer Scott Snyder.

Snyder's 2015 "Superheavy" *Batman* arc saw Gordon himself playing the role of Batman in a robotic suit when the Dark Knight was thought dead. "Jim Gordon is sort of the stand-in for the everyman," says Snyder. "He's a guy with kids, he's got a real job. There's red tape, there's bureaucracy, and yet he's the biggest fan and friend to Batman. That's all of us readers."

Commissioner Gordon's first appearance on screen was in the 1949 *Batman and Robin* film serial, in which he was played by Lyle Talbot. (Talbot would also go on to play the screen's first Lex

Luthor in 1950's *Atom Man vs. Superman* serial.) Neil Hamilton played a lovably inept Gordon in the 1966 *Batman* TV series and feature film, while Pat Hingle portrayed the commissioner in Tim Burton's 1989 *Batman* movie and its three sequels (with the exception of Michael Gough's Alfred, he is the only actor in all four films).

The most layered Gordon in films thus far is in Christopher Nolan's Dark Knight trilogy. Portrayed by Gary Oldman as a younger man than in his prior screen incarnations, this Gordon was directly inspired by the conflicted detective in *Year One*. So too was the youngest-ever screen Gordon, played by Ben McKenzie on TV's *Gotham*—the first live-action production with Gordon as its lead character.

A traditionally older commissioner is played by Oscar winner J.K. Simmons in 2017's *Justice League* movie. The more idiosyncratic live-action Gordon can be found in *Saturday Night Live*'s "Commissioner Gordon Learns Batman Has No Boundaries," a 2011 digital short starring Steve Buscemi as the commissioner opposite Andy Samberg's Batman, lampooning the Dark Knight's habit of sneaking up on and abruptly leaving his bewildered friend.

In cartoon form, Gordon first appeared in 1968's *The Batman/Superman Hour*, voiced by Ted Knight. The definitive animated Gordon debuted in 1992's *Batman: The Animated Series*. *McHale's Navy* star Bob Hastings voiced the series' commissioner through 1998's *The New Batman Adventures*, which included the nightmarish "Over the Edge," an imaginary tale in which Gordon blames Batman for the death of his daughter when Barbara is killed in action as Batgirl. An appropriately harrowing image of their dissolution is seen when Bane sends both men to their deaths by swatting them off the roof of GCPD headquarters with the symbol of their partnership, the Bat-Signal.

Other notable animated Gordons include *The X-Files*' Mitch Pileggi in the 2004 series *The Batman*, *Breaking Bad*'s Bryan

Cranston in 2011's *Batman: Year One* adaptation, and *Twin Peaks*' Ray Wise in 2016's *Batman: The Killing Joke* adaptation.

Appearing in more Batman comic books than any character except the Dynamic Duo, Gordon is the Dark Knight's most vital ally in his war against crime. Without the commissioner's support, the Gotham City Police Department would have long ago hunted him down as a criminal. While Alfred Pennyworth and the various Boy Wonders have kept Bruce Wayne from falling into the abyss, Gordon has made it possible for Gotham City to have a Batman.

9 Gotham City

More so than any one criminal, Gotham City created Batman. And it's Gotham he's vowed to save, refusing to let evil consume it.

The name Gotham, derived from the old English words for "goat" and "home," was originally given to a small town in Nottinghamshire, England, famous for its "Wise Men of Gotham"—so named because its citizens pretended to be simpletons in order to prevent King John from building a highway through their town. The town's name became synonymous with New York City when Washington Irving used it to describe the burgeoning metropolis in his 19th century satirical magazine *Salmagundi*.

It's no surprise then that the Dark Knight's earliest adventures took place in New York, which Batman co-creator Bill Finger renamed Gotham in December 1940's *Batman* #4 ("The Case of the Joker's Crime Circus"), introducing the name on the front page of the city's newspaper, the *Gotham City Gazette*.

Throughout the Golden Age of the 1940s and the Silver Age of the 1950s, Gotham was a twin of New York, with its own Statue of Liberty, a skyscraping "State Building," and various ethnic neighborhoods. Also like Manhattan, it was described as an island founded by Dutch settlers, who gave their new home a mascot, Father Knickerbocker.

What distinguished Gotham was its vernacular architecture—buildings and rooftop advertising displays shaped like giant household items, across which the Dynamic Duo chased their enemies. In those fanciful days, the city also housed a Batman Museum, celebrated Batman Day, and had a Lincoln Memorial–like statue of Batman in Gotham Park. The Gotham in the *Batman* film serials the 1966 TV show is as fabricated as that of the era's comics, shot on studio lots and soundstages.

As Batman's comics grew more serious in the late 1960s and 1970s, Gotham too became a more somber place, and landmarks like the Wayne Foundation Building (in December 1969's *Batman* #217), Arkham Asylum (in October 1974's *Batman* #258), and Crime Alley (in March 1976's *Detective Comics* #457) were established. With writer-artist Frank Miller's 1986 limited series *The Dark Knight Returns* and 1987's *Batman: Year One*, Gotham again mirrored Manhattan, albeit a more crime-ridden one.

Tim Burton's 1989 *Batman* brought a level of fantasy back to the city with production designer Anton Furst's Academy Award–winning vision of Gotham. Furst's conception of the city—inspired by architect Hugh Ferris' work and by Fritz Lang's *Metropolis*—emphasized to a greater extent than ever how Gotham was both a reflection of Batman's psyche and its raison d'être.

The comics incorporated Furst's designs, in Wayne Tower (first seen in February 1992's *Batman: Legends of the Dark Knight* #27) and the numerous gargoyles that appeared throughout the city. Furst's successor, Bo Welch, took things a step further by referencing fascist architecture in Burton's sequel *Batman Returns.* Both films were shot on soundstages, at Pinewood Studios and Warner Brothers, respectively, as were director Joel Schumacher's

Batman Forever and *Batman & Robin* (which gave the city its own theme song in R. Kelly's "Gotham City").

But as Gotham grew more ornate on screen it became less impactful. Christopher Nolan's Dark Knight trilogy made audiences *care* about the city again. By shooting in real cities such as Chicago and London, Nolan captured the verisimilitude he admired in the 1978 *Superman* movie, bringing as much life to Gotham's slums as its stock exchange. Drawing on comic storylines like 1999's "No Man's Land," in which an earthquake cuts off Gotham from the rest of the U.S., Nolan's work coincided with writer Scott Snyder and penciler Greg Capullo's run on the *Batman* comic. Their celebrated collaboration included epics such as "Zero Year," in which the city is flooded and transformed into a post-apocalyptic wasteland by the Riddler.

On TV, 1992's *Batman: The Animated Series* occupied a middle ground between Burton's expressionism and Nolan's later realism. Though it doesn't offer *The Animated Series*' omnipresent airships, TV's *Gotham* explores more of the city than prior screen incarnations, albeit without the presence of Batman.

And Gotham needs its savior, just as Batman needs Gotham—a city as layered, ever-changing, and unpredictable as the Dark Knight himself.

10 The Bat-Signal

A beacon of hope to the people of Gotham and a sign of dread to the city's underworld, the Bat-Signal has long served as Commissioner James Gordon's primary means of calling on the World's Greatest Detective for assistance.

The signal, a searchlight overlaid with the Bat symbol, first shone in the pages of February 1942's *Detective Comics* #60 ("Case of the Costume-Clad Killers," by writer Jack Schiff and penciler Bob Kane). It was described as "a gigantic cone of light [that] pierces the dusk of day and etches an eerie symbol against a black cloud—the silhouette of a giant bat!"

"That's coming from the searchlight on the roof of police headquarters!" says a pedestrian. "Yes," replies another, "they're calling the Batman!" Driving in his car, Bruce Wayne and his ward also see the symbol. "We've got business to attend to, Dick," says Bruce.

The signal appeared time and again in comics throughout the decades that followed. It first appeared on screen in the 1949 *Batman and Robin* film serial, in which it was small enough to be kept in Commissioner Gordon's office, and wheeled to the window when it was needed. The signal appeared again in the 1966 *Batman* TV series, though it was primarily used when Bruce Wayne was away from home, as Gordon most often used the Batphone in his office to contact Batman.

The origin of the signal varies from one continuity to the next. In the 1989 *Batman* film, the Dark Knight gives it to the Gotham City Police Department. In 2005's *Batman Begins*, the signal is created by Gordon, after Batman nabs mob boss Carmine Falcone and mounts him to a searchlight atop police headquarters, casting a bat-like silhouette in the sky.

Occasionally, the signal is used by Gordon to provide comfort for Gotham's citizenry and to terrify its criminal population, as in the 1986 limited series *The Dark Knight Returns* and the 2008 film *The Dark Knight*.

"I always thought the Bat-Signal was a *warning*," says Batman comic book artist Kelley Jones. "That's how the city of Gotham would see it. It wasn't a call to Batman. He was the most dangerous of all these crazy villains. They didn't know he was a hero. That was his angle."

From time to time, Batman's enemies have seized control of the signal and used it against him. Sometimes literally—as in the *Batman: The Animated Series* episode "Over the Edge," when an enraged Bane hurls the signal at Batman and Gordon, knocking them off the roof of GCPD headquarters.

Though the scenario in "Over the Edge" is ultimately revealed as a nightmare of Batgirl, thanks to the Bat-Signal and the force it summons, the sleep of Gotham's citizens is—more often than not—untroubled.

11 The Batcave

Comics began in a cave, as prehistoric drawings. So it's more than appropriate that Batman's career should start there. But the Batcave is more than a point of origin, or the nerve center of the Dark Knight's war on crime. Like his costume and car, it's the physical manifestation of his core being.

Like all things buried deep in the earth, the Batcave was revealed slowly, introduced layer by layer over the course of time. Bruce Wayne first stored his Batmobile in a barn located near Wayne Manor, where he kept his Hall of Trophies and crime lab. Then in August 1942's *Batman* #12 ("The Wizard of Words," by Batman creators Bill Finger and Bob Kane), the Dynamic Duo head to their "secret underground hangars," where they keep their Batplanes and Batmobiles, which are pulled up a steep incline into the barn via winch.

In the second chapter of the 1943 *Batman* film serial, the underground lair was formally introduced as "The Bat's Cave." It housed live bats and a crime laboratory, but at this point it was

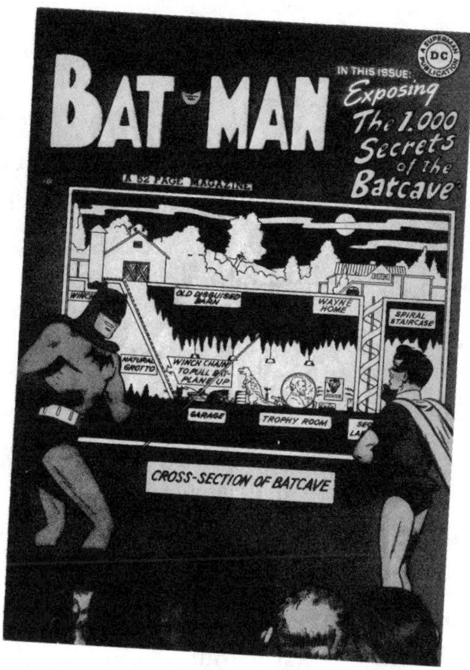

The Batcave has long provided Batman and Robin a place to store their suits, vehicles, and arsenal.
(Cover art by Win Mortimer)

little more than a glorified office space, dominated by a large desk with a bat symbol looming behind it. It was here, however, that its secret entrance—hidden behind a grandfather clock in the study of Wayne Manor—was established.

Shortly thereafter, the cave first appeared in print, in the October 29, 1943, installment of the *Batman* newspaper comic strip ("The Bat Cave!"). Its first official appearance in a comic book came the following year, in January 1944's *Detective Comics* #83 ("Accidentally on Purpose," by writer Don Cameron and penciler Jack Burnley). When an alarm goes off in Wayne Manor, Dick Grayson exclaims, "The alarm from the Bat Cave! Someone must be down there!" (That someone turns out to be Alfred, using its gym.)

When the Hall of Trophies (or Trophy Room, as it would be called) became part of the Batcave, it grew substantially. Its two best-known prizes—the huge robotic dinosaur and giant penny—were souvenirs from June-July 1946's *Batman* #35 ("Dinosaur Island") and September-October 1947's *World's Finest* #30 ("The Penny Plunderers"). They were joined by a collection of the Penguin's trick umbrellas and an enormous mask of the Joker's face, as well as the Red Hood costume worn by the Joker in his first criminal guise, as seen in February 1951's *Detective Comics* #168 ("The Man Behind the Red Hood!").

The most poignant item in the collection, however, was a Bat costume worn at a costume party by Bruce Wayne's father shortly before his murder, revealed in September 1956's *Detective Comics* #235 ("The First Batman"). "Gee, Daddy," says a young Bruce in a flashback sequence, "I wish I could wear a suit like that!" "I'll save it for you, Bruce," Dr. Thomas Wayne replies, "to wear when you grow up!" While wearing the suit, Thomas was abducted by bank robber Lew Moxon, who wanted him to remove a policeman's bullet from his arm. But Thomas wound up sending Moxon to prison. Upon his release, Moxon hired Joe Chill to murder Thomas and his wife, as the Batman finds out shortly before hunting down Moxon in his late father's costume.

Another costume memento first appeared in Frank Miller's 1986 miniseries *The Dark Knight Returns*—the suit worn as Robin by Jason Todd. Though the series itself isn't considered canon by DC, Jason was later killed in the 1988 Batman story arc "A Death in the Family," and his glass-encased costume became a permanent fixture of the cave.

When the first Robin went off to college, in 1969, Bruce Wayne decided to seal up the Batcave and move into the penthouse of the Wayne Foundation building in downtown Gotham City, where he lived for most of the 1970s. The building's sub-basement served as his base of operations during this time (prefiguring Batman's HQ in Christopher Nolan's 2008 film *The Dark Knight*). Yet this wasn't the first alternate Batcave—August 1952's *Detective Comics* #186 had introduced "The Flying Batcave," from which

Batman and Robin patrolled the streets of Gotham. And by the 2000s, satellite Batcaves existed as safe houses throughout Gotham.

The history of the original Batcave has, like so much of the Bat mythos, evolved over the years. "The Origin of the Batcave" was first told in March 1954's *Detective Comics* #205, in which it was established as the former secret headquarters of 17th century frontiersman Jeremy Coe, who spied on Native Americans for settlers. This same story explained that Bruce Wayne discovered the cave by accident when he purchased Wayne Manor, planning to use the barn in back of the property as his headquarters. But later tales showed him growing up on the property, and *The Dark Knight Returns* established that six-year-old Bruce fell into the cave, terrified—and later inspired—by the many bats residing there.

That depiction informed the Batcave's appearances in 1989's *Batman* movie as well as Nolan's Dark Knight trilogy. But whether it's the foreboding lair of those films or the bright base of operations in the 1966 *Batman* TV series (as cheery as any home housing an atomic pile), the Batcave will always be the one place where Bruce Wayne can hang his cowl.

12 Alfred Pennyworth

The one man to whom both Bruce Wayne and Batman can always turn for advice, Alfred Thaddeus Crane Pennyworth has served as butler, chauffeur, chef, medic, and mechanic. But above all, he's Bruce's surrogate father, and a surrogate grandfather to the Robins who Batman has taken under his wing.

When first introduced in April 1943's *Batman* #16 ("Here Comes Alfred," by writer Don Cameron and penciler Bob Kane),

Alfred arrives in Gotham City on a ship from England, heads straight to Wayne Manor, and informs Bruce Wayne and Dick Grayson that he's their new butler. The son of Bruce's father's butler, he explains that although he "forsook the family calling to be an actor in the music halls," his father's dying wish was that his son should again serve a Wayne.

When burglars break into Wayne Manor, Alfred, in the resulting scuffle, accidentally discovers the Batcave. "I've always admired the Batman as a brother criminologist," says Alfred in his first appearance. Intended as comic relief, the character enjoyed his own series of backup stories as a bumbling amateur sleuth. Promoted on the cover of *Batman* #22 as "The Adventures of Alfred," his strip ran for 13 installments, all of which were penciled by Jerry Robinson.

A short, portly, clean-shaven Brit, Alfred was sent to a health spa in January 1944's *Detective Comics* #83 in order to more closely resemble actor William Austin, who played the character in the 1943 *Batman* film serial. He reemerged as a slim gentleman with a pencil mustache. In *Detective Comics* #96, his last name was revealed to be Beagle, though it was confirmed as Pennyworth decades later in *Batman* #216 (which also introduced his niece Daphne).

For a time, Alfred tried his hand at writing fiction, and penned a series of stories about a grown-up Dick Grayson fighting crime as the second Batman, with the son of Bruce Wayne and Batwoman Kathy Kane—Bruce Wayne Jr.—as his sidekick, the second Robin. The last such story was featured in May 1964's *Batman* #163, and the tales prefigured the similar saga of Batman and Superman's "Super-Sons," as well as writer Grant Morrison's 2009 run on *Batman and Robin* (which saw Dick, as Batman, partner with Bruce Wayne's son, Damian), and the 2010 *Batman: The Brave and the Bold* episode that adapts Alfred's tales, "The Knights of Tomorrow!"

In the 1960s, the idea of three bachelors living together in Wayne Manor began to raise some eyebrows. So, once more playing the role of investigator in June 1964's *Detective Comics* #328, Alfred joins the Dynamic Duo on a case, and is killed pushing them out of the way of some falling rocks. Dick's heretofore unseen Aunt Harriet then moved into Wayne Manor as Bruce and Dick's housekeeper.

When the *Batman* TV show debuted in January 1966, both Aunt Harriet and Alfred—played with a constant twinkle in his eye by Alan Napier—were seen living at Wayne Manor, causing some frustration at DC Comics over the decision to kill him off. Two years later, in *Detective Comics* #356, it was explained Alfred had been revived by a scientific procedure that gave him an alternate personality, and that he had unknowingly spent many months battling his former masters as the mysterious Outsider.

April 1981's *Detective Comics* #501 saw the first appearance of Alfred's long-lost daughter, Julia, whose mother, the French superheroine Mademoiselle Marie, had a liaison with Alfred in France during World War II. With an interest in both Bruce Wayne and Batman, Julia became, for a time, the principal romantic rival of Bruce's on-again, off-again girlfriend Vicki Vale, until she was written out of DC continuity in 1985's *Crisis on Infinite Earths*. She was later reintroduced in 2014 as an SSR agent in the pages of *Batman Eternal*, a part of DC's "New 52" initiative.

Alfred's history has been refined several times since his introduction. At one point, it was stated that he'd served as an intelligence agent in World War II. But in 1987's *Batman: Year One*, his history was rewritten entirely, so that he'd served Thomas and Martha Wayne and raised their son after their deaths. This Alfred became much more of a father figure to Bruce, and inspired the versions of the character played by Michael Gough in the 1989 *Batman* movie and by Michael Caine in *Batman Begins*.

In 2012's *Batman: Earth One Volume 1*, writer Geoff Johns and artist Gary Frank introduced a very different Alfred, a Royal Marine who'd befriended Thomas Wayne while serving in the Middle East. After suffering a leg injury and getting discharged, this Alfred is offered a job as Wayne Manor's head of security, and upon Thomas and Martha's deaths is appointed legal guardian of Bruce. It's the *Batman: Earth One* Alfred who inspired the versions of the character in TV's *Gotham* (played by Sean Pertwee), the animated *Beware the Batman* (voiced by JB Blanc, he acquires a goddaughter—Batman's partner Tatsu Yamashiro), and *Batman v Superman: Dawn of Justice* (played by Jeremy Irons).

Though Oscar winner Ralph Fiennes voiced a memorable Alfred in 2017's *The LEGO Batman Movie*, the most beloved animated incarnation of Wayne Manor's majordomo is in *Batman: The Animated Series*, voiced by Efrem Zimbalist Jr. Admonishing and administering affection in equal measure, Zimbalist's Alfred is the ideal parent, and the calm in the eye of Batman's storm.

13 The Utility Belt

Though he's developed his body and mind to the peak of perfection, Batman has no superpowers. Instead, he has something equally fantastic: his utility belt.

Reports vary as to the belt's origins. In its early appearances, it was the creation of Bruce Wayne himself, then as skilled in engineering and design as in criminology. By the time of Christopher Nolan's Dark Knight trilogy, it's a product of Wayne Enterprises' weapons division. But in any case, it's packed with more gadgets than a dozen James Bond movies.

The bright yellow belt is first seen when Batman makes his debut appearance in May 1939's *Detective Comics* #27 ("The Case of the Chemical Syndicate," by Batman creators Bill Finger and Bob Kane), though here it's merely used to hold up the hero's pants. In the following issue, ("Frenchy Blake's Jewel Gang," again by Finger and Kane), it's revealed to contain his Batrope, the first tool in his arsenal. When Batman appears for the third time, in *Detective Comics* #29 ("The Bat-Man Meets Doctor Death," written by Gardner Fox with pencils by Bob Kane), it's revealed to hold "choking gas capsules," which aid Batman against the first supervillain he faces, a mad scientist.

The belt's design evolved in the stories of the 1940s. Its round buckle became square, and the number of compartments the belt contained—usually depicted as slender tubes—varied from artist to artist (though 10 was eventually decided a suitable number). The contents of the tubes also varied, depending on what Batman needed to escape each issue's death trap. Bat-Bolas, lock picks, recording devices, and his signature tool, the Batarang, were among the most common items.

In July 1952's *Detective Comics* #185 ("The Secret of Batman's Utility Belt!" by writer David Vern Reed and penciler Dick Sprang), a more consistent inventory for the belt emerged, including a tiny microscope, a miniature camera, "strange chemicals," smoke pellets, the aforementioned gas capsules, a tiny flashlight, a silken rope in the belt lining, and a disc sewn into its fabric. Should he ever find himself in a trap from which he could not escape, Batman could pour a chemical onto the disc, and it would reveal his secret identity to those who found his corpse, thus preventing any criminal from impersonating him and committing crimes in his name.

The utility belt's tube-studded design was maintained for most of the following 30 years, though some of those tubes were replaced with square pouches in the 1966 *Batman* TV series, in which the belt's inventory expanded to include such tools as the Anti-Mesmerizing Bat-Reflector, the oversized Bat-Shield, and a Bat-Container of alphabet soup.

Frank Miller's *The Dark Knight Returns* reintroduced Batman's earlier, more simplified costume design, and with it a utility belt with military-style pouches and gadgets less fanciful. The belt design of the 1950s, 1960s, and 1970s was still used, however, in Tim Burton's 1989 *Batman* movie and its sequels. The 1989 film added a grappling gun, from which the Batrope is fired. Stored at the back of the belt, it's slid to the front via a small motor. *Batman Begins*, in keeping with Christopher Nolan's more realistic approach, made its utility belt as tactical as any real-world military equipment, comprised of compartments that held an assortment of grapple guns and razor-sharp Batarangs.

Like the Batsuit and Batmobile and other elements of the Dark Knight's world, the utility belt has mirrored the different eras in which he's operated. But, like Batman himself, its purpose is as clear today as it was when first strapped on.

14 The Batarang

Captain America has his shield, Wonder Woman her lariat, and Thor his hammer. But the Dark Knight has something better than all three put together. The amazingly versatile, always dependable, and downright indispensable Batarang. As swift and silent as its namesake, it's the perfect tool for the Caped Crusader.

Batman threw his first Batarang in September 1939's *Detective Comics* #31 ("Batman Versus the Vampire, Part 1," by writer Gardner Fox and pencilers Bob Kane and Sheldon Moldoff).

Modeled after the Australian bushman's boomerang, the device misses its mark the first time it's thrown—at the villainous Monk—but later helps Batman escape his very first death trap. When the Monk captures him in a gigantic net and lowers him into a pit of snakes, Batman uses the Batarang to knock over the unnecessarily slow dipping mechanism's lever and shatter a chandelier, cutting himself free with its shards.

In his early noir-infused career, Batman's Batarangs were usually used to bop bad guys on the head and hurl his Batrope atop buildings. But with the introduction of Robin, his stories acquired a lighter tone, and the Batarangs grew increasingly colorful. In June 1957's *Detective Comics* #244 ("The 100 Batarangs of Batman," written by Batman co-creator Bill Finger and penciled by Sheldon Moldoff), the device's origin was first revealed in a flashback sequence.

While on the hunt for a criminal at a circus, Batman runs across Australian boomerang expert Lee Collins, who creates a diversion with his boomerang that allows Batman to catch his quarry. Impressed by Collins' skills, Batman asks him to teach him everything he knows about boomerangs. "I want to have absolute control," says the Caped Crusader, "since I'm going to use this not as a weapon, but as a sort of extension-arm!" When Batman grows as skillful as his instructor, Collins presents him with a boomerang he's designed, with bat-like wings.

Back in the present, the Dynamic Duo introduce readers to an assortment of customized Batarangs they've used in their cases. Among these are the Magnetic Batarang, with which they snatched a counterfeit mob's engraving plates; a Seeing-Eye Batarang that helped them find a trio of hidden bandits; and a Whistling Batarang that alerted Commissioner Gordon to an attempt on his life.

The Flash-Bulb Batarang and Rope Batarang also appear in this story, as does the most impressive Batarang seen up until that point, one so powerful that Batman and Robin keep it under lock and key in the Batcave behind a special door that bears its name: Batarang X. A giant Batarang, launched from a catapult, Batman uses it to infiltrate the island headquarters of a group of thieves who've built Batarangs of their own—Bomb Batarangs!—to loot Gotham City. Quietly arriving at their storage shed, Batman takes out their explosives and alters their wings so the criminals' plan backfires on them.

The Batarang's popularity influenced Batman's fellow Justice Leaguer Green Arrow in fashioning his Golden and Silver Age arsenal of trick arrows (Oliver Queen also drew inspiration from his friend in building his 1940s "Arrowcar" and "Arrowcave"). But when Frank Miller's *The Dark Knight Returns* limited series launched a darker era for superheroes in 1986, the most overt symbol of this change was the Batarang.

A smaller version of the tool was introduced, no longer based on a boomerang, but rather a ninja throwing star, or shuriken. Razor-edged and lethal, this new Batarang proved popular in the comic stories of the 1990s, eventually becoming the primary Batarang used by Christian Bale's Batman in 2005's *Batman Begins* and its two sequels.

15 Dick Sprang

The 2016 direct-to-video animated film *Batman: Return of the Caped Crusaders*—a continuation of the 1966 *Batman* TV series—features a fight scene, like so many in the show, in which sound effects burst across the scene as onomatopoeic graphics. Amidst the BOWs, BAMs, and WHAPs, one word flashes by that may go unrecognized by most viewers. But for Batfans who cherish the comics of the

1940s and 1950s, it's a name as significant as any in the Bat mythos: SPRANG.

Dick Sprang didn't create Batman, but he perfected him. He took the stiff, sometimes crude figure rendered by Bob Kane and fortified by inker Jerry Robinson, and made him a lantern-jawed, barrel-chested bastion of justice. Like all early Batman artists, Sprang was forbidden by Kane from putting his name on his work, since Kane's arrangement with DC stipulated that he alone receive credit for Batman. But just as Carl Barks came to be known as the "good" artist on "Walt Disney's" Donald Duck, so too did Sprang come to be recognized as the "good" Batman artist.

Born Richard W. Sprang on July 28, 1915, in Fremont, Ohio, to William and Hannah Sprang, he was a largely self-taught artist. Upon graduating from high school, Sprang took a job in the art department of the Scripps-Howard newspaper chain in Toledo, for which he supplied a steady stream of advertising for five daily editions. "I learned the value of meeting a deadline," says Sprang in a 1987 interview with Ike Wilson published in December 2002's *Alter Ego* #19. "You grew up fast in that atmosphere. That was better training than could be found in the majority of art schools of the day."

Eager to expand his horizons, Sprang moved to New York City and freelanced for four years as a pulp magazine illustrator. But he recognized the pulp era was coming to a close. A fan of the newspaper comic strips *Terry and the Pirates*, *Prince Valiant*, and *Flash Gordon*, he sought work at DC Comics. Assigned a Batman story by Whitney Ellsworth, Sprang impressed the editor with the cinematic quality he brought to his work. After illustrating the Dynamic Duo on the cover of August-September 1943's *Batman* #18, his first Batman stories appeared in *Batman* #19.

The years Sprang spent as an illustrator, coupled with his love of films, established his vision of Gotham City as the most vital and vivid of the Golden Age. His panels pulled readers in with varied depth, scope, and focus. "Now, this had been done before, of course," says Sprang in a 1989 interview with Lou Mougin in David Anthony Kraft's *Comics Interview Super Special: Batman* (published by Fictioneer Books Ltd.), "by several men, most notably [*Terry and the Pirates* creator] Milton Caniff—moving the camera around, using the movie techniques, using the frozen frame; moviemakers call the apex of action the still shot. So I continued with this…I went all-out with my ideas on page composition, of the flow and rhythm of sequential panels. And [DC] liked it."

Fans liked it, too. Among Sprang's designs were the second Batmobile, the Batplane, and the Batmarine, as well as one of the Batman's most popular foes—the Riddler. Sprang's own favorite villains were the Penguin and the Joker, the latter of whom he distinguished with a grin that took up half his face. "I loved them both," says Sprang in *Alter Ego* 19. "They were great to move around through their crazy projects of crime."

Sprang left New York with his wife, Lora Neusiis—who often lettered his work under the name Pat Gordon—in 1946, eventually settling in Sedona, Arizona. The couple divorced in 1951, but Sprang continued to work on *Batman* and *Detective Comics*, on which DC paired him with inker Charles Paris. Sprang, with his sturdy draftsmanship and dynamic lines, and Paris, with his bold inks, sent their heroes and villains hurtling over every giant prop writer Bill Finger could come up with. Their Batman and Robin traveled the globe, the details of each locale meticulously researched. A history buff, Sprang relished the opportunity to explore other eras in time-travel stories scripted by science fiction writer Edmond Hamilton. By the late 1950s, Sprang and Paris worked exclusively on *World's Finest*, in which the Caped Crusaders were paired with Superman in a string of epic adventures.

But by 1963, Sprang had had enough. In his third marriage, to Elizabeth Lewis (his second wife, Dudy Thomas, having died of a brain tumor in 1958), he suffered from depression, and tired of the

Dick Sprang is cited by many as their favorite illustrator of Batman. His style is encapsulated brilliantly in his "Secrets of the Batcave" lithograph. (Art by Dick Sprang)

grind of comics. Keen on exploring the Southwest, he retired, and found fame carving paths and discovering Native American Anasazi ruins. He wound up in Phoenix with his fourth wife, Marion Lyday, with whom he lived for the last 28 years of his life.

"More than anything else," says Sprang in *Alter Ego*, "I wanted to get out in the hills and the mountains and the canyons, and run the rivers in my own boat, explore the West, research its history, and come to know its isolated regions as well as any man—which I've done, and am doing in great measure. Comics paid my way, so bless 'em."

Sprang's style fell out of favor with some Batfans due to their disapproval of the 1966 *Batman* TV show, which took many of its visual cues from his work. By the late 1980s, however, his name had become known at last to fans, and DC began commissioning him pin-up art and covers. In 1995 and 1996, he illustrated a pair of limited-edition lithographs for Gotham Graphics, of which his "Secrets of the Batcave" is an especially stunning salute to decades of gadgets, vehicles, and casework.

Sprang died on May 10, 2000, at the age of 84 in Prescott, Arizona. Northern Arizona University—in its Richard (Dick) Sprang Collection—notes that Sprang "was considered an authority on the canyon country of southern Utah and Northern Arizona," but his legacy is forever entwined with Batman. An influence on generations of creators, his art and aesthetic served as the basis for 2008's *Batman: The Brave and the Bold.*

"Dick Sprang's work, as well as the work of Chester Gould, the *Dick Tracy* artist, I kind of see them as cut from the same cloth," says *The Brave and the Bold* producer James Tucker. "They're very dynamic storytellers, but they're almost abstractionists in the way they draw up characters. They revel in grotesqueness. Even Dick Sprang's noble heroes look kind of weird—the big lantern jaws and impossibly wide shoulders. They drew in extremes, so you could generally tell what a character was just by looking at the outline of the way they drew it. There was no subtlety. They were showmen in the way they designed their characters. Every character was distinct...The Dick Sprang stuff was just amazing."

16 Batman's "New Look"

What a difference an emblem makes.

After beginning his career as a humorless vigilante, Batman's exploits took on a lighter tone with the introduction of Robin in the 1940s. Dr. Fredric Wertham's crusade against comics in the 1950s saw sci-fi stories and tales of the extra-dimensional Bat-Mite supplant the evil of Two-Face and the Scarecrow. By 1961, children of America grew disinterested, and sales reflected it.

Looking to revive interest, Batman editor Jack Schiff allowed veteran villains such as the Joker and the Penguin to return in 1962 and 1963, the year the alien invasions finally stopped. But by then Schiff's bosses—DC Comics (then National Periodical Publications) editorial director and publisher Irwin Donenfeld and president Jack Liebowitz—had decided to replace him with editor Julius Schwartz. Considered the father of DC's Silver Age for his rebooting of Golden Age heroes the Flash and Green Lantern, Schwartz was tasked with similarly updating Batman and Detective Comics, alongside his *Flash* artist Carmine Infantino.

"Irwin told us that Batman was in terrible shape," said Infantino in his 2000 autobiography *The Amazing World of Carmine Infantino* (published by Vanguard Productions). "He said, 'I'm going to give you six months to save the character. If you can pull it out, fine; but if you can't get the sales up, we want to drop it.' That's how bad it was."

Infantino altered the ears and nose of Batman's cowl, and Schwartz suggested adding a yellow oval behind his Bat-symbol chest emblem. The result was heralded on the cover of May 1964's *Detective Comics* #327 ("The Mystery of the Menacing Mask!" written by Gardner Fox and penciled by Infantino) as Batman's

"New Look." At the time DC's top artist, Infantino demanded Bob Kane's signature, which until then had been added to the work of the Batman co-creator's "ghost" artists, be kept off his pages. It was the first time such a request had been made, and Schwartz had the power to grant it. Eventually, Kane's name was left off of all Batman artists' work.

Besides the oval, Schwartz initiated other changes. In June 1964's *Batman* #164 ("Two-Way Gem Caper!" written by Ed Herron and penciled by Sheldon Moldoff), Batman replaced the large, single-rear-finned Batmobile he'd driven for years with a convertible sports car. Designed by Infantino, this Batmobile was no longer hoisted out of the Batcave on a winch, but blasted through an automatic garage door onto a hillside and a highway. And the secret entrance to the Batcave, a set of stairs behind a grandfather clock in Wayne Manor, was replaced with an elevator tucked behind a hidden wall panel. "Two-Way Gem Caper!" also saw the introduction of the Batmobile's hot-line phone, which connected directly to Commissioner Gordon's office. ("It'll take only a moment to find out what's going on!" exclaims Robin.)

That same issue's "The Mystery Analysts of Gotham City" introduced a group of detectives who aided Batman in his casework; under Schwartz, the Caped Crusader again became a detective, albeit one who frequently operated in broad daylight. But few complained when those daylight scenes were rendered by Infantino, whose sleek layouts and bold designs brought a renewed vigor to the streets of Gotham City. Infantino also designed new foes Poison Ivy and Blockbuster, and Batgirl Barbara Gordon.

Sales reflected readers' approval of the changes. But sales would *explode* two years later, when the Dynamic Duo made their TV debut.

Gotham Gazette Exclusive

Carmine Infantino

Artist Carmine Infantino was responsible for some of DC Comics' most beloved Silver Age characters, including the Flash and the Elongated Man. He brought his sleek design sense to Gotham City with the "New Look" Batman of 1964 and the Barbara Gordon Batgirl. Infantino passed away in 2013 at the age of 87. The following interview was conducted in 2002.

Who influenced your work?
Hal Foster and Milt Caniff. And then, after Caniff, I went off on my own. That's when it really changed. Then when I studied with John McNulty at the Art Students League, he got me involved with Degas and the Impressionists. That was the real influence for me.

This was in the late '50s?
Yeah, that was the group I really studied. McNulty put me onto it, and all of the sudden I saw a whole world opening up there. And that was part of the design work—the Impressionists.

Your Silver Age work is known for its design, its fantastic layouts.
McNulty was a genius at this, and he really banged the helm with me. He'd hammer away, hammer away. It broke down to the simplest terms: everything has to direct where you want the eye to look. That's basically the whole thing—composition. So he got his point across, I think, to his youngest student. I was always focusing on composition.

How much of Batman's "New Look" was your idea?
The only thing I did was...[Editor] Julie Schwartz asked for a circle around the Bat emblem. That was it. But Batgirl I designed. The Batmobile I [re]designed.

Batgirl was the first woman in Batman's universe whose popularity rivaled that of Catwoman. How did you come up with her look?
Well, they just said to me, "[The TV show producers] want a new character." So that led to Batgirl, and that was it! And then the car. I

redesigned the car. It had looked stupid—it had a big bat head symbol on it. Then I designed a couple of villains. Poison Ivy, I created her.

Was her look inspired by any particular actress?
No, no. She was just a really sexy girl… And I designed Blockbuster. Remember Blockbuster? Those were the [Batman] characters I created.

The quality of your Silver Age work was consistently very high.
I was diligent. I didn't fool around. If I did it, I did it. It was hard work, but I did it. The work ethic was important. What happened was, I was starting to get very sloppy at one point, and that's why I went back to school at night. That changed it around. That's when the new style came out, and everything came out of it. It gave me a new vision in the work. I think an artist has to have that every once in a while.

Is that when your work started getting crazier, with its anthropomorphic caption boxes and so forth?
I had become a designer more than anything else. I gave up the art and became a designer. I stopped being an artist. If you look carefully, you'll see there's no drawings in that stuff—it's pure design.

Your work also had a keen respect for superheroes. You treated them casually, as though they really existed.
Oh, yeah, we couldn't kid around on the thing. If you made fun of it, then you lost the quality. So you had to take it serious. And you had to make it seem very serious. If you didn't, and it looked silly, then it didn't work.

You've said you were frustrated when the 1966 *Batman* TV show debuted.
They were pushing us to do more of that "BAP! POW! ZAM!" thing. I didn't do it. I just didn't do it.

You've contributed a great deal to pop culture. Looking back on your work, how do you feel about it?
I don't relate to it anymore.

You don't think too much about it?
No. It's over and done with, and you can't relive it. I just can't relate to it, in all honesty. It was nice doing it at the time, but I'm at a different point in life now, and I'm enjoying it just as much. Once in a while I'll do a recreation of the old covers, and that's about all. I literally don't enjoy it anymore. I had enough years of it. I've done everything that I wanted to do with it. I have nothing more to say, and just to be redundant, to keep doing the same thing over and over and over...I just can't do it. So I'd rather let it stop at that level, let it be, and let it have a life of its own. It makes more sense, I think. I'm just having a good time in life.

17 The 1966 *Batman* TV Series

It's been said that 1960s pop culture consisted of three B's: the Beatles, Bond, and Batman.

But while John, Paul, George, Ringo, and 007 have been universally beloved since their midcentury heyday, the 1966 *Batman* television series was, for a long time, the most polarizing of phenomena.

The show was sparked by the theatrical re-release of the 1940s *Batman* film serials in art houses, where the Z-grade affairs offered laughs for the decade's hipsters. No less a cultural tastemaker than Hugh Hefner glommed onto them, with a screening of the 1943 serial at Chicago's Playboy mansion. In attendance was an ABC executive, who, according to Batman co-creator Bob Kane, saw the audience's delight at the unintentional campiness and hit upon the idea of a deliberately campy Batman. After the idea reached ABC vice president Douglas Cramer, a call was made to film and

TV producer William Dozier. Though Dozier had no love for comic books, he picked up a copy of May 1965's *Batman* #171, "Remarkable Ruse of the Riddler!"(written by Gardner Fox and penciled by Sheldon Moldoff)—which featured the villain's first appearance since the 1940s—and saw the potential for a series that functioned on two levels: serious adventure for children and uproarious comedy for adults.

Actor Adam West had recently appeared in a Nestle Quik TV commercial as a James Bond–like character named "Captain Q," demonstrating an ability to be simultaneously funny and suave that convinced Dozier he could play both the intensely focused Batman and his easygoing alter ego, Bruce Wayne. Acting neophyte Burt Ward complemented West perfectly as Wayne's ward, the overly enthusiastic Dick Grayson / Robin the Boy Wonder. The cast was rounded out by English actor Alan Napier as their devoted butler, Alfred, Madge Blake as Dick's perennially flustered Aunt Harriet, and Neil Hamilton and Stafford Repp as the well-meaning but inept Gotham City police commissioner James Gordon and chief Miles O'Hara, respectively.

The Riddler was, naturally, selected for the show's pilot, "Hi Diddle Riddle" (which was based on "Remarkable Ruse of the Riddler!") and comedian/impressionist Frank Gorshin was cast. Jill St. John played the first of the series' many gun molls—most of whom found Batman irresistibly groovy—appropriately named Molly. When it premiered on January 12, 1966, faux pompously narrated by Dozier, audiences watched Batman enter a go-go bar while hunting for the Prince of Puzzlers, get slipped a mickey, dance the Batusi, and then get stopped by police for being too drunk to drive in pursuit of a kidnapped Robin. The public went crazy, but serious comic fans thought their hero was being made fun of. They were right.

At the time, Batman was an easy figure to mock. The character's light sci-fi era had ended, but stories like that in *Batman*

The Batman *television series, starring Adam West and Burt Ward, has retained its place in pop culture since it debuted in 1966.* (Newscom)

#171, stiffly drawn by Batman co-creator Bob Kane's "ghost" artist Sheldon Moldoff, were still in abundance, despite talented penciler Carmine Infantino having introduced the sleek "New Look" Batman a year before the show debuted. The character's flailing comic sales had picked up as a result, but those sales *skyrocketed* after the show arrived. Untold numbers of viewers purchased their first comic book, and the merchandise was nearly limitless. From bubblegum machine buttons to kitchenware, from peanut butter to trading cards, Batman, Robin, and their rogues gallery were everywhere.

Much of the show's appeal comes from its "special guest villains," including Gorshin's unhinged and hyperactive Riddler (the version that ensured the character's longevity), Cesar Romero's jubilant joy-buzzing Joker, and Burgess Meredith as that imitation avian/aristocrat, the Penguin. Yes, alliteration was a thing, as were the Dutch angles that framed each villain's lair, including that of the curvaceous Catwoman, played by Tony-winning Broadway star Julie Newmar.

West, however, was the show's chief draw. Tearing into each line of Batman's dialogue with the fervor of someone born to be the Caped Crusader, it's no wonder he was typecast ever after, reduced to getting shot out of a cannon at an Indiana carnival in his Batsuit, before his career resurgence in the 1990s. A true artist, he invented, patented, and sold his own unique cadence in the role, his own body language. Giving lessons in civic duty to Robin or solemnly vowing to foil whatever menace threatens Gotham, he deftly balanced his responsibilities to both of the show's intended audiences, maintaining an endearing earnestness.

"Haven't you noticed how we always escape the vicious ensnarements of our enemies?" West's Batman asks Robin after they escape one of Catwoman's death traps. "Yeah, because we're smarter than they are!" replies the Boy Wonder. Smiling, West turns Batman's response into a thing of beauty: "I like to think it's because our hearts are pure."

Equally beautiful was *Batman*'s catchy one-word theme music by Neal Hefti (later covered by the Who and the Kinks and referenced in the Beatles' "Taxman"), as well as each episode's Nelson Riddle score, eye-popping production design by Leslie Thomas (one of many ways, including its animated opening, in which the show capitalized on the recent appearance of color TV in American homes), and car customizer George Barris' jet-engined, atomic-powered Batmobile, the epitome of Cold War automotive cool.

While the show offered much more than camp, it introduced the aesthetic to mainstream America. It was a fact that may have delighted the host of gay talents who guest-starred, including Romero, Roddy McDowall, Liberace, Van Johnson, Maurice

Evans, Victor Buono, and Tallulah Bankhead (Dozier, who'd been married to Joan Fontaine, had a Rolodex stuffed with Golden Age vets)—to say nothing of the many stars who popped out of windows for a cameo whilst the Dynamic Duo Bat-Climbed their way up building walls.

With the exception of "Hi Diddle Riddle," *Batman*'s first season—in which its stories are comprised of two episodes, a cliffhanger separating them—is almost played straight. Or at least as straight as the giant props of the era's comics allowed. (Here those props are as faithfully adapted as many of the books' stories.) But the *Batman* film spun off of that first season amps up the comedy. And the second season, which contains a couple of three-parters, revels in it. Gorshin sat out the second run, but Newmar's Catwoman purred through more episodes, developing her kooky, endearing relationship with Batman.

Audiences, however, grew tired of the joke by the end of the show's second year, which combined with budget cuts to make the third season a largely lackluster affair. Despite the addition of Yvonne Craig's appealing Batgirl, and the admirably diverse casting of racially mixed singer and political activist Eartha Kitt as Catwoman, the third season would be the show's last.

But if a show's success can be measured by how often it's referenced more than 50 years later, then *Batman*'s is absolute. "To the Batmobile," "Atomic batteries to power, turbines to speed," "Same Bat-time, same Bat-channel," "Correct, old chum," "Riddle me this," "The worst is yet to come," and any number of Robin's "Holy…!" exclamations have made their way into the lexicon of everyday life.

Today, it's remarkable how contemporary *Batman*'s humor feels, how much of it has found its way into the comedy of recent decades. Its deadpan is echoed in the films of the Coen Brothers, its fastidious labeling mirrored in the work of Wes Anderson. Its influence has caused it to age better than Tim Burton's movie blockbusters, despite their initial embrace from fans as a return to Batman's dark roots.

One of the reasons so many hardcore comic book fans hated the show was because it became synonymous with the words "comic book." As a result, any public reference to superheroes was, for decades, prefaced with some combination of "Biff!," "Bang!," and "Pow!," after the series' onomatopoeic-laden fight scenes. (Stunt doubles Victor Paul and Hubie Kerns deserve almost as much credit as West and Ward, however easy they are to spot in the HD era.)

But it wasn't *Batman*'s fault that a superhero satire won wide acceptance before more solemn efforts—that the commentary, essentially, achieved fame before the text. Though it's understandable that comic readers, fearing the world would never take costumed heroes as seriously as they did, came to hate the series. Since it was the only live-action version of Batman for 23 years, they had no reason to think it wouldn't remain the official screen version forever. Indeed, much of the Bat mythos that followed *Batman* was either a reaction to or against its success.

Times change, however, and after Christopher Nolan's somber Dark Knight trilogy, the world was more than ready to reconsider the light escapism *Batman* offered when it landed on home video in 2014 after decades of legal disputes between 20th Century Fox (which owned the series) and Warner Bros. (which owned the characters). By then it gave viewers the same respite from reality it had Vietnam-era audiences when it premiered.

When DC's *Batman 1966* spinoff bowed in 2013, comics having evolved along cultural, racial, and gender lines, it was right at home alongside titles like *Lumberjanes* and *The Unbeatable Squirrel Girl*. The animated *Batman: Return of the Caped Crusaders* in 2016 (featuring the voices of West, Ward, and Newmar) even had the opportunity to poke meta fun at how dour the character had become since 1986's *The Dark Knight Returns*.

After TV's *Batman: The Brave and the Bold*, after the mere *existence* of Harley Quinn, it's easy to see that a humorous approach to Batman is as valid as any other.

"It's one of those shows that grows with you," says *The Brave and the Bold* producer James Tucker. "Because it works on so many levels. It works on the kid level, and then you hit adolescence and the hormones make you lose all sense of humor, and then by college age maybe you're indulging in some alternate substances, and suddenly you rediscover the show and go, 'Wow, I didn't notice all this stuff.' Then it just kind of ripens with you...The attention to detail on that show, and the art direction on that show...It was like no other television show before it, and it influenced so many shows after it. It is one of the more literal translations of comics, of the comics that existed at the time it was produced. I think DC may have done a disservice to people by downing that show so much. Because they really negated its influence for a lot of years and tried to diminish it and belittle it. And I'm like, 'This show is why a lot of people even *read* comics.' The villains and all those characters that we now know as commonplace to the Batman franchise, a lot of them hadn't been in comics for decades prior to the TV show. So I will *always* defend that show."

Plenty of actors have followed Adam West's generation-defining performance, but how many of them will one day inspire the mayor of Los Angeles and the L.A. Police Department to shine the Bat-Signal over City Hall, as they did when West passed away in 2017? Both West and the show he made famous are in a class by themselves. *Batman* is lounge lizard hedonism, beach blanket kitsch, and Elvis movie merriment poured over atomic age gadgetry into a glass of vitamin D, whole-grade American milk. Pure of heart, and twice as groovy.

Gotham Gazette Exclusive

Adam West

In the title role of the 1966 *Batman* TV series, Adam West made a mark so bold it's impacted the character for more than 50 years. West returned to the role in the 2016 animated film *Batman: Return of the Caped Crusaders*, and its 2017 sequel, *Batman vs. Two-Face*. West passed away in June of 2017 at the age of 88. The following interview was conducted in October of 2016.

Why has your Batman remained popular for more than five decades?
Joe, I have no idea. It could be my legs. Not too many guys can wear tights effectively. Errol Flynn maybe. Or [Rudolf] Nureyev. I don't know. It survived because I'm the funny Batman, the Bright Knight. Not the Dark Knight. That seems to be more…affection-getting. So people who grow up with it want to share it with their own children and their grandchildren. So I've just gotta hang on, Joe!

As amusing as your Batman is, you're also quite commanding in the role. What choices did you make when deciding how to play him? Were there any particular influences?
That's a very good question. I wish my wife felt that I was commanding. [Laughs.] Some of my influences were Sherlock Holmes / Basil Rathbone. People like that who were always musing and deducing and pacing, and suddenly…just a thunderbolt of deduction! I used that in a comedic way. You know, you borrow from everything. You do borrow a lot of stuff as an artist or an actor or whatever. Now I'm painting, and I've borrowed a few things. I borrowed one ear from Picasso. [Laughs.] But it's very difficult for an actor in my case to talk about acting. You just assimilate what you can and then you cook with it and you just do it.

Did the absurdity of the scripts help you in your approach?
Absolutely. I mean our pilot, our first script, "Hi Diddle Riddle," was written by Lorenzo Semple Jr., an award-winning screenwriter. Lorenzo was terrific, because we all got kind of married to the same

concept, and a sense of how we'd reflect the late '60s, and the kind of satire and tongue-in-cheek fun we'd have with it. Not really making fun of Batman, but making him funny for the adults. So if you laugh, you really are an adult. [Laughs.]

It's been said that '60s pop culture was defined by the three Bs: the Beatles, Bond, and Batman...
Isn't that amazing? I was asked to do a Bond movie. I played Batman and then I was asked to do Bond...If I'd played drums with the Beatles, I would have been the three Bs of the '60s. A whole hive! [Laughs.]

When you were cast in *Batman* you'd recently done a Nestle Quik commercial in which you played a James Bond–like character...
Yes. As a matter of fact, I think that commercial was responsible for them asking to see me about *Batman.* They cast me right away. I read the pilot script, had a conversation, and they just immediately cast me. It was wonderful after all those rejections. Oh my god!

Did you have a sense of the phenomenon you were creating when you started working on the show?
Oh, absolutely. Yeah, from the very beginning. When I read the pilot script, I was interviewed and we had a lot of discussions, and we really were of one accord and goal with this thing, and what the tone was going to be. Yes.

Was it a challenge to balance the appeal your Batman held for both grownups and children? To walk that tightrope?
Yes, it seemed to me in the beginning very difficult. Then as I got into it, it became easier. Then I realized, "Hey, if I can just make that cape work for me..." Our writers were really good. They understood. They got it.

The ultimate example of that cape working for you was when you created the Batusi.
[Laughs.] Oh, you're still dancing it?

Oh, hell yes.
Good! It was a global dance craze.

You worked with so many Hollywood icons on *Batman*. Do you have a favorite?
I have several. Very much Frank Gorshin, because he was mad, and Cesar Romero, because of his great energy and professionalism. And I liked "Pengy Baby" a lot. [Laughs.] Burgess Meredith, my god, I loved him...

I must ask you about Catwoman. You worked with three of the most beautiful women of the 20th century in that role...
Please, Joe, don't. I'm getting excited. [Laughs.]

Have you a favorite of the three?
It wouldn't be honorable to say. But Julie [Newmar] was wonderful because she was the first, and she has the world's tallest legs. Her legs are 6-foot-3. [Laughs.] It was wonderful working with all of them, really.

It was remarkable to see so many different actors complement your work so well.
Well, it was people who determined that whatever they were playing should be almost Shakespearean. They really knew what they were doing, and I loved it because it was a challenge every day to play nose to nose with these people.

Of course, you had the most wonderful gadgets.
All labeled.

All properly labeled. As they should be.
Right? [Laughs.] Otherwise you might make a *terrible* error!

Were you especially fond of the Batarang?
Well, no, because...It embarrassed me. I kept throwing it at the roof and it kept bouncing back at me. [Laughs.] It may have been my favorite. But I really liked the Batboat, because it was fun to run

around in on the open ocean. And the Bat-Shield, because it was so outsized and ridiculous. All of these things were really exaggerated, which made them funnier.

As the props and the situations became more outlandish, did that give you more of a license to enlarge your performance?
It certainly did. When you have that kind of environment, it really works for you. But I've always thought bigger than life anyway.

You recently returned to the role in the animated film *Batman: Return of the Caped Crusaders.* Was it easy to play the character again?
No, it was easier. Because I had no cape to fool with, and no itchy tights and no utility belt that cut into me. [Laughs.] It was much easier, because other people drew me. The character comes back very quickly. It's just kind of a speech pattern, a rhythm, and it works. With good writing and wonderful animation it becomes very simple, at least if you know what you're doing.

It really is a wonderful thing about animation and what they've done. You can do so much more than live-action, even live-action that's computer-enhanced and all those wonderful digital things they do now. The simple, clever, artistic animation...I think it's really good, and they did a great job with this movie.

Fans had the chance to see your Batman on the big screen again when the film was released in theaters.
Isn't that nice? The wonderful thing is the critics, after 20 or 30 years, have finally caught up. There was a time when they were saying things like, "Oh, it's just camp" and "It's nonsense" and "It's just a lucky thing." Now we're getting wonderful reviews, with our older movie, the new one, the series. It's terrific. I can finally come out of my Idaho Batcave and show my face.

The show has aged better than some of the Batman screen incarnations that followed it.
Joe, let them keep trying. I'll just do my thing. [Laughs.]

In *Batman vs. Two-Face*, you're squaring off against William Shatner's title villain. Shatner, of course, is another pop icon, one we've never had the chance to see you confront.
I know, I love it. [Laughs.] I think when you can put two people from the '60s together who've had the kind of success we've had—who were on a very limited time and yet had shows that have lasted and people have really enjoyed for so many years—and get us together, it's probably a good idea. And Bill has a great sense of humor. We get along beautifully. But I think I hate him now. [Laughs.] I'm preparing.

Would you like to do more Batman animated films?
Oh my god, yes. Just send the check! It would be nice, yes. Because there are so many different ways you can go with Batman, directions and universes he can exist in. Yeah, I'd like that.

These films are winning you a new generation of fans.
Yes, absolutely. But you know, because of the entire family spectrum to whom we played, it never went away. The touching thing is some of these kids have grown up and—whether they're lawyers or cops or whatever—to a man they come up to me and they say, "You changed my life. I would have never done this if it hadn't been for you." Then others come up and they say, "My father died and you became my father." These things are very touching, Joe.

Very few actors have the opportunity to touch people like that.
Well, that's the thing. I really feel like I'm the luckiest actor alive. To be able to have done what I do this long, and to have created a character that's had this longevity, and amused or pleased or instructed so many people.

Gotham Gazette Exclusive

Burt Ward

Bursting with all the energy and enthusiasm of youth, Burt Ward brought the first Robin, Dick Grayson, to life in the 1966 *Batman* TV series. More than 50 years later, he remains the quintessential live-action Boy Wonder.

Why do you think the 1966 *Batman* has endured? What accounts for its sustained popularity when there have been so many iterations of Batman and Robin?
I'll tell you what it is...When we came out on January 12, 1966, we were the first television series in history that actually interacted with the audience. When you sit there and watch a television show, there's a separation. You know the people on television aren't really communicating with you. If it's a doctor show, they're trying to save a patient's life. If it's a police show, they're trying to catch a criminal. But with *Batman* we did something different...We used to say that we put on our tights to put on the world. We wore our underwear on the outside of our clothes. We played this hilariously written script seriously, so kids took it as serious hero worship, and the adults looked at it with the nostalgia of the Batman comic book that they grew up reading. And the college kids and teenagers—which at that time was an audience that almost no television station could capture—because of the double meanings and the insinuations, they just loved it. I mean I've heard so many stories of college kids in dorm rooms fighting for seats. Getting there an hour and a half early on Tuesday and Thursday nights, just so they'd have a seat to watch *Batman*.

We came out with something that—instead of a situation where you're behind a glass wall looking at something that isn't relating to you—was a show that you *knew*. It was colorful and big, with great music. Everything was inspiring, reaching through the scene and grabbing the people and saying, "Hey, do you *really* want to see what's going on?" You can't say, "Oh, that's outdated." We were ahead of our time when we came out.

With all that, the two lead performances really anchored the show.
Well, let me tell you something, Joe...We got lucky in one respect. When we did the screen test, Adam and I had an immediate chemistry. Within five minutes of meeting each other, he and I were both laughing. I found him hilarious and fun and zany and wild, and he found me like a seltzer water—effervescent. He was Mister Suave. He thinks of himself like Maurice Chevalier or the prime minister of England, and he really is who he plays.

In my case, when they hired me, they said, "Burt, we interviewed 1,100 young actors. Do you know why we picked you? Because—forget television—if there really was a Robin, you would be it. So we don't want you to act, we just want you to be yourself and to be enthusiastic." That's what I did for 120 episodes.

That's why I think we were such a hit, the chemistry is irreplaceable. You can try all you want...And Adam has got this wild and crazy mind. He doesn't see things like normal people. He'll say things and eyebrows go up...A typical fan will come up and—let's say it's a cute girl—he'll say something like, "My ears are stiffening up. I'm beginning to feel strange stirrings in my utility belt..." My god, you don't even know exactly what to do with that, you know? But people laugh and they get red in the face, and I guarantee you—they don't forget meeting Adam and me. Nobody forgets that.

Is it true you did many of your own stunts, resulting in frequent trips to the emergency room?
Yeah. I'll give you a perfect example...The very first shot, the very first day—this was back in 1965 in Bronson Canyon—the Batmobile was coming out of the Batcave. The famous shot, everybody's seen it a million times. So I'm on the set at 5:00 AM, in makeup, and at 7:30 they're gonna get the first shot. They say, "Okay, Burt. You're gonna go in the cave, hop in the Batmobile, and we're gonna shoot this." So I go in there. It's a little hard to adjust your eyes to the light at first. But I get in the Batmobile and I look over to say hi to Adam, and...I can see it's not Adam! It's hard to make out in the dark, but I can tell it's not Adam. I say, "Who are you?" and he said, "My name's Hubie." I say, "Oh, well what are you doing here?" "Well," he says, "I'm a stuntman and this is a very dangerous stunt. They don't want to use Adam West because he might get hurt." "Oh," I say, "do I have

a stuntman?" "Oh yeah. Yeah…" "Oh. Well, where is he?" "Oh, well he's over there having coffee with Adam West."

Now you can hear someone say, "Okay, let's get ready to roll!" I say, "Whoa, whoa…wait a minute. I think there's a terrible mistake." The second-unit director comes over and says, "What's the matter, Burt?" I say, "I think there's a mistake! This man—he's a stuntman—he's telling me this is dangerous. Why am I sitting in here? If I have a stuntman, why isn't he sitting here?" "Because," he says, "we can't use him. He doesn't look like you." "Well, why did you hire him if he doesn't look like me?!" "Couldn't find anybody to look like you."

So I had no answer. I gotta do this stunt. Then the stuntman told me one thing I'll never forget. Boy, you talk about making this a white-knuckle trip…Just before we go, he says, "You know something? The more broken bones I get, the bigger the paycheck I get." How unsettling is that, right? How unsettling…

So we come out at the camera at 55 miles an hour, and he does it perfectly. But at the last second, he makes this sharp turn to the left—and my door flies open! It hits this giant, 20-foot-tall arc lamp. Knocks it right over. The camera that's sitting in a little camera chair gets knocked over. As I'm flying out the door I reach back, and my little finger hooks around the gearshift knob of the Batmobile. It keeps me from falling out, but it pulls my finger completely out of joint. I don't know if you've ever had that happen to you, Joe, but that's an incredibly painful thing…

So they stop, they run over. They're picking lights up. They say, "Burt, are you okay?" I say, "I'm okay, but my hand is *killing* me." They look at my hand and it's still in my glove. I can't even get the glove off. They say, "Oh my god, it looks like you pulled your finger out of its socket! We gotta get you to the hospital." I say, "Oh please. Thank you. It's killing me." They say, "Well, we will, Burt. Just as soon we get the shot." I said, "Wait a minute. What does that mean?" "Oh, we've got a crew here. It's $30,000 an hour"—back in 1965—"We can't leave. We gotta get this shot." "How long's it gonna take?" "We don't know. Probably another 45 minutes to light." It's 8:00 in the morning. I got to the hospital at noon.

That was the first of four days in a row of different explosions. First-degree burns, second-degree burns. Every possible thing that could go wrong. Two-by-fours landed on my nose and broke my nose...Today, they're more careful. But let me tell you something—you know it's a bad sign when you're tied down to a table, you can't move, and a wall is gonna be blown apart, and at 8:00 in the morning, when the special effects guys who are gonna handle the explosion walk past you, you smell liquor on their breath. You *know* it's a bad sign!

Do you have a favorite version of Robin's catchphrase?
Oh, well we had 378 "Holy..."s. We had a lot of stuff like that. What was so great was they really let me do the character. There wasn't anybody directing me to take my fist and hit it into my glove, or jump out of the Batmobile over the door instead of opening the door. All of this stuff I did. I guess they were so worried about everything else so they just let me do what I wanted. And because it was not something I planned, it came across as natural. That's part of why it worked so well. Now I probably would never have thought to do it because of the cost of that Batmobile. But I'd jump up on the back of it and walk along the edge of the fin. And because I was having such fun with it, I just did what I felt was right. I wasn't acting. I just got into the story. I related to the character.

And everybody else had fun too. Boy, did I find out—when I made my first public appearance in Tacoma, Washington. I was by myself—because Adam was at Shea Stadium—in a big shopping mall. They handed out raffle tickets, and they told me at the end of the weekend that they had handed out over 310,000 tickets. People couldn't get within six blocks of my appearance. You couldn't drive because people were camping in the streets.

You also had the opportunity to do a fight scene with Bruce Lee when he appeared on the show...
I knew Bruce Lee outside of *Batman*. He and I lived in the same condominium complex, and he and I used to spar together. Because I was a black belt in karate, and he was the ultimate martial artist. We would go down together—with his wife, Linda, and [his son] Brandon, who at the time was like six months of age—to Chinatown. We'd order all this food...A piece of trivia for you is that Bruce Lee's first filmed fight scene of his career was fighting me. The guy who became probably the most famous martial artist in the world, right? His very first scene was fighting me.

That was in the show. Our executive producer, William Dozier, was producing *The Green Hornet.* So there was an episode, a two-parter, where Van Williams and Bruce Lee—as the Green Hornet and Kato—were introduced in our show. We had a great fight scene.

You had a number of memorable guest stars.

Batman was such a hit and everybody was so excited to be on the show...The producers would tell me they were deluged with requests from every major star. Frank Sinatra wanted to be the Joker. Well, he couldn't, because they'd already cast Cesar Romero. But every major star wanted to be in that show because their own kids were hammering them about it. So, because there was no way you could have that many villains, they created the walking-up-the-wall scene. We're climbing the wall and a window opens and there's Sammy Davis Jr. There's Dick Clark. There's Betty White. There's Don Ho. There's Colonel Klink. There's all these different stars from all these other television shows and feature films. Everybody wanted to be a part of something that was so big. But the biggest thing about *Batman* was that it was totally universal.

18 Denny O'Neil and Neal Adams

Before writer Denny O'Neil and artist Neal Adams got hold of him, Batman could impress. He could excite, intimidate, charm even. But in their hands, the Dark Knight *breathed.*

In 1968, the Adam West–starring *Batman* TV series was cancelled after three seasons, and the Batmania it had so quickly fueled just as immediately sputtered out. The Batman comics had made a halfhearted attempt to copy its camp treatment of the Caped Crusader, but with the show gone the books suffered an identity crisis. Readers—tired of the "Biff! Bang! Pow!"—began clamoring for the detective of old, as did one of DC's hottest young artists, Neal Adams.

A lifelong comic book fan, Adams had worked for Archie Comics in the early 1960s before honing his superb draftsmanship in the world of advertising and illustrating the *Ben Casey* comic strip. Returning to comics in 1967, he contributed stories to Warren Publishing's horror magazines *Creepy* and *Eerie*, covers for DC's superhero titles, and ended the year as the penciler of the company's award-winning *Deadman*. His star on the rise, he asked Batman editor Julius Schwartz numerous times if he could draw the Caped Crusader. But Schwartz declined. Adams was instead given the opportunity by Murray Boltinoff, the editor of DC's Batman team-up book *The Brave and the Bold*. The cover of January 1968's *The Brave and the Bold* #75 features Adams' first work on Batman, with May 1968's *World's Finest* #175 ("The Superman-Batman Revenge Squads—To the Victor Comes Death!" written by Leo Dorfman), showcasing his first Batman interior art. The breakthrough, however, came in September 1968's *The Brave and the Bold* #79 ("The Track of the Hook," written by Bob Haney), when Adams paired Batman with Deadman in a story set—like most of the artist's work on the title—at night.

With fans asking for Adams' nocturnal Batman to appear in the character's solo books, Schwartz announced in June 1969's *Detective Comics* #388 that a "*big* change" would soon come into Batman's life. That change occurred in December 1969's *Batman* #217, in which Dick Grayson finally left Wayne Manor to go to college and Bruce Wayne and Alfred moved into the Wayne Foundation building in the heart of Gotham City. Adams illustrated the issue's cover, with a grim Dark Knight telling his friend, "Take a last look, Alfred—then seal up the Batcave...FOREVER!"

Reporter and political activist Denny O'Neil had won work at Marvel and Charlton Comics after writing a newspaper article about the industry, and he followed Charlton editor Dick Giordano

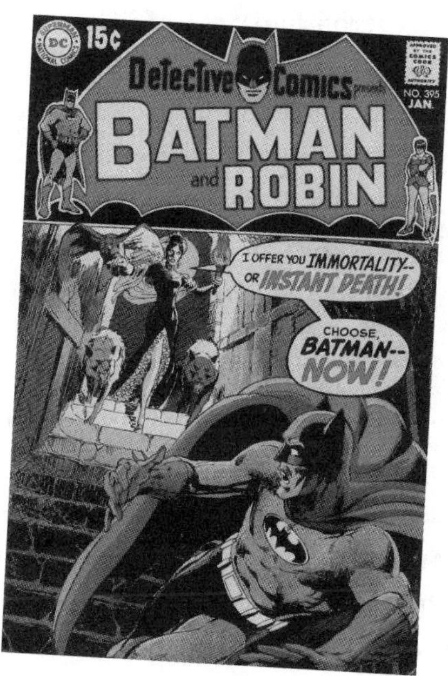

After the cancellation of the Batman *television series, Denny O'Neil and Neal Adams took Batman back to his less campy roots in the comics, beginning with January 1970's* Detective Comics *#395.* (Cover art by Neal Adams)

to DC, where he scripted *Wonder Woman* and *Justice League.* Schwartz asked O'Neil to write Batman during the TV show's run, but O'Neil, no fan of the camp approach, passed. With Schwartz implementing his big change, he again turned to O'Neil. This time, partnered with Adams (as penciler) and Giordano (as inker), O'Neil penned January 1970's *Detective Comics* #395 ("The Secret of the Waiting Graves"), and the nocturnal avenger was born anew.

The first of a dozen Batman collaborations between O'Neil and Adams over the next several years, the story finds the hero in Mexico—without the support of Robin, Alfred, or Commissioner Gordon—where he encounters a wealthy couple who appear to be immortal. Ripe with gothic horror—just one of the genres the creators would explore in their work—the tale wastes no time in announcing its redefined hero.

"A bleak hillside in Central Mexico...a pair of open graves... and the shadow of the dread...Batman...mark the beginning of an excursion into the eerie, the terrifying, the deadly! Stand still, and hear the wind howling like souls in torment…See the rise of an ashen moon…Breathe deeply and sniff the scent of death…As you prepare to learn…The SECRET of the WAITING GRAVES."

Henceforth, Batman was *the* Batman. The towering, athletic, driven detective. The sexy, jet-setting ladies' man. The dryly humorous, grimly determined, foreboding figure of righteousness. Obsessive but accessible, as capable of cracking wise as cracking heads. Adams captured all facets of the character in his pencils, bringing a level of craftsmanship to the character that hadn't been seen since the Golden Age work of Dick Sprang. O'Neil and Adams' Batman was as much at home in a cemetery as he was in the cockpit of a World War I fighter plane (*Detective Comics* #404's "Ghost of the Killer Skies!"), the snow-capped Himalayas (*Batman* #232's "Daughter of the Demon"), or the desert of Africa (*Batman* #244's "The Demon Lives Again!").

The latter two stories saw the Batman confront Ra's al Ghul—invented by O'Neil, Adams, and Schwartz—who allowed his adventures to play out on a global scale, as he fell for his enemy's daughter, the beguiling Talia. But the team brought the same level of excitement to Gotham. "Half an Evil" (in *Batman* #234) saw Two-Face return for the first time since 1954. "The Joker's Five-Way Revenge!" (*Batman* #251)—a tale penciled *and* inked by Adams—restored the Clown Prince of Crime's homicidal tendencies (absent since the Golden Age). And "Night of the Reaper!" (*Batman* #237) told the story of a Holocaust survivor seeking revenge against the Nazis on Halloween. It marked a sea change from the days of Shark Repellent Bat Spray.

Adams also gave the Batman a new no-frills Batmobile (a customized Corvette Stingray) and included a flashback to his origin in *Batman* #232. In it, he restored one small detail present in the tale's first telling (in *Detective Comics* #33) but absent in other versions: Martha Wayne does not suffer a heart attack upon seeing her husband shot by Joe Chill, but is also gunned down. It was a simple, powerful statement from the creator, concretizing his long-held dreams for the character.

"Neal Adams," says Batman artist Norm Breyfogle, "was the figurative father to so many comics artists of my generation. He influenced so many of us. In the same way that Jack Kirby influenced a lot of people, in terms of storytelling. But Neal Adams definitely had the biggest impact on the visualization and motivation for the Batman artists that followed him. I can never give him enough credit."

O'Neil produced plenty of singular Batman stories without Adams, among them *Detective Comics* #457's "There Is No Hope in Crime Alley!" (which introduced Bruce Wayne's surrogate mother, social worker Leslie Thompkins), penciled by Giordano, *DC Special Series* #15's "Death Strikes at Midnight and Three" (the first illustrated Batman prose story), delineated by Marshall Rogers, and numerous tales developing Ra's al Ghul. In 1986, he'd succeed Schwartz as editor of the Batman titles, overseeing landmark stories such as *Batman: Year One*, *The Killing Joke*, "A Death in the Family," and "Knightfall."

Likewise, Adams would create memorable Batman tales without O'Neil, including a pair of action-packed, horror-flavored yarns—"The House that Haunted Batman" (*Detective Comics* #408) and "Moon of the Wolf" (*Batman* #255)—both of them scripted by Swamp Thing and Wolverine co-creator Len Wein. Adams also co-created Man-Bat, illustrating his introductory trilogy (in *Detective Comics* #402, 404, and 407), scripted by Frank Robbins. His impact was felt across all Batman comics, as every artist from Irv Novick to Bob Brown to José Luis García-López strived to draw the character as he did. The scalloped, billowing cape in which Adams' panther-like Batman was cloaked (which took its cue from Christopher Lee's Dracula) was suddenly everywhere.

But great as they were apart, there was something special about O'Neil and Adams together. Something alchemical that made them, for a brief while, the Lennon and McCartney of Batman comics. Though their pairing also resulted in an award-winning run on Green Lantern / Green Arrow and the 1978 one-shot *Superman vs. Muhammad Ali*, Batman is their masterpiece. The character they broke down, rebuilt, and gave to all who followed them.

19 Ra's al Ghul

"I long for a better world—not one commanded by fools! This is my dream!...And when my world is realized, you will sit at my side along with my daughter!"

So vows Ra's al Ghul in *Batman* #240's "Vengeance for a Dead Man!" One of the archcriminal's earliest encounters with the Dark Knight, it was written by Denny O'Neil, who co-created Ra's with artist Neal Adams. The two were tasked with creating a new villain by editor Julius Schwartz, following the slump in comic sales after the cancellation of the 1966 *Batman* TV series. Schwartz needed a character who could serve—as had the Joker—as a Moriarty to Batman's Sherlock Holmes, and the editor came up with the name Ra's al Ghul—"demon's head" in Arabic.

O'Neil conceived of a character in the tradition of Dr. Fu Manchu, the Chinese supervillain who'd featured in the "Yellow Peril" novels of Sax Rohmer, and had been played by Christopher Lee in a series of films from England's Hammer Film Productions throughout the late 1960s. Ra's' desire for his daughter to marry the Dark Knight is prefigured by Ian Fleming's 1963 James Bond novel *On Her Majesty's Secret Service* and its 1969 film adaptation, which feature international crime lord Marc-Ange Draco, who wants Bond to marry his daughter, Tracy.

"Denny came up with a man," says Neal Adams. "He was okay—obviously very smart—but he was just a guy with an interesting name. I realized that Julie was fishing for a more interesting character and we really hadn't gotten it. Then I thought, 'What about the idea of taking a real man and giving him just enough character to carry him over that edge?' In other words, to turn him into a slightly visually stunning character."

"I thought, 'First of all, I'll give him a receding hairline, because people do respect a high forehead. Then, the idea that he's not of a given culture. In other words, he has sort of an Arab name, but the truth of the matter is that there's no reason to think that he's an Arab. There's no reason to think that he's of any given culture. What if we took it all and mixed it all together? An international person represents all cultures. Well, what would he look like? He would have high cheekbones, he would have slightly slanted eyes. The eyes would be dark.' I started to design a thick brow and high cheekbones, and a long face, and very cold eyes under it. I thought, 'I'm going to take the eyebrows off. And his clothes could be slightly exotic, but not really truly exotic. He'd still wear suits, but maybe he would care to wear a cape.'"

Ra's is first mentioned in May 1971's *Detective Comics* #411 ("Into the Den of the Death-Dealers!" written by Denny O'Neil), in which Batman rescues Talia from a renegade member of Ra's' League of Assassins, Dr. Ebenezer Darrk. An editor's note tells readers "Al Ghul signifies a mischief-maker, and appears as the ghoul of the *Arabian Nights*!"

On Adams' cover for June 1971's *Batman* #232 ("Daughter of the Demon," written by O'Neil and penciled by Adams), Ra's appears for the first time, looming atop Batman and Robin. As the Boy Wonder takes a bullet to the stomach, Ra's proclaims, "When I decide Robin must die—he dies!"

The story begins when Ra's steps out of the shadows of the Batcave and tells a startled Batman, "I am presently known as Ra's al Ghul! You shall be seeing much of me!" He explains that he's discovered the Dark Knight's secret identity by tracing the sales of his equipment to Bruce Wayne. He then enlists him in a mission to find Dick Grayson and Talia, both of whom, he says, have been kidnapped. Following Ra's to a remote Himalayan outpost, Batman learns the kidnapping was a ruse to see if he was worthy of marrying the villain's daughter.

Batman rejects Ra's offer of Talia's hand, and, over the course of several encounters, learns he's set on establishing a criminal dictatorship, aided by his Lazarus Pit (first seen in *Batman* #243), which restores life to the dead. "I have been called criminal and genius...and I am neither!" he says in September 1972's *Batman* #244 ("The Demon Lives Again!"). "I am an artist! I have a vision... of an earth as clean and pure as a snow-swept mountain...or the desert outside!" The story culminates in a shirtless sword fight between Batman and Ra's beneath the hot desert sun.

The nobility Ra's demonstrated in dueling the Dark Knight (whom he addresses as "Detective" out of respect for his abilities) rather than executing his foe distinguished him from most members of Batman's rogues gallery. And his desire to wipe out most of humanity—so he could extinguish its evil and build a better world—was understandable, if mad. As were his repeated attempts to wed Talia and Batman, culminating in his capturing the Dark Knight and administering marriage while the hero was unconscious (in June 1978's *DC Special Series* #15).

In the 1987 graphic novel *Batman: Son of the Demon* (written by Mike W. Barr and illustrated by Jerry Bingham), it was revealed that Talia's mother, Melisande, was killed by a rogue member of the League of Assassins. The 1992 graphic novel *Batman: Birth of the Demon* (written by O'Neil and illustrated by Norm Breyfogle) explains that Melisande wasn't the first woman Ra's loved, and tells the story of his origin, explaining how he was born hundreds of years ago in the Middle East. A brilliant young nomad, he became a doctor and married a woman named Sora. He learned to create a Lazarus Pit in an attempt to cheat death, but when he used the pit to save the life of a prince, the prince emerged in a maddened state and killed Sora. The prince's father sentenced Ra's to imprisonment alongside the corpse of his wife. Ra's, however, escaped and killed both the king and prince, destroying their city with the help of his tribe, at which point he gave himself his name/title, eventually establishing himself as the literal head of the criminal organization The Demon, of which the League of Assassins is a part.

Ra's almost achieved his goal of destroying the world when he released the virus Ebola Gulf-A (aka "The Clench") in the 1996 storylines "Contagion" and "Legacy," at which time he also considered Bane as a potential heir. He succeeded in driving a wedge of distrust between the Justice League and Dark Knight when he used Batman's secret fail-safe plans—developed in case League members were compromised—against the team in the 2000 *JLA* storyline "Tower of Babel."

Talia eventually turned against Ra's. In 2003's *Death and the Maidens* limited series, she encounters her older half-sister, Nyssa Raatko, whose Russian mother was abandoned by Ra's in the 18th century. Ra's also rejected Nyssa when she found him years later. Though he gave her a Lazarus Pit to extend her life, he left her family to die in a concentration camp when he partnered with the Nazis in World War II. Nyssa has her revenge by killing Ra's, and replacing him as head of The Demon with Talia. The dying Ra's claims he's pleased by their partnership.

Ra's had also rejected a son, the White Ghost (Dusan al Ghul), who brought his father back to life in 2007's "The Resurrection of Ra's al Ghul" storyline. The albino is thwarted in his attempt to place Ra's' spirit in the body of Talia and Batman's son, Damian (conceived in *Son of the Demon*), and so gives his own body to his father. Shortly after, the man Ra's had once put in charge of the League of Assassins, the Sensei, is revealed as Ra's' father. He too dies, after attacking Batman and Ra's. Since then, Ra's has battled each of the first three Robins—Dick Grayson, Jason Todd, and Tim Drake—all of whom have triumphed against his treachery.

Ra's has enjoyed almost as many lives on screen as he has in print. He first appeared on TV in the 1992 *Batman: The Animated Series* episode "Off Balance," voiced by David Warner; Warner played the character in each of his return appearances in the DC Animated Universe (in which the League is renamed "The Society of Shadows"). His swan song, *Batman Beyond*'s "Out of the Past," shows Ra's at his wickedest, when he transfers his mind from his decaying body into Talia's and kills her so he can live on.

Ra's also appeared in animated form in *Young Justice* (voiced by Oded Fehr), *Batman: The Brave and the Bold* (Peter Woodward), and *Beware the Batman* (Lance Reddick). Dee Bradley Baker provides the voice of Ra's in *Batman: Arkham City*, in which the character orchestrates the video game's events.

In live-action, Ra's made his debut in 2005's *Batman Begins.* Played by Liam Neeson, this Ra's, who leads the "League of Shadows," is responsible for mentoring Bruce Wayne before he becomes Batman. Matthew Nable played the character in TV's *Arrow* (in which he was a recurring character throughout the show's third season), while *Gotham*'s Ra's is Alexander Siddig, the first actor of Arabic descent to play the role on camera.

The casting that took Ra's al Ghul full circle happened in comic book form. In artist Mike Allred's cover for *Batman '66 Meets Wonder Woman '77* #4 (which partners Adam West's Batman with Lynda Carter's Wonder Woman), the villain is styled after none other than Christopher Lee.

Gotham Gazette Exclusive

Denny O'Neil

No living writer has affected the course of Batman's evolution like Denny O'Neil. First in his legendary 1970s collaborations with artist Neal Adams—which took the character back to his roots, making him the *dread* Batman—then as editor of DC's Batman comics in the 1980s and 1990s. The co-creator of Ra's al Ghul, Talia al Ghul, Leslie Thompkins, and Azrael, O'Neil is the world's foremost authority on the Dark Knight.

When did you discover Batman?
I would have been five or six. I was a young kid, and for some reason my family was not a bunch of readers. But my dad read the newspaper and he did buy me comic books. On Sunday morning usually, on the way back from Mass, we would stop into a little neighborhood store, and he'd order milk for the family and I could have a comic book. I remember being a little puzzled by Batman, because did he or did he not fly? I couldn't tell. My reading skills were pretty rudimentary...That was my first encounter with Batman.

But there have been, give or take, about five different Batmans. Most everybody is doing a version of a guy who is obsessed by a childhood tragedy, that has motivated himself to physical and mental perfection. Add the technology to that—which I was reluctant to do, but which certainly has a place in the mythology—and you've got Batman.

There was what Bill Finger and Bob Kane started out with, which was a gentleman crimefighter. There were quite a few of them in the mass media back then—a rich guy, who, to put it crudely, got his jollies solving crimes. Five issues into it, Bill Finger gave him an origin. I once had a chance to change that if I wanted, and I didn't. Because it sure ain't broke. It's a perfect explanation of who, what, and why he does what he does. He started as a vigilante. The Depression and World War I had shaken people's faith in authority figures. So you had the private eye, the guy who was not really a member of the establishment and made his own rules. Then, with

Robin 11 months later, he became a father figure, or at least the big brother you wish you had.

By the end of war in 1945, he was a cop. He had a platinum police badge—I guess gold wasn't good enough for him. Without any explanation as to what the mechanics of that were, he was a glorified law enforcer. The country, having just gotten through a really horrendous military experience, was not in the mood for vigilantes. So he became an authority figure.

In the '50s they were scared to death, because comics had gotten blasted in editorial pages, and Senator [Estes] Kefauver had hearings about them in Lower Manhattan, and Fredric Wertham had written a book, *Seduction of the Innocent*. So [Batman] became a daytime character, what I think of as light science fiction—you know, the occasional time-travel story, things like that. There was very little mention, if any, of the murdered parents. He was Gotham's most prominent citizen. It may have been perfectly appropriate for its time. It's not my favorite Batman period, but I'm not gonna throw rocks at it either. The writers and artists had to at least try to do stories that wouldn't possibly offend anybody, and they had to make a living.

Then came the comedic Batman in the '60s, when the country was in a rebellious mood. That was fertile ground for comedy, but not so much for comic book guys. I asked Stan Lee the morning after the first *Batman* television show episode aired, "How did you like it?" He said he liked the 30 seconds of animation in the beginning and not much else. But the show was enormously popular for two years. It crept into the third year not so popular, and then it was gone. The joke was basically, "This is what I loved when I was a kid, and now that I'm a 28-year-old Wall Street guy with a mild drug habit and a closet full of Brooks Brothers clothes, look how silly it is…" Because the TV show was having an influence on the circulation of the comics, they tried to follow its suit, and not too successfully. Then when it was gone, it was gone. At that point [editor] Julie Schwartz, [artist] Neal Adams, and I enter the story.

How did you come to work on the character?

Neal and I were flavors of the week in 1971 and tended to be getting the good jobs. I went in for my weekly talk with Julie, and he asked me if I would like to do Batman. He'd made that offer a year earlier, and I didn't think I was up to camp. I wasn't judging it, I just didn't know if I was able to do that kind of material. But I did write a sort of straight Batman story themed on New Orleans jazz, which Julie loved. Then I wrote "The Secret of the Waiting Graves" [*Detective Comics* #395]—no gimmicks, no Robin, strong supernatural bent. And Neal did, I think, an extraordinary job on the art.

In fact, Julie even made me put in a caption of the kind that were in Ellery Queen stories—"Ellery now has all the information he needs to solve the murder in the sewing room. How about you, reader?" So with [*Detective Comics* #410's] "Vow from the Grave" [April 1971], I did a classic "Dear reader, if you're really paying attention..." kind of thing.

You blended a number of different genres in your run.

Well, I had a remarkably astute editor and I had a lot of freedom. I was not consciously exploring genres. I was really working from month to month. But I had my own internal kind of schema of what kind of stories Batman could and could not do. What I put off-limits to myself and later to the people who worked for me was the kind of stuff they did in the '50s—SF lite, time-travel stories, alien invasions...But Batman is a pretty good storytelling tool. Without violating the premise of the character, there's a lot of different kinds of stories you can tell. So that's what I was doing. I was taking advantage of the fact that I had an editor who never got in the way. So I had all those possibilities, and on a practical level I had to come up with one story a month. Somewhere in that mix was a desire to keep it interesting for me.

In one instance, the artist suggested a story, and that was a story about Batman being on a train, and there was no reason on earth not to put Batman on a train. That artist was Marshall Rogers. Then in other instances there were crossovers with the Shadow. There was a real-life connection with the Shadow. Bill Finger was pretty frank about saying that Walter Gibson was his major influence. Pretty recently Tony Tollin—who's in the midst of republishing all the Shadow novels that Gibson wrote—found something that's absolutely the plot of the first Batman story. It's the same story, the same death trap. Bill had always said he was a big Shadow fan, and in this case Tony found that—allowing for the difference that one was a 50,000-

word novel and the other was an eight-page comic book—it was the same story. Anyway, that's probably a tortured and semi-incoherent answer to your answer.

Not at all. You also reinvigorated the Dark Knight's rogues gallery, including the Joker.
Almost every myth system I know about has its trickster figure. In a way he represents chaos. You take Batman, who, for all his theatrical flamboyance, is pretty much the face of logic and order—you couldn't have a better villain than the Joker to put against him. For most villains, there are principles and rules. We don't know what the Joker's reasons are. But that's okay. That becomes the reason...What we have now, who is perfectly embodied by Heath Ledger [in *The Dark Knight*], is the greatest trickster figure in pop culture. Probably my best Joker story is "The Joker's Five-Way Revenge," the first one I did. By that time the people who hated comics had gone away and I was able to actually make him a murderer.

The archvillain you're most often associated with is your own co-creation, the ageless ecoterrorist Ra's al Ghul.
Julie had the name—Ra's al Ghul, which means "head of the demon." I have no idea where he got it, but I went home and began to work with that. We introduced Talia before we introduced her daddy [in May 1971's *Detective Comics* #411]. Bob Brown drew that story, and I must have had Ra's in mind when I wrote it. But in those days we didn't plan six months ahead. We didn't plan *a month* ahead. Comic books were literally done from month to month. But we had begun to emphasize continuity a little bit. That was the way comic books and pop culture were trending.

Working on that story, I guess I began to see another opportunity to talk about some of the stuff that was really concerning me. So we gave Ra's a benevolent motivation. You can certainly quarrel with his methods—he wants to eliminate 90 percent of the people on earth so that the remaining 10 percent can rebuild and undo the damage that's been done to the environment—that's actually a commendable end. In a way, he is more noble than Batman, who really has no interest other than catching crooks. He has no grand vision. But Ra's is a loony bird. He's been alive for 400 years and he's become a maniacal sociopath, and he has this daughter who is obviously the one person in the world that Bruce Wayne should mate with. But they each have their hang-ups. She has a daddy hang-up and he has a refusal to consider consorting with a known criminal. That stuff has been changed with other writers' interpretations. And bless them, none of this is eternal and engraved in stone.

But I didn't provide character notes for either of those two new villains. It was one of the times when Neal Adams was really on his game. Instead of a guy in a mask and a spandex suit, which was the way supervillains were, he gave Ra's something that was exotic but believable, and he gave the character gravitas that no other comic book villain had. So what we did was decide it was time to create a new major character, and it worked. Most of the major characters have been created on the fly by guys working month to month and solving plot problems. In this case, we kind of, with malice aforethought, set out to create what in fact we did create.

The movie version of Ra's omits the immortality, and that's fine. My personal image of Talia would have been the actress Angie Harmon, and we got Marion Cotillard in the *The Dark Knight Rises*. But that's a perfectly valid thing for Chris Nolan and his people to have done.

Were Ian Fleming's James Bond novels an influence on the creation of Ra's?

Yeah. That has eaten my lunch a lot. I wondered about that. Also, Fu Manchu has been suggested as an influence. I am prepared to state that I never read a Fu Manchu novel. Did I see any of the movies? I don't know. I think I may have seen one. I was not aware of the similarities until the journalists asked me about [*Batman Begins*]. Then recently somebody observed the possible James Bond connection. Those I did read, and I saw all the movies. It's a guilty pleasure. I'm a liberal hippie pacifist who likes stories about a killer who doesn't question and just obeys orders. There wasn't any conscious influence. I was far more acquainted with Bond than I could have possibly been with Sax Rohmer's work. Maybe someday I'll go back and look at what movies were around when I was going to lots of movies, and see. But I don't think in either influence there was a conscious attempt to be influenced by anything. The ideas we're talking about are not unique to those characters. I would have sworn on a stack of Bibles that I was at that particular time never influenced by anything. Who knows what goes into your subconscious? Who knows what form it comes out in? I just don't know. I wish I did, because it sometimes drives me nuts. But I don't. So there was no conscious influence. I kind of doubt there was much of a subconscious influence but I don't know.

In addition to Neal Adams, you collaborated with other esteemed Batman pencilers throughout the 1970s, including Dick Giordano in *Detective Comics* #457's "There Is No Hope in Crime Alley!"—one of the best explorations of Batman's origin.

I think Dick really hit his pinnacle with that. That was a bad period in my life, and I don't know that I was doing much good work. But there was an obvious hole in the Batman backstory. Let's say he was eight when his parents were murdered in front of him. *X* years later he shows up as Batman. What about the intervening years? Then half of that springboard was that I really don't much believe in violence. I don't think it often solves problems. I'm certainly not prepared to say never. I've changed my mind a little bit about that in the last 10 years, with the fanatics out there in the world who believe they will not be saved unless they kill people like me. You can't reason with those people because they are creatures of faith. They know they're right. Well, okay, we have to defend ourselves against people like that.

But generally…Take a look at what's happening in the Middle East right now. This stuff goes on for generations, and war after war it seems that nothing gets permanently settled. Well, at that time I was involved with a group called the Catholic Worker, a group that did two things. In the best Christlike tradition, it fed the hungry and it clothed the naked. They had a building over in I guess what is now the East Village. We knew it as the Lower East Side and it was not a very choice neighborhood. But it was run by this remarkable woman, Dorothy Day, who was the close friend of the mother of my first wife, and the godmother of one of my two or three best friends. So I was aware of Dorothy, and I was certainly aware of the philosophical underpinnings of the peace movement. I had this backstory that needed filling. So we created Leslie Thompkins, named after Tompkins Square Park, which was a big hippie Village hangout in those days. I live about four blocks from it. We created that story to fill that hole in the Bruce Wayne biography, but also to introduce into the continuity a dissenting voice. Someone who tells Bruce Wayne, "What you're doing isn't right. You're doing it for the right reasons, but violence is not an answer." I just wanted that sentiment in there. We weren't trying to build any stories around it. We weren't going to mention it much. But just for the sake of a rounded characterization, if nothing else, it didn't hurt to have it there, and Leslie turned out to be a pretty interesting character on her own. So we came up with that. I guess I didn't have any idea who was gonna do the art. I probably didn't much care. We ended up with that story, which is one I'm very happy about.

When you took over as editor of the Batman books in 1986, one of your first tasks was overseeing Frank Miller's *The Dark Knight Returns*.
Frank Miller darkened [Batman] a lot, changed the emphasis, with *Dark Knight Returns*. It was certainly the next step in the evolution that began with Neal and myself. But it was well under way before I took the job that Dick Giordano offered me. It was started before I got there, more than half done. My job was not to influence the content. I facilitated the publication of that book, and then talked to the writer about why I was probably not going to refer to it again. We didn't say it didn't happen, and later writers have put it solidly in the continuity. And I don't know that the writer ever forgave me for that... But one of the things that editors get paid for is to make those kinds of decisions. We're not talking about right or wrong here, but we are talking about consistency.

***Batman: Year One* was planned as a graphic novel, but you convinced Frank Miller and artist David Mazzucchelli to publish it first in the monthly Batman comic.**
One of my jobs, as I interpreted the conditions of my hiring, was to kind of redo Batman. *Year One* was obviously going to be a different kind of Batman story, done by two creators I had great faith in and had worked well with. So I went to Dave and Frank and said, "If you let me publish this as a serial in the comic book first, we will guarantee it will be in hardcover within six months or so. You won't

suffer financially or any other way, but it will be the best possible message I can send to the readers that this is not their fathers' Batman.

***The Dark Knight Returns* helped inspire the 1989 *Batman* movie...** When the first Tim Burton movie happened, I may have had quibbles. There are some things Burton doesn't do as well as he does other things. But you can always quibble about anything. It was a huge hit, a big honkin' success—I made more royalties from that comic book adaptation than anything I'd done up until that time—and it took Batman seriously. Later I found out that [producer] Mike Uslan had something to do with that. The second one seemed to be two movies. But again they delivered on a certain level. They're what you want when you go into a movie theater on a hot July afternoon. The editor in me might have itched to do a rewrite, but basically I had no quarrel with Burton. Then came Joel Schumacher.

Joel is one of the nicest people on Earth. He was enormously gracious when I went to visit the set in L.A. When all the Time Warner executive types were gathered in New York, he came in, walked down the table, and embraced me as the Batman guy. It was very nice of him. He didn't need to do it...I don't agree with his interpretation of the Batman mythos. Some of that he's blamed on interference, and I don't doubt that that happened. Even with Chris Nolan. It's a given when you're doing this kind of job that there's going to be merchandising, and you might have to make some minor concessions to that. I don't think that Chris made many.

The Dark Knight Rises was the only Batman movie since 1989 that I hadn't seen an advance script for. I was marched into the theater by security and I had no idea what to expect. Later I found out that my wife, Marifran, and I were sitting in front of Christopher Nolan and his wife...Nolan got Batman right. The guys who did *Batman: The Animated Series* got it right, within the limitations of what they were working with—which is television animation. Those guys did a terrific job...With Nolan, it really all came together. He's a talented director who was respectful of the source material but realized he was working in a different medium. You can't just move something from one medium to another, because different media have different requirements, strengths, and weaknesses. He had 70 years of Batman to choose from, and I think he picked judiciously. One of the rumors I heard was that the Joker was going to be in the third movie, and that didn't happen because Heath Ledger died. Whether that's true or not, I thought they made good use of the comic books but delivered movies that by any reasonable standard were good movies. Whether they were about Batman or Little Orphan Annie. *The Dark Knight* is the first movie of that kind I can remember that does not end with two guys bashing each other. It ends with Batman running off and Gordon having a somber voiceover. It was a good movie, well thought out, beautifully acted.

The third one, as I said, I didn't know what to expect walking into that theater. I have only one quibble about *The Dark Knight Rises*—I would have cut the last 30 seconds. And if I had known that Christopher Nolan was sitting behind me, by God, I'd have turned around and dealt with the matter—"Listen, Chris, you gotta get rid of that thing in the café. What are you thinking about? The movie's about redemption. Come on!" [Laughs.] But Nolan did it exactly right.

20 Steve Englehart and Marshall Rogers

The rivalry between Marvel Comics and DC Comics is the teeter-totter on which the superhero comic book business has, for good or ill, seen itself balanced for the better part of the last hundred years. The two companies have routinely poached writers and artists from one another, each briefly ascending as their competitor falls. When the Marvel Universe was born in the 1960s, DC, the older of the two, continued to dominate. But as the years rolled by, Marvel's fresh, psychologically complex characters grew in popularity with teenagers and adults, while DC's old guard, designed for children, began to grow stale. Even Batman, the most layered of all DC's champions, wasn't immune to calcification.

Several years after writer Denny O'Neil and artists Neal Adams and Dick Giordano had transformed the cheery crusader of the 1950s and 1960s back into the creature of darkness he had been in his first year, Batman's adventures had again become tired. But even as Adams drifted away from DC, the New York studio he formed with Giordano, Continuity Associates, served as home for a new wave of creators, two of whom—Marshall Rogers and Terry Austin—would follow them in reviving Batman.

Steve Englehart—one of Marvel's hottest writers in the 1970s on books including *Doctor Strange* and *The Avengers*—had a falling out with the company. So DC seized the opportunity to grab him, as Marvel had done with so much of DC's talent. Englehart, however, had already made plans to leave the industry, but agreed to give the company one year of his time on *Justice League* and *Detective Comics.* Looking to exit the business with a bang, Englehart planned the ultimate Batman storyline, one that fortified the character's future by delving into his past, and brought the same mature perspective to his exploits that Englehart had employed at Marvel.

The first two issues of what became an eight-issue run were penciled by Walt Simonson and inked by Al Milgrom. But neither artist operated at his best, since Simonson's workload at Marvel limited the amount of time he could spend at DC. Still, May 1977's *Detective Comics* #469 ("...By Death's Eerie Light!") and #470 ("The Master Plan of Doctor Phosphorus!") introduce a new supervillain with a radioactive touch, and a potentially greater threat in Gotham City Council chairman Rupert Thorne, a crime boss blackmailed by Phosphorous into banning Batman. More importantly, they introduce Silver St. Cloud, a smart, beautiful, worldly socialite with whom Bruce Wayne is immediately smitten, resulting in Batman's first sexual relationship in comics.

In *Detective Comics* #471 ("The Dead Yet Live"), Simonson and Milgrom were replaced by Rogers and Austin for a story that

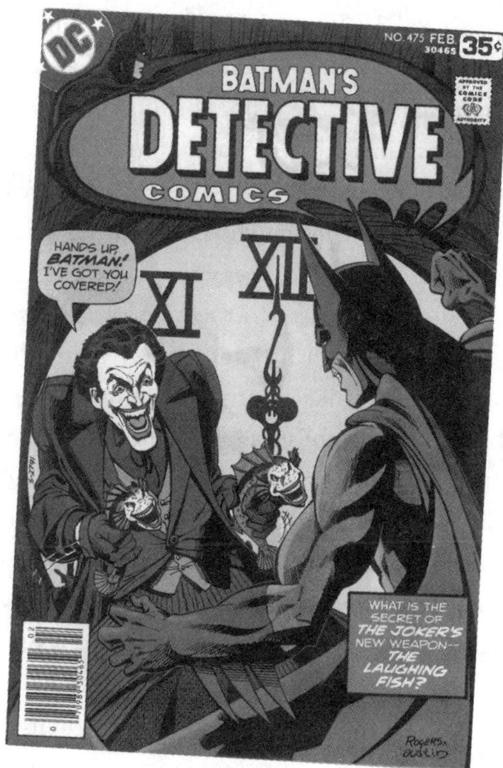

Steve Englehart crafted one of the greatest Joker stories of all time beginning with Detective Comics *#475 in 1978.* (Cover art by Marshall Rogers, Terry Austin, Tatjana Wood, and John Workman)

brought back one of Batman's first recurring enemies, Dr. Hugo Strange. Taking advantage of Batman's injuries from Phosphorous, Strange captures and unmasks him, leaving him drugged and imprisoned in the Wayne Foundation building as he impersonates Bruce Wayne and attempts to ruin him financially. A call from Silver to Dick Grayson sends Robin to the rescue in #472 ("I Am the Batman!"), though not before Strange is tortured to death by Thorne when he tries to auction off his knowledge of Batman's secret identity. Strange's "ghost" later returned to drive Thorne mad, prompting him to confess his crimes to the police.

While most every attempt since the 1966 *Batman* TV show to make the Penguin once more a formidable foe had failed, *Detective*

Comics #473 ("The Malay Penguin") succeeded. And #474 transformed Deadshot—a character who'd appeared only once prior, as a foppish, would-be crime lord in June 1950's *Batman* #59—into an assassin in a red jumpsuit and tracking-scope-mounted mask (an incarnation that lasted through 2016's *Suicide Squad* movie). The issue also saw Silver, who'd suspected Bruce was keeping secrets from her, deduce his alter ego.

But Englehart saved the best for last, as *Detective Comics* #475 ("The Laughing Fish!") and #476 ("Sign of the Joker!") told a two-part tale that ranks on any serious list of the top three Joker stories of all time, establishing his emotional dependency on Batman. Starting with the Clown Prince of Crime trying to copyright fish he's poisoned with his grin and climaxing in a rain-soaked duel with the Dark Knight—after which Silver decides she's had enough and kisses Bruce/Batman good-bye—Englehart and Rogers returned the Joker to his rightful place as Batman's greatest enemy, a position he's maintained ever since.

Rogers, with his slick, detailed pencils and energetic layouts, and Austin, with impeccable embellishments and a copious use of Zip-A-Tone (giving Gotham a layer of grime that matched the New York of the 1970s), remained on *Detective Comics* for several more issues, and eventually illustrated the *Batman* newspaper comic strip. Yet the two artists wouldn't reunite with Englehart on Batman until their 2005 six-issue *Batman: Dark Detective* limited series. Sadly, Rogers finished just one issue of *Dark Detective II* before he died of a heart attack in 2007. His long-eared rendering of Batman, wrapped in a storm cloud of cape, has influenced scores of other artists, including Todd McFarlane and Kelley Jones.

"Like in a short story," says Jones, "sometimes you can say more briefly than if you have big magnum opuses. Marshall Rogers touched upon the rogues gallery brilliantly. His Joker is definitive.

His Penguin is definitive. Everything that was in that spoke beautifully to me as a comic book fan. Reading it made me a Batman fan. To this day, when I'm recommending Batman, that's the run I always point out to people."

The impact of Englehart's storyline (collected in the trade paperback *Batman: Strange Apparitions*) was so great he was recruited to write the earliest drafts of the 1989 *Batman* movie's script. While Englehart is uncredited in the film, his contributions are still evident in, among other things, the Joker's scheme to poison Gotham, which incorporates even the dialogue of "The Laughing Fish!"

"It's one part of a binary compound," the comic's Batman says of the Joker's lethal gas, "each part harmless itself...but when they're mixed, they create a poison!" "The poison only works when the components are mixed," says Michael Keaton's Batman of the Joker's Smylex products.

With the exception of O'Neil and Adams' work, Englehart and Rogers' run on *Detective Comics* remains the version of Batman most admired by connoisseurs. The proverbial flame that burned twice as bright and half as long, its warmth radiates to this day.

"I said to myself," says Englehart of when he began writing his storyline, "'Okay, this is my shot at the Batman. But it's a limited time. I'm not gonna be the Batman writer forever and ever. So I really need to come up with the best possible stuff and fit it all into eight issues.' Which turned out to be kind of a benefit in that it just distilled everything to the essence."

Gotham Gazette Exclusive

Steve Englehart

No Batman comic book writer has done so much in so short a span of time as Steve Englehart. In just eight issues, six of which were superbly penciled by Marshall Rogers, Englehart introduced Rupert Thorne, Silver St. Cloud, and the modern version of Deadshot, as well as penning quintessential tales of Hugo Strange, the Penguin, and the Joker.

Who was your favorite Batman creator when you were growing up?
Dick Sprang. His art was amazing. Particularly for the '50s, which was when I was a kid. The extreme perspective and so forth really made Batman a very special thing. Dick Sprang's art was always spectacular. And Batman was the most interesting of the characters I had available to me.

How did your run on Batman begin?
I considered myself a Marvel writer. But there was some editorial changes at Marvel and I left the company. My wife had traveled around Europe for a year before she met me, and I thought that sounded like a good idea. So when I left Marvel, I said, "Let's set it up so we can go to Europe for a while." Then Jenette Kahn, who had just become the publisher at DC, called me up and said, "I'd like you to come over and do *Justice League*. We'd like you to do what you did on *The Avengers* and give them all personalities and stop them from being simply icons." I said, "Okay, I can give you a year. Then I'm out of here. But since we're negotiating, I would also…" That's how I got Batman, and that's why I only did the eight issues of Batman at that time, and the 12 of Justice League. Because I was only gonna be there for a certain amount of time.

In that time, you created a classic female lead in Silver St. Cloud, and in Rupert Thorne succeeded in making a mobster an intriguing Batman villain. How did they come about?
Whenever they would reprint the early Batman stuff I really liked the look of it. It was very dark and they had vampires and giant monsters

and stuff like that. I thought that pulp feeling had really been lost. Among the many things that got lost over the years was that real sense of him being a pulp character. So I really wanted to do the Joker and the Penguin and all of those guys. The other thing was I really wanted to find out who Bruce Wayne was, because he had been this icon. Denny O'Neil and Neal Adams had done some stuff, but he was still a rich playboy and that was pretty much the end of the story. I wanted to see who it was who was wearing that mask. So that's where Silver St. Cloud came from. I thought, "The best way to humanize this guy is to give him a sex life." I thought giving him a strong woman who could be his equal—who wasn't just Vicki Vale, who showed up whenever they needed a girlfriend for a story—was something I could do. In driving that home, I really wanted to have sex in there.

Now, this was under the Comics Code Authority in the '70s, so there couldn't be sex like there might be today. But it was clear, there are definitely scenes where she's lying around in a negligee in bed saying, "I had a great time last night." That's about the best you could do under the Comics Code, but it was pretty daring for the Comics Code. The thing was, because of the Comics Code, nobody had even *considered* portraying a sex life. So it was not only unheard of, it was kind of unthought of. So I did take a lot of pride in breaking down that door.

Then as far as Rupert Thorne goes...Batman had been accepted as part of Gotham City's crimefighting apparatus. He had his friend Commissioner Gordon. I thought, "Yeah, but politics is politics. There's gotta be corruption. Because of the whole pulp thing anyway, there's gotta be corruption in Gotham City."

Gotham City was the third prong there, of trying to expand his world. Trying to delineate his world, the idea was that the city council was corrupt and Rupert Thorne was the boss of the city council. Then he just kind of took off. Because of the plot structure, the corruption of the city council was something that played throughout. But when I got to the end, where Rupert Thorne and the Joker show up in the same men's room and all that, that just kind of wrote itself as the series went along.

Your two-part Joker story was groundbreaking. Were you looking to revitalize the character?
Yeah. In his first year, in *Detective Comics* back in 1939, the Joker was a homicidal maniac. That was very clear. Those early stories are very interesting because they were right at the cusp of inventing comics, so they were trying different things. But the first eight to 10 Joker stories, as they appeared consecutively in the various *Batman* and *Detective Comics* and *World's Finest*, every one of them ended with him either dying or being thrown in jail, and every one began with him not having actually died or getting out of jail. It was an ongoing sort of thing. That's part of what made the Joker so fabulous, what really imprinted him on people's minds in 1939, that he was larger than life and all that. So making him a homicidal maniac was just making him what he had started out to be. Then in 1940 they added Robin and they started to turn Batman into an icon. I love all those guys—Jerry Robinson and Bill Finger and Bob Kane—but as they were doing it in the spur of the moment it seems like they or DC realized they had a marketable property, and they began to soften the edges. They began to back away from the vampires. Batman shot somebody back in those days, and then they came up with a rule that he never shoots anybody. It reached a point in the '50s, when I was introduced to Dick Sprang's fabulous art, where we were far more into the Joker's "Ha Ha Hacienda" period, when he was just a clown who committed clown crimes. That kind of thing.

I didn't say to myself, "I'm gonna write the definitive Batman that will change him forever." But in effect that's what I was doing, in that I said, "This is what the Joker ought to be and I'm gonna make him that. This is what the Batman ought to be and I'm gonna make him that." In the time, I thought, "This is gonna be my shot. I'm gonna do this thing, and then I'll go away and somebody else will take him on and it'll just be whatever it is." But it turned out to be much bigger than that. I think everybody else was driven by my thinking, "This is what it ought to be."

In addition to the Joker, you revitalized Deadshot.
Again, I was only gonna be there for a year, and at that point a year meant seven issues. It was bimonthly and there was one extra issue

in the summer. Then the initial issues sold so well that they came and said, "We're gonna do another extra issue in the summer, so now you have eight issues." I had plotted the thing in my head. I tend not to be dogmatic about plotting, but I knew I only had seven issues so I was gonna make sure that we actually had an ending by the time we got to seven issues. So things were kind of blocked out as to what was gonna happen. When they said, "You're gonna put another one in there," I was like, "Huh. Okay." I said, "I've got Penguin and Joker and Hugo Strange," and Julie Schwartz suggested Deadshot. I have no idea why, because he was a very obscure character. In his original incarnation he wore a tuxedo and six-guns. [Laughs.] But we got to reinvent him, and I give most of the credit for that to Marshall Rogers for coming up with the new design for him…All of the sudden I was able to say, "You know, I could do a scene that's just Bruce and Silver sitting in a restaurant talking to each other. I can expand on some of the character bits. Take longer with some of the things I was gonna do and get deeper into them." In the end, it was sort of easy to expand a little in the middle and throw in Deadshot and come up with a story for him and then sort of expand the things I was gonna do. But originally there wasn't going to be a Deadshot issue.

Why did you and Marshall complement one another so well?
And [inker] Terry Austin as well. We all loved the Batman. We all kind of looked at it as "Here's our shot to do the Batman." I went first. I wrote the scripts, and then they illustrated them. So whatever I did, they were then able to be inspired or horrified by that while they were doing it. That was basically it. Because I didn't know either of them. In fact, I got those scripts written and then I did go to Europe. So I never met Marshall and Terry until a year later, when everything had been done. I had started with Walt Simonson and Al Milgrom. In those days all decisions were made by the editors. I was perfectly happy with Walt and Al, but I guess Julie Schwartz decided he wanted a different look. So when we switched after two issues to those guys I don't think I even knew. I was just writing the scripts and the *Justice League* scripts and the other stuff that I had to get done before I got out of town. So it's not like I knew Marshall and Terry were fabulous Batman artists or anything, or ever knew them at all. But I can still

remember…Having traveled around Europe all summer and fall, we went to ground in Majorca for the winter. One day I got this package and it had all the issues in it, and I remember I said, 'Thank you, God." [Laughs.]

I will wrap this up by saying, I didn't know until we were doing *Dark Detective* years later that in those days, every month, they were called in and told what a terrible, terrible art job they were doing. [Laughs.] DC did not like what they were doing at all, because DC does kind of work in terms of icons. I mean, these are the guys who redrew Jack Kirby's Superman because it didn't look like Al Plastino's Superman. [Laughs.] So they did not like Marshall's style. They did not like Terry's style of inking. So it's even more to their credit that they stood up for it and did what they wanted to do. Then, once it was all over everybody's going, "This is great!" But they had a lot of trouble.

You adapted your run into your draft of the 1989 *Batman* movie's screenplay. Did DC recommend you to Warner Bros.?
It was more the producers. Michael Uslan, who at that point had produced one or two *Swamp Thing* movies, he had an arrangement with DC to do superhero movies. He said—after reading the stuff, and particularly because of Silver St. Cloud—"Now, I can see how we could do Batman for adults." So he set out to do a Batman movie. It was all work for hire, so I wasn't involved in it. I just heard about it, and in 1986 DC called me up and said, "We've had three or four actual Hollywood screenwriters adapt your stories, but they don't get the vibe right. We want you to come on board." So at that point I did, and then did my own adaptation. I'm not a Hollywood guy but I know how this works. When I got there they said, "Oh, we're gonna have the Joker and the Penguin and Robin in this thing. So adapt your story, but put all those guys in there." I said, "That seems a little crowded," but I did it. Then cooler heads prevailed and we did further drafts where we didn't have the Penguin and we didn't have Robin. The Joker—if you're gonna do a Batman movie, to get it off the ground you're always gonna have the Joker in there. But we did have Rupert Thorne and we did have Silver St. Cloud. Then right before filming somebody decided to change Boss Thorne to Boss Grissom

and change Silver St. Cloud to Vicki Vale. I believe that's pretty much because they wouldn't have to pay me for those characters. There are royalties involved in this kind of thing, and I'm pretty sure it was a business decision. A very typical decision for DC. They're very corporate.

I was very happy with the first movie. Today, Marvel has totally figured out how to do things. From 1986 to 1989 people were still sort of trying to figure it out. So that movie could have been sharper here or there or done this or that, but for what it was at the time I was really happy with it...I have always said that Batman is not crazy. To me, Batman puts as much pressure on himself as he can possibly stand, and then he stands it. He's out there on the edge but he is standing there on the edge. When other people said later on, "He's actually crazy to be doing all this kind of stuff," I'd go, "No. Because what's the counterpart to the Joker?" It's the fact that the Joker's crazy and the Batman's not that makes for the interplay. Michael Keaton's character gets to say, "I'm not crazy." So it was pretty true to the original material. It was sent through the Hollywood rewrite mill with different people having input and so on, but I could look at it and see my stuff pretty clearly. So I was happy with it, and it did show a lot of people how you could do superheroes for adults.

You've said you felt *The Dark Knight* also drew from your work, that it wound up incorporating elements from your reunion with Marshall Rogers, the *Dark Detective* limited series, and your unpublished sequel.

Yeah. When *Batman Begins* was coming out, DC decided they wanted a lot of ancillary Batman material. So for the first time in 30 years... Again, DC is DC, and Marshall and Terry and I did a Batman run which was acclaimed and we were never asked to do it again. [Laughs.] People would go, "Why don't you do Batman?" I'd say, "Because I don't own Batman. DC doesn't want us to do Batman, so we don't get to do Batman." So for the first time in 30 years they came in and said, "Hey, we want you to do some Batman." We did that, and as it turned out, some of that was so that they could have stuff to work with for the movies. Marshall and Terry and I were gonna do *Dark Detective II*, and then Marshall died and DC didn't publish it. But then parts of it showed up in the movies. On the one hand, I'm very proud of that kind of thing. On the other hand, I could say, "Yeah, they ripped me off." [Laughs.] Marshall and Terry and I still loved doing the Batman. We had a real good time doing *Dark Detective*. I wrote all the scripts for *Dark Detective II* and Marshall drew the first issue before he died. In terms of just doing comics, we continued to have a good time at it. We weren't expecting to be ripped off.

Why do you think Batman has endured?
I just think he's a great character. He doesn't have any superpowers, so everything he does is based on strength of will, and strength of body obviously. I never did sit around and go, "I could be Batman." I don't think of how I could turn into a superhero. But I'm sure it's in the back of a lot of people's minds that he's not an alien from another planet. He's not a princess from a lost island. He's just a guy from Gotham City who turned himself into this character. I also think that visually he's great. He's black and white really. Everybody else needs a blue costume or a red costume or whatever they need. But the Bat symbol, all that stuff, is just very cool. So I think there's just more to him. He's a meatier character. I will say to top that off that obviously I like the idea of a sane, human guy doing all this stuff. He may be a very *intense* sane human guy, but this fascist robot that a lot of the stuff now depicts him as, I don't find that to be the character that interests me particularly. I'm savvy enough to know when old guys go, "Yeah, that's not the way I would do it," and that's pretty much bullshit usually. But I just got to say fascist robots don't do much for me. [Laughs.]

21 The Dark Knight Returns

The comic that redefined Batman? The book that changed a genre? The epicenter of a pop culture earthquake? So much has been said, written, and analyzed about *The Dark Knight Returns* it would be understandable if the book crumbled under the weight of its legacy. But the most impressive thing about writer-artist Frank Miller's magnum opus is that it withstands most of the hyperbole it's generated.

After Denny O'Neil and Neal Adams returned Batman to his foreboding roots in the early 1970s, and Steve Englehart and Marshall Rogers brought a new layer of realism to the character by decade's end, the Caped Crusader again entered a period of stagnation, and sales of his titles declined. Enter writer-artist Frank Miller. Fresh off of revitalizing Daredevil for Marvel Comics and creating the 1983 cyberpunk series *Ronin* for DC, Miller was the hottest creator in American funnybooks, one whom DC deemed worthy of creative carte blanche. A disciple of urban noir enraged by the crime he saw running rampant through 1980s New York, Miller zeroed in on the DC hero with whom he most identified. Initially intent on retelling Batman's origin, Miller changed his plans after experiencing an early midlife crisis.

"My main motivation in doing *Dark Knight*," says Miller, "was that I realized I was about to turn 30, and Batman was still 29. I just *could not stand* him being any younger than me. So I made him old."

Setting out to depict a 50-year-old Batman's final adventure, Miller saw in his story the potential for a grand capstone to the entire superhero genre. Starting with a climactic battle between his hero and a government-abiding Superman, Miller worked backward, building up the layers of his saga. He started with an intimate tale of Batman coming out of 10 years of self-imposed retirement, triggered by the death of the second Robin, Jason Todd. After confronting his old foe Two-Face, now completely consumed by his evil side, he faces a gang of mutant punks terrorizing Gotham, and acquires a new sidekick in 13-year-old Carrie Kelley (comics' first female Robin). Hunted by a rookie police commissioner, he battles a reinvigorated Joker to the death before engaging in a final showdown with his old friend the Man of Steel.

Inked by Klaus Janson with watercolors by Miller's then-wife Lynn Varley, *The Dark Knight Returns* was released in four 48-page, square-bound, prestige-format issues (dated February to June 1986). Its release sent shockwaves through the industry, nabbing coverage from media outlets that had previously dismissed comics as kid stuff. An operatic fable of the form, *Dark Knight* thrilled superhero devotees, offering epic action scenes and the first acknowledgement of the Clown Prince of Crime's psychological dependence on his archenemy. Moreover, it revealed to non-fans the genre's potential for social and political satire. From fame-hungry psychiatrists to a delusional Ronald Reagan, no one is spared in Miller's Mort Drucker–inspired cartooning. For many young readers, it was the first time they'd seen an authority figure questioned, let alone the president of the United States mocked.

Initiating as seismic a shift in comics as *The Lord of the Rings* and *Stars Wars* had in their respective mediums, *The Dark Knight Returns*' popular and critical success resulted in a deluge of mainstream comics aimed at mature readers—and a wave of idiosyncratic reimaginings of Batman. Brian Augustyn and Mike Mignola's *Gotham By Gaslight*, Alan Moore and Brian Bolland's *The Killing Joke*, and Grant Morrison and Dave McKean's *Arkham Asylum* followed it, as eventually did Tim Burton's 1989 *Batman* movie, in turn leading to *Batman: The Animated Series* and Christopher Nolan's feature-film trilogy. The series also resulted in Miller's

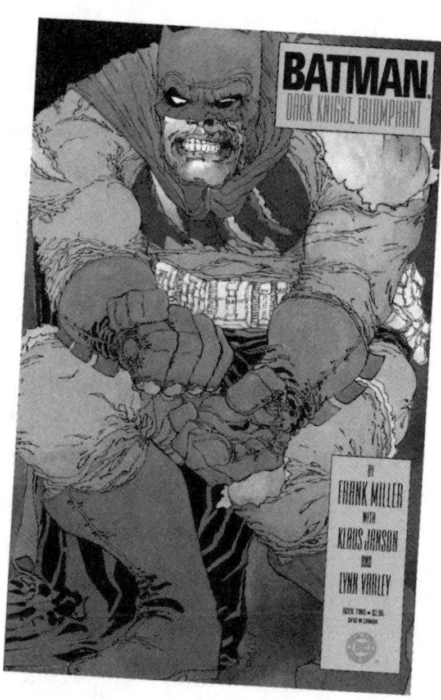

Frank Miller's The Dark Knight Returns *reimagined Batman for an entire generation of fans, and changed the future of mainstream comics.* (Cover art by Frank Miller and Lynn Varley)

Batman origin tale *Year One*, and the first new Batman monthly comic in 20 years—*Batman: Legends of the Dark Knight*, which showcased visions of the character from a variety of top creators. Suddenly there was no one correct way to portray Batman, who was reestablished as the most popular fictional character in the world.

"Gritty—graphic—grown-up," proclaimed a 1989 magazine ad for *The Dark Knight Returns*' collected edition. For better or worse, the book *did* see comics grow gritty and graphic. Yet they also grew violent and cynical, and more than a little confused sometimes as to what "grown-up" meant. An unfortunate side effect of the book's success, along with that of Alan Moore and Dave Gibbons' *Watchmen* (also released in 1986), was that the de facto mode of superhero storytelling became one of angst. Each new costumed champion acquired a tragic backstory and a lust for vengeance. What the creators of such characters forgot was that *The Dark Knight Returns* was a deconstruction, not a template, and that Miller kept his tongue planted firmly in cheek for much of its narrative—taking as much pleasure in the Joker killing late-night talk show host David Endocrine or Bruce Wayne disguising himself as a bag lady, as he did in Batman leading an army of street punks on horseback through the streets of Gotham. (All of which was brought to the screen in director Jay Oliva's vibrant 2012 animated film adaptation, featuring *Robocop*'s Peter Weller as the booming voice of Batman.)

No matter its less impactful sequels—2001's *The Dark Knight Strikes Again* and 2015's *The Dark Knight III: The Master Race* (or *Batman v Superman: Dawn of Justice* strip mining its final act)—the joy of reading *The Dark Knight Returns* remains one of witnessing a major talent at the height of his powers smashing through the presumed boundaries of his craft with the brute force of a hurricane. One swathed in a cape and cowl, embracing mortality, forging myth.

Gotham Gazette Exclusive

Frank Miller

Frank Miller changed the way the public looked at mainstream comics with 1986's grand, satirical *The Dark Knight Returns*. Miller followed it with his equally revered revamp of the Dark Knight's origin, *Batman: Year One*.

Who were your favorite Batman comic creators when you were growing up?
The best Batman I grew up with was written by Denny O'Neil and drawn by Neal Adams. I can't ignore what Denny O'Neil and Neal Adams did on the character. That influenced me a great deal coming in.

Are there any Batman creators who are especially underrated?
One is Bill Finger, who was arguably co-creator of Batman. The other is Jerry Robinson, who got very, very little credit for an astonishing amount of work, and who established a mood and a look for Batman.

Also, what Bruce Timm did [on *Batman: The Animated Series*]—and I attribute it almost entirely to him—was he took the best Batman from every period, from Dick Sprang to Neal Adams through to my stuff, everybody's stuff, and managed to mold it into this almost

(Sophia Quach McCabe)

composite Batman that was really a reminder to anybody who touches the character that Batman is essentially a force for justice. And also a big guy with a *big* jaw. [Laughs.] It's certainly closest to my interpretation. I love what Bruce did.

How did *The Dark Knight Returns* come about?

My whole career has been an exploration of the hero. I started out with openly heroic characters at Marvel Comics and at DC Comics. I always wanted to get my hands on Batman, for years on end. It was one of the big things that lured me over to work at DC Comics in the first place. But I put it off and put it off, because Batman always seemed to be too big a problem for me to try to solve. I just didn't know what I could do to refresh him, after all the different versions of the character that I'd seen growing up. Then a really strange thing happened to me. All of the sudden I realized I was about to turn 29 years old, Batman's age. Then I realized I was one year away from turning older than Batman. The more this year went on the more it bothered me that I might be older than him. So finally I [decided] to fix that, and make him older than me once and for all. So I conceived of a story where Batman was at the impossibly old age of 50. [Laughs.]

What influenced the book's look?

The biggest influence was the comic books themselves. I grew up as a comic book fan, and *Dark Knight* was a quote-unquote fan making all his dreams come true.

At first, as a comic book reader, Neal Adams was certainly an influence. As a professional, I was actually studying the much earlier versions, particularly Dick Sprang, which had a terrific effect on how I drew Batman. He drew the stockier, lantern-jawed, squarer version of Batman that I favored.

With any of these characters that have been around longer than I have, I regard what I do as part of a collective work. If it weren't for Dick Sprang there might not be Neal Adams. If it weren't for Neal Adams there wouldn't be me. I tried to contribute and have a new take.

What was your initial response to the overwhelming media coverage of the book when it was released in 1986? It may have been the first graphic novel covered on TV news programs across the country.
I was thrilled that people reacted the way they did. It certainly jump-started my career in a major way, and it gave me an amount of creative freedom that I've enjoyed ever since. So it was a winner for everybody involved. The publisher was happy, I was happy, and the audiences and retailers were happy. It was about as good a [response] as it could have had.

Why do you think *The Dark Knight Returns* is still talked about?
Well, I think it's because the character's timeless. He just needs to be updated. Who doesn't need Zorro? Who doesn't need a guy who's tougher than the bad guys to rescue us when we're in danger? The desire for a strong father figure, to go after the bad guys who are stronger than we are, is irresistible, and always will be. Best of all, he can't fly. He needs a car. So he's easy to relate to.

There's a lot of reasons. What kid hasn't run around and played in the shadows and made sure nobody can see him? And also, what kid hasn't grown up and been bullied once or twice, and wished there was somebody who could help him out, or wished that he was strong enough to take care of the bullies himself? And what person, whether from the city or the country, hasn't suffered at the hands of some form of social injustice and wished that there was someone big enough and smart enough and strong enough to take care of it? The appeal is broad-based and it's eternal.

The book introduced the first female Robin, Carrie Kelley. Was it difficult at that time to get DC to agree to her?
I'd love to tell you it was a terrible problem. I'd love to tell you that we fought every inch of the way. But no, they loved her from the get-go. [Laughs.] That was one of the ideas that they loved the most. Everything about her fit. The costume actually looks better on a girl her age, and the character is a little sprite. It was just a whole new change of atmosphere for the character. I think ultimately it helps

restore Robin to his or her proper position, which is to be the light to Batman's darkness. A grim Robin never really fit.

Arguably just as significant as *The Dark Knight Returns* was *Batman: Year One*. Did you conceive of that project at the same time?
Actually when I was finishing up *Dark Knight* I pulled out all of the notes I had put together before I started *Dark Knight*. Which were just where I wrote Batman's origin down for myself, just to figure out who he was and how he came to be, and also to set up why he retired. Those notes became the basis for *Batman: Year One*.

Do you have any favorite comic creators from among the many your work's inspired?
Just for the sake of having one of the best arguments of my life, I loved what Alan Moore did with *The Killing Joke*. Because I disagreed with everything he did. And he and I had a wonderful two-day argument about it. But it's really hard to name all the people who've done a good job with the character. There have been so many...But by and large, beyond people I've already mentioned, I have a host of favorites. I would say Archie Goodwin and Walter Simonson did some of the best Batman work in their *Manhunter* series. The list could go on for the rest of the week.

Why has Batman endured?
Batman, somewhere along the line, like Zorro, became a folk hero. Each generation wants to celebrate that folk hero because we each grew up with him...Also, there is a certain sexiness to a character who dresses up like a bad guy and throws people through windows. Batman brings an edge that most superheroes don't. Most of them were sanitized during the late '40s and early '50s.

What do you think you brought to Batman that's indelible?
We got rid of that yellow circle! It took work. [Laughs.]

22 Batman: *Year One*

After the success of his 1986 limited series *The Dark Knight Returns*, Frank Miller was the hottest creator working for DC Comics; and was again given the freedom to develop any project he chose. Deciding he wasn't quite done with the Dark Knight, Miller developed *Batman: Year One*, a retelling of the character's origin and early days.

Year One reunited Miller, as writer, with artist David Mazzucchelli, with whom he'd collaborated on the "Born Again" storyline in Marvel's *Daredevil*, another tale that broke its hero down to his essentials. Fusing the minimalism of newspaper strip cartoonists such as Milt Caniff with that of comic book artists including Alex Toth, Mazzucchelli's work in *Year One* marked the first significant reboot of Batman since the character had first appeared.

Like "Born Again," *Year One* ran in the pages of a monthly comic, *Batman* #404 to 407 (February–May 1987). Miller had conceived of the story when he proposed a line of comics retelling the origins of DC's heroes. In an interview with Peter Sanderson in *Amazing Heroes* #102 ("Dark Knight Previsited"), published on September 15, 1986, Miller remarked, "When *Dark Knight* started to take off, I mentioned that another graphic novel could be done based on my original notes…[Editor] Denny O'Neil wanted to revitalize Batman in the regular DC books and approached me to use the notes to construct a new beginning for Batman."

Year One intertwines the story of a 25-year-old Bruce Wayne—returning to Gotham after 12 years abroad—with that of Lieutenant Jim Gordon, a good man assigned to the most corrupt city in America. Abused and tormented by his boss and colleagues, the

Frank Miller's revolutionary work on the Dark Knight continued with Batman: Year One *in 1987.*
(Cover art by David Mazzucchelli)

lawman at first hunts the vigilante, but comes to find in him an invaluable ally. At the same time, Bruce realizes he alone can't rid Gotham of evil, and that Batman can inspire the just even as he terrorizes the wicked.

Year One introduced several new characters to the Batman mythos, including Mafia kingpin Carmine "The Roman" Falcone and Detective Sarah Essen (eventually Gordon's second wife). Its depiction of a determined but vulnerable Gordon and Batman were later incorporated into 2005's *Batman Begins* and TV's *Gotham*. The complete story was adapted in directors Sam Liu and Lauren Montgomery's outstanding 2011 *Batman: Year One* animated film (in which the cop and the Caped Crusader are voiced by Bryan Cranston and *Gotham*'s Ben McKenzie, respectively).

It's interesting to compare *Year One* with the Batman's first year of comic book stories, beginning with *Detective Comics* #27.

In those early days, the character's principal concern was protecting Gotham's aristocracy from the criminals who would plunder its riches. *Year One*, however, solidified Batman's role as a crusader for the downtrodden.

"If Gotham is a clean town, then Batman is a psycho," says Miller in *Amazing Heroes*. "His psychological state is extreme, but he's no psychopath. He's like Robin Hood or Zorro in his qualities of absolute dedication to a cause."

23 The Killing Joke

It's the most polarizing Batman story ever told. A tale as revered for its insight into the Joker's psyche as it is despised for its brutality toward Barbra Gordon. No one feels apathy toward *Batman: The Killing Joke*.

Prior attempts had been made to tell the Joker's origin before writer Alan Moore and artist Brian Bolland crafted their 1988 48-page comic. The most notable telling came in February 1951's *Detective Comics* #168 ("The Man Behind the Red Hood!" written by Batman co-creator Bill Finger), which revealed the character was once a laboratory worker who tried to rob the Monarch Playing Card Company, and in evading justice dove into a basin of waste chemicals that turned his hair green, lips red, and skin chalk-white.

The Killing Joke expands on that origin, revealing, in a bravura flashback sequence, that the Joker was once an unfunny stand-up comic. He joins a gang of thieves, and, on the verge of carrying out a robbery at his former place of employment, learns his pregnant wife has been accidentally killed by a household appliance. He runs

The Killing Joke*, written by Alan Moore, remains one of the most controversial stories in Batman's long history.* (Cover art by Brian Bolland and Richard Bruning)

afoul of Batman and takes an ill-fated chemical bath, after which his sanity snaps.

The book's most horrifying scene occurs years later, when the Joker escapes Arkham Asylum and arrives at Commissioner Gordon's home. He shoots Gordon's daughter, Barbara (who'd recently retired as Batgirl), through the spine, disrobes her, and takes photos of her naked, bleeding body. He then shows the photos to Gordon after dressing him in S&M attire and imprisoning him in a deranged funhouse. With Barbara crippled, the Dark Knight chases after the Joker, catches him in his amusement park, and hears one final joke from the lunatic, laughing along with him.

In the book's final panels, police cars arrive and the laughter stops. For decades most fans assumed that meant the Joker was returned to Arkham. But in an interview on filmmaker Kevin Smith's *Fatman on Batman* podcast, comic writer Grant Morrison revealed his theory that the Dark Knight actually *kills* the Clown Prince of Crime, hence the story's title. It's a sound argument, albeit a heartbreaking one, for it implies that, in the end, Batman's only option in preventing his greatest enemy from taking another life is to kill him in cold blood.

Bolland, who'd made his name illustrating Judge Dredd in *2000 AD* and DC's *Camelot 3000*, spent years crafting the book's exquisite imagery, resulting in the best work of his career, and the best selling. Not everyone was a fan, however; Moore disowned his tale, claiming it had little to say beyond emphasizing how Batman and the Joker were reflections of one another.

The idea, however, resonated with Tim Burton, who incorporated it into his 1989 *Batman* movie. And in 2008's *The Dark Knight*, Christopher Nolan borrowed *The Killing Joke*'s suggestion that anyone can wind up like the Joker depending on their circumstances. Scores of other creators have been influenced by the book, which was adapted into a 2016 animated film. Adding to the tale's controversy, the *Killing Joke* movie puts Batman and Batgirl in a sexual relationship before she's maimed.

No matter how one feels about *The Killing Joke*, there's no denying its effectiveness in portraying a Joker as vulnerable and vile as any in the character's history.

"Do I think it's the greatest story ever written or the greatest Joker-Batman story ever written?" says Paul Dini, writer of Joker favorites such as *Batman: Mask of the Phantasm* and *Mad Love*. "No, I don't. But it is certainly a classic, iconic story. If you read no other story with Batman and the Joker in it, you read this one."

24 Tim Burton's *Batman*

At a time in which cultural phenomenons are born of marketing campaigns and consumed like corn chips, it's not easy to describe the level of excitement that greeted director Tim Burton's first *Batman* movie. To say it was the perfect four-quadrant film—appealing to men and women, young and old—is putting it mildly. The World War II generation had thrilled to the character's adventures in comic books, his 1966 TV series held a special place in the hearts of baby boomers, and a good chunk of Generation X, weaned on Saturday morning's *Super Friends*, had discovered comics weren't just for kids with Frank Miller's *The Dark Knight Returns*. By 1989, the whole world knew about Batman, and eagerly awaited the most hyped movie of the decade.

It had been in development for years. Producers Michael Uslan and Benjamin Melniker bought the film rights to Batman in 1979 from DC Comics in the wake of *Superman: The Movie*'s success. A lifelong fan of the character, Uslan was determined to do him justice, and numerous screenplays were drafted. Comics scribe Steve Englehart wrote a detailed treatment incorporating mob boss Rupert Thorne and Bruce Wayne's girlfriend Silver St. Cloud, two characters he'd created during his tenure on *Detective Comics*. Screenwriter Tom Mankiewicz crafted a script using the template he'd followed for *Superman*.

Uslan and Peters wound up taking the project to Warner Brothers, of which DC was a division, and which was partnered with producers Jon Peters and Peter Guber, responsible for 1980s hits such as *Flashdance* and *Rain Man*. Fresh off the success of his debut film, Warner Bros.' *Pee-wee's Big Adventure*, Tim Burton won the job of directing, and recruited screenwriter Sam Hamm.

"I had sat down with Tim," Hamm told Jeff Gelb in *David Anthony Kraft's Comics Interview* #70, "and the first thing we talked about was that we wanted to do it straight, and scary and psychological and all this kind of stuff."

Rather than begin with young Bruce Wayne witnessing his parents' murder, Hamm and Burton decided that the film should open with Bruce having already donned the mantle of the Bat. It would slowly introduce filmgoers to his world and origin (which had never been depicted in live action before). They were also determined to make Gotham as much a character as Batman himself. Production designer Anton Furst was tasked with creating a city in the tradition of Fritz Lang's architectural wonder *Metropolis*, incorporating the Los Angeles decay of Ridley Scott's *Blade Runner* and the retro-futurism of Terry Gilliam's *Brazil*. He also conceived of the most fearsome Batmobile yet seen and the high-flying Batwing, earning an Academy Award for his efforts. *Excalibur* costume designer Bob Ringwood was responsible for creating a Batsuit that was just as intimidating.

Though his casting was initially greeted with skepticism, Michael Keaton's take on the Dark Knight in Tim Burton's Batman *and* Batman Returns *has become one of the most popular versions of the character on film.* (Newscom)

"The place is Gotham City. The time, 1987—once removed," begins the first draft of Hamm's script (dated October 20, 1986). "The city of Tomorrow: stark angles, creeping shadows, dense, crowded, airless, a random tangle of steel and concrete, self-generating, almost subterranean in its aspect…as if hell had erupted through the sidewalks and kept on growing. A dangling fat moon shines overhead, ready to burst."

Hamm was raised on comic books, Burton was not. But both men were drawn to the Batman books then making headlines: *The Dark Knight Returns*—from which Hamm used Frank Miller's idea that Batman's chest emblem was a target intended to draw fire to the armor beneath it—and Alan Moore's *The Killing Joke*, which retold the Joker's origin. Both stories saw Batman as someone almost as psychotic as his archenemy.

After Englehart submitted his final treatment, Hamm used Bruce Wayne's on-again, off-again girlfriend Vicki Vale in place of Silver St. Cloud and morphed Rupert Thorne into crime lord Carl Grissom. Days after Hamm turned in his fifth draft, the 1988 Writers Guild of America strike occurred, prohibiting him from further work on the film. British screenwriters Warren Skaaren and Charles McKeown, who'd scripted Burton's *Beetlejuice*, were enlisted, and proceeded to add the film's controversial twist—in which the Joker is revealed as the killer of Bruce Wayne's parents.

Sean Young was hired to play Vicki Vale, but suffered an injury prior to shooting and was replaced with Kim Basinger. Jack Palance was cast as Grissom, Hammer Films regular Michael Gough as Alfred, and Pat Hingle as Commissioner Gordon. Billy Dee Williams landed the role of Harvey Dent, intended to evolve into Two-Face in a sequel.

Numerous names were considered for the roles of Batman and the Joker, which eventually went to Michael Keaton and Jack Nicholson, respectively. The latter was an obvious choice given his roles in Warner Bros.' *The Shining* and *The Witches of Eastwick*, and the producers had courted him for several years.

"Jack Nicholson's performance," says Zach Galifianakis, who voiced the Joker in *The LEGO Batman Movie*, "has so many non sequiturs that were just so wonderful. Jack Nicholson's over-the-top cartoony performance was an inspiration for me."

Fans were initially less enthusiastic about Keaton. A short, comic actor best known for his roles in films such as *Beetlejuice*, news of his casting prompted fans to flood DC's offices with letters of protest. Nevertheless, production took place at England's Pinewood Studios from October of 1988 to January of 1989.

Most fans who balked at Keaton's casting fell silent when *Batman* opened on June 23, 1989, the character's 50th anniversary year. After hearing Danny Elfman's iconic theme play over its moody opening credits, audiences were stunned to see Keaton, and the film itself, take Batman as seriously as the most fervent of comic book devotees. Indeed some felt the movie took things a little *too* seriously. With a Dark Knight who bombs the Joker's hideout—killing all of his men in the process—it offered a Batman bloodthirstier than the decade's comics. A fact even Prince's pop song contributions—among them the No. 1 hit "Batdance"—couldn't mask.

Not that filmgoers were bothered by a Dark Knight who at times resembled Dirty Harry. Or the fact that Alfred lets Vicki Vale into the Batcave without Bruce Wayne's permission. Or that the Joker remembers killing Batman's parents when he doesn't know Batman is Bruce Wayne. Overproduced and spottily written though it is, *Batman* earned $411.3 million worldwide, and was the first movie to gross $100 million in the first 10 days of its release. Moreover, it showed the world what comic fans had long known. That Batman, as he was originally created, was not a hero who tolerated laughter.

25 Batman: The Animated Series

"Definitive" is a dangerous word where the Dark Knight is concerned. But it's rarely been as appropriate as in the case of *Batman: The Animated Series.*

The optimal screen version of the Caped Crusader began when Warner Brothers hired Hanna-Barbera executive Jean MacCurdy as the president of its new animation division. The medium was then undergoing a renaissance at Disney, generating films such as *The Little Mermaid* and *Who Framed Roger Rabbit?* and TV shows such as *Duck Tales.* MacCurdy had produced the Emmy-winning *Tiny Toon Adventures* under executive producer Steven Spielberg. With its whipsmart comedy and meta commentary, it launched a new era for the company.

During her time at Hanna-Barbera, MacCurdy and writer Alan Burnett had tried developing a Batman series that was darker than the company's *Super Friends* efforts, but nothing came of it. She asked her new staff to brainstorm ideas for several Warners properties, including Batman.

Artist Eric Radomski and animator Bruce Timm conceived of a design for the Dark Knight that worked with a Gotham City comprised of Radomski's "Dark Deco" backgrounds. Utilizing the aesthetic of the Fleischer Studios *Superman* cartoons of the 1940s, Radomski spray-painted his cityscapes with acrylic paint onto black paperboard, giving Gotham a look unlike any environment in TV animation history. Like Tim Burton's 1989 *Batman* film—which helped sell the series to the Fox network—Timm and Radomski reveled in retrofuturism, but abandoned Burton's gothic sensibilities for the clean lines and textures of classic noir.

Upon watching their presentation reel, MacCurdy made Radomski and Timm producers, and gave them an unprecedented amount of freedom in realizing their vision. Tasked in November 1990 with producing 65 episodes, they recruited *Tiny Toons'* Ted Blackman to design the look of their Gotham City, all imposing skyscrapers and police blimps. The key to the show's visual success, however, came in Timm's eminently animatable figures, steeped in the tradition of cartooning rather than the quasi-realism of 1980s cartoons like *G.I. Joe* and *Transformers.*

A lifelong comic fan, Timm reached out to several creators from the field to help design the show's characters. He designed Batman (who, along with Bruce Wayne, would be voiced by the stalwart Kevin Conroy), Catwoman (Adrienne Barbeau), Commissioner Gordon (Bob Hastings), Two-Face (Richard Moll), and an original character, Harley Quinn (Arleen Sorkin); while Kevin Nowlan designed the Joker (the magnetically mad Mark Hamill), Alfred (Efrem Zimbalist Jr.), and Robin (Loren Lester). *Hellboy* creator Mike Mignola designed Mr. Freeze (Michael Ansara) and the Riddler (John Glover). Radomski and Timm's opening title sequence (animated by TMS, one of several overseas studios that produced the show's animation) was designed to resemble a living, breathing Art Deco poster.

Burnett joined as the series' third producer, and coaxed Dini—who'd drafted an early version of its bible—away from his job as *Tiny Toons* story editor to do the same for *Batman.* They chose to avoid referring to the Dark Knight's oft-told origin, and instead explored how his psyche was reflected in his villains, and how Gotham created them as it had him.

With Shirley Walker on board as composer—retaining Danny Elfman's *Batman* movie score for the opening sequence—the premiere episode "On Leather Wings" was broadcast in prime time on September 5, 1992, introducing audiences to Man-Bat, the first tormented soul to occupy one of *Batman: The Animated Series'* 85 original episodes. The majority were first broadcast as part of the Fox Kids programming block, 22-minute, precision-cut diamonds fitted into a three-act cinematic structure. As lean and as muscular examples of short-form visual storytelling as anthology classics such as *The Twilight Zone* or *Alfred Hitchcock Presents*, they exercise the show's limitless potential like the best episodes of *Star Trek* and *Doctor Who*. Like Sean Connery's James Bond, their Batman is outfitted with gadgetry but must ultimately rely on his wits to defeat his opponents. He survives by the skin of his teeth because his own tragedy allows him to see the world through the eyes of his foes, even as his will and moral clarity allows him to rise above it.

A much acclaimed monthly comic book tie-in, *The Batman Adventures*, launched at the same time as the show with October 1992's *The Batman Adventures* #1. It ran 36 issues, and—when

To many Batfans, the best tales of the Dark Knight ever put to screen appeared in Batman: The Animated Series. (Production art © Warner Brothers Animation)

Batman: The Animated Series' name was changed in its second season to *The Adventures of Batman & Robin* (due to its increased use of Robin)—was rebranded *Batman & Robin Adventures.* In 1997, a continuation, *The New Batman Adventures,* premiered as a part of Kids' WB on the WB network, which allowed for a greater level of violence and frightening imagery than Fox. *The New Batman Adventures* redesigned the original show's characters in the even more minimalistic style that had since been introduced in the spinoff *Superman: The Animated Series.* In *TNBA*, Dick Grayson has matured into Nightwing (again voiced by Lester), and a new Robin, Tim Drake (voiced by Mathew Valencia), takes his place, while Batgirl (Tara Strong) is made a regular. Its tie-in comic, *Gotham Adventures*, ran for 60 issues.

A further continuation, set in the future of the DC Animated Universe, arrived with 1999's *Batman Beyond*, which saw an elderly Bruce Wayne mentor a new Batman, teenager Terry McGinnis. *Justice League*, from 2001, and 2004's *Justice League Unlimited* surrounded Batman with a multitude of fellow teammates; *Justice League* also introduced an enjoyable sexual tension between Batman and Wonder Woman. All three series demonstrated Kevin Conroy's versatility as an actor—capable of painting in innumerable shades his decades-long portrait of the Dark Knight—as well as that of the world Timm and company had designed.

For children of the 1990s and the new millennium, these series *were* Batman. But they're unbeholden to any time. Existing outside the confines of form and period, perpetual in movement and memory, they elevate an already archetypal character and his world to the purest form, condensing a half century of comic book stories into one thrilling, coherent narrative. One that's definitive in every way.

Gotham Gazette Exclusive

Mark Hamill

Mark Hamill became a pop culture icon as *Star Wars* hero Luke Skywalker. But in 1992's *Batman: The Animated Series* he proved just as effective at villainy, when he voiced what many consider the definitive screen version of the Joker. He returned to the role in *Batman: Mask of the Phantasm*, *Batman Beyond: Return of the Joker*, the *Batman: Arkham* video games, the *Killing Joke* movie adaptation, and, most recently, TV's *Justice League Action*.

When did you first become interested in voice acting?
I saw a Walt Disney TV program about how cartoons were made, and to see Clarence Nash at a microphone doing Donald Duck...The light bulb went off in my head. I was in maybe kindergarten or first grade, and I thought, "Wow, somebody goes to work and does Donald Duck as a job." [Laughs.] I thought, "I wanna do that job!" I thought, even then, "Wouldn't that be great? I'm sort of scared of getting in front of an audience. But this would be perfect because I'd do the voice and nobody would know it was me." That was very appealing—the anonymity of it all.

Because I knew early on what I wanted to do. I tried to keep it a secret. I have four sisters and two brothers who would have ridiculed me to no end if they knew that I wanted to do what I wanted to do. But I did know very, very early on.

So your Joker was the natural outcome of that lifelong passion?
Absolutely, absolutely. In fact, even the approach. I mean, I didn't do it consciously at the time, but I think I was so enamored of the voices in the old Universal horror films. Whether it was Bela Lugosi or Boris Karloff. Even Laurel and Hardy. I thought, "Where did these guys come from?" I couldn't understand the dialect, you know? I went to nine schools in 12 years, because my dad was in the Navy. So we moved from coast to coast to coast to coast, and I would notice regional accents and so forth. But I loved trying to imitate these actors. One of the actors who I think is really fundamental—at least in terms of laying down the foundation of the Joker—is Claude Rains,

the Invisible Man. I remember there was a line I used to do, trying to do Claude Rains—"Crazy? You think I'm crazy? I'll show you who's crazy!" He had such power in his voice, because you couldn't see him. I'm sure that's one of the reasons they cast him, because of his incredible power in that voice.

Now, what a lot of the voice actors do is they start with a foundation. You're not really trying to do an imitation of Claude Rains, but he's certainly in the mix. And you add a little Blue Meanie from *Yellow Submarine*—"Lovey dovey!" You can add certain aspects of any characters to make a new whole. It was a technique that I had done for several different characters, and once I got really comfortable with other voice actors, I'd say, "You know, that character's sort of a mix of Howard Cosell and Jay Leno. But the way it comes out the other end, people can't tell that's where it came from, because it sounds like neither of them." But I shouldn't have been surprised. A lot of the voice actors said, "Oh, that's very common." Then they would point out influences on famous voices they had done and you could see it. You'd say, "Oh yeah, okay. I can get that."

But I've really been blessed to be able to be a character actor in voiceover. Because the only reason I went to Broadway was to do character parts that I couldn't get on camera, whether it was *The Elephant Man* or *Amadeus*. In *Room Service* I played the sleazy producer rather than the innocent playwright—which is what the critics thought I was cast as when they came to see it, and were pleasantly surprised for the most part.

I did one cartoon series when I was still on a soap, when I was a teenager, and then I didn't work in voiceover for 20 years. It just never occurred to me. But being a huge fan of comic books and comic-related shows, when I heard they were doing *Batman: The Animated Series*, and that their model—to strive for in terms of quality—was the Max Fleischer *Superman* cartoons, I said, "I really want to be a part of this. I really want to get into this." So that was the thing that really landed me in the voiceover community. Because that was the first thing I'd done since what I had done as a teenager—*Jeannie*, the [1973] Hanna-Barbera cartoon.

As you know, the *Batman* animated series turned out to be a benchmark in that type of cartoon, in terms of the writing, the design, the music, the cast...just everything. I kind of got spoiled, because I thought, "Where has this been all my life? This is so great." I missed out on the Golden Age of radio, and here you had a whole group of actors who did the show in real time, from page one to the end. Everybody in the cast was there. It was like doing old-time radio in a sense. It was just a great thrill.

There's a great liberation in not being seen. It frees you to make choices that you probably would never make if you were on camera. You get to play characters that are unlike you physically. In animation, they cast with their ears, not with their eyes. So I was very lucky.

You continued to play the Joker in many other productions. Why do you think so many fans consider your interpretation the definitive one?

Well, I don't know about that, because I've never seen a Joker that I didn't like. I loved Cesar Romero and I loved Jack Nicholson and Kevin Michael Richardson, Jeff Bennett, Brent Spiner, Michael Emerson, Heath Ledger, Jared Leto…I would say it's the character more than it is me. There's something about a character that is so committed to anarchy and chaos. That takes great delight in other people's misery and fear. It's just the antithesis of a good person. He's insane! And because he's insane he's unpredictable, and because he's unpredictable he's rarely boring. So that's why it's been so hard to quit him.

Because after the *Arkham* games did so well—I mean, they were making upwards of a billion dollars on these things—I said, "I should go out on a high note. If I've learned anything from George Costanza, it's go out on a high note and don't look back." [Laughs.] So I very foolishly announced my retirement from the role. Because I didn't think it would come up again. But when they ask you back, you know, if you say no, someone else will do it. Troy Baker does it spot-on, he does my version of the Joker. He's versatile enough to do anything—he plays Batman, he plays villains, he plays heroes. He could come up with an original Joker I'm sure, but they cast him [in *Batman: Arkham Origins*], where they had Roger Craig Smith of *Regular Show* play Kevin Conroy's Batman and he played my Joker. It was astonishing. I thought, "Oh my gosh, this is so spot-on!"

But I really love doing it. It's hard to let it go because I have so much fun doing it. That's why I decided to go back and do *Justice*

League Action. It also brings it full circle. Because—after the R-rated *Killing Joke*, where eight-year-olds are coming up to you saying, "I can't wait to see the new Joker movie!" and you have to tell their parents, "Don't let them see it!"—at least *Justice League Action* is geared toward a younger audience. So we've come full circle back to the sort of old-school comic book Joker from the original *Batman: The Animated Series*.

Gotham Gazette Exclusive

Bruce Timm

Animation maestro Bruce Timm used his lifelong love of Batman and encyclopedic knowledge of comic books to create the award-winning *Batman: The Animated Series* and the films and TV shows that followed it in the DC Animated Universe. As DC Animated supervising producer, he oversaw many of the DC Universe Animated original movies. And as the co-creator of Harley Quinn, he illustrated her origin story, *Batman Adventures: Mad Love*, along with *Batman: Harley and Ivy*.

Many consider *Batman: The Animated Series* the definitive screen version of the character. Do you think Batman is better suited to animation than live-action?
Clearly animation has the advantage in doing a character as outlandish looking as Batman. It's a lot easier to make him cool-looking without having to worry about, "Oh, does his head look too big for his body? Do his muscles look weird? Does it look like he's wearing rubber muscles? Does his cape look bizarre?" Animation is much more forgiving that way, because it's just a purely hand-drawn medium. And fortunately, Batman has *the* best superhero costume ever. It totally lends itself to animation.

What are your favorite iterations of Batman?
I've got a lot. David Mazzucchelli's version from *Batman: Year One*, that was a real touchstone for me, going forward from that point on.

I always kind of kept that in the back of my head as almost my ideal Batman when we were doing *Batman: The Animated Series.* I love the Dick Sprang comics a lot, Neal Adams' version, Jim Aparo, Marshall Rogers definitely. The Marshall Rogers and Steve Englehart version is great. Walt Simonson did a handful of really great Batman stories. And Trevor von Eeden. I never mention Trevor Von Eeden in these interviews, but that *Batman Annual* [#8] he did in [1982] that Lynn Varley colored, that's killer. That was a big influence on me in *Batman: The Animated Series.*

Do you read contemporary Batman comics?
I don't read very many comics at all anymore. I don't have the time really. I look through a lot of them but I don't sit down and actually read them, I'm sorry to say.

How did Harley Quinn's design come about?
Paul [Dini] initially had a completely different look in mind for her. In his head he had a kind of '60s, Adam West–style, kooky Harley Quinn kind of idea. He actually did a rough sketch of her. I looked at that and went, "No, we're not doing that." [Laughs.] So I just did some research on the classic harlequin outfits and did a kind of simplified, stripped-down, streamlined superhero version of the classic harlequin outfit. With the ruffles and the jester hat and the white greasepaint and the diamond pattern. The alternating red and black actually kind of comes from the comics. Especially the Golden Age Daredevil character, the Lev Gleason version, with the red-and-black alternating costume. I think that's where I got that motif from.

What do you make of Harley's rise to fame?
I'm pleased by it, obviously. It's really cool to see that many people interested in her. But don't ask me to explain it. I kind of scratch my head. When people say, "What's the appeal of Harley Quinn?" I'm like, "The hell if I know..." Maybe that's the thing. Maybe it's how different she is from all the other superheroes/famous female characters. She really is kind of unique in that regard. Because she's really unpredictable and really weird and funny, and has this kind of weird and uncomfortable backstory, which fortunately is just kind of like an echo right now. It's not something they play up anymore, her

weird relationship with the Joker. I think that's part of the reason why she's broken out so big right now. In the comics they've detached her so much from the Joker that she really is kind of her own person now. I can't really explain why she's so popular, but clearly she is.

(Joseph McCabe)

***The Animated Series* also gave us a very popular Batmobile. You even used it in the animated adaptation of *The Killing Joke*.** That's the one place where we deviated away from the Brian Bolland comic deliberately. Because in the comic when he shows up at the carnival at the end he's driving this really deliberately old-school Batmobile from like 1950 or even earlier. Brian's such a great artist he can make that work. But we looked at it and said, "We're gonna get a laugh. If we have Batman show up in his final showdown with the Joker driving that car people are gonna titter and giggle instead of going, 'Yeah!'" So we said, "Okay, we can't go that way if we want a cool Batmobile." The *BTAS* Batmobile wasn't my first choice. I said, "It shows up in one scene. Let's look at all of our stock Batmobiles from all of our previous versions. Because there's been a zillion of 'em in all the different movies and the TV shows. We pulled them all out, we looked at them. We kind of went, "Okay, I don't really like that one...I *really* don't like that one..." The *BTAS*mobile was the one where I went, "Okay, you know, that one still looks cool. So we'll just make it the *BTAS*mobile."

Why has Batman endured?
You know, you'd think I'd have a good answer for that. After all these years, I don't have the answer.

Why have *you* loved him for so long?
He looks cool. [Laughs.] I'm sorry, but ever since I was a kid...I don't know what exactly about it is. I don't know what the constant is between them—the first version of Batman that I ever saw was Adam West, and I love the Adam West version as much as I love the Neal Adams version as much as I love the Frank Miller version. And they're not really connected in any way, shape, or form except by the costume. He's got the coolest costume of anybody in comics. So I think that's a big part of it. He's the good guy who dresses like the bad guy.

Gotham Gazette Exclusive

Kevin Conroy

No actor has played Batman as many times as Kevin Conroy. In *Batman: The Animated Series*, *Batman: Mask of the Phantasm*, *The New Batman Adventures*, *Batman Beyond*, *Batman Beyond: Return of the Joker*, *Justice League*, *Justice League Unlimited*, the *Batman: Arkham* video games, and *Justice League Action*, he's defined the Dark Knight on screen.

Were you new to the world of Batman when you were cast in 1992's *Batman: The Animated Series*?
Yes. [Voice director] Andrea Romano had to kind of fill me in on the background of the character—the loss of his parents as a child, avenging their deaths, this moral obligation he feels throughout his life, and how he evolves at the cost of a normal, fulfilled life. But he turns that disability into a great force of good. I said, "Wow, this is the arc of so many great tragic characters. This is an almost Hamlet-like character, or like the great Greek tragedy characters." Bruce Timm liked that take. I had trained in theater work, so I really approached it from a purely theatrical, stage-actor direction, and just used my

imagination. Because I had no preconceptions in that sound booth that day, I felt completely liberated to use my imagination and come up with a sound that I thought would be appropriate for the character. It put me into a darker and deeper and huskier place, which just sounded to me so mysterious and secretive. It seemed appropriate, and they loved it. Andrea told me later they had seen about 500 people. So I was just very, very, very lucky to have made the right choice that day.

John Lennon said, "Life is what happens to you when you're busy making other plans." I never planned on doing this much animation. You never know that something's gonna snowball that way and go on. I get asked all the time now, "Did you see this 25 years ago? Did you see where you would be now?" I always say, "Are you kidding? There's no way that you could have possibly seen this." It's just life unfolding as you keep jumping from rock to rock. Actors are always thinking the job they have is the last one they're gonna have. I'm just very grateful that this has lasted as long as it has. I really am.

Does Batman's voice come from your stomach?

Yeah, the voice really comes from his gut. It's really from the deepest place in him. The one trick I found to playing the character was Batman is not the mask. Batman is who he really is in his soul. So that voice, when he goes down to that deep husky voice, that has to be in your deepest, darkest corner of your gut, because that's who he is. When he puts on a suit and faces the world and becomes charming Bruce Wayne, that's where I would use my upper register and put a lot more color in the voice, because he's performing for the world. I think that kept the Batman sound very grounded and very believable and rooted. Sometimes when they do a Batman voice it sounds too forced and theatrical. The trick I found was that's not the performance. The performance is Bruce Wayne.

How closely were you able to identify with Batman? You've said in past interviews that, like Bruce Wayne, you didn't have the easiest childhood...

Well, no one has an easy time. Life is just a hard journey. It's how you deal with it. I had a lot of difficulties growing up, but I wasn't starving to death. I had alcoholic parents, and I've been on my own since I was about 17. But that's not as bad as some kid who's growing up in the middle of a war. So it's all relative. But I really do believe that everyone has a hard time. Because life is just hard. It's a hard journey. That's why people relate to Batman the way they do. Because he's a man who faced a crushing tragedy as a child and didn't let it crush him. He turned it around and became a beacon of good. Everything in the world is so gray that people love the fact that there's not a lot gray about Batman. He's very pure. He has a very strong moral compass. He's a noble character...The episodes I've loved playing the most are the ones that deal with his conflict. Like "Perchance to Dream." It's an episode in which he's forced, after being drugged, to go into his own childhood and face his demons. In that I got to do the voices of young Bruce, middle-aged Bruce, Batman, and Bruce Sr. I was doing voices that had to be distinctly different but had to be believably related. So that was a real challenge for an actor.

In your performance you bring the same sense of decency that Christopher Reeve brought to Superman.

Oh yeah. There's no question of him being the most decent person. The wonderful thing in all the series I've done—Batman never kills. After a fight, if someone falls off a building, they have what's called the "stay alive groan." [Laughs.] So that the audience understands that Batman did not kill this person...He won't kill.

It's funny you bring up Christopher Reeve. Because we were at Juilliard at the same time and we knew each other. He was a couple of years ahead of me, a bit older. What a wonderful, wonderful, funny, talented guy. He was a great, great guy.

Superman and Batman together...

I know, isn't that funny? We almost roomed together actually. I looked at an apartment that he wanted to split with me, but I was a full scholarship student living on money I made as a mail boy when I was 17. So I had nothing to spend on rent.

The two of you must have stood out at school. You're both pretty tall.

Yes, we're both pretty tall. But he was a lot better looking than me. [Laughs]

You've had the opportunity to perform with a wide range of actors as Batman.
Word got out pretty quickly that there were these great recording sessions going on at Warner Brothers. Andrea Romano told me she could get anyone she wanted into those shows, because everyone wanted to be in those recording studios. It was kind of unique in that Warner Brothers always likes the actors to record together. Some studios like to get completely separate takes. But Warner prefers to get people working together, and that's a great thing because actors feed off each other. The energy enhances your performance. I'm much better opposite Mark Hamill than I would be if he wasn't there. And I think that I help him be a better Joker. So the bookings of these sessions—with Roddy McDowall and Efrem Zimbalist Jr. and Paul Williams—they just got to be so much fun. All these people were coming in.

With *Batman Beyond*, you had a different version of Bruce Wayne to play, an elderly mentor. Did you call on a different side of your theater background? The elderly Bruce is reminiscent of King Lear.
Exactly. That was exactly what my visual image was. I've done two productions of *Lear*, one was for Jack O'Brien at the San Diego National Shakespeare Festival and one was for John Houseman at Lincoln Center. That was actually exactly the quality—the *Lion in Winter* character. That was my visualization, that he was still enormously powerful. He could do *Lear*'s "Blow, winds, and crack your cheeks!" But he just didn't have the strength to fight the fights anymore. But he still had the epic passion of a great tragic character. So that was a lot of fun to play.

When it came time to do *Justice League*, how did a large regular ensemble affect your performance?
That was strange. Because suddenly I went from being the center of the action of every episode to being one of five or seven characters, and the role I played as Batman evolved. He was suddenly the outsider. So the action often centered around Superman or one of the other characters, and Batman would sort of be the conscience, brooding in the corner and commenting on the action. Batman was always kind of an outsider to the Justice League.

***Batman Beyond* and *Justice League* also gave you the opportunity to sing.**
That was done specifically because they know I like to sing. [Laughs.] They were looking for an excuse. And the only appropriate song they could have me sing in *Justice League* was "Am I Blue?" So the audience really got a kick out of that.

Were the *Arkham* games difficult, since you didn't have a traditional narrative or record with other actors?
I can't explain to you how difficult it is compared to traditional acting. Because in traditional acting you have a linear storyline. You have a reality you're living in, you have other characters to feed off of. It was really like doing a radio play. The games are just done in pieces, and you have to be alone for the most part. Because they need completely clean takes on every line. And you're doing line after line after line after line after line. Then they say, "Great. Now can you do it with a little irony?" Line after line after line after line after line. They say, "Great. Keep the irony, now with a little more anger." Line after line after line…And to do this for four hours at a time trying to keep the Batman character alive, trying to keep that voice pure, and to act… It's exhausting. After four hours you get an hour's break, and then you go in for another four hours. *Arkham Knight*, the last game, it took two years to build, two years to record, and there were 37,000 lines of dialogue. It was a vast undertaking. So recording the games is not fun. But then when you see it you're so proud of what you've been a part of. But it's definitely not why you go to Juilliard. [Laughs.] It's a ballbuster, but it looks great when it's done.

Can you share some of the more memorable feedback you've had from fans over the years?
Oh my god, I have such incredible fan encounters and fan stories. It's why I love going to Comic-Con. Batman has the most amazing fans. They invest so much in him. They use him as a role model for so many things.

I had a young woman come up to me in Chicago, at a convention, and say, "Can I just hold you?" I hugged her and she got very emotional. She said, "I grew up in the projects on the South Side of Chicago, and I just want you to know that everyone I grew up with is either dead or in prison. The only reason I'm not, and that I have a life and a career, is because of Batman. I had him every day. I came home from school and there you were, and you got me out of those projects." I said, "Now wait a minute, you got yourself out of those projects, and God bless you for doing it. That's amazing." But wow, what an honor to be part of something that's affected people like that. Batman was a tool she used.

I do hear stories like that. I've had homeless people come up to me on the street and say, "You're Kevin Conroy!" I think, "How could they possibly know?" It's because of publicity and the Internet. They say, "Do it! Do it! Do 'I am vengeance...'" And you're doing, "I am vengeance. I am the night..." standing in a parking lot in the middle of the night with a homeless guy and his face is beaming and tears are coming to his eyes, and you think, "This is a great blessing I have, to be able to share this with people." He touches people in a very, very intimate place. I meet working-class people, college professors, really rich people, really poor people—who all have an equally passionate experience with Batman. His audience is very democratic.

I give panel discussions at the Cons. The [DC Animated] characters in general I equate to the great mythological stories that the Greeks and Romans had. They used those characters to teach morality to their young people. The Shakespeare plays started out as passion plays and morality stories. Batman is Orestes. Superman is Achilles. It's just the way we teach morality to young people. The need to tell those stories hasn't changed in thousands of years.

Why do you feel so many regard your Batman as definitive? What's your sense as to why he's resonated the way he has?

I like to believe it's because I'm such a good actor that I deserve it. [Laughs.] But the fact is I think it's just because I'm the voice of the animated character, as opposed to the live-action version, and the character really is most alive in animation, because people can invest their own imaginations in the character. My voice became associated with the cartoon, so I get to ride that wave for 25 years. Whereas Michael Keaton or Val Kilmer or Christian Bale or Ben Affleck, they get much more hemmed in by the physicality that they have to exhibit than they would in a cartoon. So that really advantages me. I think that has everything to do with it actually. But I'd like to think my acting has something to do with it. [Laughs.]

Do you ever see yourself retiring from the role or is it too much a part of you?
I love playing the character, and as long as they ask me to I will continue to play him. The only times I don't is when a director comes on and wants to do his own take on the role—he'll hire another actor. But then they usually ask that actor to imitate me. [Laughs.] I love doing the character. So as long as they keep asking I'll keep doing it.

26 Harley Quinn

The popgun-firing, mallet-swinging, hyena-cuddling Harley Quinn has, in the 25 years since her creation, evolved from put-upon minion to the fourth-most-popular hero in the DC Universe (after the Trinity of Superman, Batman, and Wonder Woman). Much of her success comes from being the most understandable of comic characters; at heart, she's as much a fan as any reader.

Writer Paul Dini created Harley while scripting "Joker's Favor," an episode of *Batman: The Animated Series*' first season (originally broadcast on September 11, 1992). In fashioning a henchwoman for the Joker, Dini conceived of a character who could bring out a different side of the Clown Prince of Crime. Lighthearted and fun-loving, clad in a black-and-red jester costume and domino mask (designed by series producer Bruce Timm), Harley drew the ire of "Mister J" by getting bigger laughs. Dini found the perfect voice for the character in a friend, actress Arleen Sorkin, who'd played a similar role in a dream sequence in an episode of the soap opera *Days of Our Lives*. Sorkin gave Harley a brash, bubbly Brooklyn accent, reminiscent of actress Judy Holliday.

Harley's ill-advised devotion to her "Puddin'" was explored throughout the series' run. But she proved popular enough to star in episodes of her own, most notably "Harlequinade"—which partnered her with Batman in a riff on *48 Hours*—and "Harley's Holiday," in which she's released from Arkham Asylum for a day. Both were written by Dini, who also gave her a much needed gal pal in Poison Ivy, in the episode "Harley and Ivy."

Dini also scripted Harley's finest moment on *The New Batman Adventures*, "Mad Love," an adaptation of his Eisner- and Harvey Award–winning comic of the same name, illustrated by Timm. The story details Harley's origin, explaining how she was once Dr. Harleen Frances Quinzel, a psychologist looking to make a name for herself. After interviewing the Joker in his cell at Arkham, she ends up falling head over heels for the maniac and breaking him out of the asylum.

Harley made her comic book debut in the September 1993 issue (#12) of the show's spinoff title *Batman Adventures* ("Batgirl: Day One," written by Kelley Puckett and penciled by Mike Parobeck). She was made a part of DC continuity in October 1999's *Batman: Harley Quinn* #1. Written by Dini and penciled by Yvel Guichet, it sported a cover by Alex Ross featuring Harley dancing with a tuxedoed Joker—an image recreated in 2016's live-action *Suicide Squad* movie—and its story saw Harley gain superpowers, courtesy of Ivy. Harley won her first ongoing series with December 2000's *Harley Quinn* #1 ("A Harley Quinn Romance," written by Karl Kesel and penciled by Terry Dodson). Running 38 issues, the book saw her leave the Joker and become an integral part of the DCU in her own right. So did the 2000 flash-animated web series *Gotham Girls*, in which she starred alongside Poison Ivy, Batgirl, Catwoman, and Zatanna. Catwoman and Ivy also joined Harley in 2009's *Gotham City Sirens* comic, co-created by Dini and artist Guillem March.

Harley made further appearances in animated form in 2004's *The Batman* (voiced by Hynden Walch), 2008's *Batman: The Brave and the Bold* (as a black-and-white, Betty Boop–style flapper voiced by Meghan Strange), and 2015's *DC Super Hero Girls*—voiced by Tara Strong, who replaced Sorkin as the character's principal voice in 2011's *Batman: Arkham City* video game. Harley first appeared in brick form in 2008's *LEGO Batman: The Videogame* (voiced by Gray DeLisle), before starring in 2017's big-screen hit *The LEGO Batman Movie* (in which she's voiced by Jenny Slate).

Batman: Arkham Asylum, in which Sorkin voiced Harley for the last time, gave the character a more provocative look, suiting its more sinister universe. It consisted of a corset, fishnets, and pigtails. A variation of the outfit appeared in most of the other games in which Harley appeared, and was transferred to comics when DC relaunched its universe in 2011's "New 52." Harley earned a new ongoing series—written by Jimmy Palmiotti and Amanda Conner, and penciled by Chad Hardin—with February 2014's *Harley Quinn* #1 ("Hot in the City"). One of biggest-selling "New 52" titles, its Harley was given a new origin, in which she's dumped into a vat of acid by the Joker, which bleaches her skin white and dyes her hair blue and red. No longer wearing a mask, she favors dark eye makeup, and a pair of roller-derby skates.

This iteration saw romance begin to bloom for Harley and Ivy (as did 2015's *DC Comics Bombshells* series). It also saw her drafted by Amanda Waller into the *Suicide Squad*, and become a regular in the team's new book in November 2011's *Suicide Squad* #1 ("Kicked in the Teeth," written by Adam Glass and penciled by Federico Dallocchio). Harley had a friends-with-benefits relationship with teammate Deadpool, and the two featured in the Squad's 2014 animated movie *Batman: Assault on Arkham* (in which she was voiced by Hynden Walch).

The short-lived 2002 TV series *Birds of Prey* introduced Harley to live-action, as a criminal mastermind played by Mia Sara, though without her jester costume or joie de vivre. Infinitely more popular was 2016's *Suicide Squad* movie. Margot Robbie played the blockbuster hit's Harley, with cotton-candy hair, hot pants, satin bomber jacket, and a torn baseball tee with the words Daddy's Lil Monster emblazoned across it. The look matched her weapon of choice, a wooden baseball bat, and was reflected in August 2016's *Harley Quinn* #1 (a part of DC's "Rebirth" relaunch). Her *Suicide Squad* costume was also the year's most popular cosplay outfit.

But then Harley has long been a favorite of cosplayers, who share her boundless enthusiasm for her work and total devotion to whatever she pursues. With Robbie set to reprise her role in—as well as produce—the *Gotham City Sirens* movie, Harley Quinn's set to leave both comic and film audiences laughing for a long time to come.

When they created the character of Harley Quinn for Batman: The Animated Series, *Paul Dini and Bruce Timm had little idea she would become one of DC's most popular characters.* (Production art © Warner Brothers Animation)

27 Two-Face

The theme of duality informs many of the characters in Batman's world, from Bruce Wayne's own alter ego to those of his costumed friends and foes. But the walking embodiment of this theme is Two-Face, the Dark Knight's most tragic enemy.

The character was inspired by Robert Louis Stevenson's horror novella *Strange Case of Dr Jekyll and Mr Hyde*, specifically its 1941 film adaptation starring Spencer Tracy. It was released a year prior to Two-Face's first appearance in August 1942's *Detective Comics* #66 ("The Crimes of Two-Face!" by Batman creators Bill Finger and Bob Kane). "In each of us," Stevenson wrote, "two natures are at war—the good and the evil. All our lives the fight goes on between them, and one of them must conquer."

Introduced as handsome district attorney "Harvey 'Apollo' Kent," Two-Face's story begins when Kent takes mobster "Boss" Moroni to court, with Batman testifying on the witness stand. The hearing is interrupted when Kent produces the mobster's lucky two-headed coin as evidence against him—and Moroni hurls a bottle of concentrated sulfuric acid at his head. Hideously scarred on one half of his face, Kent finds his fiancée can no longer bear to look at him.

"Look! Look again!" he cries. "A face divided into beauty and ugliness! Queer…Frightening, isn't it?" Kent goes mad, marks one side of Moroni's coin, and henceforth flips it to make every decision. Resigning as D.A., he pursues a life of both altruism and crime, his misdeeds based on the numeral 2.

Two-Face's debut story was resolved two months later, in *Detective Comics* #68 ("The Man Who Led a Double Life!"). He reformed and cleared his name in September 1952's *Detective*

Comics #187 ("The Double Crimes of Two-Face!"). By then, his name was changed to Harvey Dent, to avoid confusion with Batman's fellow crimebuster, Superman/Clark Kent.

Almost 20 years passed before Dent showed his faces again. Writer Denny O'Neil and penciler Neal Adams revived him in August 1971's *Batman* #234 ("Half an Evil"), in which Two-Face's good side proved his undoing. Dent appeared frequently throughout the 1970s and 1980s, and threatened Gotham in 1986's landmark *The Dark Knight Returns* limited series. The early 1990s, however, were the character's true Golden Age.

In 1990's *Batman Annual* #14 ("The Eye of the Beholder," by writer Andrew Helfer and penciler Chris Sprouse), Harvey's origin was altered, and he was explained to suffer from dissociative identity disorder, brought on by an abusive father—who flipped a two-headed coin every night when deciding whether or not to beat his son. Child abuse has since become a hoary cliché in supervillain origin stories, but here it works as a means of explaining the rage inside Harvey, and the second personality that results from it. It also serves to deepen his connection to Bruce Wayne, whose childhood trauma summoned up a creature beholden to justice instead of chance.

"Why are we doing this?" asks Two-Face when he confronts his old man, holding a gun to his head, about to flip his silver dollar (one side now marked). "Because now *we* are two faces...One good, the other bad, fifty-fifty, half-and-half. Opposite yet equal. Because we're *deadlocked.* And when that happens we let the coin decide..."

Helfer's story furthers the symbiotic relationship between Batman and Harvey Dent prior to the latter's accident, again caused by Maroni (his name now spelled more sensibly), after he brings a container of acid into court upon realizing he will lose, and that a gun will set off the metal detectors.

Elements of "The Eye of the Beholder" were utilized in the 1996 limited series *Batman: The Long Halloween* (which functions as an extended origin for Two-Face) and in the 1992 two-part

"Two-Face" episode of *Batman: The Animated Series*, in which the character is voiced by Richard Moll. Like much of the show, "Two-Face" was enriched by greater psychological complexity than had been previously seen in children's television. One of *The Animated Series*' finest episodes, it's the definitive screen portrait of the character. Almost as good is *The New Batman Adventures'* episode "Judgment Day," in which Two-Face develops a *third* persona, the Judge (voiced by the 1966's *Batman* show's False Face, actor Malachi Throne).

Of course, there have been attempts to do Harvey Dent justice in live-action. Billy Dee Williams played the character in Tim Burton's 1989 *Batman*, but his day as Two-Face would have to wait until he voiced the villain in 2017's *The LEGO Batman Movie*. Instead, Tommy Lee Jones took over the role when Burton and Keaton were succeeded by Joel Schumacher and Val Kilmer with 1995's *Batman Forever*. Jones' Two-Face is even more over the top than his co-star Jim Carrey's Riddler, working only as an example of how *not* to do camp. Aaron Eckhart fares much better in the role in Christopher Nolan's 2008 *The Dark Knight*, though he's overshadowed by Heath Ledger's scene-stealing Joker.

Two-Face was almost a part of the Adam West–starring *Batman* series, but was presumably deemed too gruesome for TV audiences of the time. The episode in which he would have appeared, "The Two-Way Crimes of Two-Face" (written by Harlan Ellison), finally reached Batfans in comic form, in November 2014's *Batman 1966: The Lost Episode* (scripted by Len Wein and penciled by José Luis García-López). Two-Face at long last confronts West's Caped Crusader on screen in the 2017 animated movie *Batman vs. Two-Face*, voiced by another icon of 1960s television—William Shatner.

Comedy and tragedy are the twin masks of theater. But in the opera of Harvey Dent's life, there is only room for the latter. No matter the face he wears it on.

28 Batman Begins

By the time Batman entered the 21st century, two B-grade film serials, a comedic TV show, and a series of flashy but narratively vacant big-budget movies had made the character a cultural icon. But there was something for which hardcore Batfans still yearned: a definitive live-action version of their hero. On June 15, 2005, their patience was rewarded with *Batman Begins.*

As bad as it was, director Joel Schumacher's 1997 *Batman & Robin* deserves some praise, because by burning Warner Brothers' film franchise to the ground, it allowed for its reconstruction. With billions of dollars in merchandise revenue on the line, and Fox's *X-Men* and Sony's *Spider-Man* proving the public's thirst for superhero cinema had not yet been slaked, there was never much doubt that Gotham City's savior would be born anew. The question was how.

English-American filmmaker Christopher Nolan first won the affection of movie lovers with his 2000 breakthrough *Memento,* a gritty suspenser about a man searching for his lost identity. Nolan's follow-up, 2002's *Insomnia,* proved he was capable of working with big stars and a Warner Brothers budget. So when word that the studio was interested in rebooting Batman reached Nolan, the writer-director pitched a vision of the Dark Knight as far from the neon miasma of Schumacher as possible, one that took full advantage of Batman's core asset: his humanity.

A longtime fan of the character, Nolan was nonetheless unfamiliar with much of the lore Batman had accumulated since Frank Miller's game-changing 1986 limited series *The Dark Knight Returns.* So Nolan turned to David Goyer, a veteran comics writer who'd enjoyed a long run on DC's *JSA* and scripted Warner Bros./

New Line Cinema's *Blade* films. Together, Nolan and Goyer, inspired by director Richard Donner's *Superman: The Movie*, fashioned a tale of Bruce Wayne's early days, from the moment he discovered the Batcave as a young boy (a scene straight out of Miller) to the night his parents were murdered, from his training abroad to the creation of Batman. Working closely with his *Insomnia* production designer Nathan Crowley, Nolan conceived of Gotham as a real city. Unlike the Gothic fantasyland of Tim Burton's movies, theirs incorporated the steel and concrete of real urban centers into a battleground befitting a nocturnal warrior. Equally important was the Dark Knight's technology, rooted in actual military hardware and cutting-edge science, made manifest in their design for a new Batmobile, aka the Tumbler.

"I felt," says Nolan in Claudia Kalindjian's 2005's *Batman Begins: The Official Movie Guide* (published by Time Inc. Home Entertainment), "that we had never before seen the specialness and otherworldly nature of the character against an ordinary world, so that the audiences would be as astounded by this character as the inhabitants of the cinematic world. That's the key to adopting a realist approach."

In *American Psycho* star Christian Bale, Nolan found someone who had the acting range to portray Bruce Wayne's public playboy persona as well as his private turmoil, and the physical presence for an almost bestial Batman, enhanced by the biggest, most versatile cape yet sported in a Batfilm. As Donner had done in his film, Nolan backed up his young star with an array of veteran actors: Michael Caine as loyal-but-forthright manservant Alfred Pennyworth, Morgan Freeman as Wayne Enterprises' tech-head/armorer Lucius Fox, and Gary Oldman as Batman's police liaison James Gordon (bearing a startling resemblance to the young Gordon of Miller's *Batman: Year One*). As Bruce's mentor and would-be seducer to the dark side of vengeance, Liam Neeson was cast as Henri Ducard, who (spoilers!) emerges as Ra's al Ghul. All four men are surrogate fathers to someone still learning to be both myth and protector. With so many heavyweights in the cast, it's no wonder that Katie Holmes, as Rachel Dawes, a romantic interest concocted for the film, looks a little out of her element as Bruce's childhood sweetheart turned Gotham assistant DA.

Batman Begins' script sweeps viewers along on Bruce's journey, as he uses every tool and technique available to combat crime and strike terror in the hearts of his enemies. It borrows elements from not only Miller's work but Jeph Loeb and Tim Sale's 1996 limited series *The Long Halloween* and Denny O'Neil and Dick Giordano's story "The Man Who Falls" (from DC's 1989 anthology *Secret Origins*).

"I would say that 'The Man Who Falls' is very, very important," says Nolan in *The Official Movie Guide*, "leading into *Batman: Year One*, which makes up part of the middle act of our film, along with elements from *The Long Halloween*, [then] moving on to our own idea of where the story could lead."

Shot on location in Iceland, London, and Chicago, as well as at England's Shepperton Studios, the film has the look and feel of the 1970s blockbusters Nolan admired, maintaining a staccato rhythm (helped in no small measure by Hans Zimmer's pulsating score) all its own. If *Batman Begins*' climax—hinging on a plot by Ra's al Ghul to poison Gotham with a fear toxin developed by Cillian Murphy's twitchy Scarecrow—feels, like the film's fight scenes, slightly less focused than what surrounds it, it's no less compulsively watchable.

With a worldwide box-office gross of $374.2 million, *Batman Begins* met the approval of both audiences and critics, bringing its hero back from the cinematic graveyard in which he'd been left for dead. More importantly, it left fans hungry for more. Little did they know, the main course had not yet been served.

29 The Dark Knight

If *The Dark Knight* didn't exist, it would be necessary to invent it.

Writer-director Christopher Nolan's 2008 film is many things: a sequel to *Batman Begins*, an Oscar-nominated crime drama, and one of the most praised movies of the 21st century. But first and foremost, it's Batman's finest live-action adventure.

Co-scripting this time with his brother Jonathan (from a story co-written by David Goyer), Nolan returned to Gotham to expand the world he'd developed and examine real-world issues, like the price of post-9/11 security and the "War on Terror." He found the perfect means to do so in Batman's greatest enemy, the Joker, here a self-described "agent of chaos" and one of the screen's most compelling portraits of insanity. Nolan centers *The Dark Knight* around Bruce Wayne, who looks for a way to save his city and sees its possible redemption in the form of district attorney Harvey Dent, an idealist whose black-and-white view of good and evil is corrupted by the Clown Prince of Crime.

"Batman's developed himself into an extraordinary individual," says Nolan, "but one in a very terrible place with a terrible responsibility that he's now having to take on. And this film, I think, pushes that further and further and suggests that perhaps that's going to be inescapable."

Nolan amped up his visuals to suit his narrative, shooting on location in Hong Kong and Chicago (again forming the basis for Gotham City), and at England's Pinewood Studios.

"We wanted to push even further in the direction of making Gotham feel like a real, contemporary city," explains the filmmaker. "And so we shot much more on location than we did on the first

Christopher Nolan's The Dark Knight *was a seismic shift in the world of comic book movies, proving that a sophisticated take on the subject matter could please fans and critics alike.*

film, including our interiors. As much as possible we shot in real places to achieve a real-world scale."

The Dark Knight boasts no fewer than four scenes lensed in IMAX, the first time the format had been used in a feature film production. Chief among them is the opening sequence, a heist scene worthy of Michael Mann, and the truck chase, which introduces the next generation of Batcycle—the Bat-pod. Conceived by Nolan himself and created by production designer Nathan Crowley, this escape vehicle is steered by its driver's shoulders, and contains engines in its wheels. The film's other design highlight was the first movie Batsuit (post–Adam West) that allowed its wearer to turn his head.

As Bruce Wayne and his alter ego, Bale surpassed his work in *Batman Begins*. Some might be put off by his raspy Batman voice, but he exhibits charm, rage, horror, grief, and a zen focus as he fights to save Gotham from spinning out of control.

"He's matured," says Bale. "He was an angry young man before. He was somebody aspiring to do good. He had great altruism, but a lot of naiveté as well. This is somebody who's matured. He's become more worldly. He has the burden of responsibility of having attained the power that he was looking for before. It's a very different position to be in, holding onto power rather than trying to get it."

As Bruce's three surrogate fathers—Alfred Pennyworth, Lucius Fox, and James Gordon—Michael Caine, Morgan Freeman, and Gary Oldman again delivered first-rate performances, as did Aaron Eckhart as dashing "white knight" Harvey Dent and Maggie Gyllenhaal as Bruce's lost love Rachel Dawes (replacing *Batman Begins*' Katie Holmes).

But it's Heath Ledger's performance that's the stuff of legend. Viewed almost 10 years on from the actor's tragic death six months before the film's release (and the critical reception that earned him the only acting Oscar ever awarded a superhero film), his work is even more impressive. Unlike Jack Nicholson in Tim Burton's *Batman*, Ledger underplays his role, ushering filmgoers into his performance with nervous tics and twitches and a hypnotic delivery. Like the film itself, his Joker is a mammoth achievement, as compelling a human monster as Anthony Perkins' Norman Bates or Anthony Hopkins' Hannibal Lecter.

"Everything about the character," says Nolan, "really seems aimed at keeping the audience on the back foot, not knowing exactly what to expect."

The only downside to *The Dark Knight*'s Joker is the rash of blockbusters that copied his character—among them *Skyfall*, *Star Trek Into Darkness*, and Marvel's *The Avengers*—each of which featured charismatic villains who get imprisoned as part of their master plans.

Unlike most thrillers, however, *The Dark Knight*'s suspense hinges not so much on who lives or dies (though what other superhero movie has the audacity to kill off its leading lady halfway through?), but on the choices its hero makes. Just as compelling is the sense of what's happening off screen, of a group of artists pushing the limits of their form. For their efforts, *The Dark Knight* netted eight Academy Award nominations and grossed $1 billion dollars worldwide, making it the highest-grossing film of 2008.

As superhero fans, we often hunger for the validation long denied our favorite genre. But *The Dark Knight*'s ultimate accomplishment is that it transcends awards and box office receipts. It knows it's enough just to be a damn good Batman movie.

Gotham Gazette Exclusive

Christopher Nolan

Writer-director Christopher Nolan created the first wholly successful superhero film trilogy with his *Batman Begins*, *The Dark Knight*, and *The Dark Knight Rises*. The following interview was conducted upon the release of 2008's *The Dark Knight*.

***The Dark Knight* is the first Batman film without "Batman" in its title...**
There was something very evocative about the phrase "The Dark Knight" that really is synonymous with Batman but also makes you think about Batman in a certain way that seemed very relevant to the story, in terms of expressing who Batman is in relation to Gotham. That seemed what the film was about. I think it fits quite nicely. It also prompted us to try and make this some kind of definitive statement about the character. A definitive account of what we think Batman is.

How did you feel when you saw the response to Heath Ledger's performance as the Joker?
I simply feel a bit of a sense of relief that people are receiving the performance the way I know he intended it to be taken. My responsibility as a director has been to make sure that we were crafting a performance in the right way. You always feel that responsibility to someone who's given you a great performance on set. But we obviously felt that responsibility many, many times over in the post-production on this film.

How does writing for the Joker compare to writing for other characters?
Once you start writing for a character like that, it's hard to stop. It's just fun. It's fun to hear him talk. It's fun to hear him pontificate, really. Then there's a certain amount of discipline that has to come in, in the writing and indeed in the editing—to try to pull that back, actually. But he had such a fantastic voice and such a fantastic way of

looking at the world that it was interesting to find out what he had to say.

In *The Dark Knight*, Bruce Wayne/Batman is headquartered within Gotham, instead of at Wayne Manor...

With Bruce Wayne and Batman, there's inherently quite a bleak sense of who he is that in the past has been portrayed in a very Gothic manner, with this mansion he's in. It's all wood paneling and grandfather clocks and things. We wanted to try and do it in a very modern fashion. We show this extraordinarily opulent penthouse, but the bleakness of it, that you get from the modernism of it, it expresses his state of mind quite nicely.

What informed Heath Ledger's performance?

Johnny Rotten, Sid Vicious, these kinds of punk influences were some of the things we talked about. We also talked about the character of Alex in *A Clockwork Orange*. He's very anarchic and yet somehow has great charisma, both in the book and in the film. We talked about a lot of different influences, and he talked about an extraordinarily diverse set of influences like ventriloquist dummies. The way they would talk and the way they would move and all kinds of peculiar ideas that I wasn't really able to get a handle on until I saw him start to perform the scenes, and start to show how the character moved and how the character gestured and how the character spoke, with this extraordinarily unpredictable voice. The range of the voice, from its highest pitch to its lowest pitch, is very extreme, and where it shifts is unpredictable and sudden.

The thing with the tongue was...He had this prosthetic that was covering his lower lip and it would come unglued sometimes. I'd seen him sort of sticking it back with his tongue, and it was only after a few weeks of shooting that I realized that wasn't what he was doing, that he had started to adopt that actually as part of the character. It was an interesting balance, editing the performance, because he has all kinds of interesting facets, all kinds of mannerisms and things. What I like about them all is they all feel that they come from the character. They don't feel like actorly touches. I read them as genuinely part of the fabric of a real human being.

What surprised you about him?
Well, it certainly didn't surprise me that the performance was as great as it was. I really expected that from him because I had seen his other work. What really surprised me was how easy he was to work with. Because he's somebody who puts so much in his performances and has given such intense performances, I was a little worried he might take himself very seriously. And he didn't. He was very warm and fun to have around and a great collaborator. Really, just a lovely person.

What went into Two-Face's design?
Hopefully for audiences it's more morbidly fascinating than repulsive. We had looked at more restrained versions, and they were more stomach-churning. They were more depressing. They were a little too real. It felt like we needed to have a very extreme approach with a little movement and detail in it that would be a little bit more fanciful, a little bit more removed from reality.

Some have drawn a political parallel between the film's Batman and Joker and America and Iraq...
Well, I'm not sure there is, which is why it's an interesting story point. Because Batman's an extraordinarily powerful fighter. And yet, as the Joker says to him in the interrogation scene, "You have nothing to do with all your strength. There's nothing to threaten." You can't threaten somebody and intimidate somebody who is not bound by any conventions—or any rules of engagement, if you like—and does not in any way respect your authority or your rules. That's what the Joker is. He's a pure force of anarchy.

If the film is written and made, as we tried to, in a very sincere way—where the filmmakers are trying to engage with the things that excite them, the things that frighten them in real life, and trying to have some real texture to the thing, so that it's personal to us and relevant to us—there will inevitably be political parallels in retrospect. But the key is not to be self-conscious about that, to not force that. The key is really just to try and make a great film, tell a great story. But if you're creating from your place in this world, from genuinely the way you see the world, after the fact, looking back at the film, then you see parallels.

Gotham Gazette Exclusive

Heath Ledger

Heath Ledger's performance as the Joker in director Christopher Nolan's *The Dark Knight* is astonishing not only for its portrait of insanity but for how its fire rises above the tragedy of the actor's death on January 22, 2008, and the fanfare of his posthumous Oscar victory, to continue burning in our collective consciousness. The following interview was conducted in November of 2007, when Ledger was promoting *I'm Not There*, the Bob Dylan–inspired musical drama in which he co-starred.

What do you look for in the film roles you take?

It takes up so much of your time and energy to go away from your life for a few months. I get really obsessed with it, and I kind of lock myself down. So it really has to be worth it, and it has to be something that challenges me—that has an element of fear attached to it. And something that I feel is going to teach me something. That's gonna further me. Otherwise, what's the point?

You've gone on record as saying you weren't a huge fan of comic books. What attracted you to *The Dark Knight*?

Yeah. The only reason I wasn't [was] I grew up in a household of girls. So there were very few Batman comic books lying around. There [was] mainly *Archie*. So that's probably the only reason why I never grew up reading Batman.

But I really loved *Batman Begins*; and the character of the Joker was just too good to turn down. I've said this before, but...if Tim Burton was doing *The Dark Knight* and asked me to play the Joker I wouldn't have taken it. Because to try and even touch what Jack Nicholson did in Tim Burton's world would be a crime. So when Chris [Nolan] came to me, and...I knew how Chris was. He had already set up the world for me. I'd seen what world it was that I would be playing in. So I knew it was open for a fresh interpretation. I also instantly kind of had something up my sleeve, which happened to be exactly what Chris was kind of looking for. We sat down and kind of shared ideas, and they were the same. So we just went with it.

Gotham Gazette Exclusive

Christian Bale

In 2005's *Batman Begins*, actor Christian Bale brought a level of ferocity to Batman that hadn't been seen in a live-action film. The following interview was conducted after Bale completed work on the film's sequel, 2008's *The Dark Knight*.

How do you approach playing a man who dresses up as a bat?
You have to take a leap of faith and just really do what you believe to be right. For me that was that it *is* ridiculous—a man dressing up as a bat—and it *is* silly and it *is* laughable. So the only way to play it is like he's a demon himself. Like he's a beast.

I never really got that from the other [Batman movies] that I've seen, and so it was clear to me. When I did the screen test I did it like that. I just thought, "I don't really want to play it any other way. I just want to do it that way, and if they want to do that, then great. I want to do the movie. And if they don't want to do that, then I don't really want to do it anyway."

So then you manage to tread this line where you can actually be a man dressed as a bat and not have it be absolutely silly. Of course, it's fantastic. It's fantasy. But it's great, this weird world that we've created, where you can actually believe that this man with issues genuinely believes that dressing up as a bat is the best way to combat crime in the city—and it actually ends up working. Other people believe him too.

Did you enjoy the earlier Batman movies?
I was never really a fan of the previous Batman movies. But I'm very proud of what we did with *Batman Begins* and—not to sound too full of myself—I think we did a good job with the first one. I think we've done even better with the second one.

Batman is motivated by a desire to fight crime. To what extent do you identify with that?
I think that it's a damn shame if we're in any society where people don't attempt to do that kind of thing themselves. Whilst I've never truly been

tested, I'd be hideously disappointed with myself if I didn't step up to the plate in situations like that. At heart, I think probably everybody has that desire and would like to answer that question of—if push came to shove—would they be able to stand up and rise to the occasion.

Your Batsuit was redesigned for *The Dark Knight*. Is it more comfortable?
I wouldn't call it "comfortable," but it's far more comfortable than the first one. I can sit in it for a long time without feeling like I'm gonna have rubber-suit rage. It's much cooler and more agile. It's heavier, but it meant that I could breathe much easier in it. The other one I could never really take a deep breath in at all. The cowl was constricting, and it was difficult to breathe inside of that as well. With this new one I was able to do much more. The fight sequences could be more dynamic because I had so much more energy. I could do all of them myself. So it's better in every way.

What was it like working with Heath Ledger as the Joker?
Our first scene was in an interrogation room together, and I saw that he's a helluva actor who's completely committed to it and totally gets the tone that Chris [Nolan] is trying to create with this. We're not going for actors revealing their enjoyment of playing a wacky caricature. We're treating this as serious drama. You go into character and you stay in the character. I love that. I find that so ridiculous that I love it, and I take that very seriously. Heath was definitely embracing that. When he was in the makeup and the garb he was in character the whole time; and when he took it off he was absolutely fantastic company to be around.

As you see in the movie, Batman starts beating the Joker and realizes that this is not your ordinary foe. Because the more I beat him the more he enjoys it. The more I'm giving him satisfaction. Heath was behaving in a very similar fashion. He was kinda egging me on. I was saying, "You know what, I really don't need to actually hit you. It's going to look just as good if I don't." And he's going, "Go on. Go on. Go on..." He was slamming himself around, and there were tiled walls inside of that set which were cracked and dented from him hurling himself into them. His commitment was total.

Were you ever worried about being upstaged?
No, not at all. Because it was exactly the point that I had a problem with in all of the other Batman movies. Especially after reading Frank Miller's *Batman: Year One* and various other graphic novels. I asked myself, "Well, how come it's always been that he's the most boring character?" I'd never found him to be intriguing at all. Whereas these graphic novels depicted him as by far the most fascinating of them. I feel like we gained that back with *Batman Begins*—that he's a character with substance. So I have no problem with him competing with somebody else. Because that can only make for a better movie, if you have these other fascinating characters arriving on the scene too.

30 The World's Finest Team

They're the world's greatest superheroes. The Man of Steel and the Dark Knight. And though they appear to be opposites—symbols of light and darkness, reflecting their respective missions—for most of their careers they've been the best of friends.

Their first joint appearance saw a smiling Superman and Batman, joined by Robin the Boy Wonder, marching in unison on artist Jack Burnley's cover for July 1940's *New York World's Fair Comics* #2. For an encore, the three leapt across a city skyline on Fred Ray's cover for March 1941's *World's Best Comics* #1. The heroes appeared in solo stories beneath those covers, though there were many to follow. With its second (June 1941) issue, *World's Best Comics* became *World's Finest Comics*, and Superman and Batman occupied its cover for the remainder of the 1940s.

The first time they would appear in the same story was when they joined the Justice Society of America in October 1941's

All-Star Comics #7 ("$1,000,000 for War Orphans," by writer Gardner Fox and artist Everett E. Hibbard). But they were relegated to honorary/reserve member status, with the book focusing on second-stringers like Hawkman and Atom. The true first meeting of Superman and Batman occurred in the March 2, 1945, episode of *The Adventures of Superman* radio drama, the third chapter of "The Mystery of the Waxmen" serial. Batman (voiced at first by actor Stacy Harris) and Robin became a staple of the daily show in order to give actor Bud Collyer the occasional break from playing Clark Kent and his alter ego.

Come the next decade, fans would finally *see* the two champions join forces, with June 1952's *Superman* #76 ("The Mightiest Team in the World," written by Edmond Hamilton and penciled by Curt Swan). July 1954's *World's Finest* #71 ("Batman—Double for Superman!" by writer Alvin Schwartz and penciler Curt Swan) was the first issue of the team's run in the comic that exclusively chronicled their partnership through 1986. Its genesis was detailed in June 1958's *World's Finest* #94 ("The Origin of the Superman-Batman Team!" by Hamilton and penciler Dick Sprang). Their bond was tested time and again, most notably by the many world-threatening menaces they faced as members of the Justice League, by Lex Luthor and the Joker when they formed an alliance in May 1957's *World's Finest* #88 ("Superman's and Batman's Greatest Foes!" also by Hamilton and Sprang), and by "The Superman-Batman Revenge Squads" in May 1968's *World's Finest Comics* #175 (written by Leo Dorfman and penciled by Neal Adams).

They shared a TV series in Filmation's 1968 *The Batman/Superman Hour*, and 1970s fans watched the two battle alongside Wonder Woman and Aquaman in TV's *Super Friends*. But although Superman sometimes referred to Batman as his "best friend" in the Bronze Age of comics, that friendship came to halt after 1986's *The Dark Knight Returns*—which saw Superman tasked by the U.S. government with halting an older Batman's outlaw activities, resulting in a duel to the death between them. They were then reduced to frenemies—occasional, uneasy allies against common threats in stories that erected philosophical differences between them.

"Frank Miller's *The Dark Knight Returns* popularized the idea," says comics artist Alex Ross of the Superman-Batman division. "But, visually, as soon as Neal Adams did his design overhaul, there was always this thought in mind that Batman was this more aggressive, darker character. His characterization in the 1970s began that way, and Frank just kind of cashed in on that, giving that symbolism full action in a story that separated them. For contrast, he cast Superman in a position of being a status quo representative. Which is never anything I would have put upon him, that he would have turned a blind eye to injustices. That was something that's a failing of the story, that had to serve Batman by making Superman look stupid."

Ross and writer Mark Waid's own possible-future limited series, 1996's *Kingdom Come,* brought Superman and Batman's feud to an end, in a tale of violent vigilante metahumans whose actions bring back the old guard. In its collected edition, *Kingdom Come* ends with Wonder Woman asking Batman to be the godfather of the child she's having with Superman.

With June 2003's *Superman/Batman* #1 ("The World's Finest," written by Jeph Loeb and penciled by Ed McGuinness), the two won a new monthly team-up, the first storyline of which was adapted for the 2009 animated film *Superman/Batman: Public Enemies.* In 2013, DC's "New 52" reboot brought with it *Batman/Superman,* which ran for 32 issues.

Critically savaged upon its release in 2016, *Batman v Superman: Dawn of Justice* (which took its cue from their fight in Miller's *Dark Knight Returns*) marked the two champions' first meeting in live-action. But a more rewarding screen depiction of that meeting is in the three-part 1997 "World's Finest" episode of *Superman: The Animated Series*. True to its name, it finds a happy medium between the reluctant comrades of recent decades and the good buddies of yesteryear.

31 Batgirl

Batman and Robin inspire for how they've turned tragedy into triumph. But personal trauma is by no means a requirement for heroism. The shining example of how anyone can be a hero in Gotham City is Batgirl.

Five young women have donned the mask of Batgirl, the first of whom, Betty Kane—operating under the name "Bat-Girl"—was the niece of the original Batwoman, Kathy Kane. Intended as a sidekick for Kathy and a romantic interest for Robin (as Kathy was for Batman), Betty debuted in April 1961's *Batman* #139 ("Bat-Girl!" written by Batman co-creator Bill Finger and penciled by Sheldon Moldoff). The blonde teenager fashions a costume for herself—a red dress, boots, and Bat mask, with green belt and short scalloped cape—after visiting her aunt and learning her secret. Armed with her gadget-filled "Crime Compact," she rescues Batman, Robin, and Batwoman from the notorious Cobra Gang. Kathy then trains her as a way of keeping her out of trouble, but Betty surprises the team by locating the gang's hideout. Bat-Girl's first appearance isn't devoid of the era's rampant misogyny ("Not bad—for a girl!" Robin tells her), but even in this early incarnation, the character subverts expectations by pretending to faint when the King Cobra pulls a gun on her only to judo chop it out of his hand.

Betty Kane—like Batwoman, Bat-Mite, and Ace the Bat-Hound—was all but erased from DC Comics when editor Julius Schwartz revamped the Batman titles in 1964. (She later resurfaced as "Bette Kane" in post–*Crisis on Infinite Earths* continuity, aka Flamebird, a member of the Teen Titans' Titans West.) Betty was followed, however, by the most famous Batgirl of all.

The *Batman* TV series was an enormous success when it debuted in 1966, but by the end of its second season, its ratings had tumbled. In an attempt to replicate the success of Catwoman, one of its most popular recurring characters, executive producer William Dozier asked Schwartz for more female characters. The editor conceived of a new ally for Batman and Robin, and tasked *Detective Comics* artist Carmine Infantino with designing her costume.

"It was Julie's idea that she be Commissioner Gordon's daughter," says Infantino in his 2000 autobiography *The Amazing World of Carmine Infantino* (published by Vanguard Productions). "He asked me to design what she would look like in and out of costume. I also designed her motorcycle."

Dr. Barbara Gordon first appeared in January 1967's *Detective Comics* #359 ("The Million Dollar Debut of Batgirl!" written by Gardner Fox and penciled by Infantino). A bespectacled librarian at the Gotham City Library, she's introduced sewing up a Batman-inspired costume for the Policeman's Masquerade Ball—a black bodysuit with yellow boots, gloves, Bat emblem, and thigh-hugging belt, topped with a blue cape and cowl, from which flowed her trademark red hair. "I made my PH.D. [sic] at Gotham State University!" she muses en route to the ball. "I graduated summa cum laude! I wear a brown belt at Judo! But tonight will be the highlight of my life!"

How right she is. She immediately stumbles upon Killer Moth's Moth-Men attacking Bruce Wayne, as part of a protection racket scheme. Buying the millionaire enough time to change into his Batman costume, "The Dominoed Daredoll" later aids Batman and Robin in taking down the Moth gang. A hit with readers, Barbara's popularity soared when she joined the *Batman* show.

Played by former ballerina Yvonne Craig, she debuted on September 14, 1967, in the third-season premiere, "Enter Batgirl, Exit Penguin." Craig brought loads of charisma to the role, even if, instead of punches, she was limited by the producers to "ladylike" kicks in fight scenes. Clad in a form-flattering costume identical to her comic counterpart's, but colored a shimmering purple, Craig's Batgirl was more than the equal of Batman and Robin, whom she fought alongside in the show's opening credits. She was the first female superhero—from DC or Marvel Comics—to appear on screen.

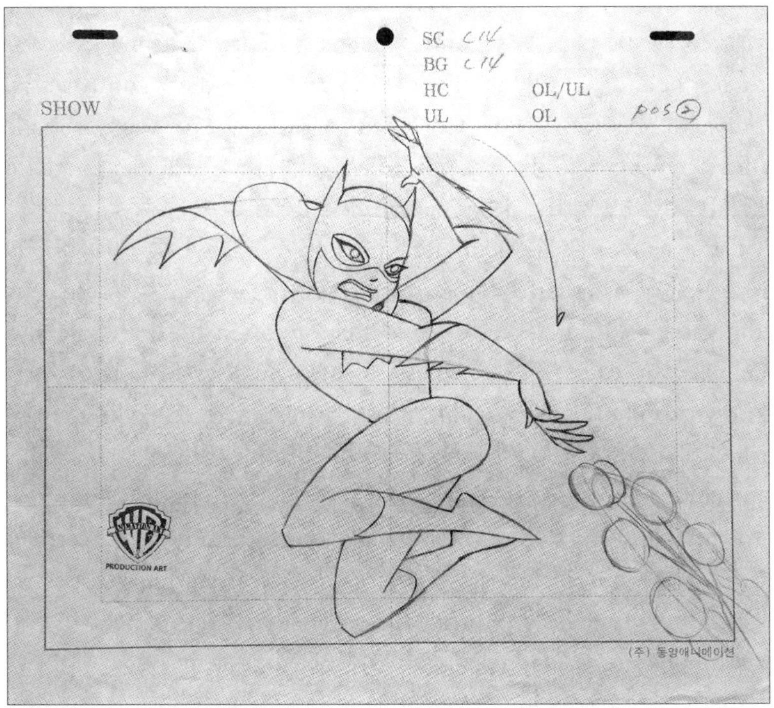

Motivated by altruism rather than personal trauma, Batgirl has long been an inspirational figure among Gotham's crimefighting heroes. (Production art © Warner Brothers Animation)

Unfortunately, Batgirl's popularity wasn't enough to save the series, and *Batman*'s third season would be its last. But Barbara returned in the 1969 animated *The Batman/Superman Hour* (voiced by Jane Webb), and starred in her own backup feature in *Detective Comics* in the early 1970s. Eventually abandoning library science for politics, she became a member of the House of Representatives. In the late 1970s, she partnered with Robin, whom she dated, for a series of adventures in the *Batman Family* comic, before enjoying another long run in *Detective Comics* in the early 1980s. In the wake of 1985's *Crisis on Infinite Earths* limited series and 1986's *The Dark Knight Returns*, Barbara's history was retconned and she became Commissioner Gordon's niece, whom he and his wife adopted after her parents' deaths. She retired from her role as Batgirl in May 1988's *Batgirl Special* #1 ("The Last Batgirl Story," written by Barbara Kesel and penciled by Barry Kitson). She was then shot and crippled by the Joker in that same year's controversial *Batman: The Killing Joke*. Confined to a wheelchair, she was made into a new hero, Oracle (thanks to writers John Ostrander and Kim Yale), in 1989 in the pages of *Suicide Squad*.

Eleven years after Barbara hung up her cowl, Batgirl briefly returned in March 1999's *Batman: No Man's Land* #1 ("No Law and a New Order—Part One: Values," written by Bob Gale and penciled by Alex Maleev) in the form of Helena Bertinelli—best known as the post-*Crisis* Huntress—after an earthquake demolished Gotham City. Wearing a suit like Batman's own, Bertinelli's career as Batgirl was cut short when she refused to follow his orders. Fortunately, "No Man's Land" also introduced her successor, Cassandra Cain, in July 1999's *Batman* #567 ("Mark of Cain, Part One," by writer Kelley Puckett and penciler Damion Scott), who became Batgirl when Helena retired from the role in August 1999's *Batman: Legends of the Dark Knight* #120 ("Assembly," written by Greg Rucka and penciled by Mike Deodato Jr.).

The daughter of League of Assassins member David Cain and martial arts master Lady Shiva, Cassandra (named after the mythological seer) was raised by her father to be Ra's al Ghul's bodyguard. In order to optimize her killing prowess, she was taught to read body language instead of a written or spoken language. But she rejected her role, and, as a teenager, fled to Gotham, where she became a courier for Barbara Gordon. In return, Barbara taught her to read and speak, and Cassandra wound up saving Commissioner Gordon from her father, earning a job as the first Batgirl with her own ongoing comic, premiering with April 2000's *Batgirl* #1 and running for six years. Cassandra was also the first regular Asian character in Batman comics. In an all-black suit, its emblem the yellow outline of a bat, with a mask that covered her entire face, Cassandra trained with Barbara and, eventually, Lady Shiva, whose conflict with her daughter caused a civil war within the League of Assassins, climaxing with a fight in which Cassandra left her mother to die, after which she quit her role as Batgirl and her solo title ended its run (with April 2006's *Batgirl* #73).

Following that year's "Infinite Crisis" storyline (before which Dick Grayson proposed marriage to Barbara), Cassandra reemerged as a villain and leader of the League of Assassins, a move criticized by fans and later explained away as a result of being drugged by Deathstroke. She again became Batgirl, and joined the Titans and the Outsiders. When Batman disappeared in 2008's "Final Crisis" storyline, Cassandra relinquished her role, later rejoining Batman in 2010's *Batman Incorporated*, as Hong Kong's Black Bat.

Stephanie Brown, who'd served as Spoiler and, briefly, the fourth Robin, became the next Batgirl, eventually wearing a more traditional suit and cowl, albeit with Spoiler's purple highlights. Mentored by Barbara, Stephanie was also granted her own comic series with October 2009's *Batgirl* #1 ("Batgirl Rising: Point of New Origin, Part One," written by Bryan Q. Miller and penciled by Lee Garbett). The title ran for two years, before Stephanie was retconned out of existence in DC's reboot of its universe in 2011's "New 52." When fans complained, she returned as Spoiler in 2016's "DC Rebirth."

As with any business, marketing concerns take precedence over all in comics. And so Barbara, the best-known Batgirl, ultimately resumed her role as the Daredoll in the "New 52," finally earning her own regular title with November 2011's *Batgirl* #1 ("Shattered," written by Gail Simone and penciled by Ardian Syaf). This series retconned Barbara's background so she recovered two years after the events of *The Killing Joke*. It won the character a multitude of new fans, both in its initial form and after it was revamped and Barbara was made a PhD student in issue #35, which began the "Batgirl of Burnside" arc. Written by Brenden Fletcher and Cameron Stewart, who shared penciling duties with Babs Tarr, this storyline gave Batgirl her most utilitarian, cosplayable costume yet: a purple leather jacket, yellow gloves, hiking boots, and a snap-on black-and-yellow cape. It was popular enough to survive DC's "Rebirth" relaunch, in which Batgirl got her *fifth* series, with September 2016's *Batgirl* #1 ("Beyond Burnside, Part One," written by Hope Larson with art by Rafael Albuquerque).

Next to Yvonne Craig's groundbreaking portrayal, Barbara's most popular screen iteration is in 1992's *Batman: The Animated Series*, in which she's voiced for several episodes by Melissa Gilbert, and 1997's *The New Batman Adventures*, in which she's a regular (sporting her classic 1960s comic look) voiced by Tara Strong. In 1999's *Batman Beyond*—which takes place 50 years later—she follows in her dad's footsteps as Gotham's police commissioner (voiced by Stockard Channing). She's also a regular (voiced by Danielle Judovits) in the two best seasons—three and four—of 2004's *The Batman*.

Bruce Timm, co-creator of *Batman: The Animated Series*, remarks on the difference between Batman and Batgirl: "They come at the crimefighting profession from different angles. He's all about vengeance. He's all about making criminals pay. Whereas she has a deep-seated sense of morality instilled in her by her parents, specifically Commissioner Gordon, who's the top cop in Gotham. She's young. She's healthy. She's athletic. And she gets a kick out of going out and beating up criminals. Whereas Batman doesn't really do it for that reason. He's just focused on punishing every criminal in the world for killing his parents. So it's oil and water. Sometimes [their relationship] works out well. Sometimes it doesn't."

With the exception of the 1966 *Batman* series, live-action has been less kind to Barbara. She appeared in the short-lived 2002 *Birds of Prey* TV series as Oracle and, in flashbacks, Batgirl; both were played by Dina Meyer. Alicia Silverstone played her (as Barbara Wilson, Alfred Pennyworth's niece) in 1997's execrable *Batman & Robin*. But Babs' big-screen future is looking brighter. Following her winning turn—again as police commissioner (voiced by Rosario Dawson)—in 2017's *The LEGO Batman Movie*, writer-director Joss Whedon is, at the time of this writing, planning the first Batgirl solo film.

As one of the DC Universe's sharpest minds, Barbara would no doubt agree that the evidence is conclusive. No matter the era, history demands a Batgirl.

"Batgirl," says voice actress Tara Strong, "is an important part of the history of this franchise, and of women empowerment. She's someone you can relate to. Someone you want to hang out with. Whom you feel is a kindred spirit. It's like, 'Batgirl's a really cool chick...Oh, and she's kicking bad guys' asses? We love her!'"

Gotham Gazette Exclusive

Tara Strong

Tara Strong occupies the unique position of having voiced two of Gotham's best-loved residents: Barbara Gordon—in *The New Batman Adventures*, *Batman Beyond: Return of the Joker*, *The Killing Joke*, and *Beware the Batman*—and Harley Quinn in the *Batman: Arkham* games and *DC Super Hero Girls*.

How did you come to be cast as Batgirl?
I had moved from Toronto to Los Angeles maybe a year and a half before they had casting notice for that. I went in as if it were any other audition, except I knew the weight of this role, and was pretty darn hopeful to book it. It's such an iconic character, and a strong girl who can really inspire other girls, and I was more than anxious to be a part of that franchise. [Laughs.] The waiting room was totally intimidating. There were on-camera celebrities, voiceover stars. But I felt like I had just as much of a shot as anyone else in the room. I went in and pretty much did her as my own voice. To be honest, Batgirl is the closest thing in my career to my own voice that I've done. So I guess something in my own sound was appealing to Bruce Timm and [director] Andrea Romano. They just sort of liked the authenticity of what I brought to the table. So I really got lucky. Every single time I went in to do that job, I was pinching myself to sit beside Mark Hamill and Kevin Conroy and Arleen Sorkin. It was a pretty magical time.

What was it like recording with them?
Mark and Kevin are forces to be reckoned with. They're just so brilliant, and even though Mark was known for primarily on-camera work…Most people in voiceover have done on-camera, but when you have a superstar come in, the chances are they're not gonna be that great. Because they're super-successful and confident in their world. You're asking a tap dancer to do ballet, and not every one of them does. So he happens to be one of those on-camera superstars who can authentically deliver a brilliant voiceover performance. I can't imagine anyone else in that role. Of course I love all the people that I

work with, but as far as I'm concerned there is one Batman and that's Kevin Conroy and there is one Joker and that is Mark Hamill.

You say Barbara is the closest to your own voice, yet you sound much less intense than she does.

Personality-wise I'm not as dark as she is, but the timbre of my voice is hers. If Tara was in the situations Batgirl is in, my timbre would probably sound like hers. But not so much my attitude—I'd probably be more positive than she is. [Laughs.]

Do you have a favorite Batgirl story?

Well, my favorite *Batman* episode was "Girls' Night Out." No question. For the same reason I wanted to book Batgirl. It was such a great empowering women episode, where we could have a little spa day at home and then go out and kick ass. It was just so much fun. I love the images from that episode. I love teaming up with Supergirl, and I loved that concept. It was sort of ahead of its time. Now we have the *DC Super Hero Girls* and different variations of women kicking butt together. But "Girls' Night Out," in animation, was one of the first.

"Girls' Night Out" also featured Arleen Sorkin's Harley Quinn. How did you eventually approach voicing Harley?

When I was approached to do Harley, it was brought to my attention that they wanted to take her to different places and different levels and I should not do an impression. That made me both terrified and relieved. Relieved because Arleen is alive and well and a brilliant actress and there's no reason to replace her. Terrified because if I'm not doing an impression and it sounds different…are the fans going to get angry? [Laughs.] I was pretty scared that they weren't going to like my version, and my version was directed by the people who were working on *Batman: Arkham City*. So they wanted a lot more craziness to her and big energy, highs and lows, and just a slightly different timbre than Harley originally had…I really love Arleen, and she was so gracious in interviews. She said, "If I ever wanted anyone to take over it would be Tara." It's really hard to have someone else do a role that you've done and you love. So I'm very grateful to her. Luckily, a lot of fans loved what I did.

Are games more demanding than TV shows?
Video games are definitely vocally more challenging than TV series. When you're doing a series you're with other actors, you're playing off them, you get little breaks. When you're doing a video game, it's just you for four hours, and often there's 8,000 death sounds. It's grueling…I will say, though, I don't know what it is about Harley and video games but I never get cranky. I never get tired. And when I have a video game session with her I am so happy I feel like it's my therapy. [Laughs.] I can just get out all my frustrations and be crazy Harley. It's sort of like coming home, and the wicked side of myself gets to come out and play.

Going back to Barbara…was the adaptation of *The Killing Joke* a difficult project in which to voice her, because of the adult subject matter?
There was a little more of wanting to make sure the fans really loved what I did and identified with her. I did the film before reading the comic, because we didn't want it to influence my performance. Then afterward when I read it I was like, "Oh my god, this is the greatest comic book ever. Wow!" [Laughs.] It's brave, and I really loved everything about it. When I saw it I called Bruce and said, "I think I'm most proud of this. It's such an amazing piece." Of course people took issue with the romantic part. I would just say, "You know what? She's a grown woman and Batman is not her relative. So everybody just chill out." [Laughs.] I really, really love that movie a lot.

There are several versions of Batgirl. Why do you think Barbara remains so popular?
She's by design a very lovable character. She's a very real character. Harley's more like a character that your crazy side relates to, but not on a daily basis…During my run, they always directed me to be very real. That's another important part of what's attractive about her. She's just a real girl. There's nothing over the top that could annoy you or take you out of the moment. When you're watching episodes from our run, with Mark and Kevin, even though they're extraordinary situations, they're believable because the acting's so real. She just fits in with that world…And with so many male superheroes, it's just nice to have a girl. [Laughs.]

32 Visit the Batcave

Nestled within Hollywood's Griffith Park are the city's famed Bronson Caves, one of which served as the most famous cave in all of fiction—the 1966 *Batman* TV series' Batcave.

Carved out of the 100-foot-tall stone wall of a quarry, the Batcave is easily accessible to visitors. Just take Canyon Drive from Hollywood Boulevard, head north into Griffith Park, and park your car in the lot on the right that you encounter at the end of the road. Then hike on the trail that leads southeast. After a quarter of a mile, you'll hit a fork in the trail. Bear left and you'll see the tunnel out of which the Batmobile roared in the beloved show.

Fans can visit the mouth of the Batcave, made famous in the 1966 Batman *television series, anytime they're near Griffith Park in Los Angeles.* (Joseph McCabe)

It's only 50 feet in length. But your friends won't know that when they see the photo you take of yourself standing by its mouth—ready to hitch a ride with the Dynamic Duo on their way to Gotham City.

33 "A Death in the Family"

Since he first leapt off the cover of *Detective Comics* #38, Robin the Boy Wonder has served as the one steady source of light in the Dark Knight's universe. But what if that light was snuffed out? What if Batman's greatest enemy was responsible? These questions are answered in "A Death in the Family," a story that changed the Dark Knight forever.

Originally published in October 1988's *Batman* #426 through January 1989's *Batman* #429 (written by Jim Starlin and penciled by Jim Aparo), "A Death in the Family"—according to DC editor Denny O'Neil in his afterword to the tale's 1988 collected edition—was born out of DC Comics' desire to test new telephone polling technology as a way of interacting with readers. It would allow fans to decide the fate of Jason Todd, the second Robin, whose popularity had faded since his introduction in 1983.

Intended by his co-creator, writer Gerry Conway, to serve as a street-smart, rebellious alternative to straight-laced Dick Grayson (who grew beyond his position as sidekick into the adult hero Nightwing), Jason didn't differ all that much from his predecessor until he was retconned following the events of the 1985 limited series *Crisis on Infinite Earths*. Reintroduced as the orphaned son of a drug-addicted mother and a criminal henchman father, the new Jason never fully caught on with readers.

In "A Death in the Family," Jason grows careless in the field as he wrestles with his parents' deaths, prompting Batman to remove him from active duty. The lad learns, however, that the woman he thought was his mother was, in fact, not; his real mom is one of three women living overseas. Without telling Batman, he sets off in search of the women, but he soon reunites with his mentor, who follows the Joker to the Middle East after he steals a cruise missile. After ruling out two of the three women, Jason meets the third, Sheila Haywood, a medical doctor in Ethiopia who indeed proves to be his biological mother. Jason learns that Haywood is a disgraced surgeon who has been embezzling funds—and in turn is being blackmailed by the Joker into stealing medical supplies—when she turns her son over to the Clown Prince of Crime. After brutally beating the young man with a crowbar, the Joker betrays Haywood, ties her up, and leaves her with her bloodied son in a warehouse containing a ticking time bomb. With his last ounce of strength, Jason frees his mother and stumbles with her to the exit, only to find the door locked.

In a first for comics, readers then saw, on the last page of *Batman* #427, a full-page ad that invited them to call one of two 900 numbers (each costing 50 cents) to determine whether Jason should live or die. The results were counted, and, by just 72 votes (5,343 to 5,271), Jason's fate was sealed. In the opening pages of *Batman* #428, amidst the rubble of the explosion, the Dark Knight finds Jason's mother. She explains how he threw himself in front of her to take the main brunt of the blast. "Such a…good boy," she says with her last breath. "Must have…really…loved his… mother…" Then the Dark Knight finds his sidekick's shattered body "already getting cold to the touch."

"A Death in the Family" was the first Batman comic to become a national media event. Despite a hailstorm of criticism, editor Denny O'Neil—who'd commissioned two versions of the story's outcome and voted in favor of Jason's survival—defended it as "part of an occasionally bumpy process" in keeping the Dark Knight's adventures vital. Years later, however, O'Neil expressed regret upon learning that one voter may have programmed their computer to repeatedly dial the "death" number.

Jason's demise had been foreshadowed by the character's absence in 1986's *The Dark Knight Returns*. It also loaded a mountain of guilt onto Bruce Wayne's already constant sense of loss, creating a more driven Dark Knight than had been seen previously. Coupled with the Joker's crippling of Barbara Gordon earlier in the year (in *The Killing Joke*), it cemented the villain's reputation as a homicidal maniac without peer, a position he maintained when he appeared on cinema screens in the following year's *Batman* movie. The death of the second Robin would also influence later films like *Batman Beyond: Return of the Joker* and *Batman v Superman: Dawn of Justice*; it also prefigured the death of another Boy Wonder, Damian Wayne.

"I didn't think it was a particularly creative response to the material," says Gerry Conway of the call-in stunt. "It seemed to me to be kind of dismissive of the character and dismissive of the creative intention behind the character. So from that point of view, I was kind of offended by it. If they had actually tried to do it in a way that was intending to be meaningful, that would have been great. As it turned out, I think it *did* have meaning, despite the kind of cavalier attitude that the creators brought to it. Certainly Jason has gone on to be a fairly memorable character in his own right as time has passed."

Jason was brought back decades later as the Red Hood (since no superhero death is guaranteed permanent). But "A Death in the Family" marked a turning point in mainstream comics, both in its depiction of the loss of innocent life and the complicity in that loss that it coaxed from readers.

34 Robin II: Jason Todd (aka Red Hood)

Few characters in the DC Universe have taken a path as circuitous as that of Jason Todd, the second person to serve as Batman's partner Robin. But then few have for so long teetered between good and evil.

Jason was introduced to Batfans in the pages of March 1983's *Batman* #357 ("Squid," by writer Gerry Conway and penciler Don Newton). The son of Joe and Trina Todd, Jason and his parents were acrobats in the Sloan Circus. When the circus was targeted by a protection racket, the first Robin, Dick Grayson, enlisted Joe and Tina's help in bringing down the racketeers. This led to their deaths at the hands of would-be mob kingpin Killer Croc.

In his guilt, Dick took Jason to Wayne Manor, where the young man found the Batcave. He fashioned his own Robin costume, and attempted to avenge his parents' murder. But Batman took him under his wing, trained him, and made him his new Robin in December 1983's *Batman #366*. Jason even dyed his reddish-blond hair black, resembling the young Dick Grayson in appearance as well as origin. The supervillains Jason and Batman battled together included the vampirish Nocturna, to whom Bruce Wayne temporarily lost custody of Jason.

The similarities between Bruce Wayne's two wards dissolved when the DC Universe was rebooted following the events of the 1985 limited series *Crisis on Infinite Earths*. Jason was reintroduced in June 1987's *Batman* #408 ("Did Robin Die Tonight?" written by Max Allan Collins and penciled by Chris Warner) as the son of a drug-addicted mother, Catherine, and a criminal father, Willis. Living on the streets of Gotham, he tries to steal the tires off the Batmobile when Batman parks it in Crime Alley on the anniversary of his own parents' deaths. Hoping to spare Jason a life of crime, the Dark Knight places him in Ma Gunn's School for Boys, though he soon learns the school is run by a gang of criminals employing its students as thieves.

Batman and Jason busted the crime ring, and Jason underwent six months of intensive training, at the end of which he was installed as Robin. In time, Jason learned his father was killed by Two-Face, whom Jason then tried to kill. Angry, vengeful, and rebellious, Jason was not afraid to disobey the Dark Knight's orders. Yet he won the support of Nightwing, the adult Dick Grayson, and became a member of his superhero team the Titans.

This new persona of Jason proved unpopular with fans, never more so than when he allowed a rapist to fall from a building to his death (or perhaps deliberately pushed him). Bruce suspended Jason from his duties as Robin, but the boy's life took another dramatic turn in the 1988 storyline "A Death in the Family," in which he learns his biological mother is *not* Catherine Todd, but is instead Sheila Haywood, a medical aid worker in Ethiopia. After finding Sheila, he discovers she's partnered with the Joker, and blackmailed into giving the Clown Prince of Crime medical supplies. Heartbroken, he watches his mom turn him over to the Joker, who proceeds to beat him senseless with a crowbar, then lock him and his mother in a warehouse with a ticking time bomb. DC readers then voted on Jason's fate—resulting in his death.

With Jason's suit in a glass case in the Batcave (a move foreshadowed in 1986's *The Dark Knight Returns*), Batman entered one of the darkest periods of his life. He considered Jason's death his greatest failure, one that would haunt him for many years to come. During the 2005 "Infinite Crisis" crossover event, the continuity of the DC Universe was once more reshaped, resurrecting Jason.

As explained in the 2005 storyline "Under the Hood" (written by Judd Winick with art by Doug Mahnke, Eric Battle, and Shane Davis), Jason spent a year in a coma, and was found by Talia al

Ghul, who put him in one of her father's restorative Lazarus Pits, from which he emerged with a white streak in his hair and an insatiable bloodlust. The 2010 limited series *Red Hood: The Lost Days* (also written by Winick) told how Jason took the original criminal identity of his killer, the Joker, to become the antihero the Red Hood, an inverse of Batman who believes the end justifies the means.

In his new persona, Jason sought to eliminate Gotham's gangs by taking over the underworld. He also plotted revenge against Batman, whom he blamed for not avenging his death by killing the Joker. While Jason wound up beating the madman with a crowbar, just as he himself was beaten, the Dark Knight refused to let him kill his enemy.

In the years since, Jason and the Bat family have continued to butt heads, but they've also united to confront mutual enemies. In August 2009's *Batman and Robin* #1, the Red Hood acquired a sidekick of his own—Scarlet—a teenage girl with whom he tried to reveal Dick Grayson's identity to the world (after Dick became Batman when Bruce Wayne was believed dead). When Jason was sent to Arkham Asylum, it was Scarlet who busted him out. But Jason soon forsook his evil ways. In DC's 2011 "New 52" reboot, he was awarded his own monthly comic book, *Red Hood and the Outlaws*, partnering him with two of his fellow former Titans, Starfire and Arsenal. In July 2012's *Batman Incorporated* (Vol. 2) #1, he took on the role of the titular organization's Wingman. In DC's 2016 "Rebirth," *Red Hood and the Outlaws* was relaunched, and Jason joined the Amazon warrior Artemis and the imperfect Superman clone Bizarro to form a "Dark Trinity."

Jason hasn't made as many appearances on screen as his predecessor Dick Grayson or his successor Tim Drake. But he received a film of his own in the 2010 direct-to-video animated *Batman: Under the Red Hood.* Well worth a watch, it examines Jason Todd's life as a young man (voiced by Alexander Martella), a teen (Vincent

Martella), and an adult (*Supernatural* star Jensen Ackles). Jason was also given the title role and served as the main villain of the third *Batman: Arkham* video game, *Arkham Knight*.

Whether enemy or ally, the path walked by Jason Todd has always been his own.

35 The Batman Newspaper Strips

In the 1930s and 1940s, newspaper comic strips were the favored big brother of comic books. They featured better art, their creators were paid more handsomely, and they were read by far more people. Superman was first intended to be a newspaper strip character, and made the leap to the funny page in 1939. To the delight of his fans, Batman followed four years later.

Initially titled *Batman and Robin*, the daily adventure strip was launched on November 1, 1943; a Sunday comic strip followed on November 7. Featuring the last steady concentration of work by Batman co-creator Bob Kane (whose art would usually be drawn after that time by the "ghosts" he hired), the strip, in its first incarnation, ran through 1946. It was written by Kane's fellow Batman creator Bill Finger and comic writers Don Cameron, Jack Schiff, and Alvin Schwartz. Assisting Kane on the art were Batman comic pencilers Jack Burnley, Fred Ray, and Dick Sprang.

Several years after the *Batman and Robin* strip finished its run, it was relaunched by Walter B. Gibson, the pulp magazine writer who'd created the Shadow, the vigilante who'd helped inspire Batman's creation. By 1953, he was editing *Arrow* (a short-lived Sunday comic supplement), in which the Caped Crusaders' strip adventures, written by Gibson, ran exclusively.

A third version of the comic strip, *Batman with Robin the Boy Wonder*, hit newspapers at the height of the *Batman* TV series' popularity in 1966. It was written by DC Comics' Whitney Ellsworth—who'd served as producer and story editor on the *Adventures of Superman* TV series—and comic book writer/editor E. Nelson Bridwell, with art by DC artists Sheldon Moldoff, Joe Giella, Carmine Infantino, and Al Plastino. At first campy, like the TV series, it grew more serious over time. Its Sunday edition ran until 1969, and its daily until 1972; at that point Batman vacated the strip, though Bruce Wayne stayed on, and its focus shifted to a new character, the superhero Galexo. It finished its run in 1974.

The fourth comic strip to feature Batman, *The World's Greatest Superheroes*, debuted in 1978. The Dynamic Duo shared this strip with their friends Superman, Wonder Woman, the Flash, and Black Lightning. Eventually its name changed to *The World's Greatest Superheroes Present Superman*, *Superman*, and finally *The Superman Sunday Special*, as it came to focus on the Man of Steel. It ended in 1985.

With a new wave of Batmania generated by the 1989 *Batman* movie, a fifth Batman strip, the most recent to date, was launched that same year. Titled *Batman*, its first storyline, co-starring Catwoman, was drawn by acclaimed artist Marshall Rogers and scripted by mystery writer Max Allan Collins. The two were succeeded by writer William Messner-Loebs and artists Carmine Infantino and John Nyberg.

Like any Sunday guest, the Batman strips were generally better behaved than their disreputable monthly sibling, and often too polite for their own good. But they helped maintain the character's visibility even when sales of his comic slumped, meriting their inclusion in any history of the Dark Knight.

36 The Penguin

Oswald Cobblepot. The funny little man with the funny little walk. Though the umbrella aficionado adopts the affectations of the aristocracy, he couldn't be more unlike the blue-blooded Bruce Wayne.

Batman creators Bill Finger and Bob Kane offered different accounts of the Penguin's genesis. Finger claimed he was based on emperor penguins and intended as a parody of upper-crust society, while Kane maintained he was based on Willie, the top-hatted mascot for Kool cigarettes.

In any case, December 1941's *Detective Comics* #58 ("One of the Most Perfect Frame-Ups," by Finger and Kane) introduces the Penguin as an art thief going by the name "Mr. Boniface." He joins a gang of racketeers, but murders their boss and seizes control for himself when he realizes he prefers giving orders to taking them. Tuxedoed like his namesake, sporting a top hat, monocle, and cigarette holder—and carrying an array of tricked-out umbrellas—he proves one of the most cunning adversaries Batman and Robin have faced when he frames the Dark Knight for extortion. His audacity immediately catapulted him into the spot of Batman's second-greatest opponent, after the Joker.

In 1946, the *Batman* Sunday newspaper comic strip revealed the Penguin's real name, Oswald Chesterfield Cobblepot, much to his chagrin. In time, his crimes took on an avian theme. They also grew less lethal throughout the 1940s and 1950s, when his umbrellas—which had sprayed acid, knockout gas, and bullets—instead became a means of transportation, serving as parachutes, pogo sticks, and portable helicopters and rockets.

The Penguin's predilection for birds was explained in "The Origin of the Penguin!" in March 1981's *Best of DC Blue Ribbon*

Danny DeVito's version of the Penguin in Tim Burton's Batman Returns *is the most repulsive ever captured on film.* (Newscom)

Digest #10 (by writer Michael Fleisher and penciler Romeo Tanghal). This story established that Cobblepot grew up in his parents' pet shop, and that his nickname was coined by those who tormented him as a child. His penchant for umbrellas came from his mother, who insisted he carry one wherever he go.

Despite his cunning, the Man of a Thousand Umbrellas is sometimes portrayed as one of Batman's more sympathetic archenemies, with a soft spot for the ladies. From 1987's *Batman Annual* #11 ("Love Birds") to September 2008's retelling of his origin in *Joker's Asylum: Penguin* #1 to the 2011 miniseries *Penguin: Pain and Prejudice*, he falls for women, only to, more often than not, have his heart shattered. Yet that heartbreak never lasts long, and the Penguin's unfeeling intellect is his principal weapon. He's even operated a successful business (albeit one that's served as a front for his shady dealings)—Gotham's Iceberg Lounge.

On screen, the Umbrella Man was first played by two-time Oscar nominee Burgess Meredith in the 1966 *Batman* TV series and film. Meredith's "Pengy," with his trademark waddle and "Waugh waugh" laugh, remains the most enjoyable live-action version, informing every portrayal that followed—even Danny DeVito's dark turn in 1992's *Batman Returns.* In that Tim Burton film, the Penguin's a deeply unsympathetic outcast, as grotesque in his consumption of raw fish as his plan to murder Gotham's firstborn children. As the character tells Michael Keaton's Batman, "You're just jealous because I'm a genuine freak and you have to wear a mask."

In animation, the Penguin was well served by *Batman: The Animated Series.* Launched the same year as *Batman Returns*, the show's early seasons retained the film's depiction of Cobblepot as a mutant with flipper-like hands. But in its final season (when it was redesigned and renamed *The New Batman Adventures*), the series employed the character's traditional form. It better suited the performance of singer-songwriter Paul Williams, who wrapped his voice around phrases like "ornithologically inspired entoilment" with the best of them.

Gotham, however, offers the most satisfying screen portrait of Penguin since the 1966 series. Premiering on television in 2014, actor Robin Lord Taylor cuts a taller, thinner Penguin than fans are used to, but he delivers what is by far the show's most charismatic performance.

"I learned that the Penguin was a bullied kid, that he was tormented as a child by his peers for his interests and the way he looked," says Taylor. "Immediately, I was like, 'That's the humanity.' That was my way into his world and making him real. It was my entry into making that character three-dimensional, as opposed to just some sort of archetypal supervillain."

Taylor's Penguin rises above his station as a limping errand boy for the mob to become Gotham's most successful gang leader. He's the ultimate opportunist, a model capitalist—one who channels his sadism into his work ethic.

In any guise, the Penguin proves appearances are deceiving. And that a flightless bird can soar as high as a bat.

37 Batwoman

She cuts through the night like blood-stained lightning. An alabaster and ebony cacophony clad in a cape. Red and black, the Hebrew colors of war. She is Katherine Rebecca Kane. She is the Batwoman.

The evolution of Gotham City's fiercest fighting female mirrors that of society's, and pop culture's, regard for women. She began at a time when America's feminine ideal was all too frequently ornamental. But as early as her debut story, in July 1956's *Detective*

Comics #233 ("The Batwoman," by writer Edmond Hamilton and penciler Sheldon Moldoff), Kate—or "Kathy" Kane as she was then called—knew how to turn the ornamental on its ear.

A brunette in a yellow jumpsuit, with red boots, belt, gloves, cape, and mask, she busted a pair of bandits with the aid of a large powder-puff in her handbag/utility case. "She shook a whole cloud of powder in my face—*achoo*—can't stop sneezing!" cries one of the thugs, before Batwoman locks a steel handcuff disguised as her charm bracelet around his wrist.

"Whoever you are—you can't crusade against crime!" says Batman. "The law of Gotham City says that nobody can wear a Batman costume!" "You're wrong, Batman," she replies. "The law says, 'No man can wear it.' I'm a woman!"

On her next case, Batwoman blinded a jewel thief with her compact mirror before he could shoot Batman, then nabbed the rest of his gang with a perfume flask full of tear gas. "Batman, she's making you look bad!" says Robin, as a newspaper's headline proclaims, Batwoman Saves Batman. "I don't care about that but I do worry about the risks she's taking!" says Batman, attributing her success to "good luck."

As Kathy muses in her Batcave, a converted mine tunnel running beneath her mansion, we learn she was once a daredevil circus acrobat who yearned to use her skills to fight crime like Batman, and got the opportunity to do so when her uncle died, leaving her an inheritance. Like Bruce Wayne, she poses as a socialite while living a double life. Though Bruce and Kathy are attracted to each other, they refuse to divulge their secret identities. It's telling, however, that by story's end, while Batman determines hers, Batwoman refuses to learn his.

Batwoman continued to work with Batman throughout the Silver Age, eventually getting her own sidekick, Bat-Girl (who was smitten with Robin). But when editor Julius Schwartz took control of the Dynamic Duo's titles in the 1960s, Kathy vanished, along with other elements of Batman's world deemed unnecessary. Reappearing occasionally in the 1970s, she was killed by the Bronze Tiger in September 1979's *Detective Comics* #485, though her Earth-Two counterpart appeared in January 1982's *The Brave and The Bold* #182 to join Batman in fighting Hugo Strange.

Since nature abhors a vacuum, Batwoman was rebooted for a new generation of readers as flame-haired Kate Kane in September 2006's *52* #9. As revealed in a stunning 2009–10 run of *Detective Comics* issues by writer Greg Rucka and artist J.H. Williams III (collected as *Batwoman: Elegy*), Kate was the child of two career soldiers. When she was just 12 years old, her mother was murdered by enemy agents, who abducted her twin sister, Beth, setting her on a path that led to becoming Kate's archenemy, Alice, High Madame of the Religion of Crime. Her father remarried into wealth (again making the character an heiress), and Kate enlisted as a Marine cadet, becoming senior elite in gymnastics. But she resigns when she falls in love with another cadet, and her colonel tells her she's violated the military's code against homosexuality. After years of training her mind and body, she launches a one-woman war on crime in a tactical suit built by her father and inspired by the Dark Knight's own (originally designed by artist Alex Ross, who'd intended it to be used for Batgirl).

Kathy Kane was reintroduced into DC's continuity by writer Grant Morrison during his run on the Batman titles. This new Kathy, an assassin for the UN covert operations agency Spyral, joins Batman Incorporated in battling Talia al Ghul.

The Kate Kane Batwoman received her own sadly short-lived title written and illustrated by J.H. Williams—the best original comic book in DC's "New 52" line—and became a part of the Bat Family when she too joined Batman Incorporated. But no matter how many allies she surrounds herself with, Kate is unique. A soldier on many fronts, she fights a war waged in Batman's world and our own.

Gotham Gazette Exclusive

Alan Brennert

Screenwriter and novelist Alan Brennert is responsible for just a handful of Batman stories, but each is a gemstone of storytelling, from *Detective Comics* #500's landmark "To Kill a Legend" to the "Elseworlds" one-shot *Batman: Holy Terror.* All are collected in *Tales of the Batman: Alan Brennert.*

Your first Batman story was "To Kill a Legend." How did it come about?

I had friends from my days in comics fandom, and one of them was Paul Levitz, who by that time, 1980, had ascended to the editorship of the Batman titles. We got together for dinner in L.A. and I told him about an idea that had recently popped into my head for a Batman story. I said, "If you like this, you can hand it to one of your writers to write." He looked at me and said, not unreasonably, "You're a writer. Why don't you write it?" I had not written a full-length comic script before that, and certainly not a major character like Batman. That story ultimately became "To Kill a Legend." I handed it in and Paul liked it. I figured, "Well, this'll wind up as a fill-in issue somewhere." The next thing I knew it was the lead story in *Detective Comics* #500. I was kind of gobsmacked. I really had not expected it to be in such a prestigious slot, much less a prestigious anniversary issue. But Paul liked the story a lot and then put it in there, and then that story was reprinted a zillion times in various DC collections. That led to me writing other stories for DC when Dick Giordano took over the editorship of *The Brave and the Bold.*

Up until that point there hadn't been many retellings of Batman's origin. Certainly not one that explored it as your story did, considering what would happen if Bruce Wayne's parents weren't murdered. What inspired your tale?

Two things. The story "The First Batman" [from *Detective Comics* #235] was about Batman tracking down the killer of his parents, Joe Chill. It also relayed a lot of previously unrevealed backstory about how Chill was really working for an industrialist named Lew Moxon. That story always impressed me as a child because it had an absolutely awesome panel in which Batman is telling Joe Chill, "You murdered these people. You shot Martha and Thomas Wayne in cold blood. A child was there and watched his parents die before him." Chill says, "How do you know that?" In the next panel he throws off his mask and says, "I know because I am Bruce Wayne. I am that child!" That was a moment that you didn't see often in comic books. That kind of raw emotional power. It was interesting because it came at a time when Batman was no longer the feature it started out to be. It was a lot sunnier. He had Robin. Every once in a while the Joker would pop up, but he wasn't really a killer anymore. So in the middle of this you had this raw nerve of story that really went to the very root of who Batman was. Of course it was written by Bill Finger, who co-created Batman and who actually created Bruce Wayne and the origin of Batman.

So that inspired it, along with the concept of the Multiverse, which I'd loved ever since it was introduced in the story "Flash of Two Worlds!" I was a stone-cold fan of the JLA/JSA crossovers, and I'd always loved the concept of parallel worlds. I loved the idea that there were worlds where superheroes were middle-aged, they'd gotten married, they had children, and they had to continue to fight on. To me that was just a really powerful magnet of a concept drawing me to it. I started looking at the dates. The original Earth-Two Batman debuted in 1939. You could arguably say that the Earth-One Batman started about 20 years later or so, in the 1950s. That's when DC started chronicling the Earth-One Batman. I thought, "We were always told that events happened first on Earth-Two and then on Earth-One. What if there's another Earth out there where these events haven't yet happened?" So I was kind of following a Gardner Fox–created idea, that of these events rippling their way down through the Multiverse. Once I got the idea of this being a world where Thomas and Martha Wayne have not yet died, the rest of it just fell into place.

Your love of the Multiverse also informs "The Autobiography of Bruce Wayne!" from *The Brave and the Bold* #197, in which the Batman and Catwoman of Earth-Two fall in love and marry.

Yeah, Paul Levitz had established in *All Star Comics* that Bruce Wayne had married Selina Kyle, laid down the mantle of the Batman, and become Gotham City's police commissioner. The backstory was told in the Huntress origin that he wrote. I loved the story and all of Paul's *All Star* stories. I thought, "They started out as enemies. How did they get from being enemies with something of a sexual tension going on between them to somebody that they would want to marry?" I just worked backward from that, and I thought what it would be like for him about 15 years into his career, which is where I set the story, about 1955, and how he was frozen into this sham identity of Bruce Wayne, the idle fop who pumps Jim Gordon for information but his real life is as the Batman. And he wonders, "What will become of Bruce Wayne? What's to become of me when I'm too old to be Batman? Is there no me left?"

From there it led to the idea of bringing in the Scarecrow to aggravate his worst fear—his fear of being left alone. Which is what happened to him in Crime Alley that night, when his parents were gunned down in front of him. He was all alone, and he worked his entire life surrounding himself with people, and with this life of adventure and conflict in order to avoid being alone again.

Your "Interlude on Earth-Two," from *The Brave and the Bold* #182, also embraced Silver Age staples, such as the original Batwoman.
I grew up reading those stories; '61 was about when I started reading comic books. That was the tail end of [editor] Jack Schiff's era of Batman—"The Zebra Batman!," "The Gorilla Boss of Gotham City!," all those great outrageous stories. But at the same time I appreciated the "New Look" Batman when [editor] Julie Schwartz took it over. I really appreciated when Denny O'Neil and Neal Adams came in and turned him back into *the* Batman, the Dark Knight. So it was kind of a nice thing to be able to play simultaneously with a darker Batman, the Earth-One Batman, but also with the props at least of the Silver Age Batman. All of which I got from those giant annuals.

Why did you elect not to do more comic stories?
I got busy. I stopped writing for *The Brave and the Bold* largely because it got canceled, and I got a gig as executive story consultant on *The New Twilight Zone,* which consumed all of my work time for the next two years.

You penned a Batman graphic novel in 1991's *Holy Terror*, a tale that's more relevant than ever with America's religious fundamental movement gaining political power.
My politics were evident even in my earlier stories. If you look at my Batman/Creeper story it's about this creature made of origami being animated by a demagogue, a conservative TV host who's against anybody who's different. Which is, as you say, frighteningly relevant today. Then my Batman/Hawk and Dove team-up also had politics in it. That was written at the height of the Reagan administration and that had aspects of that. So *Holy Terror* was a continuation of that theme, but writ large. I was able to create an entire world in the shape of what some evangelical Christians really wished the world looked like. I was also trying to push the envelope as far as I could. Freedoms were opening up. You could get away with a lot more in terms of language and theme. It's a darker book than any of my other comic stories. That's partly a function of my politics and partly a function of the new freedom that I had in writing it.

Do you still read Batman comics?
I've read a few of the stories. There is room for a number of different interpretations of Batman. Because the character is so complex you can make of him what you want. But the Batman I've been seeing lately is just so grim and humorless that I don't know how you write that. I watched *Batman v Superman: Dawn of Justice*. It was very nicely made and all of the actors were fine, but, I'm sorry, *my* Batman would never say, to anyone much less Superman, "Do you bleed? You will." Batman does not want to see people bleed. People bleed when he beats them up because he's doing it to get information. But he's not a sadist…Then the absolutely laughable scene in which they discover that their mothers are both named Martha. "Well, I guess this makes us friends!" [Laughs.] I sat there going, "Really? Somebody pitched that in the room and nobody started laughing?" So yeah, I am not a fan of the DC movies that are being done. But I am a *huge* fan of the DC television shows. I love *Supergirl*, I enjoy *The Flash*, and I enjoy *Legends of Tomorrow*. They're getting it right.

38 The Dark Knight Rises

Whether telling a one-issue tale or one that spans years, superhero comic books are designed to keep readers buying them. Endings are uncommon. So any ending imagined for the Dark Knight in his native medium—be it Frank Miller's *The Dark Knight Returns* or Mark Waid and Alex Ross' *Kingdom Come*—is usually explained away as an imaginary tale. In the concluding chapter of his cinematic trilogy, however, writer-director Christopher Nolan was afforded an opportunity long denied most Batman storytellers: closure.

In 2005's *Batman Begins*, Nolan had suggested his hero might one day quit fighting crime when Gotham no longer needed him. In 2008's *The Dark Knight*, Bruce Wayne almost entrusts his crusade to district attorney Harvey Dent. *The Dark Knight Rises*, released in 2012, starts with Wayne (played for the last time by Christian Bale) having hung up his cape and cowl following the deaths of Rachel Dawes and Dent in the preceding film, confident that Gotham is secure at last. A recluse in his mansion, he's coaxed out by the arrival of terrorist Bane (Tom Hardy), who breaks the Bat and uses the late Ra's al Ghul's League of Shadows to take over Gotham. Calling out to the city's disenfranchised, Bane proclaims himself their liberator, while secretly planning to destroy Gotham for (spoilers!) Ra's' revenge-minded daughter, Talia (Marion Cotillard). With the aid of James Gordon (Gary Oldman), Lucius Fox (Morgan Freeman), Alfred Pennyworth (Michael Caine), and two new allies—young cop John Blake (Joseph Gordon-Levitt) and master thief Selina Kyle (Anne Hathaway)—the Dark Knight indeed rises.

For his third Batman film, Nolan sought to create an epic, driven by an antagonist who for once was Batman's physical equal. Since the bestselling comic storyline "Knightfall" featured the Dark Knight's most memorable defeat—in which his spine was snapped by Bane—it made sense to incorporate the masked mercenary genius (who'd previously appeared in 1997's regrettable *Batman & Robin*). *The Dark Knight Returns* inspired the film's portrait of a Batman coming out of self-imposed retirement, and 1999's "No Man's Land" storyline informed its depiction of a besieged Gotham unable to call on the U.S. government for help.

Again filming a large portion of his movie in IMAX, Nolan shot much of *The Dark Knight Rises* in Pittsburgh (its final Bane-Batman fight was lensed at Carnegie Mellon University)—and in Chicago, Los Angeles, New York, New Jersey, England, and Wales—significantly expanding Gotham. India's Mehrangarh Fort served as the location of Bane's prison "Pit." In scope, scale, and running time (165 minutes), *The Dark Knight Rises* is by far the biggest of the trilogy. It announces its ambitions with an opening sequence that rivals that of *The Dark Knight*—a midair plane heist shot over Scotland's Cairngorm Mountains—and climaxes with a spectacular chase through the concrete canyons of Gotham featuring the latest addition to Batman's armory, the assault aircraft known as "The Bat."

Hardy's performance doesn't have the critical cachet of the late Heath Ledger's Joker in *The Dark Knight*, but it's no less compulsively watchable. With half his face obscured by Bane's maw-like mask, his voice—a kind of camp aristocrat's—eerily contrasts his wrestler's build. Hathaway, swathed in a multifunctional, state-of-the-art catsuit, reinvents Catwoman as a 21st century femme fatale (through whom the film gives a voice to the Occupy movement). Cotillard and Gordon-Levitt hold their own against returning vets Bale, Caine, Freeman, and Oldman, all of whom bring their A game.

In the kind of creative collaboration that could only exist in the Internet age, composer Hans Zimmer (working this time without James Newton Howard, his partner on the prior films) invited Batman fans worldwide to submit recordings of themselves via ujam.com, chanting the Moroccan words "Deh-shay, deh-shay bah-sah-rah, bah-sah-rah," which he fused into a chorus on the soundtrack's stirring "Rise" chant.

Sadly, *The Dark Knight Rises*' release date, July 20, 2012, was marked by a far greater horror than any fiction—the Century 16 theater shooting in Aurora, Colorado, in which 12 people were killed and 70 more injured by a deranged gunman who identified himself as the Joker. It once more called into question the United States' inadequate gun control laws.

Where *The Dark Knight Rises* received the most criticism from fans was in its stated eight-year-gap in continuity following the events of *The Dark Knight*, and in Bruce Wayne's decision to retire at film's end, leaving his legacy to Blake (aka "Robin"). The complaints were understandable, since the Bruce Wayne of the comics has long vowed to spend his entire life warring on criminals. But film is a different medium, with different narrative possibilities and requirements, and a movie trilogy demands a three-act structure with an emotional payoff. So if one views Nolan's films as their own version of the mythos, imbued with their source material's spirit but shorn of its structure, they offer as definitive a Batman as any.

39 Filmation's *The Batman/ Superman Hour*

Batman: The Animated Series might be the definitive cartoon realization of the Dark Knight, but it's far from Batman's first foray into animation. The path was forged by Filmation's *The Batman/ Superman Hour.*

First broadcast on CBS on September 14, 1968, exactly six months after the last new episode of the 1966 live-action *Batman* TV series had aired, this Saturday morning cartoon show followed Filmation's *The New Adventures of Superman*, *The Adventures of Superboy*, and *The Superman/Aquaman Hour of Adventure* in bringing DC's heroes into the homes of children across America, many of whom had never before seen the company's costumed champions. Produced by Filmation founders Norm Prescott and Lou Scheimer and directed by their fellow founder Hal Sutherland, the series was the first of many to feature actors Olan Soule (who'd appeared in the 1966 *Batman* episode "The Pharaoh's in a Rut") and Casey Kasem as the voices of Batman and Robin. Alfred, Commissioner Gordon, and most of the male villains were voiced by Ted Knight (best known for his work in *The Mary Tyler Moore Show* and *Caddyshack*).

Batgirl (voiced by Jane Webb), Joker, Catwoman, Penguin, Riddler, Mr. Freeze, and the Mad Hatter also made their first animated appearances on the show, while other characters such as the Scarecrow, Tweedledum, and Tweedledee appeared for the first time on screen, in episodes that used comics talents like *The Brave and the Bold* writer Bob Haney. Thirty-four Batman stories in all were produced through January of 1969, with the Caped Crusaders' half of the show consisting of one six-and-a-half-minute story and one two-part story, each of its halves also six-and-a-half minutes. For kids distraught over the cancellation of their favorite live-action series, it functioned as a continuation (albeit without the former show's camp), complete with Chief O'Hara and Robin's ubiquitous "Holy…!" expressions.

The Batman installments of *The Batman/Superman Hour* were repackaged in the fall of 1969 into another series, the 30-minute *Batman with Robin the Boy Wonder.* When its run ended, the Dynamic Duo guest-starred in two 1972 episodes of Hanna-Barbera's *The New Scooby-Doo Movies* ("The Dynamic Scooby-Doo Affair" and "The Caped Crusader Caper"), both of which were parodied in the *Batman: The Brave and the Bold* episode "Bat-Mite Presents: Batman's Strangest Cases!" The Caped Crusaders also appeared in Hanna-Barbera's 1973 *Super Friends* (again voiced by Soule and Kasem) before returning to Filmation in 1977's *The New Adventures of Batman.* The latter series—which aired concurrently with 1977's *The All-New Super Friends* (the first time that animated series airing on two different TV networks featured the same characters)—saw Adam West and Burt Ward return to voice the Caped Crusaders. The characters' design employed the same model sheets as the 1968 series (reminiscent of comic artist Carmine Infantino's versions of Batman, Robin, and Batgirl), but the latter show's science fiction stories were similar to those of the 1950s Batman comic books, including Whirly-Bat helicopters and extra-dimensional imp Bat-Mite (voiced by Scheimer).

Filmation's animation process was notoriously cheap, even by the standards of its day, the result of it being the only major TV animation studio to produce its work entirely in America. As such, it endlessly reused stock footage of the characters throwing Batarangs, swinging on Bat-ropes, and speeding off in the Batmobile. But Filmation's efforts helped keep Gotham City alive on screen in the 21 years between the Adam West series and Tim Burton's 1989 *Batman* movie. For that reason alone, Batfans are in Filmation's debt.

40 Bat-Mite

No character is more emblematic of Batman's surreal sci-fi period in the 1950s and early 1960s than Bat-Mite. A nigh omnipotent extra-dimensional, Batsuit-clad imp, his visits to Gotham City have proven as frustrating for the Caped Crusader as they have entertaining for fans.

Just as Batman was created as a response to the success of Superman, so Bat-Mite, introduced in May 1959's *Detective Comics* #267 ("Batman Meets Bat-Mite," by Batman co-creator Bill Finger and penciler Sheldon Moldoff) began his career as a copy of Superman's nemesis, Mister Mxyzptlk. But while Mxy left the 5th Dimension to torment the Man of Steel, Bat-Mite was Batman's self-proclaimed biggest fan—the ur-nerd of pop culture.

"I'm not a pest at all," he proclaimed to Mxyzptlk (his sometimes rival, sometimes partner) in November 1960's *World's Finest* #113 ("Bat-Mite Meets Mr. Mxyzptlk!"). "I help Batman and Robin! Because I admire them so, I want them to do their best feats and stunts! That's why I use my magic!"

Unfortunately for the Dynamic Duo, Bat-Mite's magic often involved giving superpowers to criminals and bringing giant inanimate objects to life, all in an effort to make Batman and Robin's fights more impressive. Along the way, the pixie pest developed a crush on the Silver Age Batwoman, gave Batman's dog Ace the Bat-Hound superpowers, and, after getting rejected one too many times, created a superhero from scratch to steal the Dark Knight's thunder—complete with an image of Bat-Mite on his chest.

When Julius Schwartz became editor of the Batman comic titles in 1964, Bat-Mite (along with Ace and Batwoman) were phased out in favor of more "realistic" detective stories. But the

An imp from another dimension obsessed with Batman, Bat-Mite is a product of 1950s sci-fi. (Cover art by Sheldon Moldoff and Ira Schnapp)

scamp has made a number of memorable return appearances. In *Detective Comics* #482 ("Bat-Mite's New York Adventure"), he visited our Earth (Earth Prime) and tried to convince DC Comics to publish a book about his exploits. In the 1995 one-shot special *Batman: Mitefall* (a parody of the popular "Knightfall" storyline), his home dimension was invaded by Bane-Mite. In the 2000 one-shot *World's Funnest*, his war with Mxyzptlk leveled the entire DC Universe. And in writer Grant Morrison's 2008 story arc "Batman R.I.P.," Bat-Mite is revealed as a figment of Batman's imagination, aka "the fifth dimension."

Though Bat-Mite was one of the regular characters in Filmation Associates' 1977 *The New Adventures of Batman* animated series (in which he was voiced by Filmation founder Lou Scheimer), his definitive screen incarnation is in 2008's *Batman: The Brave and the Bold.* Voiced by Pee-wee Herman himself, Paul Reubens, he gets the spotlight in four of the show's best episodes: "Legends of the Dark Mite!," "Emperor Joker!," "Bat-Mite Presents: Batman's Strangest Cases!," and the series finale "Mitefall!" All but "Emperor Joker!" were written by Paul Dini, who brought similarly vibrant life to Mxyzptlk in *Superman: The Animated Series.*

Angel, devil, or something of both, Bat-Mite, with his unbridled love of the Caped Crusader, has more in common with Batfans than almost any other Batman character.

41 Batman Returns

In 1989, some filmgoers had not yet received the news (heralded by so many media outlets) that comics were no longer for kids, and were thus put off by the violence in Tim Burton's first *Batman* movie. But any objectionable material in that film paled in comparison to what they found in 1992's *Batman Returns*, the film that altered the course of the Batman movies for more than a decade.

In the wake of his first blockbuster's success—and as a way of wooing him back to direct another (which would help secure star Michael Keaton)—Burton was granted much more creative control of the sequel by Warner Brothers, so long as he included the Penguin, then regarded by the studio as the Dark Knight's second-most-popular enemy (such was the influence of the 1966 *Batman* TV series even 26 years later).

But the Penguin suited Burton just fine, who saw in Oswald Cobblepot the kind of misfit he preferred to traditional heroes and villains. He also responded to Catwoman, the Batman's longstanding lead femme fatale, torn between good and evil. Screenwriter Sam Hamm, who'd co-written the original film, drafted a script utilizing both criminals. Burton, however, elected to bring Daniel

Waters onto the project after seeing his black comedy *Heathers*. Waters' script included a new character, Max Shreck (named after the star of F.W. Murnau's *Nosferatu*). A parody of yuppie tycoons, Shreck abuses his employee Selina Kyle, prompting her transformation into Catwoman. Waters also added the Penguin's campaign for mayor of Gotham (a story told in the 1966 series' episodes "Hizzoner the Penguin" and "Dizzoner the Penguin," and later depicted on TV's *Gotham*).

Wesley Strick (uncredited in the film) was then recruited to rewrite Waters' script, and introduced the Penguin's plan to kill Gotham City's firstborn sons. A mutant child so hideous his own parents attempted to drown him, Burton's Penguin, played by Danny DeVito under layers of Stan Winston–designed makeup, would be a grotesque in every sense of the word.

Annette Bening was chosen to play Catwoman, but became pregnant and was unable to take the job. Burton wound up hiring Michelle Pfeiffer, who ably takes her character from fragile executive assistant to fierce, sexy antihero. Christopher Walken was given a Beethoven wig to play her boss. *Batman*'s Michael Gough and Pat Hingle returned as Alfred and Commissioner Gordon, respectively. Bo Welch replaced Anton Furst as production designer and crafted a more simplified Gotham City on Warner Brothers' Burbank lot, and Danny Elfman returned to compose an even more elaborate score than he had for the 1989 film.

Keaton and Pfeiffer display terrific chemistry in their scenes together, and the latter's character emerges as the film's most interesting. But DeVito's Penguin, who eats raw fish whole with his bile-blackened teeth, bites the nose off a campaign manager, and thinks nothing of slaughtering infants ("Male and female! Hell, the sexes are equal with their erogenous zones blown sky high!"), polarized audiences. He also—along with Catwoman's dominatrix-inspired attire and climactic electrocution of Shreck—traumatized Warner Bros. execs hoping for a family-friendly summertime hit.

Despite earning more in its opening weekend than any film had up to that point, *Batman Returns*' $266.8 million total gross was a mere fraction of the original's. When parents complained about the inappropriate marketing of a McDonald's Happy Meal tie-in, the studio was forced to issue a statement. The next time Warners greenlit a Batman movie, licensing concerns took firm precedence over art.

There's plenty of the latter in *Batman Returns*. Selina's costume gave her a ragdoll quality, one that anticipated *The Nightmare Before Christmas*' Sally, and there's a sweet absurdity to the Emperor Penguin pallbearers carrying Cobblepot's corpse to its grave. But it's a Tim Burton film first and a Batman movie a distant second. Like most of the filmmaker's output, it's preoccupied with the freaks and outcasts of society, but at the expense of a hero hell-bent on justice. As in his first *Batman*, Burton's Dark Knight kills his enemies, using the Batmobile's rear exhaust to set fire to one of the Penguin's henchmen and blowing up another with a fistful of dynamite. Worse, Waters and Strick's script is so overripe with trailer moments and one-liners (each of them, from "Life's a bitch, now so am I!" to "Just the pussy I've been lookin' for!" just begging to be put on a bumper sticker, coffee mug, or Hot Topic T-shirt) that the sad song in its heart struggles to be heard.

Burton cemented the mainstream acceptance of Batman as suitable entertainment for grown-ups. But decades later his films can be as difficult for 21st century Batfans to watch as the 1966 series was for 1980s comic book readers. Ever the frustrated art director, his Batman movies are much more concerned with conjuring up evocative visuals than with presenting coherent detective stories or rousing action sequences. Like the hero who marches through them—who's so frequently overshadowed by his enemies—they're "split, right down the center."

42 Joel Schumacher's *Batman Forever* and *Batman & Robin*

In 1993, Warner Brothers executives' heads were still reeling over the previous year's *Batman Returns*. The film didn't come close to earning as much as Tim Burton's first *Batman* movie, and the studio worried the outcry from some parents over its violence and S&M-influenced Catwoman had hurt toy sales. When Burton agreed to step back and merely produce a third Batman movie, the sighs of relief emanating from the studio's Burbank offices could be heard worldwide.

Eager for a family-friendlier film that wouldn't ruin a McDonald's promotion, the studio recruited Joel Schumacher, a former costume designer who'd directed *The Lost Boys*, *Flatliners*, and Warner Bros.' then-recent hits *Falling Down* and *The Client*. Akiva Goldsman, *The Client*'s screenwriter, was hired to draft a script, after Lee and Janet Scott Batchler turned in an initial draft focusing on the Riddler.

Fast-food chain considerations are literally at the forefront of Goldsman's screenplay for 1995's *Batman Forever*; Batman's first line in the film, as he prepares to exit the Batcave in his flashy new Batmobile, is "I'll get drive-thru." Other Bat-groaners include "You trying to get under my cape, Doctor?" and "It's the car, right? Chicks love the car."

Upon reading Goldsman's script, Michael Keaton decided he was done with Batman. "It sucked," said Keaton on the January 3, 2017, episode of *The Hollywood Reporter*'s *Awards Chatter* podcast. "The script never was good. I knew it was in trouble when he [Joel Schumacher] said, 'Why does everything have to be so dark?'"

Warners replaced Keaton with Val Kilmer, who'd recently won acclaim for his turn as Doc Holliday in *Tombstone*. Nicole Kidman won the role of love interest / criminal psychologist Dr. Chase Meridian. Tommy Lee Jones, who'd starred in *The Client*, accepted the role of Two-Face at the request of his son, a Batman fan, even though Billy Dee Williams had played Harvey Dent in Burton's *Batman*. Jim Carrey—on fire with hits *Ace Ventura: Pet Detective*, *The Mask*, and *Dumb and Dumber*—beat out Robin Williams for the role of the Riddler/Edward Nygma. The role of Robin, originally intended to be introduced in *Batman* and *Batman Returns*, went to Chris O'Donnell.

Kilmer, who looks and acts more like the Bruce Wayne of the comics than Keaton, is given a bit more detective work to do as Batman than his predecessor, as well as more action scenes. But his efforts are undermined by a subplot involving repressed memories that goes nowhere, most of it left on the cutting room floor. In its place are a few too many scenes of Carrey and a miscast Jones (in Day-Glo purple makeup) chewing, swallowing, and spitting out the neon-soaked scenery in a nonsensical plot about Nygma

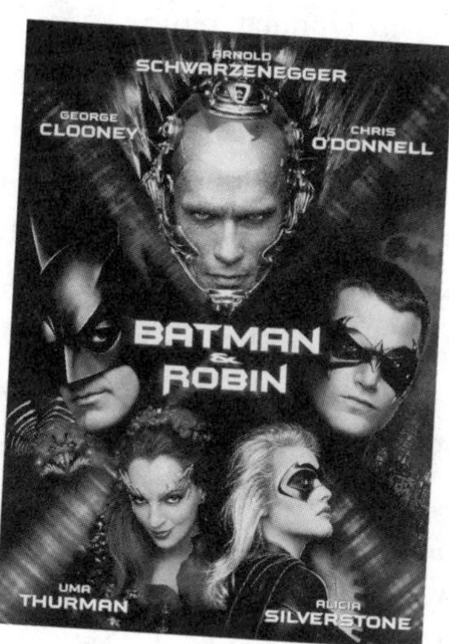

Joel Schumacher's pair of Batman films represented an attempt to "lighten up" the Dark Knight.

stealing the brain waves of Gotham's citizens. Kidman, a talented actress, plays a psychologist so unprofessional she uses the Bat-Signal in an attempt to seduce the Dark Knight. And O'Donnell is just too old to be playing the newly hatched Robin.

The less said about Batman's infamous Bat-nipples, the better.

Schumacher never commits to any one tone, resulting in a film that wants to be liked by too many and ended up being loved by too few. Lacking the high comedy of the 1966 *Batman* TV series, the gothic moodiness of Burton's movies, and the suspense of Christopher Nolan's Dark Knight trilogy, it's a studio picture in the most compromised sense of the word.

Batman Forever earned $70 million more than *Batman Returns*, making it the second-highest-grossing film of 1995. As a result, Schumacher and Goldsman were invited back to Gotham City, but their 1997 follow-up, *Batman & Robin*, is even worse. It's a garish nightmare of Bat-credit cards and silver Bat-codpieces that squanders $125 million in an unsuccessful attempt to replicate the camp of the 1966 show.

O'Donnell returned as Robin, though Kilmer, who hadn't gotten along with Schumacher, did not. He was replaced by George Clooney, whose film career had just begun after he departed TV's *ER*. Clooney looks great in Bruce Wayne's turtlenecks, with the biggest chin of any live-action Batman up to that time, and he projects genuine warmth in his scenes with Alfred. Yet his lighter Caped Crusader is saddled with the worst script in the series, concerning Mr. Freeze's efforts to ice the planet so Poison Ivy can repopulate it with plants. Arnold "You are not sending me to the cooler" Schwarzenegger's Victor Fries is a hammy, inferior knock-off of the tragic scientist in *Batman: The Animated Series*' Emmy Award–winning episode "Heart of Ice," while Uma Thurman, to no avail, channels Mae West as Pamela Isley / Poison Ivy.

Pro wrestler Robert "Jeep" Swenson's Bane—just a few years after the character made his comic debut—is shoehorned into a film already overstuffed with secondary characters, each of them swallowed by its cartoonish sets. Also present is Alicia Silverstone as Batgirl (the character's film debut), John Glover (*The Animated Series*' Riddler) as Ivy's boss Dr. Jason Woodrue, model Elle Macpherson as Bruce Wayne's girlfriend Julie Madison, and the returning Michael Gough and Pat Hingle as Alfred and Commissioner Gordon, respectively. Silverstone won the Razzie Award for Worst Supporting Actress, one of the film's 11 nominations.

"If you do anything that could be considered cheesy or camp, you have to believe it," explains producer James Tucker, whose *Batman: The Brave and the Bold* is a much more satisfying tribute to the 1966 series. "There's a part of you that has to think it's cool, too. You can't be looking down your nose at it and then expect the audience to respond. *Batman Forever* kind of straddled the line. But *Batman & Robin* tainted people's opinions of *Batman Forever*. People who liked *Batman Forever* saw *Batman & Robin* and went, 'Oh wait, *that's* what they were doing in that last movie?'"

Schumacher, to his credit, issued an apology to Batfans in the *Shadows of the Bat* documentary on the film's home video release. "If there's anybody watching this," he says, "that, let's say, loved *Batman Forever* and went into *Batman & Robin* with great anticipation, if I've disappointed them in any way, then I really want to apologize. Because it wasn't my intention. My intention was just to entertain them."

"I actually thought I destroyed the franchise," admitted Clooney in a 2015 interview on *The Graham Norton Show*. "But I thought at the time this was gonna be a very good career move. It wasn't."

Grossing $238.2 million—almost $100 million less than *Batman Forever*'s $336.5—*Batman & Robin* didn't exactly destroy the franchise. But in keeping with its villains' plans, it put it on ice.

43 Be Like Bruce Wayne

In his lifetime, Batman co-creator Bill Finger never received appropriate compensation for his mammoth contributions to pop culture. But there now exists an organization to help provide a financial safety net for the comic book creators who are still with us, an organization through which today's superhero fan can acknowledge the importance of the field's creators, and, like Bruce Wayne himself, be a humanitarian.

Created in 2000 by a group of comic publishers, the Hero Initiative is a federally recognized, nonprofit charity devoted to aiding comic book creators in need. Since these creators are responsible for characters that generate billions of dollars in film, television, and video game revenue, a donation to the Hero Initiative is the most effective way to say thank you for the entertainment they've given us.

The Hero Initiative maintains a presence online and at comic conventions around the country, selling art and limited edition comic books; and hosting writers and artists, who raise funds for the organization by signing autographs and sketching for fans. Famed Batman writer Denny O'Neil sits on Hero's Fund Disbursement Board, and Hero sponsors an annual Lifetime Achievement Award—which had been won by such Batman artists as Nick Cardy, Neal Adams, and Walt Simonson. The charity also administers the Dick Giordano Humanitarian of the Year Award (named in honor of the late Batman artist and executive editor of DC Comics), the recipients of which have included Dark Knight delineators Jerry Robinson and Tim Sale.

To learn more about the Hero Initiative or to make a donation, visit www.heroinitiative.org.

44 Robin III: Tim Drake (aka Red Robin)

Tim Drake is the Robin who most emulates the detective side of the Dark Knight.

Introduced in August 1989's *Batman* #436 ("Batman: Year Three—Different Roads," by writer Marv Wolfman and penciler Pat Broderick), Tim, unlike his predecessors Dick Grayson and Jason Todd, wasn't discovered by Batman. Instead, he sought out his future mentor. Having once witnessed Dick perform in the circus, a nine-year-old Tim realized Dick was Robin after seeing him perform a quadruple somersault while fighting crime. He then deduced Batman's secret identity. But he kept the secret to himself, and, inspired by the Caped Crusaders' example, trained his mind and body.

He had plenty of time to do so, since Tim's parents, Jack and Janet Drake, often neglected their son when he was growing up, enrolling him in boarding schools while they focused on their careers. When Jason Todd was killed, Tim noticed Batman operating without Robin and growing disturbingly violent. He wound up helping Batman and Nightwing fight Two-Face after donning Jason's old costume in December 1989's *Batman* #442, the final chapter in the "A Lonely Place of Dying" story arc. Yet he was not officially accepted by Batman as the third Robin until he underwent many months of training—later detailed in the 1991 *Robin* limited series—and saved him from the Scarecrow in December 1990's *Batman* #457 ("Master of Fear," by writer Alan Grant and penciler Norm Breyfogle).

Clad in a costume designed by legendary Batman artist Neal Adams, one sleeker and more practical than that worn by Dick and Jason, Tim emerged as the smartest of the Robins. A genius hacker, he focused on solving problems rather than punching them in the face. Unlike his predecessors, he was drawn to fight crime by a sense of righteousness instead of vengeance, though he was tempted by the latter, especially after his mother was killed and his father paralyzed by the villainous Obeah Man.

Tim acquired his two principal weapons—a Bo staff and a throwing star in the shape of his "R" chest emblem—in the 1991 *Robin* limited series (in which he trained under the assassin Lady Shiva). The book proved successful enough to spawn two follow-up miniseries, and a regular monthly series kicked off with November 1993's *Robin* #1, running 183 issues before concluding in 2009.

Along the way, Tim suffered other losses, including that of his girlfriend Stephanie Brown (aka Spoiler, who briefly replaced him as Robin), his best friend Superboy in the 2005 *Infinite Crisis* limited series, and eventually his father, who was killed by Captain Boomerang in the 2004 limited series *Identity Crisis*.

With Superboy and the speedster Impulse, Tim founded Young Justice, a team of teen champions he led. When Young Justice dissolved, Tim joined the Teen Titans, and eventually led them as well. Following Superboy's death, Tim fashioned a new uniform for himself, in red and black, the colors of his fallen friend.

Though Tim had originally rejected Bruce Wayne's offer to adopt him, he allowed his mentor to do so in February 2007's *Detective Comics* #826. Unlike Dick, Tim saw himself one day retiring his alter ego and leading a normal life. Yet he forged a new crimefighting identity for himself when Bruce was believed to be killed in 2008's *Final Crisis* limited series.

Since Dick Grayson then became Batman and appointed Bruce's son Damian as his Robin—reasoning that Tim was an equal, not a sidekick—Tim donned the black cowl of Red Robin. Beginning in August 2009's *Red Robin* #1, Tim searched the globe for signs of Bruce, whom he believed was alive, and defended

Wayne Enterprises from Ra's al Ghul, becoming for a time the head of the company.

When Bruce returned, reclaimed the mantle of the Bat, and formed Batman Incorporated, Red Robin was appointed leader of the organization's black-ops team, the Outsiders. When the DC Universe was rebooted in 2011's "New 52" event, and again in 2016's "Rebirth," Tim's origin was retconned so he'd never taken the name Robin, but begun his career alongside Batman as Red Robin. In "New 52," Tim exchanged his cowl for a domino mask and acquired a winged suit. In "Rebirth," he wears a suit much like his original Robin costume, albeit with an emblem comprised of two Rs instead of one.

Tim debuted on screen as Robin in the 1997 animated TV series *The New Batman Adventures*, in which he's voiced by Mathew Valencia. Sadly, this incarnation of the character (incorporating elements of Jason Todd's Robin) suffered a tragic fate, revealed in the 2000 direct-to-video movie *Batman Beyond: Return of the Joker* (in which he's voiced as an adult by Dean Stockwell). In the second season of TV's *Young Justice*, Tim replaces the first season's Dick Grayson (and is voiced by Cameron Bowen). Red Robin (voiced by Yuri Lowenthal) first appeared on screen in the 2015 direct-to-video film *Batman Unlimited: Animal Instincts*. Tim has also proved popular enough to be the Robin in the blockbuster *Batman: Arkham* video games (voiced by various actors).

The first Robin to earn his own comic book title, Tim Drake has proven time and again that brains are every bit as important as brawn, and that one need not witness one's parents' murders to defend Gotham City.

"I wanted Tim to be the antithesis of all the other young characters who were sort of orphaned," says Tim's creator Marv Wolfman. "I didn't want him having this big grudge on his shoulder. I didn't want him to be Batman. And I wanted him to *want* to be Robin."

Gotham Gazette Exclusive

Norm Breyfogle

No artist defined Batman in the late 1980s and 1990s like Norm Breyfogle. His run on the character, most of which was scripted by Alan Grant, introduced Tim Drake's Robin, the Ventriloquist, Scarface, Anarky, Mr. Zsasz, and two of the sleekest Batmobiles in comic history. Though Breyfogle suffered a stroke in 2014 that now prevents him from drawing, his enthusiasm for the comic book medium remains palpable.

A large percentage of young Batman fans were introduced to comics through your work, because you were the regular Batman artist when the character's 1989 movie debuted.
That's right. I really lucked out in that regard. I had been waiting since I was 15 for a Batman film. That was great. I was like a celebrity. When I'd go to conventions I'd have lines that would go out the convention door and all the way around the block. Sometimes twice around the block. It was crazy. But I was young and had a lot of energy, so I would stay there until every last person got a signed copy.

You must have made quite a few people happy. Which version of Batman appealed to you when you were a kid?
Neal Adams is what really hooked me on comics. I still consider him by far to be the best American comics artist of his generation…It's amazing. He's 19 years older than me and he's still going strong, and here I am with a stroke and I can't draw. [Laughs.]

I can't imagine how difficult that's been for you.
It's been a real blow. It squashes a man's ego, as Charlton Heston said, looking at the universe at the beginning of *Planet of the Apes*. I've had a number of ego-squashings in my life. But you know, they've always been good for my soul. They've knocked me off my high horse and put everything in perspective.

When you turned pro, you began drawing Batman almost immediately.

Yes. I went to college and got an illustration degree. So I was pretty much at a professional level after graduating. I'd been sending originals of my stuff, a big box of framed paintings to DC Comics. [Laughs.] It was really nice of them to send them back to me, because you just don't send originals through the mail. I knew that, but I didn't have the money to take photographs or slides. Then I did one tryout story, so a couple of months later [vice president / executive editor] Dick Giordano called me in and asked me to be the regular artist on *Detective Comics*. I said, "Oh god, yes!" There was a lot of Batman in my portfolio, because I always drew a lot of Batman.

From the start, your Batman work was distinct in its liquid-like fluidity.

At first that was a compromise for me, for years, due to trying to meet deadlines on a regular basis. I always wanted to do much more detailed Neal Adams / Dick Giordano / Jim Aparo work. I was always trying to do that under deadline pressure. But out of necessity I did simplify it into an almost animation-like style. That's why a lot of people consider that first Batman animated show to be influenced by my work. There was a similarity. I think it's because animation is composed of more simplified drawings, and I had simplified my style. But I always tried to maintain the drama as much as possible.

You and Alan Grant formed one of the great artist-writer partnerships on the character.

It was serendipity. Alan had always wanted to write Batman, and he was already big on *Judge Dredd.* Denny O'Neil, as editors always try to do, was looking for a way to bring in a new look, or something to keep the characters alive. So he told Alan Grant to write it, and Dick Giordano called me to draw it. But as far as I know it was Denny O'Neil's choice to bring us both together.

I would have worked well with any writer, but Alan was a real pleasure to work with. Alan was an ideal comics artist's writer, in that he left a lot of what should be left up to the artist. His scripts were direct and to the point, and it was amazing how much he could get across in an economical piece of work.

In your run, you introduced a handful of new villains.
The reason Alan created so many new characters was that the delivery system for American comics in Scotland, where he lived, was very spotty. So he was never sure what was going on in terms of the continuity, and which characters he could use and which characters he couldn't use because they were already being used in some other Batman-related book. So he just took that opportunity to create new villains. Those were all done by Alan. He created all these new villains and I drew them first, so I co-created them, and some of them have lasted to this day. Anarky, the Ratcatcher, Mr. Zsasz...

When I first read the Ratcatcher script, I was thinking that the Ratcatcher sounded like a Judge Dredd villain. Alan described him as wearing a World War II gas mask, and I gave him the long boots for wading through the sewer. That was the first in a series of characters Alan Grant created out of the blue for Batman, and I was lucky enough to design them visually and to draw them for the first time for a publication.

In the beginning of your run, you introduced the Ventriloquist.
That's right. I remember the first Batman job I did—a Crime Doctor job—I think Mike Barr wrote that one. But the Ventriloquist storyline was the first storyline with Alan Grant and John Wagner. They were a writing team at that point.

Alan described the Ventriloquist as being a mild-mannered accountant type. So I gave him thick bottle glasses and a tiny little mouth, which was to contrast against Scarface's loud, '40s-gangster-era attitude and dialogue. It was really fun to design the characters Alan came up with, and that was one of the most fun ones to design. It was the first one we designed together. I remember he described Scarface quite thoroughly. He described him as an Al Capone doll, but he also described him as carrying a little piano. That's why he was carrying a piano in the first issue. But that just got in the way, so it disappeared soon...He also would have him holding machine guns and stuff. That was funny, because I would have the Ventriloquist holding the machine gun, and Scarface's floppy arm would just be holding his hand. He was described as having a pinstripe suit and a carnation.

The Ventriloquist may have made the quickest leap of any villain from his first appearance in comics to 1992's *Batman: The Animated Series.*

That's true. When I read the first script with the Ventriloquist, I thought, "Oh my god. This is brilliant. It's an *obvious* villain for Batman that nobody has come up with before." There had been chilling depictions of ventriloquist dummies in media. I think there were two or three of them in *The Twilight Zone*. And there was a movie, *Dead of Night*, a black-and-white movie from the '40s, and the most horrifying element was a ventriloquist doll. So I was amazed that nobody had ever thought of that for Batman before. The mark of a great creator, especially on a well-known character like Batman, is to be able to bring together different concepts that nobody had thought of before but that are obvious once you see them. Alan was really good at that.

Anarky also made a big impact.

Alan described him simply as looking like the "Spy vs. Spy" characters in *Mad* magazine. The other reference he gave me was *V for Vendetta*. So he said Anarky could be a cross between *V for Vendetta* and "Spy vs. Spy." That's basically what I had for it. He also described Anarky as a kid, so he had a contraption to make himself look taller. His mask was an extended neck. My challenge was to make it look like there was something funky about Anarky when you first meet him, and you later discover why. Because he's got this contraption to make himself look taller, like an adult. That quickly disappeared when he went into a miniseries, because it just got in the way, and Anarky was growing up. So I figured he was growing into the role, so to speak. Plus it was more expressive after a while to have the face mask show expressions, just like Batman does in his mask.

I added the gold face mask to symbolize Anarky's "pure" motivations, and also the purity of youth, which hasn't yet discovered the nuances of good and evil. So he had a really black-and-white attitude about good and evil. That's really the essence of what Anarky is all about. I also gave him a long, dark-red flowing costume.

You mentioned Anarky's eyes. Your Batman is also known for his very expressive eyes.
That's something they've only begun to get right in movies now, with CGI—making the masks really expressive. I think I was the first one to really take advantage that much, of not just the eyes but the expression lines around the nose and the expression lines in the forehead. Neal Adams showed the expression through the face mask really well. So I was really inspired by that. But I was of course also meeting deadlines and developing my own style. So I just took Batman's mask as being part of his face. Just like his cape. It's not just a costume. It's part of his preternatural being. It's all very expressive. I left it up to the fans at that point, or anybody else if they wanted to, to describe how that could be done realistically. The best explanation would be that it's nanotechnological to some degree, and that's why it suits his expression.

Your cape was equally expressive.
I just had an intuitive sense of Batman, and I was welding it together with my own development as a comics artist under the pressures of deadlines. So it was kind of an alchemical mix of those two things. Frank Miller did one Batman Christmas story, and I really liked that cape's depiction. Then Todd McFarlane did a little bit of Batman just before I came on, with the Reaper. Todd really went overboard with the cape. I thought he went too far, but that was also an influence. The main thing for me was to find an exciting balance between realism and expressionism. So I wanted to take advantage of the cape, but I didn't want to go too far. In retrospect, I think I did go too far a number of times. But it's all a matter of opinion, really.

The best aspect of drawing Batman, in fact, was his cape. Most artists will probably say the same thing. It's what makes drawing Batman so much fun. Because you can use the cape as a gigantic design element, literally and figuratively. Not only in the panel but with the whole page. Neal Adams was doing that way back when I first saw his work in *The Brave and the Bold*. A lot of people think I was the first one to make the eyes expressive or to use the cape in certain ways, to frame panels. But that's not true. Neal Adams was the first to do that.

As difficult as it is to come up with new villains, it's also difficult to come up with new cars. Yet you designed more than one memorable Batmobile.

I took the initiative entirely on that myself. The scripts by Alan Grant or Denny O'Neil's editorship didn't have anything to do with it. Things were more flexible back then. Artists had more artistic license. I had an intuitive feel for how far an artistic license could be taken on Batman. So I felt like I could design any kind of Batmobile I wanted. It had just gotten to the point where the Batmobile had begun to open up a little bit in the design. The design that had been used for years before I got on that was starting to feel a little tired, I thought. Alan Grant's Batman stories were pretty unconventional at the time, so I just felt intuitively and logically that Bruce Wayne was a millionaire and Batman was a rough-and-tumble guy who'd probably gone through a lot of Batmobiles. So he'd probably have a lot of different designs. So I thought that was a perfect opening for me to just come up with any design I wanted. At first I tried a number of different designs. Then I started zeroing in on what I felt the Batmobile should be like.

[Toy maker] Corgi put out two of their Batmobiles based on my design. One from the earlier version of my design, and one from the later version of my design. Man, they really nailed both of them. Especially the second one. It's a beautiful little car. To this day it holds up against any of the more recent Batmobiles. The Tumbler is a brilliant change for Batman. I think that's probably gotta be the best Batmobile. But outside of being a military vehicle, I think my design has been the best of all the Batmobile designs. I was going for just an ultramodern sports car feel.

After *Legends of the Dark Knight*, *Shadow of the Bat* was the first new Batman comic book to come out in some time. You kicked it off by introducing Victor Zsasz and Jeremiah Arkham.

Alan described that Arkham Asylum was based on a traditional maze. It was a circular maze, almost like a crime circle. And Arkham himself…I don't think I was given any description for him. I just made him look like a doctor, a psychiatrist. He had glasses and he had a laboratory coat. Most of his character design came out of his facial expressions and the way that he treated his subjects, like Victor Zsasz. Of course most people think Zsasz was based on Hannibal Lecter. That's what I thought too. I still feel to this day that it has to be true. Because it was such a coincidence that Zsasz was created at the same time that *The Silence of the Lambs* came out. But Alan denies he had seen that movie or knew anything about that movie when he created Victor Zsasz. [Laughs.]

But I was aware of it, so I definitely was influenced to depict him in that matter. Although I ended up depicting him with these black triangular eyes, which at first were just shadows. Then I ended up taking it too far and made it look like some kind of expressionistic mask, and it didn't really work as well. The first depiction that I had of Victor Zsasz, when he comes out of the shadow and he puts his hands on the glass and he's got this maniacal expression…Facing Batman on the outside of the cell, he just looks like a normal guy, but with scars all over his body. It was all in the madness of his eyes. I think that was my best depiction of him.

You eventually had a chance to indirectly collaborate with Neal Adams, since he designed Tim Drake's Robin costume and you were the first artist to illustrate it in comics.

That's right. DC Comics hired a number of artists to come up with different costume designs for Robin. Robin was redesigned in 1989, and there were a lot of different costume designs and Neal Adams' design was the one that was chosen. There were two elements that were incorporated into Neal's design that Neal hadn't actually put into it, that I put into it. That was Robin carrying the staff, which was entirely my idea. It made sense to me that he would have a staff. Robin Hood fought Little John with a staff. They had that staff fight on the log. So I had that in mind. Also, it made sense, because he was a kid and he was fighting adults who were stronger than him and had much longer reach than him…Then the throwing star was the other thing I put into my designs that was then injected into Neal's design as well. His Robin symbol on his chest that he could use as a throwing star, that was my idea. So it was those two ideas of mine, but it was Neal Adams' design.

You illustrated two Batman graphic novels, *Holy Terror* and *Birth of the Demon.* The latter was fully painted.
That was the ideal job. When I was a kid and I wanted to be a Batman artist, that would have been the ultimate ideal—doing a fully painted Batman graphic novel. Although the one thing I was disappointed in at first was that Batman had such a little part in it. It was all about Ra's al Ghul and his origin. But once I got into it, the fact that I was able to do it fully painted really made a big difference in making the desert scenes work, because there were a *lot* of desert scenes. That could have been boring if it was drawn in pen and ink with color added...It was the only time I worked with Denny O'Neil on a Batman story. That was a dream come true too. I felt like I was right in the legacy of Neal Adams and Denny O'Neil when they first came up with Ra's al Ghul when I was 12 years old.

45 "Knightfall"

Love 'em or hate 'em, crossover stunts have fueled the American superhero comic book business since Marvel Comics' 1984 *Secret Wars* limited series pulled in most of the publisher's major characters' titles. DC followed suit with *Crisis on Infinite Earths* (1985), *Legends* (1986), *Millennium* (1988), and *Invasion!* (1989). As the publisher's most popular character, Batman was the first solo character around which a post-*Crisis* crossover revolved, 1989's "A Lonely Place of Dying," which introduced the third Robin, Tim Drake. But "A Lonely Place of Dying" involved just two titles—*Batman* and *New Titans*—and spanned a mere three months. The next such event, 1993's "Knightfall," ran the better part of a year.

With a deluge of new readers flowing into comic stores from Tim Burton's 1989 *Batman* film, its 1992 sequel, and the latter year's *Batman: The Animated Series*, editor Denny O'Neil chose to do the unthinkable by putting Bruce Wayne out of commission in an event that would, for a time, see a new Batman in Gotham. Originally intended to take place before 1992's "The Death of Superman" stunt, the first chapter of "Knightfall" was pushed back to May 1993's *Batman* #492 so as not to compete with the Superman books' similar storyline.

The principal antagonist of "Knightfall" is Bane (introduced in January 1993's *Vengeance of Bane* one-shot), a brilliant, steroid-enhanced criminal who makes it his mission to break Batman and rule Gotham. The saga's other guest player, substitute Batman Jean-Paul Valley, made his debut in the 1992 limited series *Batman: Sword of Azrael.* Valley was a grad student who discovered his destiny as the latest in a line of super-assassins when he was activated by a secret religious society known as the Sacred Order of Saint Dumas. Intercepted by Batman, he was turned away from a life of destruction—or so readers had thought.

Following months of prelude, the prologue to "Knightfall," in *Batman* #491, finds Bane breaking open Arkham Asylum and dumping its inmates on Gotham, in an effort to wear down the Dark Knight. Already experiencing a crisis of self-doubt, Batman spends several months catching the escapees. Exhausted, he heads back to the Batcave, only to find Bane waiting there for him. Bane breaks his spine in July 1993's landmark *Batman* #497 ("The Broken Bat," by writer Doug Moench and penciler Jim Aparo).

"We all wanted to have the breaking of the back," says Moench, "because it's the most dramatic and decisive and visually wrenching thing you could do. But once the idea came up... 'Well, we're gonna be bringing Bruce Wayne back eventually, so if we break his back is this a feasible thing?' One of [*Detective*

Comics writer] Chuck Dixon's relatives was a nurse and she had just been talking about this new treatment—that if you get to someone who's had a broken back within 12 hours you can have a complete and total recovery. This was a brand-new treatment at the time.

"We said, 'Well, okay. This is comic books, right? We can use that new treatment as part of the suspense. A race against time to get Bruce Wayne to a hospital quick enough for this new treatment to be done!' That sealed it. If we could write our way out of it, we'd do it."

With Bane ruling Gotham's underworld, Bruce Wayne began a long process of rehabilitation, leaving the city in Valley's care as the new Batman. Forbidden by Bruce to confront Bane, Valley at first complies, but eventually his Azrael programming is soon reinstated. He designs an armored Batsuit and breaks the super-criminal in October 1993's *Batman* #500. So ends the first volume of "Knightfall."

Volume 2, "Knightquest," is divided into two parts: "The Crusade," in which Valley (or "AzBats") goes out of control in his new role, and "The Search," which follows Bruce and Alfred as they travel the globe in search of Tim Drake's missing father and Bruce's girlfriend and therapist, both of whom were kidnapped in Volume 1. By the end of "Knightquest," Valley has once more become an executioner.

Volume 3, "KnightsEnd," chronicles Bruce's return to Gotham, his horror at what Valley has become, and his subsequent reclaiming of the mantle of the Bat, in August 1994's *Batman: Legends of the Dark Knight* #63 ("Climax" by writer Denny O'Neil and penciler Barry Kitson). Two epilogues followed: "Prodigal," which sees Dick Grayson briefly serve as Batman, and "Troika," in which Bruce returns for good in a new-and-improved black Batsuit. In 1995, Valley again reformed and earned his own 100-issue series, *Azrael* (renamed *Azrael: Agent of the Bat* in 1998).

"It was frustrating but rewarding," says Moench of the task of plotting "Knightfall" with his fellow Batman writers. "It was a pain in the ass but fun. Every two contrasting adjectives you can come up with, you could apply to doing this. I was, on balance, all for it at the beginning. But at a certain point I felt like we were extending it too much. Obviously it made money and people seemed to love it so much that it was hard to resist keeping it going."

Batman's initial confrontation with Bane (with a far different outcome) was retold in the 1994 *Batman: The Animated Series* episode "Bane," and in Christopher Nolan's 2012 *The Dark Knight Rises*, in which he also sets Gotham's criminals free. The entire "Knightfall" trilogy was adapted by O'Neil in his 1994 novel of the same name.

Amoral antiheroes like Marvel's Cable and Deadpool and Image's Spawn were ubiquitous in the comics of the early 1990s, their blades, chains, and ammo belts replacing the capes and cowls of their predecessors. Jean-Paul Valley was intended as a response to such characters, one who could have been similarly embraced. But the reaction to "Knightfall" proved that, when given the choice, Batman fans preferred a hero who *didn't* kill his enemies. In so doing, it reaffirmed the faith DC's readers and creators had in each other, and that both had in the Dark Knight.

46 Bane

The most unlikely of Internet stars, the archvillain Bane has inspired more online parodies, spoofs, memes, and GIFs than just about any member of the Dark Knight's rogues gallery. One need look no further than former *Saturday Night Live* star Chris Kattan's take on the character in such Funny or Die videos as "Bane After Batman" and "Bane the Telemarketer" to see how much a part of the zeitgeist Tom Hardy's performance in *The Dark Knight Rises* has become.

Before Christopher Nolan's 2012 trilogy topper, the public's awareness of Bane was largely limited to his subliterate strongman persona in 1997's *Batman & Robin*. But as comic book fans well know, the character's roots run far deeper than that celluloid misfire, back to *Legends of the Dark Knight*.

In the March 1991 issue of the anthology series (#16), writer Denny O'Neil kicked off his five-part "Venom" storyline, in which Batman fails to save the life of a little girl and begins taking the titular steroid in an effort to improve his abilities. Never one to shy away from addressing social problems in his work, O'Neil had the Dark Knight grow addicted to the drug, a dependency he was only able to overcome with the aid of Alfred.

Two years later, with DC's "Death of Superman" storyline a runaway bestseller, the company performed a similar crossover stunt with Batman in 1993's "Knightfall," taking Batman out of commission and replacing him with a bloodthirsty successor, from whom he ultimately reclaimed the mantle of the Bat. Tasked with finding a suitable supervillain to defeat Batman, O'Neil, as editor, teamed with writers Doug Moench and Chuck Dixon to create Bane. A criminal genius intent on destroying the Dark Knight, the character was conceived by Moench as an evil version of the pulp hero Doc Savage (himself an inspiration for Superman), with his gang of henchmen/experts mirroring Doc's "Fabulous Five." Moench suggested Bane inject Venom to enhance his physical strength, pumping it into his brain via tubes connected to a lucha libre–style mask.

"We had planned all these issues leading up to an unnamed villain," says Moench. "An unimagined villain really, except we said he would be a 'big deal in every way.' That's what led me to think of an evil Doc Savage. A big deal in every way, Doc Savage is the smartest guy on earth and the strongest guy and the best athlete and the best fighter."

The character debuted in January 1993's *Batman: Vengeance of Bane* #1, written by Dixon and penciled by Graham Nolan. This one-shot special established that the villain grew up in the prison pits of Peña Duro on the island nation of Santa Prisca, where he was forced to serve time for his late father's attempt to stage a coup against the government. Though his mother died when he was just six years old, he slowly became the most feared prisoner in Peña Duro, killing a man when he was just eight. While building his body, he sharpened his mind by reading every book in the prison, and named himself Bane. The officials tried to break his spirit by sentencing him to 10 years in solitary confinement, but Bane grew stronger, and was selected as a guinea pig when the developers of Venom required someone to test the drug on. The only prisoner to survive the testing, Bane's strength and stamina surged, though his body came to require Venom every 12 hours, necessitating his tubes and face mask. Bane then faked his death and escaped from prison with the help of his friends Zombie, Bird, and Trogg. Bird eventually told Bane of his home, Gotham City, and its protector Batman. Bane decided to crush Batman to prove his superiority and rule Gotham. Releasing all the inmates of Arkham Asylum, he became one of the few supervillains to learn Batman's secret

Bane, an archvillain fueled by the strength-increasing substance known as Venom, made a name for himself by breaking Batman's back during the 1993 "Knightfall" storyline. (Cover art by Kelley Jones and Bob LeRose)

identity. With the Dark Knight exhausted, Bane confronted him in the Batcave and broke his back.

Following the events of "Knightfall"—by the end of which he was defeated—Bane fled Gotham and became Ra's al Ghul's personal bodyguard, intent on marrying his daughter Talia in 1998's *Batman: Bane of the Demon* limited series. In time, Bane learned his father, Edmund Dorrance, was still alive, operating under the name King Snake and leading the Hong Kong street gang the Ghost Dragons. After killing him, Bane sought to end his reliance on Venom and reform. He's since formed alliances with the team of supervillains known as the Society, the Suicide Squad, and the Secret Six.

Voiced by *Ocean's Eleven* and *The Manchurian Candidate* star Henry Silva, Bane first appeared on screen in 1992's *Batman: The Animated Series*. In the second-season episode "Bane," he's introduced as a former South American inmate in a Cuban prison, who took Venom as part of a project to produce super-soldiers. He's hired by mob boss Rupert Thorne in an unsuccessful attempt to eliminate Batman. The character's at his best, however, in the 1998 *The New Batman Adventures* episode "Over the Edge," in which he's set loose on Batman by Commissioner Gordon, who blames the Dark Knight for the death of his daughter, Barbara.

"You can't believe how I've looked forward to this," Bane tells Batman. "Though I was hoping for more of a fight. But what could I expect…from a killer of children."

Considerably less successful was Bane's live-action debut, as a henchman of Poison Ivy in *Batman & Robin*. Played by the late pro wrestler Robert "Jeep" Swenson, he's portrayed as a nebbish convict named Antonio Diego who's transformed into a green-hued monosyllabic lummox. In Christopher Nolan's *The Dark Knight Rises*, Tom Hardy's erudite Bane is freed from the character's Mexican wrestling mask and tubes. Instead, he sports a breath mask that feeds him a gas to kill the pain of injuries he suffered helping Talia escape from "the Pit" in which he grew up. This Bane began his career when he was recruited by Ra's al Ghul for his League of Shadows.

Years after the laughter from the resulting web parodies had faded—each of them drawing on his endlessly imitable voice—Hardy's Bane again went viral in January 2017, when Donald Trump's inaugural address echoed the supervillain's words upon seizing control of Gotham: "We give it back to you…the people."

"I'm just thrilled every time there's a Bane LEGO set or whatever," laughs Moench. "Because it means a big fat royalty check is coming. Freelancers get no pension. But having created Bane, it's like a pension on steroids."

Gotham Gazette Exclusive

Doug Moench

In the early 1980s, Doug Moench enjoyed a run on Batman in which he created the villain Black Mask and was the first writer to script the adventures of Jason Todd's Robin. Moench returned to Batman in the 1990s—when he created the "Elseworlds" graphic novel *Batman & Dracula: Red Rain* and its sequels, co-created Bane, and crafted a memorable run on Batman with artist Kelley Jones.

Before working on Batman you were known for your work on Marvel's horror titles. Were you to drawn to Batman's darkness?
Yeah. Ever since I was very young Batman was just about my favorite character. I mean, like everyone else, when the Marvel books started I was nuts about them. But even through that I think Batman remained my favorite. Even if the issues coming out were not as good or as attractive as what Marvel was doing, the character himself was still the best. Then of course when Neal Adams and Jim Aparo and Denny O'Neil and Bob Haney started doing really good stuff with the Batman character, once again I realized, "Yeah, this is the guy I like the most."

Gerry Conway had introduced Jason Todd, but you were the writer to introduce him as Robin.
Yeah. Gerry was doing a good job, but I did not like the new Robin idea. Maybe I would have had Gerry stayed and written it and shown me what it was gonna be. But just being dropped like that into my lap, it was like, "What the hell? Why in the world do we have to do this to the most famous duo in comics? It's still gonna be Batman and Robin, but it's just a different guy. What is the point?" Nobody ever really explained that. Since I obviously didn't want to do it I didn't have a good reason for doing it, but I just tried to do the best I could the way the cards were dealt.

I did manage to talk them into not doing something that I thought was worse: they were going to take Robin out of Batman and put him in *The New Teen Titans*. At that time *Teen Titans* was selling more copies. It was a more profitable book. So it sort of had precedence. Though I thought that was all wrong. The two best sellers should be Superman and Batman. But they were gonna put Robin in there and then Jason Todd was gonna come in and he was gonna be a new sidekick. They didn't have a name for him yet. So I talked them out of that and said, "No, if Dick Grayson has to be in *Teen Titans*, he should have the new name." He became Nightwing.

Once you started writing Batman, you focused on crime stories as opposed to superheroics.

Yeah, I never thought of Batman as a superhero. He's a costumed hero. I related to him more along pulp magazine lines. More of a Shadow type than a Superman type.

You created a number of your own villains. One of the biggest was Black Mask, who's become more popular over time.

Apparently he's going to be the villain in the second *Suicide Squad* movie…I just felt like I did all the other villains and it wasn't time to redo Joker again yet. So let me deliberately try to create a new villain who's strong enough to join the best rogues gallery in comics. Again, the pulps—his name, Black Mask, was the name of a pulp magazine. I thought it was a great name. Again, getting back to the costumed hero as opposed to superhero, I always felt Batman's rogues gallery were costumed characters as opposed to supervillain costumed characters. So you always look for ways that they can have a visually distinctive identity without the spandex supervillain thing. So I would do things like face tattoos and mohawks or shave 'em bald. Some way to make them visually distinctive without looking totally outlandish. So this guy with a double-breasted suit and a gangster hat, "All right, that's not enough…Ah, a black mask!" That led to the literal ebony wood mask. Then I had the bright idea that if he's a gangster he's got a gang, and all the gang members would wear different masks. So, "Wow, I have a whole army of new villains, and new ones can be created at will using these tribal masks and evil clown masks. Whatever masks you can think of." I was very pleased with that notion. It seemed to kill 19 birds with one stone.

In addition to Black Mask, you're responsible for Bane. What led to his creation?

We worked out "Knightfall" in infinite detail at these "Bat meets," up to the point where the big driving force behind the "Knightfall" storyline would be introduced. We put that off and put that off. By the fourth or fifth Bat meet—which was not a major one, just a mini one with me, [writer] Chuck Dixon, [editor] Denny O'Neil, and one or two assistant editors—we had to come up with this character we'd been heading toward all this time. So the point of the meet was to create this character. Now, in the past Bat meets, I'd always resisted thinking ahead. I'd just wait till we got to the Bat meet, listen to people talk, and then based on that I would say things. I felt like it wasn't my place to decide things in advance before we had the meet. But by this point I realized there was a lot of wasted time doing things that way because the others were doing that too mostly. We'd all just sit there and look at each other for a while, with nobody putting any advance thought into it. So I'm driving to this mini Bat meet and I start thinking, "What should this character be like?"

By the time I got to the Bat meet I'd thought up the concept of what I called "an evil Doc Savage." A guy who has trained himself to be the best physically and mentally and who has three, four, five assistants, each one a specialist in a different area—weapons, computers, whatever. Like Doc Savage had his cadre of experts. Then I came up with the wrist thing, with the buttons and the little tube going up his arm, plugged into the back of his head, to give himself a jolt of this super drug that would pump him up even more. And the Mexican wrestler's mask. I came up with a bunch of other stuff.

I decided to keep it to myself in case anyone else had something better. So we get to the meet and Denny says, "Okay, our new villain. What's it gonna be?" We just sat there looking at each other and I waited, gave them a chance, and then I said, "Well, on the drive here I thought of an evil Doc Savage." They all said, "What?" I explained the whole thing and they were nodding. They were happy. I said, "But if this guy's so amazing how come we never heard of him before?" Chuck Dixon said, "He grew up in prison." Denny O'Neil loved that. Then I said, "Okay, how could he grow up in prison? That doesn't happen." Then they said, "Well, it can happen in other countries. It doesn't happen here." So I think Chuck came up with Santa Prisca.

By the end of this meet we had the character totally hammered out, except for one thing that changed later. I had suggested the name of the villain be Venom, because the drug was called Venom. I said, "We can use the Venom that Denny came up with to pump this guy up, make him even stronger." The drug was Denny's idea. Denny had done a *Legends of the Dark Knight* five-parter and it was called "Venom," and it was about Batman getting so debilitated that he needed a crutch, and he went to this drug.

Everybody said, "Oh, that's a good name." So we all went away. We had our new "Knightfall" villain and he was Venom. Then I got a call and they said, "Well, Venom's out. Believe it or not, none of us have apparently been reading Spider-Man. There's a new big-deal Spider-Man villain called Venom." "Really?" I said, "Okay, you want me to come up with a new name?" They said, "No, no. Chuck had to write his issue and they looked up 'Venom' in the thesaurus and they found 'Bane.'" I said, "Bane sounds good." So that was that.

After "Knightfall" you scripted a run of stories on *Batman* that were independent from such crossover storylines.

I really felt like, "I wanna be a writer again rather than part of a committee." They let me, as an experiment, separate my title, the *Batman* title, and they carried on with the other books crossing over... That was what people called the Kelley Jones run, where you could read *Batman* without having to buy *Robin* and *Catwoman* and *Detective* and *Shadow of the Bat*. I was much happier. I don't think they were too happy, but I just couldn't take it anymore. It was too much of a good thing with the crossovers.

Is that the Batman work with which you're most satisfied?

I suppose. I did this other "Elseworlds" thing with Barry Kitson called *Batman: Book of the Dead*. That I think is probably the single best Batman story I've ever done. Other than that it's probably that run. It's funny, when I argued for the separation of the books and I won the fight—and this was a big battle—they said, "Okay, your artist can be Kelley Jones." I said, "No, he's perfect for *Haunted Gotham*, this horror take on Batman. But I can tell you because I see the letters that as many readers who love Kelley's work there are just as many who hate his Batman. They're the ones who read the monthly book, and they're just gonna hate him on the monthly book. They think his Batman's too weird, too bizarre. They're right, but it's perfect for *Haunted Gotham* and *Red Rain* and *Crimson Mist* and *Bloodstorm* and *Dark Joker*."

My first thought was, "Well, I just won the fight to get separated. Now I'm not gonna have another fight about the artist." Then I thought, "After Kelley has worked with me this much he deserves a shot at these big Batman royalties and after being with me on the monthly book it'll pay off for him finally." So I didn't fight it at all. Like I said, other than that one *Book of the Dead* project, the Kelley Jones issues are probably my favorites.

Bane's been depicted several times on screen, the best known being Tom Hardy's role in *The Dark Knight Rises*.
I'm all in favor of it just based on the checks that come this way. I've not yet watched the movie, so I don't know. But I will say I've watched almost every other Tom Hardy movie and he's one of my favorite recent actors. So I'm sure he's great as Bane. I love Christopher Nolan as a director. But there's just something about having written all this stuff…When I want to unwind with a movie, I go, "Batman? Eh, I think I'd rather watch something else." So I really don't pay much attention to how Bane is being portrayed or used.

What are you up to these days?
Cashing Bane and Black Mask royalty checks. It's a wonderful thing. [Laughs.] No, actually before all this money started coming in, I had gotten fed up with the business. It's changed so much. I was spoiled when I first started by having no interference whatsoever, having no editorial guidance. No one looking over my shoulder and no one telling me what to do. Now every little thing is just micromanaged. I guess comic books became so successful that they could afford to hire all these editors. [Laughs.]

Gotham Gazette Exclusive

Kelley Jones

Working in the tradition of artists Graham Ingels and Bernie Wrightson, artist Kelley Jones channeled his love of horror fiction into the Dark Knight. With writer Doug Moench, Jones crafted the bestselling 1991 graphic novel *Batman & Dracula: Red Rain* and its sequels before enjoying a successful run on the monthly *Batman* book.

What was your first exposure to Batman?

If I had to say what made an impression on me and was my first real contact with him, it came from the Marshall Rogers run in *Detective Comics* with Steve Englehart. I still think that's probably my favorite version. Favorite story. Favorite artist. Favorite writer. Favorite everything. I was very lucky in that the first one I ever read was the definitive one in my head. All the things that made Batman work for me were there. It was specifically in Marshall Rogers' approach. It was extremely cinematic, iconic in every sense. Everything he did was as it should be. I read wonderful stuff by other people, but that always stays in my head, and when I reread them I don't see any nuts or bolts. I just get swept away all over again.

The first Batman story you illustrated was *Red Rain*.

Yeah. I came upon Doug Moench when he had read my *Deadman* stories. He had liked them quite a bit. At that time, when I was doing *Sandman*, I was working with [inker] Malcolm Jones, who was then associated with Doug on another project. That subject had come up, and Malcolm called me and said, "Do you want to hear the pitch?" I said, "Absolutely."

So I was very excited just to speak to Doug. But when he first mentioned the book, I was so excited I thought it just sounded terrible. [Laughs.] Because he told me, "Batman fights Dracula." I was thinking I was gonna get the Joker or the Penguin or any of these great rogues. Then I got his treatment in the mail and thought it was an absolute work of genius. From that point he left it open to my interpretation and we just went to town. I had no idea that it would become as successful as it became. The fact that it sold out the weekend of its release was beyond my dreams, much less that there would be two sequels. I never would have thought that. It was a miracle that I got to do it, and I thought that was the end of my involvement with Batman after I finished it. I figured I'd go back to doing monsters and horror and all that kind of stuff.

You applied a gothic horror sensibility to Batman most artists hadn't.

Yeah. I'm also very into the films of Orson Welles, and at that time I used that to be a little more symbolic, a little more cinematic. Using lights and darks, layering panels, doing foreground, midground, background, more than using traditional perspective. Just anything as an angle.

When it came to doing Batman himself, I started thinking that his first power would be fear. So I always tried to make him frightening, all the time. Other than the insane rogues gallery, once he tells you, "Don't be a criminal in my city," you wouldn't be a criminal in his city anymore. So that affected the drawing. I didn't want to be caught up in the typical things, using just simple anatomy like you would use in a comic. I thought it would be about the cape.

It wouldn't be just the physical presence of his body, but of that cape. I didn't want it static. It would always be moving. It would fit my needs for whatever I needed in that panel. I wanted the cowl demonic. I didn't think, "How would this work? How would this really be?" I didn't want that kind of realism. Everything else was gonna be real. Everything else was real. But not him.

So when I would do that I would think, "He has to be that guy who, when he appears, is already in the room with you before you know he's in the room." That kind of thing. So you try to project fear through that. If I could get that across, that opened up my style. It gives you something to work on beyond just the script. You interpret it through that lens.

Your Batman still has the longest ears of any Batman.
Why not? It's comics. If I wanted realism I can get that anywhere. I don't want to look like all the other guys. Neal Adams already did a realistic Batman. I'm *not* gonna beat that. He's an incredible draftsman and I'm not. So the only thing you can bring to the table is your own sensibility. That's the only thing original an artist really can do. That creates your own language and that hopefully will bring people into what you're trying to say.

When I first started doing it, [editor] Denny O'Neil said he thought he saw something good going on. Well, he had worked with Marshall and with Neal and with everybody else. So if he was saying that…It gave me courage.

You and Doug Moench appeared to be pretty simpatico.
Yeah. At the same time, when we came to the regular series, he didn't want me to do it. When it was offered to me, he didn't know it was offered to me. But I knew he didn't want me to do it. He wanted to continue doing other things. But I wasn't gonna pass that up. On a complete other level, as a comic book artist, you have to do something on that level of notoriety where you can plant your flag. It can't be a little run here, a little run there. Monthly comics separate the men from the boys, you know?

So I committed myself. I signed that contract. Doug was not happy. He only became happy when I said, "Look, Doug, you can now write whatever stories you want. You can write your paranoia stories. You can write your gothic stories. You can write whatever you want. It will not be what you had to do before, where you had to do more of a mainstream Batman thing. You can do that kind of odd thing you do because I'll be on your side." He said, "If you're late once, I'll kill you." [Laughs.] So I said, "All right." Other than when they moved the publishing release dates, we were on time every month…I have a lot of respect for guys who can make a monthly deadline. That was the hardest period of my career, and the best.

Your villains were as outré as your Batman.
There were surprises. I didn't realize I'd enjoy Man-Bat as much as I did. I didn't even think I'd love Scarecrow. I remember groaning when

he said he wanted to do a Scarecrow story, and I loved it afterward…I really wanted to do Mr. Freeze, and we were told no. Because the company thought Mr. Freeze was stupid. We only got one issue, but it reintroduced him and they put him in [*Batman & Robin*] after that. They changed him from the *Animated Series* version to our version. At that point, he came back as a legitimate villain. I thought he was terrifying, but tragic at the same time. So I just revamped him real quick. They said, "Okay. You never get to ask for anything ever again." [Laughs.] And I didn't. I was a good soldier after that.

I always see the rogues gallery as one big wonderful thing. They're so unique to Batman. I know other characters have their own villains, but they're all uniquely idiosyncratically interesting to Batman. You can do a story without Batman with them in it, and they're still interesting. I always found something uniquely fun about any of these villains. Every time I would draw them it was like I didn't have to follow what someone else did. I can kind of invent my own thing—and it worked! Time has been extremely kind to those stories. It was a lot of work, but I now feel pretty good about how those hold up. I always get a kick out of it when people tell me, "This could come out now." That's a good feeling.

Your work also emphasized that the world Batman inhabits is just as important as he is.

I always thought Gotham was a character. So I drew Gotham as some parts modern, some parts old. Some parts American, some parts European. It was bits and pieces of everything. Because it was a living thing to me. I told Doug once, "I think Gotham makes these people this way, so I want it to be a character. It isn't evil, because it made him. It made Batman. But it's almost Tolkienesque, this place that shapes what's around it." Doug glommed onto that, and there we went. People will say, "You drew Batman!" I say, "And Gotham too!" Because Gotham was as long-eared, as it were, as Batman was.

47 The Long Halloween

By the mid-1990s, multi-title crossover storylines, gimmick covers, and character deaths and rebirths had so come to dominate superhero comics that skeptics wondered if mere *stories* could still enrapture audiences the way they had in 1980s books such as *The Dark Knight Returns* and *The Saga of the Swamp Thing*. For Batman fans, the answer arrived in 1996's 13-issue prestige-format limited series *The Long Halloween*.

Writer Jeph Loeb and artist Tim Sale had won a following with the three annual *Batman: Legends of the Dark Knight Halloween Special* titles they'd produced from 1993 to 1995, each a seasonal treat set—like the monthly *Legends of the Dark Knight* series—early in the Batman's career. For their first extended Batman story they returned to a period shortly after that portrayed in Frank Miller and David Mazzucchelli's 1987 *Batman: Year One*, which introduced crime boss Carmine "The Roman" Falcone and featured young assistant district attorney Harvey Dent.

In *The Long Halloween*, Dent, now a DA, is caught up in a yearlong murder mystery / crime drama pitting Falcone against rival mob leader Sal Maroni, while a mysterious figure named Holiday carries out a string of apparently random underworld killings on national holidays. As Batman partners with James Gordon and Dent to put a stop to the murders, the latter meets his destiny as Two-Face, and Gotham's gangsters lose their hold on the city to the Batman's rogues gallery.

A seminal tale of the Dark Knight, *The Long Halloween* works, like most of Loeb and Sale's collaborations, by offering just enough of a spin on genre conventions for the artist's gothic-noir nightmares to flourish. Sale's reimaginings of Gotham's denizens draw from a variety of illustration and comic traditions, yet his style is among the most distinct of all Batman artists. Showcasing his work at its best, *The Long Halloween* won the 1998 Eisner Award for Best Limited Series.

The Long Halloween's depiction of the city's crime families, and of Harvey Dent, was one of the acknowledged inspirations for writer-director Christopher Nolan's *Batman Begins* and its sequel, *The Dark Knight*, as well as TV's *Gotham*. In 1998, Loeb and Sale followed their opus with a 14-issue sequel, *Batman: Dark Victory*, and in 2004 with a related limited series, the six-issue *Catwoman: When in Rome*.

"When we work together," says Sale of the duo's approach to handling iconic characters, "what we bring to it is: 'Okay, what was really cool about these guys that made them stick around for years?' That's the kind of stuff that we want to do. And tell those stories in a more contemporary way, but not get bogged down by all the bullshit of what's come to be known as continuity...At some point, both [Marvel and DC] discovered that you could fill a ton of comics by making things more convoluted. It's just not what I'm interested in doing."

Gotham Gazette Exclusive

Tim Sale

Artist Tim Sale's idiosyncratic, expressionistic vision of Gotham City in his collaborations with writer Jeph Loeb—most notably the *Legends of the Dark Knight Halloween Special*, *The Long Halloween*, and *Dark Victory*—won him a legion of admirers and informed Christopher Nolan's Dark Knight trilogy.

Your first Batman work was "Blades," the *Legends of the Dark Knight* story arc you did with writer James Robinson.
I met James at the San Diego Comic-Con. At one point we were talking on the phone, and he told me that he had sold a script to editor Archie

Goodwin for a *Legends of the Dark Knight* story. I said, "Do you have an artist?" He said, "No, I don't." I said, "What about me?" And that was "Blades." When I finished that, it turned out—I didn't know it at the time—Jeph had been jealous. Jealous that I'd gotten to work on Batman, but also that I'd worked with another writer. He's very possessive in that way. But when I was done with "Blades," Jeph—really for the first time—expressed his desire to do a Batman story.

So I called Archie and said, "Could I possibly do another one of these with Jeph?" I didn't really know what to expect, because no artist had really ever done more than one arc on *Legends*. So I thought maybe that was a rule. But Archie said, "Yeah." So the first *Halloween Special* began as a story arc, in concept, on *Legends*.

How did you and Jeph collaborate on *The Long Halloween*?
We'd throw around a lot of different ways of working in the beginning. But Jeph had never written a comic before working with me [on *Challengers of the Unknown*]. And there was a lot of artwork that got thrown away that I did thinking we could have more back and forth. Well, the problem is, his stuff is words but mine is a daylong drawing, right? If he says, "No," or what I've done gives him an idea for something else that works better, I've still spent an awful lot of time doing something. There was an awful lot of that early on. For a number of years, all the *Halloween Special* books were produced this way.

By the time we got to *The Long Halloween* it wasn't done that way anymore. But all of the *Halloween Special* books were five- or six-hour phone calls, where he would get a yellow legal pad, and take a credit card, and draw a rectangle on the legal pad, and the rectangle would be the comic page. He'd divide it up into panels and he'd make little notes and call me and describe the book to me. And I would do the equivalent on my end, drawing rectangles and making notes and saying what they were. But it was a really good way for us to get to know each other.

Frank Miller and David Mazzucchelli were big, big influences early on. But other comics, dating from the mid-'60s on, were also touch points, because we remembered when Neal Adams did that or Jim Steranko did that. We'd just riff on that...It's very seamless now. It took a long time to get there, but it was worth it. He now writes a full script.

You've described your joint approach to superheroes as a boiling down of characters and their mythology to their basic elements.
Right...In the same way that I like three panels to a page, and I like a high-contrast look in my artwork. I don't use full bleeds. I don't break the panel border, either with balloons or with artwork. I like a cleaner look aesthetically.

Let's say somebody loves the new Batman movie, and they go, "I'm gonna go check out Batman comics. I haven't seen one in 20 years." They go and they see there's a million speed lines and a million panels and a million words on a page. They're gonna go, "Okay, this is too much work." I know that *I* look at those pages and *I* think it's too much work to follow. I'm interested in being somebody where they can open my book and go, "Well, that's kind of cool. I wonder what happens next." I think one of the ways to do that is to not have it so busy all the time.

After *The Long Halloween*, you and Jeph collaborated on its sequel, *Dark Victory*.
I'm in the minority in that I much prefer it to *Long Halloween*. I know that my work is better. I was a much better artist by the time I got to it than I was when we did *Long Halloween*. I actually think Jeph's writing is better, in almost every respect. What it doesn't have is that it's not the first, and so it doesn't have blush of the first, and the sort of groundbreaking quality, as it were, of *Long Halloween*. Most people don't look at it in the same way, or consider it the bastard stepchild. But I feel the opposite way about it.

It was also great to come back to it right after doing something so completely different in *Superman for All Seasons*. To come back to Batman really felt like coming home again. I just loved drawing Batman in that world. I hope I always have the opportunity to do that. I just think he's a really great character, and I think he really fits me. Or I fit him. However that works. [Laughs.]

48 *Batman: The Movie* (1966)

Though the 1943 *Batman* film serial marked the Caped Crusaders' first adventure on the big screen, it wasn't until 1966 that Batman and Robin appeared in a feature film. In July of that year, riding the crest of the wave of Batmania spawned by their hit TV series, the Dynamic Duo starred in the first color superhero movie: *Batman.*

Their debut would have happened sooner. *Batman: The Movie* (as it's often called) was supposed to kick off their ABC show. But a dearth of quality programming prompted the network to change its plans and premiere the series first, in January of 1966. While that first season was still in production, film sets were constructed based on executive story editor Lorenzo Semple Jr.'s script. When the season wrapped, actors Adam West and Burt Ward immediately began work on the film under the direction of famously fast-working Leslie H. Martinson, who'd helmed the show's episodes "The Penguin Goes Straight" and "Not Yet He Ain't." West and Ward were joined by co-stars Alan Napier (as Alfred), Neil Hamilton (as Commissioner Gordon), and Stafford Repp (as Chief O'Hara). Matching wits with the heroes were a cadre of their most fiendish foes, including Frank Gorshin's Riddler, Cesar Romero's Joker, and Burgess Meredith's Penguin. With Julie Newmar unavailable to reprise her role as Catwoman (which she'd played in just one first-season story), a replacement was found in former Miss America 1955, actress Lee Meriwether.

With the film's budget of $1.5 million, the producers pounced on the opportunity to furnish the Dynamic Duo with new toys, including the Batcopter, a Bell helicopter customized with scalloped wings (first seen in May 1951's *Detective Comics* #151), and the Batboat (first seen in April 1946's *Detective Comics* #110). The latter, a Glastron V-174 designed by Mel Whitley and Robert Hammond, featured glowing Bat eyes, a red flashing Bat beacon, Batzooka hatches, a scalloped tailfin with glowing Bat-Signal, and, best of all, a faux jet nozzle and water squirter to make it appear the boat, like its cousin the Batmobile, was powered by nuclear energy. (One of two Batboats built can be viewed today in the Hollywood Car Stars Museum in Gatlinburg, Tennessee). The production was so enamored of the Batboat that the film's premiere was held, on July 30, 1966, at the Paramount Theatre in Austin, Texas, the home of Glastron Industries.

With a script as zany as any of the television show's, albeit packed with more zingers, *Batman: The Movie* finds its four "super-criminals" (the "United Underworld") kidnapping one Commodore Schmidlapp (played by Reginald Denny) and stealing his dehydration machine in order to capture the "United World" security council and seize control of the planet, with the aid of the Penguin's pre-nuclear

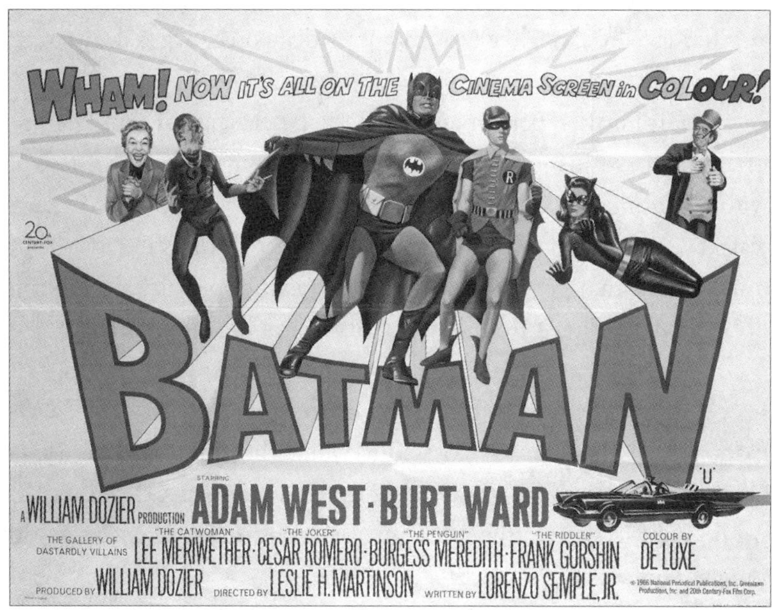

Batman, Robin, and their rogues gallery from the 1966 Batman *television series made the jump to the silver screen later that same year.*

submarine. As part of their plan, Catwoman, disguised as Russian reporter Miss Kitka, seduces Batman in his guise as Bruce Wayne in order to lure the Caped Crusaders into her cohorts' clutches.

Like the series, *Batman: The Movie* is a surprisingly faithful adaptation of the 1950s/early 1960s comics, right down to the name of Catwoman's cat, Hecate. Shot on location in Los Angeles and at Stearns Wharf in Santa Barbara, it's enormous fun, enlivened with exploding octopi, Shark Repellent Bat Spray, and a self-sacrificing porpoise. It's also capped with the nascent franchise's first stabs at the kind of political satire found in the era's *MAD* magazine and *The Smothers Brothers Comedy Hour*. "Disposing of pre-atomic submarines to persons who don't even leave their full addresses?" says a disgusted Batman on a phone call with a Pentagon official playing tiddlywinks with his secretary. "Good day, Admiral!"

The film also gave West more screen time than usual as Bruce Wayne, performing many of his own stunts. He also generates plenty of chemistry with Meriwether, as both Bond girl–esque Kitka and her catsuit-clad alter ego, the most deliciously wicked of screen Catwomen.

Regarding her performance, Meriwether says, "From the age of about six to just a few years ago, just about every night, I slept with a cat one way or another. The purr comes naturally. My purr wasn't as good as Eartha Kitt's. I don't know how she did it, but mine wasn't that good. But the meow was my specialty. It's a kind of 'Mrowrrr.' That's from having cats in my life all my life."

Sadly, the enormous popularity the series enjoyed in its first season didn't carry over to the box office, and *Batman: The Movie* made little more than it cost. But when the show was denied a home video release for many decades (over rights issues and cross-studio conflicts), the film brought the series' candy-colored world to new fans via VHS and DVD.

As Batman himself puts it in the movie's most famous scene, "Some days, you just can't get rid of a bomb."

Gotham Gazette Exclusive

Lee Meriwether

Before she starred in TV's *Time Tunnel* or received an Emmy nomination for her role in *Barnaby Jones*, former Miss America Lee Meriwether became the first actress to play Catwoman on the silver screen, in 1966's *Batman: The Movie*.

Were you a cat lover before playing Catwoman?
Oh yes! It really was an easy slide in for me, because I had cats all my life. And now my daughters have cats. So I come and visit them. [Laughs.]

So you looked at cats as your inspiration for the role?
Oh yes. I hadn't seen Julie [Newmar] perform. I was surprised that they were looking for a Catwoman for a film. Because she had done it, but she was already into another film. She was working at another studio, and I think at that time well into filming the movie. So that's why they had the audition for gals to come in and read for the part. Luckily I did all the right things. I did all sorts of purring and kneading my knees (I was sitting while reading) and licking my hand, rubbing my cheek and all of that. [Laughs.] Doing many of the cat things that I had watched my cats do for years.

Then as I left the room, I heard someone—I assume it was the director [Leslie H. Martinson]—say to the people I'd read for, "I didn't tell her to do any of that." [Laughs.] So I guess that helped a lot. Thank goodness for cats.

At that time were you already aware of what a phenomenon the 1966 *Batman* TV series had become?
No, not really. I loved watching the show. And to be even considered just a little bit for the movie, I was—oh my gosh—very, very excited about it. I was lucky. I was the lucky one. I was really very fortunate in many, many ways. Because I was able to work with the villains—the geniuses—these men, Frank Gorshin, Burgess Meredith, Cesar Romero...Oh my goodness. These men were just gems. I was so

lucky to work with them. And lucky to work with Burt and Adam as well. [Laughs.] Because they were wonderful.

What were your fellow villains like in real life? Were they as charismatic as they were on screen?

Oh yes, and I learned so much from them. I watched them work out pieces of business. Burgess worked on his cigarette holder, and the cigarette at the end of the holder—making it fall and holding on to it. He was working on holding it in his mouth, and having to say, "Run silent. Run deep." It was up high and then he has it drop. Next time you see it, just wait for that. Because he worked on that for, I'd say, easily 20 minutes. To get that just right. He was off on the side when he wasn't filming. I watched him and I thought, "Oh my, what dedication, and he's getting it right."

They worked on their roles. Frank was always exercising, because he had to jump around a lot and be nimble and all of that. So he kept himself healthy.

In one scene…I don't know how he did it because he really didn't have a chance to run through it. He wanted to show off the outfit that had been made especially for him by the costume department. He wanted to wear the jacket that came with the outfit. Because he loved it! He just flipped over it. It's got all the question marks all over it, little purple ones. He had asked permission, but the director said, "No, just leave it. Just do what you're supposed to do. We don't have the time to cover it." So he did it in one take. He walked past me, goes behind us, went to the coatrack, and there was his jacket. He put it on and stood there and said his lines, and the director said, "Cut! Okay, yes, print." Frank knew enough about film that he knew it would be taken care of and he could do it. He was great.

And Cesar…I watched him dedicate at least 15 minutes to get his wrists to turn with those joy buzzers in his hand, where he had to grab people and make them shake. He worked on that as long as Burgess worked on dropping the cigarette holder. It was wild. We had such a good time. I really was most fortunate to work with them. It was like going to film school. I saw masters at work, and I benefited from it, definitely.

And I learned from Burt and Adam. I didn't work as much with Burt as I did with Adam. But Adam…That was a fine line that he walked in that part. Because it could have been so supercilious, and it wasn't. It could have been somewhat trying on the other end of it, and he just kept going and he was just so good. I was lucky to get in the group. We all did have a good time. I was so grateful for that job.

The romantic scenes between your character and Bruce Wayne worked especially well.
Oh yes. Even though I was evil Kitka. [Laughs.] But I tried not to be totally evil. I wanted it to be possible that that relationship *could* happen. It was a fine line I had to trod too. [Laughs.] Adam made it so easy. He really did. He's a very personable guy, and, as I said, a very good actor. I've seen him in other roles on stage several times, and he's always been true to the script, true to character. They were lucky to have him.

How did you approach the role?
I tried to stay within the boundaries of the script. I saw the humor of it, and so I pulled back a touch…Burgess was hysterical. You know where he's dehydrated the [United World ambassadors] and they're little piles of dust and I've got the brush and dustpan? We're filming, and I'm starting to brush them up, and he ad-libs, "Careful! Everyone has a mother…" [Laughs.] So we had to do that over again. It was hysterical. I literally did fall over and giggle up a storm. Oh, he was funny. He really was funny. He was very witty.

The film began shooting immediately after the show's first season wrapped. Was it a very fast-paced shoot?
It was. I don't know that they were on a timeline that kept them going, but I do know the filming was completed in 18 days. Everybody stood around and went, "Wow, that went fast." [Laughs.] Heaven, I've been on other movies that have taken months, but 18 days…From what I heard, I think that they had that limit of time placed upon them. But it wasn't rigorous for us at all. We all did our job, learned our lines, got there on time, listened to the director, and had a wonderful time. I loved doing it.

Adam is always talking about how uncomfortable the Batsuit was. Was the Catsuit any more comfortable?
It was uncomfortable. Difficult to get out of. In the sun outside, my top and sides would get sunburned. It was metallic, to make it shimmer. There were metallic threads in the material. I don't know where they got them, but it conducted heat and I had [a] sunburn. [Laughs.]

Do you have a favorite scene in the film, or a favorite line of dialogue?
They jump to a scene where I had to say my name, Kitka—saying "Kitayna Ireyna Tatanya Kerenska Alisoff." I hadn't worked on it. I hadn't learned that speech. I didn't know we were doing that scene that day. So I went off in the corner and just ran the names over and over and over, praying, "Please help me remember this!" And I was able to do it. As such, I've never been able to forget those names. [Laughs.] They're emblazoned in my brain somewhere.

The final battle atop the Penguin's submarine was filmed at 20th Century Fox?
That was on the backlot. We were in a tank. I forget what the measurement of water was. But one of the stuntmen was injured by falling off and falling into the water. He hit his head. Oh my gosh, we were all so scared for him. Because they pulled him out of the water and did CPR and he was fine, but he had to go to the hospital because he was bleeding horribly. I went to the hospital. He was coming out of it after he had all sorts of stitches and things done. I said, "Do you need anything? Can I get you anything?" He said, "Just give me a kiss." I said, "Oh, you can have as many was you want!" He was one of the henchmen who worked throughout the film. He was a nice guy, so… [Laughs.]

Why do you think Catwoman remains such an icon?
I know, and I have no answers for you. It's just a wonder. [Laughs.] A lot of people gravitate toward animals. Whether they know it or not, they are partial to certain animals. For a cat to become an iconic figure is a little strange, but I understand it. I'm certainly glad that it's lasted that long.

Have you met any of the actresses who've since played the role?
Of course I've known Julie for quite some time. I've even been in a show with her. I know her well...Anne Hathaway I met in passing. But she didn't know who I was, and I just couldn't stop her to say, "I played Catwoman!" So I just let it go. And Halle Berry, she had the best costume I think of all of us. And we're very jealous. Or anyway I am. I told her that too, and she laughed hysterically. [Laughs.]

As the person who defined Catwoman in movies, what are your thoughts on the performances of those who followed you?
I think they all brought their own talents to it. They're gorgeous women and wonderful actresses. So, given another chance to play Catwoman, I'd steal any number of things from them. [Laughs.] No, that's a joke. But I admire them tremendously. They are all wonderful.

49 The Top Five Vintage Batman Collectibles

When the *Batman* TV show premiered in January 1966 it launched the first wave of Batmania. Here are five of the most coveted collectibles to ride that wave.

Marx Batman Action Figure

The Mego toys of the 1970s are much loved, but the first poseable Batman action figure was a plastic, four-inch version of the Caped Crusader from the Marx Toy Company. It came packaged with a removable cape, as well as Bat-rope, Bat-cuffs, a Batarang, and other accessories.

Topps Batman Trading Cards

In 1962, artists Bob Powell and Norm Saunders illustrated the Topps Company's infamous *Mars Attacks* series of trading cards.

Four years later, Powell penciled and Saunders provided finished paints for three series of Batman cards, offering a spectacularly violent, pulp-influenced alternative to the 1966 show's capers. In 1989, Topps reprinted the combined 143-card set in a "Deluxe Reissue Edition"—including such unforgettable images as the Riddler preparing to brand a terrified Robin with a hot iron in the shape of a question mark.

Bump-N-Go Batmobile

There's no shortage of toy Batmobiles available to fans of the 1966 *Batman*'s iconic George Barris–designed auto. The most iconic of them was made in 1966 by Britain's Corgi Toys. The coolest, however, is Azak Hamway International's Japanese-manufactured, bright-blue, battery-operated, tinplate Bump-N-Go Batmobile, featuring dazzling lights and sound effects.

Batman Utility Belt

The vintage toy most coveted by collectors—and the one most difficult to find complete in its original packaging—is the Ideal Toy Company's Official Batman Utility Belt. It featured a "Complete Set of Crime Fighting Equipment," including "Bat-a-rang," "Bat-Signal Flash" flashlight, "Bat-Gun Launcher," and "Bat-Rocket Grenade." Have money to burn? Ideal also packaged the belt with a helmet and cape in the Batman Equipment Set.

Batman Water Gun

The most absurd piece of merchandise inspired by the show is without question the 1966 Japanese-made Batman squirt gun, originally available for just 39 cents. Kids poured water into a small hole in the Caped Crusader's posterior, squeezed a trigger mounted on his crotch, and shot water out of his mouth. Even the Joker has never known such madness.

50 Robin IV: Stephanie Brown (aka Spoiler)

Robin is commonly referred to as the Boy Wonder, but two young women have donned the yellow cape and domino mask of Batman's sidekick: Carrie Kelley, in the 1986 alternative-future limited series *The Dark Knight Returns*, and Stephanie Brown, who, for a brief time, was the official fourth Robin.

The daughter of Arthur Brown, aka the second-rate villain Cluemaster, Stephanie made her debut in August 1992's *Detective Comics* #647 ("Inquiring Minds," by writer Chuck Dixon and penciler Tom Lyle). Intended as a one-off character, the blonde teenager first appears in the guise of the Spoiler, a vigilante in purple cloak and hood who leaves clues designed to spoil her father's criminal plans. Her clues are found by Batman and the third Robin, Tim Drake, who help her take down her dad.

Enjoying her new role, Stephanie continued fighting crime as the Spoiler, in part so she could see more of Robin, on whom she developed a crush. Though Robin knew her real identity, she didn't know Robin's, and so she began dating Tim. Soon after, Stephanie became pregnant with the child of her ex, and Tim helped her through her pregnancy, her delivery, and in giving her baby up for adoption. When Tim was sent by Batman on a secret mission that took him outside of Gotham, the Dark Knight revealed to Stephanie Tim's identity, and trained her with the help of the Birds of Prey and Batgirl Cassandra Cain. Batman ultimately decided Stephanie wasn't cut out to be a superhero, but Stephanie continued patrolling and dating Tim upon his return.

More tragedy invaded Stephanie's life when she learned her father had died on a mission with the Suicide Squad, leading

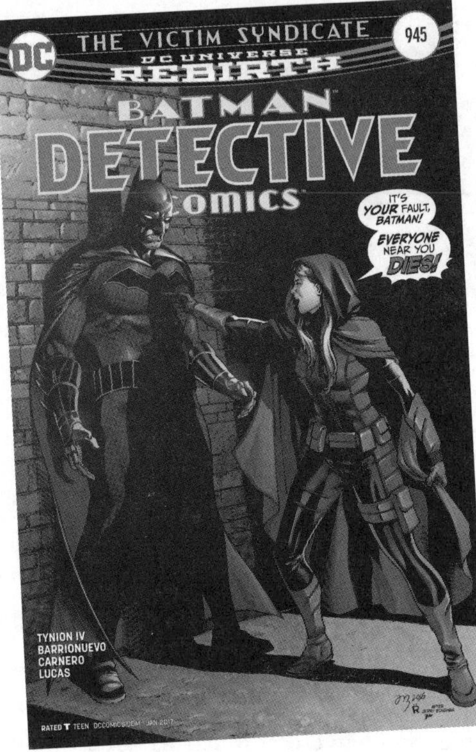

Stephanie Brown, the daughter of a criminal, adopted the vigilante persona of Spoiler and later became the fourth person officially known as Robin. (Cover art by Alvaro Martínez Raúl Fernández and Brad Anderson)

Stephanie to take out her anger on Gotham's criminal population. Tim's father then learned he was Robin and demanded he hang up his cape for good, relocating his son to a private school outside of town. In July 2004's *Robin* #126 ("A Life More Ordinary," written by Bill Willingham and penciled by Damion Scott), Stephanie mistakenly believes Tim is cheating on her. In a fit of rage, she makes her own Robin costume, breaks into the Batcave, and insists Batman make her his new Robin. To her surprise, the Dark Knight agrees. He trains her for three months, then allows her to fight by his side.

But when Stephanie ended up disobeying Batman in order to save his life, he fired her; the Dark Knight feared she'd end up like the second Robin, Jason Todd, who'd also refused to take orders. Stephanie then accessed the Batcave's computer, stole one of Batman's plans for wiping out Gotham's underworld, and inadvertently started a gang war that resulted in her getting kidnapped and tortured by Black Mask. She escaped, and received medical care from Dr. Leslie Thompkins, but her injuries were too severe. To Batman's horror, she died in the hospital.

Stephanie's death was eventually explained as the result of Thompkins' deliberate negligence, in an effort to convince Batman to end his crusade. This explanation was later changed when it was revealed Stephanie wasn't dead after all, and that Thompkins had faked her death in order to spare her any retaliation from Batman's enemies.

Following the events of DC's "Final Crisis," with Bruce Wayne believed dead, Cassandra Cain retired from being Batgirl and Stephanie replaced her in the role, winning her own series with August 2009's *Batgirl* #1. The original Batgirl, Barbara Gordon, served as Stephanie's new mentor, and gave her a vehicle of her own, the Batcycle-derived Ricochet. When Bruce Wayne returned, he gave Stephanie his blessing to continue as Batgirl.

When DC's "New 52" reboot occurred, Barbara Gordon again became Batgirl and Stephanie was taken out of continuity. But petitioning on the part of her many fans led to her return as Spoiler in the 2014's series *Batman Eternal.* The year prior, Stephanie had made her screen debut in the 2013 *Young Justice* episode "Before the Dawn," in which she was voiced by Mae Whitman.

With Stephanie back as Spoiler in DC's "Rebirth" relaunch, there's little doubt she'll remain a vital part of the Batman's world. Forever a Girl Wonder.

51 Batman on the Radio

Six years after he debuted in *Detective Comics* #27, and three years after his first movie serial premiered, superhero fans heard the Dark Knight breathe on the radio.

It happened when Batman met the Man of Steel in the latter's show *The Adventures of Superman*. Stacy Harris first voiced Batman, opposite Clayton "Budd" Collyer's Superman and Robin Liss' Robin, whom Superman met when he saved him from drowning in Metropolis' North Bay after the Boy Wonder was knocked unconscious by a gang of criminals in the second episode of the 12-part "Mystery of the Waxmen," broadcast on March 1, 1945.

"The boy…he's wearing a cape," says Superman, "and a red leather vest with the letter R on it. Why he must be…Great Scott! Up with him. Up, up, and away!"

Robin tells Superman that Batman has disappeared, and in the next episode they discover the Masked Manhunter has been captured by the evil mastermind Zoltan and placed in his wax museum as a statue. After breaking him out of encasement, Superman meets Batman for the first time in any medium. Later that year, on September 10, the two icons would properly join forces, in the fifth episode of the 14-part "Dr. Blythe's Confidence Gang."

Batman would appear regularly on *The Adventures of Superman*, giving Collyer a break from his duties as both Clark Kent and his alter ego. After his first appearance, Batman's voice was usually provided by Matt Crowley. Two attempts were made to give the character a radio show of his own, but each came to naught. The first occurred in 1943, when a pilot (now lost) was recorded with Scott Douglas voicing Batman. In 1950, a second pilot was produced—for *The Batman Mystery Club*, in which the hero, voiced by John Emery, tells a group of children about his exploits, a series of mysteries involving faux ghosts and spirits a la Hanna-Barbera's *Scooby-Doo* franchise. It's probably all for the best that the latter didn't sell.

52 Batmanga

The best action comics function as fever dreams, as though their creators have witnessed firsthand the stories they're telling. Japanese comics, or manga—longer in length and often more propulsive than their Western counterparts—are ideally suited to deliver this narrative explosion. Fortunately for Batman fans, their hero's adventures have been chronicled in both Japan and the U.S.

When the editors of the weekly manga anthology *Shonen King* learned the 1966 *Batman* TV series was coming to their shores, they asked writer-artist Jiro Kuwata to develop new tales of the Caped Crusaders for Japanese audiences. Kuwata (a disciple of Astro Boy creator and manga pioneer Osamu Tezuka) had already co-created the cybernetic superhero 8 Man, but he was unfamiliar with Batman and Robin. His editors gave him a supply of American comics to bring him up to speed.

As Kuwata explains in Chip Kidd, Geoff Spear, and Saul Ferris' *Bat-Manga! The Secret History of Batman in Japan* (published in 2008 by Pantheon Books), "My initial plan was to practice the realistic and dynamic drawing style of American comics, and then blend it into my original drawings. Even when you just look at the proportions of men drawn in American comics, it is so different from that of the Japanese, which highly interested me and made me think that practicing that style would expand my drawing a great deal. However…I ended up being too busy to try any of that. I couldn't take the time to imitate and practice Bob Kane's Batman at all and had to draw it my own way."

The resulting series was published in *Shonen King* from April 1966 to May 1967, at the height of the show's popularity in Japan. It offers a fascinating glimpse of a familiar world through a very different lens. The design of the Batmobile, for example, and of Batman and Robin's costumes are the same as those in the show and comics, but evil scientists, killer robots, and talking gorillas take precedence over the usual rogues gallery.

Some old enemies, however, reappear under new names. Popular Flash foe the Weather Wizard becomes "Go Go the Magician," and other villains, such as the Outsider and Clayface, are given new alter egos and histories (the latter derives his powers from an "alien life liquid"). Death Man, a one-off villain created by writer Robert Kanigher and artist Sheldon Moldoff for May 1966's *Batman* #180, became "Lord Death Man," the antagonist of Kuwata's first Batman story and one of the most enjoyable. It was adapted by writer Paul Dini into an uncanny pastiche of 1960s anime in a segment of the 2011 *The Brave and the Bold* episode "Bat-Mite Presents: Batman's Strangest Cases!" Writer Grant Morrison also used Lord Death Man in his *Batman Incorporated*.

Starting in 2014, three volumes collecting Kuwata's complete run of Batmanga were finally published in the U.S. by DC. Kuwata's work serves as a cross-cultural romp for readers of all ages and a shining testament to the Dark Knight's universality.

53 Batman: Mask of the Phantasm

The early 1990s were a golden age of feature film animation, with the likes of *Beauty and the Beast*, *Aladdin*, *The Lion King*, and *The Nightmare Before Christmas* packing theaters and winning raves. The decade's most overlooked animated feature, however, is one in which no character sang a note of music—*Batman: Mask of the Phantasm.*

When *Mask of the Phantasm* was released on Christmas Day 1993, some might have found it ironic that the Batman film with the most mature, coherent, and intelligent script to date was a cartoon. If so, they hadn't watched *Batman: The Animated Series*, on which it's based, and the two creators of which—Bruce Timm and Eric Radomski—served as *Phantasm*'s directors.

The film's development began when Timm and Radomski's fellow producer Alan Burnett was informed that Warner Brothers wanted a direct-to-video movie spinoff of the hit show. Burnett wanted to tell a love story, something his team hadn't done in the series. Story editor Michael Reaves suggested a tale about a woman for whom Bruce Wayne almost abandons his career as the Dark Knight.

As Burnett explained in an interview with Bob Garcia in the February 1994 issue of *Cinefantastique*, "Even though it was originally slated for direct-to-video release, I wanted it to have the feel of a movie, and felt we needed really strong emotions. So we decided that years ago, Bruce fell in love with Andrea Beaumont and wanted to marry her. She brought to his life something he hadn't had in years: happiness. Then she left town and severed their relationship."

Almost half of *Mask of the Phantasm*'s 76 minutes is told in a series of flashbacks, detailing not only Bruce (voiced, as in the show, by Kevin Conroy) and Andrea's relationship, but the beginning of Bruce's crimefighting career. Taking its cue from Frank Miller's *Batman: Year One*, *Mask of the Phantasm* shows Bruce making mistakes in his earliest attempts to stop thugs. Meanwhile, a crime drama unfolds, in which Andrea's father gets tangled up with the mob, including one gangster who will become the Joker. In the present, Andrea (voiced by Dana Delany) reenters Bruce's life, and they rekindle their romance. However, a new villain—the spectral Phantasm—appears in Gotham, targeting the city's criminal population and threatening to tear Bruce and Andrea apart once more. In the end, the film's examination of how people respond to tragedy delineates what makes Batman a hero.

"In *Mask of the Phantasm*," says Conroy, recalling his favorite moment in the film, "Batman has a wonderful scene at his parents' gravesite where he's pleading with them to release him from the vow he's made to them. Because he's finally fallen in love and he wants to have a normal life, but he knows he can't...The tragedy of the character is so relatable. That's what people love about him."

Given the freedom allowed by a PG rating, *Mask of the Phantasm* features a small amount of blood and implied sex, two elements forbidden on *Batman: The Animated Series*. Also, its Joker (voiced once more by Mark Hamill, and used far more judiciously here than in the 1989 *Batman*) is permitted to kill people, squirting acid from his lapel flower instead of gas. But what's most impressive is the tragic story it tells of lost love and unrealized dreams, brought to vivid life in a flashback scene at Gotham's shimmering World's Fair, and a gripping climax amidst its crumbling remains.

Production began on *Phantasm* in November of 1992, but it wasn't until February of 1993 that Warner Brothers decided to give the film a theatrical release. It was produced in just eight months, as opposed to the years afforded most animated features. Burnett and

Reaves were able to share the writing chores with series scribes Paul Dini (who handled most of the Joker's scenes) and Martin Pasko (who co-wrote the flashbacks with Burnett), while Timm and Radomski called on the show's directors—Dan Riba, Frank Paur, Kevin Altieri, and Boyd Kirkland—to oversee its sequences. The theatrical release boosted the film's budget to $6 million, allowing for an impressive computer-animated flight through Gotham's concrete canyons in its opening credits. It also permitted composer Shirley Walker to recruit more than twice the number of musicians with whom she recorded the show's music.

Batman: Mask of the Phantasm wound up grossing just $5.6 million upon its release, Warner Brothers' marketing department in 1993 having little idea how to promote a PG-rated animated film. But time has been kinder to it than it was to Bruce and Andrea, and the movie still possesses the tightest, smartest script of any Batman feature.

How odd that a children's film should make fewer commercial concessions than the ostensibly adult Batman epics that followed it. Yet as *Mask of the Phantasm* makes abundantly clear, the child is often parent to the adult.

54 Oracle

Physically impaired superheroes have been a staple of comic books at least as far back as DC's Dr. Mid-Nite (introduced in April 1941's *All-American Comics* #41), a blind man who gained the ability to see in the dark. Few, however, have inspired as many as Oracle.

When Gotham City police commissioner James Gordon forbade his bespectacled, bookish daughter, Barbara, from joining the police force, she slaked her thirst for justice by donning the cape and cowl of Batgirl (in January 1967's *Detective Comics* #359), and battled alongside the Dynamic Duo. But years later, after hanging up her cape and cowl, she was shot in the spine by the Joker, in writer Alan Moore's 1988 graphic novel *The Killing Joke*. Paralyzed from the waist down, it appeared her crimefighting days were over.

But in the wake of *The Killing Joke*'s release, husband-and-wife writing team Kim Yale and John Ostrander saw an opportunity for Barbara to again make a difference as the wheelchair-bound, cyberspace operative and information broker Oracle. She began her new career in January 1989's *Suicide Squa*d #23 (written by Yale and Ostrander and penciled by Luke McDonnell). Barbara anonymously served as an ally of the Squad for many months before her identity was revealed (in *Suicide Squad* #38). Two years later, she forged a new partnership with the Dark Knight and became his primary intelligence source in October 1992's *Batman: Sword of Azrael* #1 (written by Denny O'Neil and penciled by Joe Quesada). She took the name Oracle from the legendary Oracle of Delphi, High Priestess of the Temple of Apollo—the Greek god of music, healing, light, and truth.

Using her background in information science, her photographic memory, and her genius-level intellect, Oracle eventually became the head of operations for the Birds of Prey, the crimefighting team she co-founded with her friend Dinah Lance (aka the Black Canary). After teaming up in June 1996's *Birds of Prey: Black Canary/Oracle* (written by Chuck Dixon and penciled by Gary Frank), the two heroines were joined by the Huntress, and their adventures were brought to television in 2002's short-lived *Bird of Prey* series (in which Oracle was played by Dina Meyer). A version of Oracle also appeared in the 2013 computer-animated series *Beware the Batman* (voiced by Tara Strong).

Controversy erupted when, as part of DC's company-wide "New 52" reboot in 2011, Barbara was de-aged, regained the use of her legs, and resumed the role of Batgirl. By this time, Oracle had been embraced as a triumphant symbol by the disabled community, and her absence was interpreted by many as a sign of disrespect. But *Batgirl* writer Gail Simone defended the changes, claiming that Barbara continued to inspire and was now a version of the character younger than Oracle.

In addition to providing inspiration, the cyberspace goddess paved the way for such super-team coordinating superhackers as *Smallville*'s Chloe Sullivan and *Arrow*'s Felicity Smoak.

Gotham Gazette Exclusive

John Ostrander

In the *Legends* limited series (published in 1986 and 1987), writer John Ostrander introduced the modern incarnation of the Suicide Squad, as well as the Squad's director, Amanda Waller. In the ensuing *Suicide Squad* comics, Ostrander transformed former Batgirl Barbara Gordon into one of the Batman's greatest allies: Oracle.

How did Amanda Waller come about?

I wanted someone who did not have superpowers themselves but was as tough as nails, and I wanted someone of a type that hadn't been seen much. So I thought, "Female. African American. Middle-aged. Heavyset." I wanted the weight because I thought that size would give the impression of will. Because that's what would drive her. You had to get the sense that she was powerful, even without superpowers. She was called the "The Wall," and she even looked a little like a wall. So that's essentially how she came about.

With Amanda, I never thought that she was a villain herself. An antihero? Absolutely. But I never saw her as evil. She always had a very real reason for doing what she was doing. It really was about not just her power but getting the job done. And that the job was *worth* doing. Given her background, she didn't mind using the bad guys. Because she and her family had suffered at the hands of bad people. So she's not terribly sympathetic toward them. If they die along the way, well, too damn bad.

How about Oracle? How did she develop?
My late wife, Kimberly Yale, and I were writing together at that point. We had read *The Killing Joke*. I want to say right off the top that I have vast respect for Alan Moore and Brian Bolland. They are incredible artists. But neither Kim nor I particularly cared for how Barbara Gordon was treated in *The Killing Joke*. She was basically shot and treated as disposable. It looked like she had been beaten up. Possibly raped.

We got the permission to take her and use her however we wanted. So we said, "Okay, if she'd been shot at that angle and at that range…" Well, first of all, she should have been dead. But we went past that and said, "Okay, she's crippled, and that has to be the effect of that story on her. That her back is broken." But then we wanted to show how she could still be a hero. With that, it had already been established that she was very good with computers. So we set up this whole new version of Barbara as this character Oracle, who became this information broker.

We figured that if we created her correctly and interestingly enough she would find a lot of use in the DC Universe. Because other writers would go, "Oh, this simplifies my plot a whole lot." Rather than have people run around and have to find out this and have to find out that, they could just go check with Oracle, and Oracle finds it out for them. As a result, she wound up being tremendously useful in the DC Universe; and in fact was the lynchpin for *Birds of Prey*, both the comic book and the TV show.

So she was a fantastically successful character, and we got wonderful letters from people who were physically challenged, who had difficulties the way Barbara did. To show that Barbara overcame them, and that Barbara was still a hero, that was very important to them. That was very gratifying to read.

When DC restored Barbara's ability to walk, those fans spoke up.
I'm aware of the controversy at that time. In fact, Gail Simone—who's a friend and a wonderful writer—took me aside at a convention to tell me what was going to happen. She told me that she was [doing] the new *Batgirl* book for two reasons—A.) because she loved Batgirl, and B.) it was going to happen anyway, so she wanted to be the one to do

it, since she felt that she could keep it as consistent as possible with the Oracle incarnation.

Oracle appears to have inspired other information brokers in DC projects. For example, *Smallville*'s Chloe Sullivan performed a similar role in that show's continuity.
Oh yeah. And Felicity in *Arrow.* In fact, I think they were teasing around at one point where they said she needed a superhero name. The Green Arrow said, "We can't give you Oracle because that's already taken." It was a little nod of the hat to us...Yeah, Felicity is my favorite on *Arrow.* No disrespect to anyone else. [Laughs.]

55 See the Batmobile

"Atomic batteries to power. Turbines to speed..."

Batman fans don't have to travel to Gotham City to catch a glimpse of the Batmobile. A trip to Los Angeles will suffice.

Designer George Barris, the "King of the Kustomizers," sadly passed away in 2015, but his legacy lives on through the many fantastic vehicles he created for film and television, the most famous of which is the customized 1950s Lincoln Futura concept car (originally built by the Italian company Carrozzeria Ghia) that served as Batman and Robin's chief means of transportation in the 1966 *Batman* TV series.

The original prototype was sold at auction in 2013 for $4.6 million to Arizona car collector Rick Champagne. But a duplicate car fashioned out of a 1970s Ford chassis by customizer Bob Butts, which Barris often took to car shows and comic book conventions, remains on display in the front showroom of Barris Kustom

Industries (aka Barris Kustom City), located at 10811 Riverside Drive in North Hollywood, California.

You can see the world-famous convertible through the shop's front window, but pop in for a closer look. It sits alongside some of the King's other creations, including the almost-as-famous Munster Koach from another iconic 1960s show, *The Munsters.*

At the time of this writing, the Batmobiles from the 1989 *Batman* film and 1995's *Batman Forever,* as well as a Tumbler from 2012's *The Dark Knight Rises* and the Batmobile from 2016's *Batman v Superman: Dawn of Justice* can be seen in the Picture Car Vault on the Warner Bros. Studio Tour in nearby Burbank. The Batmobile from 1992's *Batman Returns* is on permanent display at L.A.'s Petersen Automotive Museum.

Batfans can get up close and personal with several Batmobiles, including the Tumbler from Christopher Nolan's cinematic trilogy, on the Warner Bros. Studio Tour in Burbank, California. (Sophia Quach McCabe)

56 Gotham by Gaslight

The DC comic books of the 1950s offered a multitude of "imaginary" stories, tales too outrageous for even that decade's fanciful sensibilities, and so disregarded as canon. Decades later, when Frank Miller's *The Dark Knight Returns* proved outré visions of Batman could result in massive sales, creators again began presenting alternate realities for the Caped Crusader, albeit considerably more adult than the 1950s tales. The first one of note was the February 1989 one-shot special *Gotham by Gaslight.*

Written by Brian Augustyn, penciled by Mike (then credited as Michael) Mignola, and inked by P. Craig Russell, the 48-page *Gotham by Gaslight* pits the Dark Knight against one of history's most infamous villains: Jack the Ripper. It begins in 1889 Vienna, with Bruce Wayne studying the human mind under Sigmund Freud, describing a dream in which his parents' murderer is stopped from killing him as well by a cloud of bats. After many years abroad, Bruce returns to Gotham, intent on starting his war on crime, only to find his home terrorized by the Ripper, who describes the city as "an overripe fruit...fat, fetid, and fit to burst." Before he can catch the maniac, he's framed for his crimes, arrested by his friend Inspector Gordon, and sentenced to hang. The twist that follows fuses the Ripper's history to that of the "Bat-Man."

Gotham by Gaslight's success led to a sequel, 1991's *Batman: Master of the Future* (again written by Augustyn, with art by Eduardo Barreto), and the creation of DC's "Elseworlds" label for similarly apocryphal tales like *Batman: Holy Terror* and *Batman & Dracula: Red Rain*. It also helped usher the then-burgeoning steampunk literary subgenre into mainstream American comics, and so paved the way for Alan Moore's *The League of Extraordinary*

Gentlemen and Mignola's original creation Hellboy. The Dark Knight's *Gaslight* costume was translated to film for a sequence in Zack Snyder's *Batman v Superman: Dawn of Justice*.

57 Batman vs. The Incredible Hulk

Hard as it might be to believe in these days of box-office battles between rival billion-dollar superhero universes, there was once a time when DC and Marvel Comics joined forces to tell stories of their costumed champions crossing over into each other's worlds. The first such union occurred in the 1976 oversized "treasury edition" title *Superman vs. The Amazing Spider-Man*, followed by July 1981's *Superman and Spider-Man*. Not content to let the Man of Steel have all the fun, the Dark Knight got in on the action a few months later. The September 1981 issue of *DC Special Series* #27 contained a 64-page story called "The Monster and the Madman," better known as *Batman vs. The Incredible Hulk*.

The unlikely pairing occurs when an old foe of the Hulk, the cosmic Shaper of Worlds, lands in Gotham City. His body damaged from his space travels, he meets the Joker, and uses the Clown Prince of Crime to acquire a gamma gun developed by Wayne Research. With the gun, the Joker is able to heal the Shaper, and, in exchange, is granted near limitless power (anticipating the "Emperor Joker" storyline that ran across DC's Superman titles in 2000). As per the rules of such first meetings, Batman and the Hulk (who calls the Caped Crusader "Pointy Ears") battle each other before joining forces to stop their common enemies.

Len Wein, who'd enjoyed his two longest regular runs as writer on the characters, scripted this landmark issue. "When I

Batman vs. The Incredible Hulk *was one in a series of stories featuring hero vs. hero matchups long imagined by fans.* (Cover art by José Luis García-López and Gaspar Saladino)

was approached by [editor] Julius Schwartz regarding the possibility of me actually handling a team-up of those two characters," Wein explains (in his introduction in 1991's *Crossover Classics: The Marvel/DC Collection*), "I set an Olympic record jumping at the chance."

As enjoyable as it is, Wein's story primarily serves as a showcase for the art of penciler José Luis García-López. One of the finest draftsmen to work in mainstream American comics, the Spanish-born artist had previously illustrated *Superman vs. Wonder Woman*, and was well-known for drawing the Last Son of Krypton in *DC Comics Presents*. But García-López preferred drawing Batman, and the DC Style Guide he created in 1982 for the company's licensees featured what became the dominant image of the Caped Crusader for the better part of the decade. Still in use today, the guide was also the basis for 1984's "Super Powers Collection" of Kenner action figures. *Batman vs. The Incredible Hulk*, however, represents García-López's finest work for DC. Inked by Dick Giordano, the artist demonstrates his immense range in scenes referencing Salvador Dali, Pablo Picasso, even Lewis Carroll.

The first intercompany crossover to showcase the Caped Crusader, *Batman vs. The Incredible Hulk* paved the way for later run-ins with Spider-Man, Captain America, the Punisher, Spawn, Aliens, the Predator, Grendel, Judge Dredd, and the Teenage Mutant Ninja Turtles.

58 *Mad Love*

Obsession is rarely more dangerous than when it's romantic. That idea runs through the heart of Harley Quinn's origin story, the tale of a young woman who makes a literal fool out of herself when she falls for the wrong guy. But *Mad Love* isn't just the definitive Harley Quinn tale—it's one of the best Batman comics ever.

Batman: The Animated Series producers Paul Dini and Bruce Timm crafted *Mad Love* when they were invited to do a special issue for the show's tie-in comic book, *The Batman Adventures.* The two had created Harley for the series' first-season episode "Joker's Favor," and this was their opportunity to give the popular "hench-wench" an origin, with Dini scripting and Timm illustrating (in what the latter calls his "mainstream comics debut"). Dini conceived of the 64-page book's central irony, explained in flashback: Harley was formerly Dr. Harleen Quinzel, the Joker's psychiatrist at Arkham Asylum. Intent on getting the killer clown to spill his secrets so she could make a name for herself with a tell-all book, she was instead manipulated and seduced into setting him free and becoming his partner in crime. In time, however, her "puddin'" fails to reciprocate her feelings, and she convinces herself

Paul Dini and Bruce Timm told Harley Quinn's origin tale in Mad Love. (Cover art by Bruce Timm)

his preoccupation with Batman is what's keeping them apart. So she kidnaps the Dark Knight, and plans to kill him with an unused Joker death trap that she's perfected. In so doing, she accidentally provokes the Joker's ire, giving Batman a weapon with which to defeat him.

Fittingly, *Mad Love* was published in February (Valentine's Day month) of 1994. Later that year it won the Eisner Award for "Best Single Story," then came full circle and was adapted by Dini into a 1999 episode of the TV series, one of the show's best. "Amazingly," as Timm proudly notes in his afterword to the story's deluxe presentation (published in 2009 as *Batman: Mad Love and Other Stories*), "it survived the transition to 'children's programming' with most of its innuendo and violence pretty much intact."

A variation of Harley's origin from *Mad Love* was presented in 2016's live-action *Suicide Squad* film. And it opened the door for an equally excellent limited-series in 2004 from Dini and Timm, the three-issue *Batman: Harley and Ivy*.

"It showed the power of the show," says Dini of *Mad Love*'s success. "That it really worked on people's imaginations. That they liked that version of the Batman character. That they really embraced Harley as a character on her own."

59 The *Batman* Film Serials

Batman is preceded by Superman in most media, but the Last Son of Krypton takes a backseat to the Dark Knight when it comes to live-action film. In 1943, just four years after his first print appearance, Batman starred in the first movie serial to feature a DC comic book superhero: Columbia's *Batman*.

Released in 15 15-minute chapters, *Batman*, directed by Lambert Hillyer, stars Lewis Wilson (the father of James Bond film producer Michael G. Wilson), the first actor to play the role of the Caped Crusader. He appears alongside Douglas Croft as Robin, William Austin as Alfred, and Shirley Patterson as Bruce Wayne's Golden Age girlfriend Linda Page. Made during World War II, the film concerns a plot by the evil scientist—and racist stereotype—Dr. Tito Daka, played by J. Carrol Naish. (Naish was considered for the role of the Joker, when the character was slated as the film's villain; the Clown Prince of Crime's presence is still felt in Daka's funhouse headquarters.) Daka schemes to create a radium-powered gun capable of dissolving any material in order to ensure Japan's victory in the war.

Seen today, *Batman*'s depictions of Asians are reprehensible. Like much of the era's pop culture, it was intended as propaganda while America was battling Japan in the South Pacific. Here, even the Dynamic Duo is a tool of the government, with Bruce Wayne and Dick Grayson operating as federal agents (since heroic vigilantes in film productions were then forbidden).

Batman's chapters are, for the most part, padded with uninvolving action in an effort to fill out its 260 minutes. (Robin falls down *a lot.*) Several longstanding elements of the Bat mythos originated here, including the Batcave (more of a Bat-office in this version) and a slimmer, more urbane Alfred than the portly comic foil who'd previously appeared in the comics. The serial's also noteworthy for introducing the idea of Batman marking the criminals he catches with the Bat symbol, a concept used as recently as 2016's *Batman v Superman: Dawn of Justice.*

Flawed as it is, *Batman*'s 1949 sequel is even worse. Directed by Spencer Gordon Bennet and produced by the notoriously cheap "Poverty Row" producer Sam Katzman (who by then had produced Columbia's first *Superman* serial), *Batman and Robin* features Robert Lowery and Johnny Duncan as the Dynamic Duo (who park the Batmobile in their home's driveway for all to see). Lyle Talbot (Lex Luthor in Katzman's *Atom Man vs. Superman* serial) portrays the screen's first Commissioner Gordon, and Jane Adams brings to life reporter Vicki Vale. The plot again concerns a high-tech invention, this time a device that can seize remote control of motor vehicles. Relying heavily on stock footage, as well as shots recycled from the first *Batman* serial, the most entertaining thing about *Batman and Robin* is its hero's Batsuit, which resembles nothing less than a turn-of-the-century devil costume. Anyone with reservations about Christian Bale's attire in Christopher Nolan's trilogy is advised to take a look.

The *Batman* serials' ultimate role in history would be played in 1965, when the first was re-released to theaters. Retitled *An Evening with Batman and Robin*, it was viewed as unintentional camp. But it paved the way for a far more enjoyable deliberately camp version of the characters—the 1966 *Batman* TV series.

60 Lucius Fox

The world in which Batman creators Bill Finger and Bob Kane lived was a monochromatic one, as were the comic books that depicted it. But in the wake of the Civil Rights Movement of the 1950s and 1960s, and the social awareness it raised, a greater number of racially diverse characters began appearing in American comics. Gotham has grown richer for the presence of Killer Croc, Shondra Kinsolving, Sam Young, Max Gibson, Jezebel Jet, Ethan Bennett, David Zavimbe, Fish Mooney, and Duke Thomas. And the first African American regular to appear in Batman comic books remains one of Bruce Wayne's greatest allies: Wayne Enterprises' Lucius Fox.

Lucius was introduced in January 1979's *Batman* #307 ("Dark Messenger of Mercy," by writer Len Wein and penciler John Calnan) as Bruce's second-in-command. With the exception of Dick Grayson and Alfred Pennyworth, Lucius became his most trusted advisor and confidante. But unlike Dick and Alfred, Lucius was responsible for a family. His daughter Tiffany, who ran Wayne Enterprises' drug-rehabilitation program, was introduced in the following issue, and his son Timothy in *Batman* #313. January 1990's *Batman* #443 saw the first appearance of Lucius' wife, Tanya, and daughter Tamara in October 2009's *Red Robin* #3. The latest member of the Fox clan is the first to headline his own comic book—son Luke Fox, better known as the second Batwing.

In 1995's *Batman: Legends of the Dark Knight Halloween Special* #3 ("Ghosts"), it was explained that Lucius first met Bruce Wayne in Paris, when Bruce saved him from a mugger. Fox then gave Bruce the idea to use his vast inheritance to create the charitable Wayne Foundation, which Fox eventually headed. But a different account of their first meeting was presented in October 1994's *Detective Comics* #0 ("Choice of Weapons"), in which, before Bruce acquires his Batsuit, he recruits Lucius from Pontefract Industries to run WayneTech. The latter version prefigures Lucius' role in 2005's *Batman Begins*, which in turn inspired the first storyline of the monthly comic *Batman Confidential* ("Rules of Engagement"). Here, Lucius begins as an engineer at Wayne Enterprises' aerospace division, a position from which he rises to become the company's CEO.

Morgan Freeman's performance in Christopher Nolan's cinematic trilogy—in which Lucius is appointed to his position at Wayne Enterprises by his late friend Thomas Wayne—is the best-known portrayal of the character; but Lucius first appeared on screen in 1992's *Batman: The Animated Series*, voiced by Brock Peters. (In the spinoff series *Batman Beyond*, it's revealed that Lucius has a son, Lucius Jr., who forms his own company, Foxteca.) Louis Gossett Jr. voices Lucius in 2004's *The Batman*, in which—as in Nolan's films and the comics published subsequently—he serves as Batman's armorer.

61 The Riddler

Riddle me this, dear readers: which member of Batman's rogues gallery can always be counted on to challenge the cerebral stamina of the World's Greatest Detective? Why, none other than the Prince of Puzzlers himself...the Riddler!

Though he was prefigured by a similar Fawcett Comics villain named Dr. Riddle—who first appeared in May 1942's *Bulletman* #5—the man known as Edward Nigma (or E. Nigma) played his first mind game against the Dynamic Duo in October 1948's

Detective Comics #140 ("The Riddler," written by Batman co-creator Bill Finger and penciled by Dick Sprang). Introduced as a cheating schoolboy who gained a reputation for his "expertise" at solving puzzles, he grew to manhood and sought greater thrills by matching wits with Gotham's smartest sleuth.

"I'll make each crime a duel of wits between myself and the law," he exclaims, "and fix the puzzles so I'll always win! But first I'll need an appropriate costume..." That costume proved to be one of the most outrageous in comic books—a skintight emerald jumpsuit covered in question marks.

The Riddler returned two months later (in *Detective Comics* #142), then disappeared for almost two decades. He was reintroduced in May 1965's *Batman* #171 ("Remarkable Ruse of the Riddler"), an issue that caught the attention of producer William Dozier and writer Lorenzo Semple Jr., when they adapted it for the pilot episode of their 1966 *Batman* TV series.

The show was a shot of adrenaline in the heart of Gotham's Count of Conundrums, brought to life by impressionist Frank Gorshin, whose manic performance perfectly complemented Adam West's no-nonsense Caped Crusader. Gorshin—who earned the show's only Emmy nomination for acting—starred in four two-part stories in the first season, the most of any "Special Guest Villain," before his Riddler joined Catwoman, Penguin, and Joker in the 1966 *Batman* spinoff film. The actor skipped the second season to focus on his film career, and his tights were filled by *The Addams Family*'s John Astin for one two-parter. Thankfully, Gorshin returned for one final third-season episode.

"As a kid," said Gorshin in the February 1994 issue of *Cinefantastique*, "I loved Batman comics and I never thought that someday I might be able to play that character that wears the question marks and left the riddles. I relished it. I wanted to do it. I didn't have to audition or anything. They asked for me, and I agreed."

One of their most venerable nemeses, the Riddler has been vexing the Dynamic Duo since his introduction in 1948. (Cover art by Win Mortimer)

The Riddler made numerous comic appearances for the remainder of the decade, but was benched once more when the Batman titles took a moody turn in the early 1970s. He made another comeback in May 1975's *Batman* #263 ("Riddler on the Move") and won a new generation of young fans as a member of the Legion of Doom in 1978's animated *Challenge of the Super Friends.* When Batman's world grew dark in the late 1980s, writer Neil Gaiman used the Riddler to sing a dirge for lost innocence in 1989's *Secret Origins Specia*l #1 ("When Is a Door: The Secret Origin of the Riddler").

The Riddler's reputation as a mastermind was rejuvenated when he manipulated Batman's deadliest enemies into attacking him in 2002's "Hush" storyline (in which he learned the Dark Knight's secret identity), and in the *Batman: Arkham* video games. His fixation with riddles, along with his name (for E. Nigma was by then revealed as a pseudonym for Edward Nashton), was stated in 1995's *Detective Comics Annual* #8 (which retold his origin) to stem from a craving for the attention denied him by his parents. *Batman: The Animated Series* writer-producer Paul Dini tweaked the character during his run on *Detective Comics* in 2006, curing him of his obsession and making him one of Batman's allies. Sadly, the alliance was short-lived.

Although the Riddler did not appear in Christopher Nolan's Dark Knight trilogy, he made up for it by holding all of Gotham hostage in *Batman*'s 2013 "Zero Year" storyline, a part of DC's "New 52" reboot. The Riddler was the first supervillain the Dark Knight faced in this continuity.

The Riddler also took center stage in 1995's *Batman Forever*, as played by orange-haired, cane-twirling, human can of Red Bull Jim Carrey. Another noteworthy live-action Riddler arrived in TV's *Gotham*, in which the character is a socially awkward forensic scientist turned psychopath played by Cory Michael Smith.

The most successful animated version of the Riddler is in *Batman: The Animated Series*, in which he's a former video game programmer voiced by *Smallville*'s John Glover. Robert Englund and "Weird Al" Yankovic also voiced memorable versions in 2004's *The Batman* and the *DC Nation Short* "Riddle Me This," respectively, while funnyman Conan O'Brien cameoed as the voice of the Riddler in *The LEGO Batman Movie*.

No screen version of the Wizard of Quiz, however, has been able to escape the shadow of Gorshin, who created an enigma all his own in the tittering, prancing madman with an undying passion for perplexing puzzles.

62 Talia al Ghul

Think your love life's a roller coaster? Try dating the devil's daughter.

Just as criminal mastermind Ra's al Ghul has his roots in author Sax Rohmer's "Yellow Peril" villain Fu Manchu, so is Ra's' daughter Talia prefigured by Fu Manchu's daughter Fah lo Suee, sometimes accomplice and sometimes enemy to her father.

Talia first appeared on Neal Adams' cover for May 1971's *Detective Comics* #411 ("Into the Den of the Death-Dealers!" by writer Denny O'Neil and penciler Bob Brown), clad in a purple cheongsam, bound to a wooden post, and surrounded by swordsmen. In the story, Batman crosses paths with her in Asia, when she's kidnapped by the League of Assassins' Dr. Ebenezer Darrk.

"I am Talia," she tells Batman, when they're imprisoned by Darrk, "daughter of he who is called Ra's al Ghul! Darrk's henchmen captured me at the University of Cairo! I study medicine there..."

After breaking free, the Dark Knight is almost stabbed by his enemy, but is saved by Talia when she shoots Darrk in the chest, hurtling him in front of an oncoming train.

When Ra's himself first appeared weeks later, in June 1971's *Batman* #232 ("Daughter of the Demon," written by O'Neil and penciled by Adams), he kidnapped Robin and took him to the Himalayas as part of an elaborate plan to determine if Batman was worthy of marrying Talia, who'd fallen in love with him, and inheriting his empire of crime. The story channeled another literary source: Ian Fleming's 1963 novel *On Her Majesty's Secret Service* (the basis for the 1969 film), in which the crime lord Marc-Ange

Draco captures James Bond and asks him to marry his suicidal daughter, Contessa Teresa "Tracy" di Vicenzo.

Talia returned several times, revealing a bloodthirsty side as she aided her father in his schemes, culminating in *Batman* #244's "The Demon Lives Again!" (again by O'Neil and Adams). Here, the brown-tressed temptress saves her "Beloved" after he's stung by a scorpion while dueling with her father. The story's final panels, in which a shirtless Batman pulls Talia toward him for a passionate kiss, are among the most iconic in superhero comics.

"When he has his dalliance with Talia," says *The Dark Knight Returns* creator Frank Miller, "that's a moment to remember. Because we don't know where this is going. We don't even know this *side* of him."

Unfortunately, Batman's feelings for Talia often landed him in trouble. In January 1975's *Detective Comics* #444 ("Bat-Murderer!"), she frames the Dark Knight for her murder, so that, hunted by the police, he'd forsake his crimefighting and join her in the League of Assassins. In June 1978's *DC Special Series* #15 ("I Now Pronounce You Batman and Wife!"), she drugs Batman unconscious so her father can marry them. ("In my nation," says Ra's, "the consent of the female and her father are sufficient for marriage!") Batman refuses to honor the marriage, and she once more helps him thwart Ra's.

In 1987's *Batman: Son of the Demon* graphic novel (by writer Mike W. Barr and artist Jerry Bingham), it is revealed that Talia's late mother was killed by one of her father's assassins. (It's later explained that Ra's met Melisande, a woman of Chinese and Arab descent, in 1969 at the Woodstock Festival.) *Son of the Demon* also sees Talia and Batman at last consummate their marriage, after which she becomes pregnant. But she pretends to suffer a miscarriage, and when Batman leaves her, she bears a child.

Like Batman, Talia has confronted the villains of the DC Universe. After Bane broke the Bat in 1993's "Knightfall" storyline, Ra's al Ghul deemed him a suitable replacement for his daughter in 1996's "Legacy" story arc. But she held no love for the villain. And when Lex Luthor became president of the United States in 2001, she ran LexCorp for him, under the name Talia Head (having at last rejected her father). Secretly sharing information with Superman, she sold LexCorp's assets to Wayne Enterprises, causing Luthor's downfall. She also used a Lazarus Pit to restore life to the second Robin, Jason Todd.

In the 2003 limited series *Batman: Death and the Maidens*, Talia's older half-sister Nyssa breaks her will by repeatedly killing her and immersing her in her Lazarus Pit. She then manipulates Talia into killing their father and taking control of his empire, after which Talia disconnects herself from Batman and becomes a founding member of the Secret Society of Super Villains. In September 2006's *Batman* #655, she introduces the Dark Knight to his son, Damian, as a means of distracting him from her activities.

At first Talia was protective of her son, shielding him from her father (who returned in 2007's "The Resurrection of Ra's al Ghul") and his plan to transfer his soul into Damian's body. But in time she founded her own organization, Leviathan, and used it to attack Gotham. Battling Batman Incorporated, she stood by while Damian's clone, the Heretic, killed her son. In the end she herself was killed by Kathy Kane, the first Batwoman. Since no one in comics is ever really dead, however, she returned in February 2015's *Robin Rises: Alpha*.

Supergirl star Helen Slater gave voice to Talia when the character first appeared on screen in "Off Balance," a 1992 episode of *Batman: The Animated Series*. British actress Olivia Hussey voiced her when Talia appeared in *Superman: The Animated Series* and *Batman Beyond*. *Gotham*'s Morena Baccarin voiced her in the animated films *Son of Batman* and *Batman: Bad Blood*, while Stana Katic voiced a memorable Talia in the *Batman: Arkham* video games.

In live-action, Talia appeared in the fifth season of TV's *Arrow*, played by Lexa Doig, and in 2012's *The Dark Knight Rises*, played by Oscar winner Marion Cotillard. The latter film presents the most unequivocally evil version of the character to date, when she infiltrates Wayne Enterprises under the name Miranda Tate. Consumed by her quest for vengeance against Bruce Wayne after her father's death in *Batman Begins*, she plots with Bane to destroy Gotham City, a self-proclaimed "knife that waits years without forgetting, then slips quietly between the bones."

But then Bruce too has wrestled with daddy issues, which may be why he and Talia find each other so irresistible. Drawn to each other's darkness, they're nonetheless unable to surrender to it.

"She's unbelievable, isn't she?" says artist Neal Adams of Talia. "Maybe she's not as gorgeous as one thinks, but she makes you *feel* like she is...There's some women that do that, and it's different women for different people. But when that hits a guy he becomes helpless, and he can't believe that he's seeing what he's seeing. That somehow, magically, another human being can be so wonderful and so beautiful. That's Talia. That's what she's about. She's the woman sitting across the table that just stops everybody from talking so they can just look at her."

63 Robin V: Damian Wayne (aka Redbird)

All of the Robins are children of Batman. But in the case of Damian Wayne, it can be proven by DNA testing.

In the 1987 graphic novel, *Batman: Son of the Demon* (written by Mike W. Barr and illustrated by Jerry Bingham), the Dark Knight finally consummates his long-simmering romance with Talia al Ghul, the daughter of League of Assassins leader Ra's al Ghul. Talia becomes pregnant with his child, but lies to Batman, telling him she's suffered a miscarriage.

The offspring of Bruce Wayne and Talia al Ghul, Damian Wayne was introduced to his biological father in 2006. He eventually took over the mantle of Robin. (Cover art by Chris Burnham)

Cut to October 2006's *Batman* #656 ("Batman & Son, Part 2: Man-Bats of London," written by Grant Morrison with art by Andy Kubert). Talia, having taken over her father's business, arrives in Gotham City and informs Batman that, as "the perfect man," he was chosen to breed an heir to her late father's criminal empire. She introduces him to their son—a spoiled, obnoxious, and foul-mouthed child named Damian, trained by the League's masters.

Telling Batman that Damian lacks "the guiding hand of a great man," Talia leaves the brass-knuckled boy in his care. But after taking him home to Wayne Manor and the Batcave, Damian beheads one of Batman's enemies, beats up Robin Tim Drake, and (in *Batman* #657) steals the deceased second Robin Jason Todd's costume, proclaiming himself his father's new sidekick. The four-issue "Batman & Son" arc concludes with Talia launching an attack on Gibraltar and telling Batman she wants them to rule the world with Damian. He refuses, and mother and son vanish, presumed dead in the attack.

The lad returned, however, and again wore the red-and-green colors of the Boy Wonder—opposite Dick Grayson's Batman—after Bruce Wayne was believed killed in DC's 2008 "Final Crisis" event. The new, albeit more dysfunctional, Dynamic Duo was born in the ensuing "Battle for the Cowl" storyline. Dick and Damian earned their own title, 2009's *Batman and Robin* (again written by Morrison), in which they confronted new foes such as Professor Pyg and Mister Toad, and battled Jason Todd, reborn as the Red Hood. With Grayson's support, Damian also joined the Teen Titans, as well as Batman Incorporated, in which he briefly operated, against his father's wishes, as Redbird.

Artist Chris Burnham, who illustrated most of Damian Wayne's adventures in the *Batman Incorporated* comic (in which he briefly adopts the name "Redbird"), explains the joy of drawing the fifth Robin: "Batman is grim and gritty and fairly realistic as far as comics go. He's got that dynamic realism. But with Damian you can really push his proportions and get cartoony with it. And he's a little kid, so you can give him that awesome little sourpuss face. I just love drawing my little buddy. He's my favorite thing to draw, bar none."

Eventually, Talia revealed the full extent of her madness when she rejected her son for siding with his father, who returned from the grave. Having cloned the boy, she bred his augmented adult replacement, the Heretic, who runs a sword through Damian in April 2013's *Batman Incorporated* Vol. 2 #8. He dies a hero, fighting to save the world from his mother, who would dismiss him as "a martyr to folly in his little cape and boots."

"It was a real drag killing him," says Burnham. "I felt really bad about it. It's a weird thing...As far as our story's concerned, he's dead and buried. But in that last issue [of *Batman Incorporated*] there's three different cliffhangers indicating how he could be brought back."

Damian was indeed brought back, and received his own series in 2015's *Robin: Son of Batman*. In DC's 2016 "Rebirth" relaunch, Damian becomes leader of a new group of Teen Titans and partners with the son of Superman in the series *Super Sons*.

The first Damian to appear on screen is the son of Batman and Catwoman in an imaginary story in the 2010 *Batman: The Brave and the Bold* episode "The Knights of Tomorrow!" (in which he's voiced by Patrick Cavanaugh). The animated film trilogy *Son of Batman / Batman vs. Robin / Batman: Bad Blood* (in which he's voiced by Stuart Allan) adapts much of Morrison's run on the character.

At just 13 years old, Damian Wayne is the most relatable of Robins. After all, who *doesn't* want their parents to stop fighting?

64 Batman Beyond

Some Batman TV shows are thrilling. Some are funny. And some, as in the case of *Batman Beyond*, are *schway.*

A continuation of the saga begun in *Batman: The Animated Series, Batman Beyond*—which won a Daytime Emmy Award for Outstanding Special Class Animated Program—began when Warner Brothers, believing *BTAS* skewed toward older audiences, asked producers Bruce Timm, Paul Dini, and Alan Burnett to develop a new series featuring a teenage Batman. With little interest in abandoning Bruce Wayne, the three were skeptical at first, but came to see the assignment as an opportunity to build a new world for the Dark Knight.

Set 50 years after the events of *BTAS*, *Batman Beyond* begins with a flashback to Bruce Wayne's last adventure as Batman. Wearing a sleek new red-and-black suit, Bruce (voiced once more by Kevin Conroy) suffers a heart attack and finds his only means of defense is a gun. So he retires. In the show's present, Wayne Enterprises has merged with industrialist Derek Powers' company to become Wayne-Powers, and most of Bruce's old friends are gone, so he's boarded himself up in Wayne Manor with his Great Dane, Ace. It's a surprisingly dark note on which to launch a series aimed at a younger audience. But the main focus of *Batman Beyond* is on its title character, high school student Terry McGinnis (voice by Will Friedle). A former juvenile delinquent trying to walk the straight and narrow, Terry's life changes when his father is murdered by Powers' bodyguard, prompting the teen to steal the gadget-packed Batsuit and bring the killer to justice. Though Bruce is initially reluctant to take on a new partner, he sees in Terry the chance to continue his work as a crimefighter, and the two join forces to fight Powers and all who threaten Neo-Gotham.

Glen Murakami, who'd served as art director on *Superman: The Animated Series*, joined Timm, Dini, and Burnett to become the fourth producer on *Batman Beyond* and was responsible for much of the show's look, creating a vibrant city of the future that takes its cue from the towers, tubes, and flying cars of sci-fi film classics. But his Neo-Gotham is by no means derivative. Nor is the show's new rogues gallery, including high-tech hypnotist Spellbinder, sonic supervillain Shriek, and, best of all, the shape-shifting Inque, a character that takes full advantage of animation's potential. Even those antagonists who do call back to the past, such as the various Jokerz gang members, function more as social commentary than imitative opponents.

Batman Beyond's first season, which premiered on January 10, 1999, establishes its cast, including Commissioner Barbara Gordon (Stockard Channing voices the retired Batgirl and reluctant ally to Terry), Terry's mom (Teri Garr), and troublesome little brother (Ryan O'Donohue)—neither of whom know he's Batman. Nor does his long-suffering girlfriend, Dana Tan (*Futurama*'s Lauren

Tom). Eschewing the corporate thriller plots of its first year, *Batman Beyond*'s second season shifts its attention to Terry's high school, and introduces the one peer who knows his identity—the brilliant Maxine "Max" Gibson (voiced by Cree Summer)—who functions as Terry's best friend and girl Friday.

Many of *Batman Beyond*'s episodes cater to tween audiences, with school-day stories of dating, peer pressure, and social ostracization. But its superhero element turns them into something universal, in much the same way that Stan Lee and Steve Ditko's *Spider-Man* and Joss Whedon's *Buffy the Vampire Slayer* offered something for all ages. The show, in fact, anticipates the entire DC live-action TV explosion, with Max (like the Batman comics' Oracle), prefiguring similar hacker sidekicks such as *Smallville*'s Chloe Sullivan and *Arrow*'s Felicity Smoak.

Batman Beyond's sci-fi setting allows it to explore a range of issues, from drug abuse to genetic engineering. And Terry's state-of-the-art Batsuit (sans cape, with a full face mask, its ears longer than the Batman of old's), which plugs into his flying Batmobile, injects some Iron Man–style innovation into the Bat mythos, with its rocket boots, retractable wings, cloaking device, and dispensable Batarangs. Science fiction also allows for the evil *BTAS* alumni who *do* reappear, including the still tragic Victor Fries (in "Meltdown") and the wickedest take on Ra's al Ghul in the DC Animated Universe (in "Out of the Past"), as well as a futuristic prototype for the DCAU's Justice League (in "The Call, Part 1"). The fate of the Joker, Harley Quinn, and Tim Drake's Robin are revealed in the outstanding 2000 spinoff film *Batman Beyond: Return of the Joker*.

Though *Batman Beyond*'s three-season run wasn't given a finale, its successor, *Justice League Unlimited*, concluded Terry's story in the episode "Epilogue." Set 15 years after the events of *Batman Beyond* (and originally intended as the final chapter in the DCAU), it sees Terry learn the truth behind his origin and set a new path for his future. Like *Batman Beyond*'s pulse-pounding title sequence (designed by the late comic book great Darwyn Cooke), its industrial/metal score (which netted a Daytime Emmy Award for Outstanding Music Direction and Composition for composers Shirley Walker, Lolita Ritmanis, Michael McCuistion, and Kristopher Carter), and of course the slang slung by its teen hero, *Batman Beyond* is totally and unutterably the apotheosis of schway.

65 The Top Five Craziest Batsuits

Batman's had his share of sleek, sexy super-suits throughout his career. But few are as memorable as the outrageous outfits of the 1950s and 1960s.

The Counterfeit Suit

"The Strange Costumes of Batman!" in November 1950's *Detective Comics* #165 (written by Edmond Hamilton and penciled by Dick Sprang) features such far-out items in the Bat-wardrobe as the polar "Camouflage Costume," the "Luminous Uniform," the "Interplanetary Suit," and the "Golden Garb." But none are as strange as the foam-rubber-molded Batsuit that allows Robin to disguise himself as his partner when Batman becomes incapacitated. Fortunately, Gotham's crooks lack the basic intelligence to recognize the symbol in the suit's chest emblem: a red-breasted robin.

The Rainbow Suit

When Dick Grayson injures his arm in March 1957's *Detective Comics* #241 ("The Rainbow Batman," written by Edmond Hamilton and penciled by Sheldon Moldoff), Batman must draw

The Dark Knight has worn some wild suits over the years, including this zebra-print number in 1960's Detective Comics *#275.* (Cover art by Sheldon Moldoff and Ira Schnapp)

attention away from Robin, whom he fears will be identified having the exact same injury. His solution? He wears a different colored costume each night, culminating with the Batsuit that transforms him into "a rainbow of dazzling action"—the Rainbow Batsuit.

The Zur-En-Arrh Suit

February 1958's *Batman* #113 ("Batman—The Superman of Planet X!" by writer France Herron and penciler Dick Sprang) saw the Caped Crusader recruited to battle alien invaders on the distant planet Zur-En-Arrh—where he manifested powers like those of Superman—by that world's own Batman. The Batman of Zur-En-Arrh wears a "futuristic" costume consisting of bright red tights and tunic, yellow sleeves, and purple gloves, boots, cape, and cowl. Bruce Wayne himself would don this uniform years later in 2008's "Batman R.I.P." In this story arc, the Zur-En-Arrh persona is revealed as a backup personality Batman adopted to prevent his mind from being destroyed by an enemy's attack.

The Zebra Suit

In January 1960's *Detective Comics* #275, the Caped Crusaders battle the Zebra-Man, a criminal with magnetic powers, in a story by writer Bill Finger and penciler Sheldon Moldoff. When Batman's exposed to the machine that gives this villain his abilities, the Caped Crusader's skin and costume are imprinted with the pattern of magnetic lines of force; thus making him "The Zebra Batman." Wondering what clothes will complement your shag carpet, lava lamp, lounge music, and mai tais? Consider the Zebra Batsuit. The ultimate in midcentury kitsch wear.

The Bat-Baby Suit

When an evil scientist creates a machine that reduces Batman's body to that of a four-year-old child while maintaining his adult mind and physical strength, the Caped Crusader continues fighting crime as Bat-Baby, the pinnacle of Silver Age silliness. May 1962's *Batman* #147 ("Batman Becomes Bat-Baby," by writer Bill Finger and penciler Sheldon Moldoff) introduced the mini manhunter, along with his uniform: black shorts and suspenders, a gray T-shirt with a Bat-symbol emblem, and little blue gloves, cape, and cowl. "So gangland is now calling me a baby!" says the once proud detective. "Well, I'll dress like a baby, and prove to them that I'm still a crimefighter—as Bat-Baby!"

66 Dance the Batusi

Batman may not have inspired as many popular songs as Superman, but he's still got it all over the Last Son of Krypton when it comes to the performing arts. He has his own dance.

Introduced in the pilot episode of the 1966 *Batman* TV series, "Hi Diddle Riddle," the Batusi is created by the Caped Crusader in the "What a Way to Go-Go" discothèque, after he's slipped a mickey by one of the Riddler's lackeys. Not wishing to attract attention, Batman accepts an invitation to dance from the Riddler's gun moll, Molly (who interests him, strangely). He escorts her to the dance floor and performs a series of moves that resulted in a new dance craze in clubs across the country, its name a play on the then-popular dance, the Watusi.

To dance the Batusi, one must first find some appropriate go-go music and attire (or a cape and cowl). The dancer begins by gyrating his upper and lower body. He must then trace the contours of his ears and forearms with his fingers. A peace sign is formed with the index finger and middle finger of each hand, and the hands move across his eyes. If a cape is worn, it may be shaken as the dancer continues to gyrate, abandoning all inhibitions in a state of euphoric madness.

Batman also performs the Batusi in the first-season episode "The Pharaoh's in a Rut," varying his moves with leaps and hops. (A Catwoman-inspired variation, the Catusi, was introduced in the second season's "Hot Off the Griddle.") Decades later, the dance would undergo a resurgence when performed by John Travolta in *Pulp Fiction*.

Batman star Adam West improvised the Batusi after learning he was required to dance in "Hi Diddle Riddle."

"I was on the way in [to work]," says West. "I was driving, and I had the script beside me, learning lines. I noticed I had to come up with something quite goofy, because Batman has been slipped a mickey, a poison drink. I was listening to jazz on the radio, and I switched around, got some different [stations]. And I began to move in my car seat, and people looked at me strangely. I was Watusiing, then Batusiing, while I drove."

"Now," he laughs, "that's not as dangerous as texting."

67 Batman: The Brave and the Bold

Ever since Frank Miller's *The Dark Knight Returns* revamped Batman for a new generation of comic book readers in 1986, the character's dominant image has been that of a grim, obsessed, often morose nocturnal avenger. While that's led to plenty of great stories, it's come at the cost of neglecting most of his adventures in the 1950s and 1960s. Tales that could charm as well as thrill. Some would say there's no going home again. No retreating to the innocence of childhood. Well, they haven't seen *Batman: The Brave and the Bold.*

The most unapologetically joyful of Batman's screen incarnations, and the most underrated, *The Brave and the Bold* premiered on November 14, 2008. At the time, Warner Brothers was looking for a kid-friendly Batman that could sell the toys Christopher Nolan's *The Dark Knight* (released just a few months prior) could not. Rather than manufacture a weekly half-hour series as commercial, however, producers James Tucker and Michael Jelenic took the opportunity to craft a love letter to the Batman's most overlooked era. Tucker and Jelenic took as their template the Silver Age

The Brave and the Bold comic. In the wake of 1960s Batmania, the book served as a Batman team-up title from issue #74 (November 1967) to #200 (July 1983), its final issue. Under writer Bob Haney, *The Brave and the Bold* was the most offbeat of the pre–Modern Age Batman's titles, with stories set in World War II, outer space, or the Old West that paid little heed to the rigors of continuity.

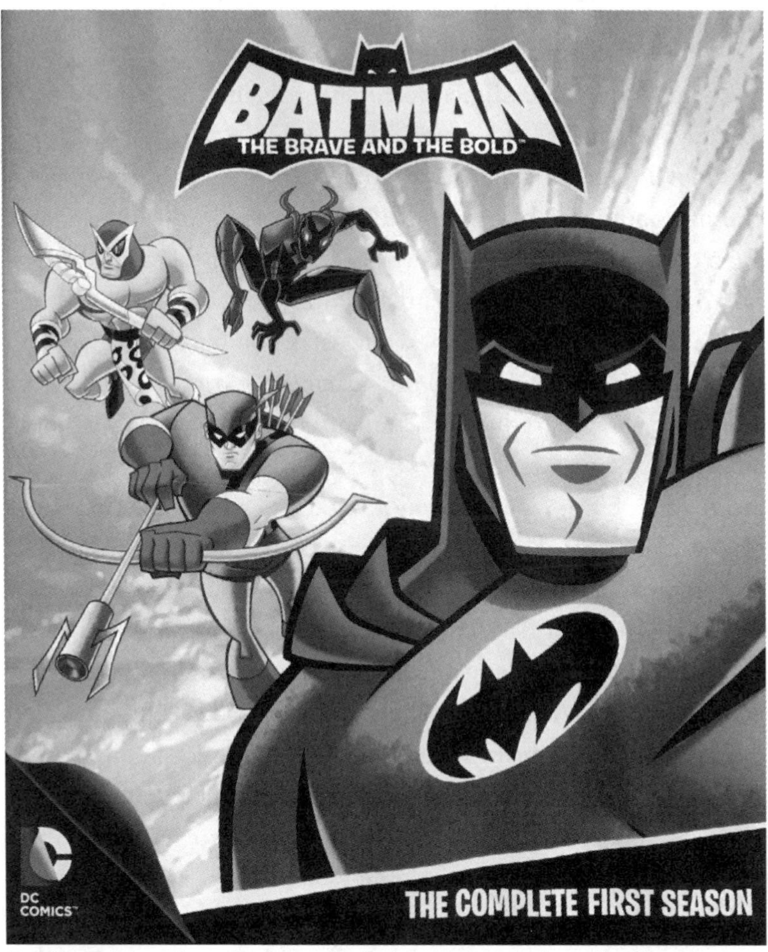

Bright, joyful, and unafraid to push the boundaries of what a kid-friendly animated series could be, Batman: The Brave and the Bold *ran for 65 episodes, from 2008 to 2011.*

Television's *The Brave and the Bold* took a similar approach, utilizing many of the same idiosyncratic DC heroes—such as the Metal Men, Deadman, and the Doom Patrol—while adding lots of equally endearing characters who'd since debuted—including Kamandi, the Outsiders, and the Justice League International. What unified everything was an aesthetic borrowed from Golden Age Bat draftsman Dick Sprang, whose bold-lined, barrel-chested Batman meshed perfectly with Silver Age staples Batwoman, Ace the Bat-Hound, and Bat-Mite.

The latter's extra-dimensional shenanigans allowed the show to add meta to the merriment. For example, in the first-season episode "Legends of the Dark Mite!" Bat-Mite is interrupted by one of a multitude of disgruntled Batman fanboys while addressing a crowd at a comic convention: "I always felt Batman was best suited to the role of gritty, urban crime detective, but now you guys have him up against Santas and Easter bunnies? I'm sorry, but that's not my Batman!" Bat-Mite responds by reading a note from one of the show's producers: "'Batman's rich history allows him to be interpreted in a multitude of ways. To be sure, this is a lighter incarnation, but is certainly no less valid and true to the character's roots as the tortured avenger, crying out for Mommy and Daddy'... And besides, those Easter bunnies looked really scary, right?"

Actor Diedrich Bader provided the voice of *The Brave and the Bold*'s Batman, an unflappable ramrod ever eager to pulverize crime with his mighty "hammers of justice." But Bader could also find the pathos beneath the cape and cowl, on full display in the second-season's "Chill of the Night!" where Batman at long last finds the man who murdered his parents. The show also provided the perfect model for developing longer storylines, as when it used its opening teasers (which usually presented adventures separate from those of the main plot) to introduce the second season's Starro invasion storyline, which climaxed with the death of a beloved character.

Bader's Batman found ideal friendly foils in Will Friedle's sometimes sidekick Blue Beetle, James Arnold Taylor's hypercompetitive Green Arrow, and John DiMaggio's perennially chipper Aquaman (the best screen realization of the sea king). The latter two, as well as Grey DeLisle's Black Canary, featured in *The Brave and the Bold*'s acclaimed musical episode, "Mayhem of the Music Meister!" Its title villain voiced by Neil Patrick Harris, it was, as Aquaman would say, "Outrageous!"

But there isn't a single episode of *The Brave and the Bold* that doesn't go for broke. And no character was too obscure. Want to watch Batman solve a mystery with Detective Chimp? Chase evildoers in the Haunted Tank? Get serenaded by the Vigilante during a Western showdown? Tucker and Jelenic have you covered. Similarly, no story is too ridiculous. Seeing Batman fight alongside Wonder Woman to the theme from her 1970s Lynda Carter–starring TV show evokes as many years of joy as watching him stop "John Wilkes Boom" from killing Abraham Lincoln on Earth-5501 in the teaser of the show's final episode, "Mitefall!" Smart, touching, and hilarious, it ranks alongside the finest TV series finales of all time, animated or otherwise, culminating in a wrap party at which Batman addresses the show's audience of children, reassuring them that he will always be there for them.

"The hammers of justice will always pound straight the bent nails of evil," says *The Brave and the Bold*'s Batman, encapsulating its mix of wit and reverence. It is a mix no other incarnation of Batman has so gloriously achieved.

"It's really a celebration of Batman," says James Tucker. "All kinds of Batman. All that Batman encompasses. I think our show kind of helped break the stalemate on allowing people to enjoy Batman on a lighter level."

Gotham Gazette Exclusive

Diedrich Bader

Actor Diedrich Bader has won big laughs for his roles in *The Drew Carey Show*, *Office Space*, *Veep*, and *American Housewife*, but he's beloved by Batfans as the voice of the Caped Crusader in the joyous *Batman: The Brave and the Bold*.

In *Batman: The Brave and the Bold*, you repopularized the idea of a lighter Batman.
People got hung up on a very dark image of Batman, and [producer] James [Tucker] turned that all around, and said, "We all have different versions of Batman, and we're allowed to." I think that was a singularity of the show, and I think that's why it didn't take off immediately. People didn't fully know where we were going, because it was so different and so lighthearted. Then we really got into a groove about halfway through the first season.

People were used to a certain type of Batman, and we defied their expectations. That's also the reason it continues to grow in interest. People get more and more open to the idea of expanding their concept of what Batman is capable of, back to the old Adam West show. I watched Adam West when I was a kid and really loved that show. But I don't know if I ever gave Batman any real thought after I was a kid. I'd read Frank Miller's Batman. That kind of piqued my interest again. But that was such a dark vision of Batman, and sort of revisionist in its way.

Your Batman voice is reminiscent of Adam West's, but you make it your own.
I was just doing a really bad Kevin Conroy impression. [Laughs.] Then just trying to hit my jokes in a way that was subtle rather than too hard. And use a little bit of Adam West. It is an odd delivery, when I listen to it, but it seemed right at the time. I highlighted the comedy probably more than others would have, but I felt like that was the tone of the show.

I'm very, very proud of my work on that. It's without a doubt the best part I ever had. It took all of my skills rather than a narrow skill set, which is a lot of what I'd been doing in the past. What's great about Batman is that of course he's got this incredible backstory, but he's also a very sophisticated and intelligent person carrying a lot of baggage around. He's deeply soulful and has his own dry sense of humor and a sense of honor that I really respect. It's a beautiful part.

Your Batman voice sets the tone for the show—both amusing and reverential.
Well, thank you! That was the thing I was trying to do: have some fun with it and yet at the same time come from a place of love and respect. Never making fun of Batman, but having fun *with* Batman.

The show pairs Batman with many different heroes. Do you have a favorite?
Oh, yeah. Aquaman was my favorite. I'm gonna go ahead and say it. John DiMaggio created something that was totally unique and cool and was a great balance to the dryness of my Batman. He went over the top and stayed there deliriously for the whole thing. I love his characterization of it—"Outrageous!"

As fun as those episodes could be, the show demonstrated the character's range in episodes like "Chill of the Night!"
Yeah, "Chill of the Night!" was an episode that was really deep. I actually broke into tears when he met his parents' killer. It meant so much to him to have this moment where he could confront him. I felt for him. I realized that I had crossed over and that the character's problems were then *my* problems. Because I was *really* into it at that moment. It was intense.

***The Brave and the Bold* also has one of the best finales of any series.**
It was an incredibly well-written episode and it was very difficult to get through that last monologue. I had to do a number of passes at it, because it was so heartfelt and so sweet and so genuine and so what we wanted to hear from Batman that I kept breaking up.

If the circumstances ever allow for it, would you like to revisit the character?
Oh, I would love to play Batman again. That would be a dream come true. But I'd only really want to do it with James. That would definitely be a dream come true. Because I think we created something really special.

Gotham Gazette Exclusive

James Tucker

Producer James Tucker—a veteran of *Batman: The Animated Series*, *Batman Beyond*, and *Justice League Unlimited*—reclaimed the fun Batman of the 1950s and 1960s by pairing him with myriad heroes and villains in the glorious *Batman: The Brave and the Bold*.

How did *Batman: The Brave and the Bold* come to be?
It started when we knew there was going to be another [Christopher] Nolan Batman film, which ended up being *The Dark Knight*. As usual, when a big franchise movie, especially a Batman movie, comes out, it usually generates a connecting cartoon. So we knew we had to do something, and at the time Warner Animation was very close to shutting down. There weren't really many other animation producers on the lot who could handle a new Batman show. So I kind of got it by default.

It's funny, because I think they wouldn't have allowed me to make the show I ended up making had the situation been any different. Meaning had there been more people to choose from in animation, and if the Nolan film hadn't been so dark that they knew they couldn't do anything approximating that. They had to go radically left of that even to be on the air, because there was no way Cartoon Network was going to take a show as dark as *The Dark Knight* ended up being.

There was an episode of *Batman: The Animated Series* called "Legends of the Dark Knight." It was a pretty famous episode in which I did the Dick Sprang section. Warner Bros. Animation president Sam Register said, "Why don't you do that?" I never in a million years thought anyone would allow me to do that. But he wanted it to be radically different from anything we had been doing. I was like, "You know, this won't be thought of as cool." [Laughs.] He's like, "That's fine."

It's so funny, because now we're almost 10 years out from that time, and I've done two Adam West *Batman* movies, *Justice League Action* is on the air, *Teen Titans Go!* is the number one cartoon on Cartoon Network. But the landscape was totally different in 2007 to 2008, when the thought of doing something that was even remotely campy—or just the word "fun"—got sneers from the fan base. Because people had done such a hit job on the '66 show for 40 years, but that's what got me into Batman. So a return to that was fine in my book.

***The Brave and the Bold* has a dry wit that doesn't fully venture into camp.**

Yeah, we always tried to ride the line of camp. I say it owes a lot to the Adam West show, and to the *100 Page Super Spectacular* books DC put out in the '70s, with gritty contemporary stories and reprints going back to the Golden Age. So you got the Batman of the late '30s, the '40s, the weird '50s stuff, and then the '60s stuff. It was almost like seeing a timeline. So that kind of became the motivating philosophy of the show—Batman is malleable. He is not fixed into this one rigid, dark, noir landscape. He's been shown multiple ways, and he's always Batman. As long as he's consistently the same guy, you can throw him into any situation.

It was weird, because the toy company wanted a Batman that could go into different environments because they wanted their Scuba Batman and their Airlift Batman and their Street Luge Batman. [Laughs.] That was always the stopping point of other Batman shows: "Why would he do that?" Whereas in my head I had a reference point of all these old issues. I'm like, "Of course Batman can have a Flying Batcave!" *100 Page Super Spectacular* was pretty much the blueprint for the show. Because it was Batman in all these ludicrous situations, in different time frames, but yet he was still cool.

BTAS had to clean the slate. It was mandated to give us a serious Batman that honors the comics of its time and goes back to the noir roots and skips all the middle stuff. Whereas we were just the opposite. We dug into the middle stuff. The stuff that people had become embarrassed by, we were like, "We claim this as our own. This is Batman too." So that became the mantra of the show.

We didn't really know it going in. There was an executive we had a meeting with, and the very first thing out of his mouth was, "No death traps." Of course the very first shot in *The Brave and the Bold* is them sitting suspended over a vat of acid. So it just goes to show we weren't listening to a lot of people. [Laughs.] It was like, "No, that's exactly what we should do."

We were timid at first. The first 13 slowly dip their toe into that weird water. Then by the second season it's just crazy. Much like the seasons of the '66 *Batman* show. The first season is campy but it's not as overtly comedic as the show became in the second and third seasons. We followed that template with our series.

What are your favorite episodes?

When I was on *Superman* and *Batman Beyond* and *Justice League*, there was a thing that Bruce Timm called a "Wednesday show." Meaning "This show didn't turn out so good, but we have to get them done." I was young and hungry going, "This should be better!" He's like, "No, it's a Wednesday show"—meaning "It's gonna air in the middle of the week." As long as you start out the week strong and end strong, you can't kill yourself over one show. Going into *The Brave and the Bold*, we just had one show a week. I went, "I don't want any Wednesday shows."

So it's hard to pick my favorite episodes, but my favorite episodes are the ones that are really ridiculous. "Aquaman's Outrageous Adventure!" I love that one. I like the ones that keep moving. I also like the one where Batman and Batwoman switch bodies. It's kind of like our version of *Some Like It Hot*. It's over the top but it's really kind of adult in its own way and it honors women's movies of the '40s. I like all the episodes where we can put in the Batman Family.

We really tried. I didn't ever want to say, "This episode is kind of meh." Not that there aren't some, but we tried our best to make them shine.

Was the idea of using each episode's teaser as a separate short adventure yours?

Yeah. Again, being a kid of the late '60s/early '70s, I remember *Space Ghost*, and when adventure shows were done in smaller chunks. The original Filmation *Superman* and *Aquaman* and *Batman* were all shorts. So for years and years I was like, "Why don't we do shorts anymore?" So I came up with the teasers, just to have a reason to introduce new heroes in a shorter form that we probably wouldn't have developed a whole episode around. It kept me interested. I'm like, "We can cut into the middle of a story or cut to the tail end of a story and we can also end it as they're about to go into action." So it was just about shaking up people's short attention spans and my own. [Laughs.]

The series finale "Mitefall!" is a mic drop.

Michael Jelenic kept pitching the teaser with Abraham Lincoln, saying, "Batman saves Lincoln from John Wilkes Booth." I kept going, "That's in bad taste. I'm a black dude. Batman's not gonna save Lincoln. That's crazy." But when he finally pitched it the last time he said, "Oh, it turns out it's Abraham Lincoln in an alternate universe." I went, "Why didn't you say that? That's great!"

My biggest contribution to "Mitefall!" was in Batman's final speech to the camera. I added the "boys and girls" line. Because I remember the Adam West show, how he sometimes talked directly to the camera. I said, "If we're gonna do a final show, I want Batman to break that wall and talk directly to the kids and the people who were kids when they first saw him." Because that's what the whole show was about: enjoying Batman, the Batman who gets you into all the other stuff. He was the gateway drug into comics for me, and for a lot of people of a certain age the Adam West show was a gateway drug into getting into comics. It was important that he addressed boys and girls because really it's the kid inside everyone that still needs to have a Batman to hold onto. I wanted it to work on that level, so that it was very much like superhero comfort food. Yeah, I'm very proud of how that episode turned out.

68 Batman Incorporated

In a decade that saw Christopher Nolan's Dark Knight trilogy released concurrently with TV's lighthearted *Batman: The Brave and the Bold*, that saw the 1966 *Batman* TV show arrive on home video as the *Batman: Arkham* video games reveled in industrial grunge, writer Grant Morrison fused all of Batman's iterations—from pulp hero to James Bond–esque globetrotter—into one glorious continuity. He capped his run with *Batman Incorporated.*

The roots of *Batman Incorporated*, like much of Morrison's work on the Dark Knight, run all the way back to the Golden Age of comics. In this case, to December 1950's "The Batman of England!" (by Batman co-creator Bill Finger and penciler Dick Sprang) in *Batman* #62. The story introduced Percy Sheldrake, the Earl of Wordenshire, and his son Cyril, who are inspired by Batman and Robin to don medieval period attire, mount horse-headed motorcycles, and fight crime as the Knight and his sidekick Squire. In *Batman* #65, another European crusader, Wingman, appeared (in "A Partner for Batman!"). And in January 1955's "The Batmen of All Nations" (in *Detective Comics* #215), writer Edmond Hamilton and penciler Sheldon Moldoff assembled an entire team, as Batman, Knight, and Squire join Australia's Ranger, Argentina's Gaucho, Italy's Legionary, and France's Musketeer.

Renamed "The Club of the Heroes" in August 1957's *World's Finest* #89, the Batmen were reunited by Morrison 50 years later in August 2007's *Batman* #667 ("The Island of Mister Mayhew"), and given a new history that included the Native American chief Man-of-Bats and his son Little Raven (who grew up to be Red Raven). They were attacked by the criminal cult the Black Glove, led by Dr. Simon Hurt (an ancestor of Bruce Wayne's), who formed a Club of

Villains and tried to kill Batman. But the Dark Knight defeated the Black Glove with an assist from Talia al Ghul's League of Assassins.

Reinvigorated, Bruce Wayne decided to expand his crimefighting operations. He publicly announced he was funding Batman and formed Batman Incorporated. Starting in January 2011's *Batman Incorporated* #1, Batman established an army of vigilantes across the globe. Joining the surviving members of the Club of Heroes were the former Robins and Batgirls as well as the African hero Batwing, the Algerian Sunni Muslim French Nightrunner, Australia's new Dark Ranger, England's Hood, Argentina's Cimarron, Japan's Mr. Unknown…and Robin's pet Bat-Cow.

Intending to rule the planet with Bruce Wayne and their son, Damian, Talia was enraged when both rejected her and Damian chose to remain with Batman Incorporated as Robin. With Leviathan (a splinter group from her father's League of Assassins), she declared war against Batman Incorporated, and stood by while her agents killed Damian. After battling the Dark Knight one last time, she was killed by the first Batwoman, Kathy Kane.

An idea machine in human form, Morrison began his stint on Batman with the "Batman and Son" storyline, followed by "The Resurrection of Ra's al Ghul," "The Black Glove," "R.I.P.," "Final Crisis," "Batman and Robin," and "The Return of Bruce Wayne." All are well worth the attention of veteran Batman fans, as they weave obscure bits of continuity and forgotten lore into narrative gold. *Batman Incorporated* is his opus, an epic that never loses sight of what lies at the heart of the Batman mythos: the yearning for family.

"The neat thing about that run," says artist Chris Burnham, who drew the bulk of *Batman Incorporated*, "is that it acknowledges every era of Batman and tries to make it a unified whole. So it's got the grim and gritty 1980s and 1990s, it's got the good stuff from the 1950s and 1960s, it's got the film noir stuff from the 1940s—and it really combines them all. The more Batman stuff you like, the more you're gonna like that run. Because it resonates more."

Gotham Gazette Exclusive

Chris Burnham

Chris Burnham illustrated the bulk of Grant Morrison's *Batman Incorporated*, drawing more versions of the Dark Knight than almost any other artist. Though Burnham began his run imitating frequent Morrison collaborator Frank Quitely, he soon developed his own offbeat look for the epic series.

On *Batman Incorporated*, you were given an opportunity few artists have had, in that you didn't just draw the current iteration of Batman but most every iteration of Batman, both geographically and chronologically.

It was immediately super nerve-wracking, because I'm a big Grant Morrison fan and a big Batman fan and a big Grant Morrison Batman fan. I was in a very good position of knowing exactly what a Grant Morrison Batman comic was supposed to feel like. I knew exactly what he was going for. Even at its most confusing, even when it was too trippy to understand, I knew how to draw a trippy Grant Morrison comic. I had somehow cracked that code by reading *The Filth* five times. I knew what I was supposed to be doing. And all the stuff he was referencing—"Oh, it should look like *The Prisoner* and like the Gerry Anderson shows"—most of the stuff he was looking for was stuff that I was fairly familiar with. I have a feel for the weird '60s British stuff. So we just meshed pretty well.

Then all the different Batmen of All Nations and Batman Incorporated...Google Images is awesome. If they're fighting in Batman Park in Australia, I knew exactly what that looks like thanks to Google Images. I don't even think they call it out in that issue as being Batman Park. I think that's just a stupid joke for only Australians to get. [Laughs.] But that is exactly the bridge there. It's super accurate. They're driving away from the city's opera house, and they drive off that bridge. All of that stuff, as far as I could get it at the time, was super accurate.

Besides Frank Quitely, who established the look of Grant Morrison's storyline, who were some of your inspirations on *Batman Incorporated*?
Years and years ago, I got into Moebius a lot. Like an idiot I was like, "I can do that!" Which is preposterous to say, but I started bringing a lot of Moebius into my art. I was sucking up all sorts of Geoff Darrow. Frank Quitely is a big Moebius and Geoff Darrow guy, they're two of his foundational influences. So having that background made it pretty easy to absorb the surface qualities of Quitely. When I started drawing Batman, I had his Batman issues taped up on my drawing board all day long. So every time I wanted to draw Damian, I was looking at his Damian, and it just naturally started to look like that. But as the series went on I was looking at my own stuff for reference, so I started to draw more like how I would naturally draw, developing my own style. But on those first couple of issues I was totally leaning into the Frank Quitely thing. It was absolutely intentional.

Did you have any favorites from among the many Batmen you drew?
I love issue #7 with Man-of-Bats on the Indian reservation. Designing his Batcave was really fun, and all the stupid little signs. It was rewardingly laborious. In the script Grant calls out a number of things, but just because he wrote it doesn't mean he gets the best idea as far as I'm concerned. So I'm always like, "Oh, you think that's funny? Here's an even funnier thing to put in the Batcave..." All the giant money in all the other Batcaves is my idea. In Wayne Tower, there's a silver dollar or a quarter. That was my idea. So in the Man-of-Bats cave there's a giant wooden nickel. Then in Batman Japan's Batcave, there's a giant one-yen coin. And in the Outsiders' there's a giant Simon Stagg coin that said, "In Stagg We Trust." That's a stupid little running joke that keeps me amused and makes me feel like it's my comic too. It's not just Grant Morrison's Batman; as far as I'm concerned, it's my Batman too.

I'm sure Grant is very open to that.
He seeks it out. The way he writes, he leaves a lot up to the artist's imagination, and it's very intentional. He won't write the next issue until the previous issue has been drawn, at least getting into the real

specifics of it. Because he wants to be influenced by what the artist is bringing to the table. With any given comic or series, if you could hop in a time machine, the first issue of *Batman Incorporated* probably would have looked pretty similar if Frank Quitely had drawn it or I had drawn it. But issue #2 would have been drastically different just because of the way that we would have influenced Grant.

You had another all-too-rare opportunity when you were allowed to redraw much of the story for its *Absolute* edition.
I don't know specifically, but I suspect that Grant was annoyed enough with it that he said, "Yeah, we can do this now. But for the big collection at the end can we make it the way we want to make it?" They were cool with it, and they actually let me redraw all the fill-in pages that had kind of popped up. That's very rare. It's kind of a waste of money, really. Because I got paid to redraw those pages after they paid people to draw them the first time. [Laughs.]

One of the reasons *Batman Incorporated* works so well is that as epic as it gets, there's a refreshing lack of pretense.
Yeah. There's a real sense of humor to it, which I think is great. Because there's something inherently goofy about men dressing up in tights, and I think it's great to acknowledge that while still telling a heartfelt, compelling story. Once you start to take it a little too seriously you definitely run the risk of it coming off as totally laughable. Like "Gimme a break, guys. You're running around in your tighty-whities here." [Laughs.]

Gotham Gazette Exclusive

Grant Morrison

Writer Grant Morrison wrote Batman in the *Arkham Asylum* graphic novel and monthly *JLA* before scripting a run—from 2006's "Batman and Son" to 2013's *Batman Incorporated*—that captured 75 years of comic history in a single narrative.

What was the driving force behind your multi-year run on Batman? The simple take was I imagined all of Batman's history was one man's biography. That opened everything up. Because suddenly you got something that was almost like a human being. Because if you have contradictions between, say, Neal Adams' Batman and Dick Sprang's Batman and Frank Miller's Batman—imagine they're the same guy. Because in our lives we've gone through periods where maybe we're a little more bright-eyed and utopian and some shit happens. Somebody lets you down. Someone dies in your family. Then suddenly you're the Dark Knight. To say there's only way of doing Batman was reductive. The pantomime, the camp Batman of the '60s, that's when he was 23. But then when he gets to 28, Robin's dead, and he says, "What have I done? What is this mission? Who am I? What am I?" Then the kind of broken, twisted, psychologically inflected Batman of the '90s makes sense. It's like, this is a guy who's getting older, and the mission that was virtually this carnivalesque attempt to subdue crime has left a trail of bodies and done psychological damage.

So for me, that character, from the 1930s on...I imagine him being, say, 20 in his first appearance in *Detective Comics*; that's just my personal take on it. So he's 20 then, and by the time he meets Talia he's 25. And by the time Jason Todd and everyone's dead he's 28. Then he's getting his back broken, and I imagine that Batman being 35 years old. He's lived all of this, and he's been all of those Batmen. He's been Adam West. He's been Frank Miller's *Year One* Batman... It just seems like such a rich character when you accommodate all of that. It became almost human. It became a thing that was generating its own personality.

Passing through the various stages of life?
Yeah, and actually representing how we all feel. How things can be different…I had Talia come back and suddenly she hates him. She's had enough. People will say, "But that's not Talia." Talia loved him when she was 19 and he was 25. Now she's old and she's got a kid. It's like, my mother once loved my father. But she ended up getting divorced and they hated each other. They tore each other apart in divorce court. For me, it was like, let the characters grow and change. Suddenly the person you loved is your worst enemy. And that's the last thing you want. Because you know each other so well, so you can hurt each other really well. I felt like all of that was made more convincing and more powerful by just taking the notion that, every story, he's lived them all. So that was my basic notion for Batman.

You really embraced the reason the character has lasted so long—the fact that he can be so many different things.
Yeah, exactly. Because we all can be. It made him more human. I find that really fascinating, and it's why I stayed with it for seven years rather than the 15 issues that they originally planned for. Because I just got so caught up in the character. He's so amazingly rich. So that was it, and everything else came from that basic concept.

Your work also showed other creators how the character can evolve. Like when you gave him a son in Damian.
Yeah. But I always just wanted to kill the kid so he wouldn't affect the future of Batman. Because I knew [writer] Scott Snyder didn't want to have to deal with the son. Because his Batman was a loner, he was a bit more human. He could screw up more. Whereas my Batman was…Okay, you've done 15 years of training. You're a zen master. You wouldn't have those hatreds anymore. The training would have bombed you out. You'd be an optimum man by this point, psychologically quite pure.

You'd have inner peace.
Yeah. So that's my Batman. He's the optimum man. He's solved his problems. But I understand why it's cool to write about a Batman who's a bit more angry and angst-driven and just dealing with the mission. So that's why I wanted Damian out of the picture—"Here's the story and then he dies and Batman can move on and you need never mention the kid again." But the kid then proved popular, and he's in there again, screwing up the continuity. So I'm kind of pleased with that. But, you know…[Laughs.]

69 Batman Beyond: Return of the Joker

When *Batman Beyond*—a continuation of *Batman: The Animated Series*, set 50 years in the future—bowed in January of 1999, the fate of several of its predecessor's characters remained unresolved. The biggest question, however, was what happened to Tim Drake, the show's second Robin, and the Batman's archenemy, the Joker. It was a long wait before fans received answers. But on December 12, 2000, they came at last in *Batman Beyond: Return of the Joker*.

On the show, Tim's costume was displayed in the Batcave, in a case similar to that which held Robin II Jason Todd's in the comics. So, many feared Tim had been killed by the Joker, and that Batman in turn had killed the Clown Prince of Crime. The answer provided by *Return of the Joker* is almost more horrifying, since it's revealed that the Joker (again voiced by Mark Hamill) and his sidekick/girlfriend Harley Quinn (Arleen Sorkin) kidnapped Tim and drove him insane while learning all of Batman's secrets (including his true identity). Grafting a rictus grin on his face, the Joker essentially takes Batman's son and makes him his own, transforming him into a living mockery of the Dark Knight. Though Batman (Kevin Conroy) and Batgirl (Tara Strong) rescue Tim, their Bat Family is destroyed.

That chilling truth comes out in a virtuoso flashback sequence midway through a gripping action movie directed by Curt Geda (who'd storyboarded some of *BTAS'* best episodes, including "Heart of Ice" and "Harley's Holiday") and scripted by Paul Dini; working from a story he'd crafted with his fellow *Batman Beyond* producers Bruce Timm and Glen Murakami. Timm and Murakami also designed the film's characters, along with Shane Glines, including a new group of Jokerz (among them the adorably lethal "Dee Dee" twins, Delia and Deidre Dennis), who become minions to the original "Mister J" when his mind takes over the body of the now-adult Tim Drake (voiced by Dean Stockwell). It's his last laugh at the Dark Knight and his legacy.

Will Friedle voices the new Batman, Terry McGinnis—a surrogate for Bruce who battles the Joker's surrogate in Tim—and Angie Harmon lends support as Commissioner Barbara Gordon

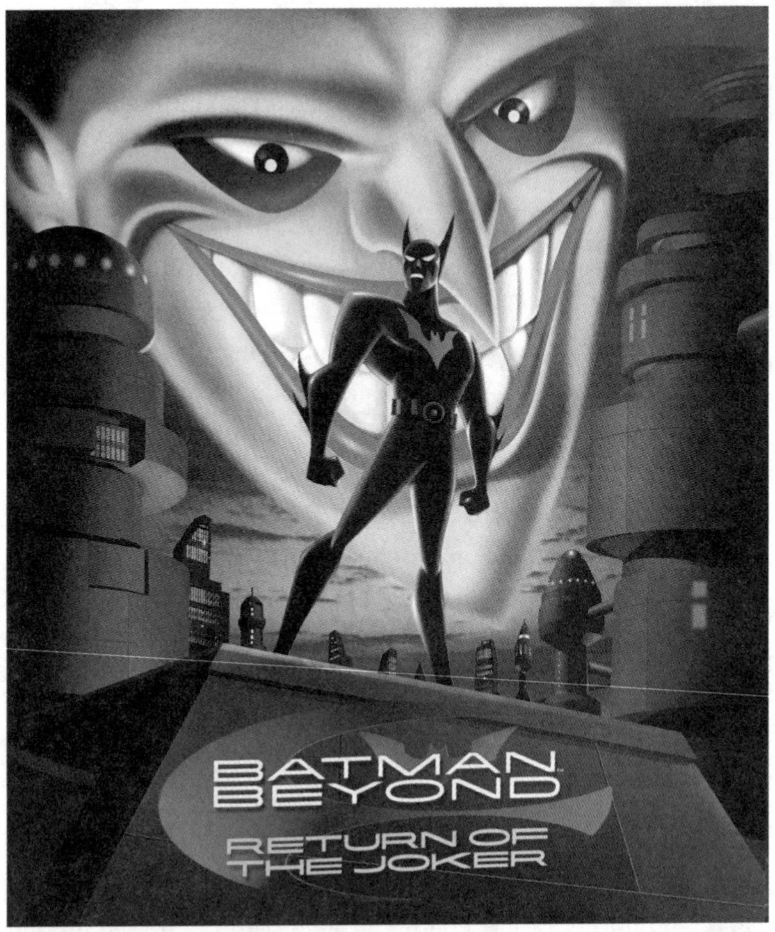

A spinoff of Batman Beyond, *set many years after Bruce Wayne had hung up his cape and cowl,* Batman Beyond: Return of the Joker *was the first animated Batman movie to receive a PG-13 rating.*

(replacing *Batman Beyond*'s Stockard Channing). But it's Conroy and Hamill who steal the show, delivering what may be their career-best performances as the Dark Knight and the Clown Prince of Crime. The latter has never been creepier, bringing his usual boisterousness down to a simmer to play an eerily calm, studiously patient psychopath.

Planned originally for theatrical release, *Return of the Joker* debuted on home video when Warner Brothers got cold feet over its content, trimming much of its violence in the wake of April 1999's Columbine High School shooting. The "Original Uncut Version" was finally released on April 23, 2002, the first animated Batman movie to receive a PG-13 rating.

In addition to plumbing the depths of its characters' psyches, *Batman Beyond: Return of the Joker* stands out for its intense action sequences and the quality and consistency of its animation. Produced by Japan's TMS Studios (which storyboarded half the film), it's on par with the best anime released this century, and marks the first time that *all* of a DC Animated Universe production's backgrounds were rendered digitally. Series composer Kristopher Carter provides the score—which employs far more orchestral music than the series' rock soundtrack—assisted by house music pioneers Mephisto Odyssey with industrial band Static-X and blues musician Kenny Wayne Shepherd.

As both a bittersweet conclusion to *Batman: The Animated Series* and a story that takes full advantage of *Batman Beyond*'s cyberpunk potential, *Batman Beyond: Return of the Joker* is required viewing for all Batfans.

70 "Hush"

One of the rock star artists who made their names at Marvel Comics in the late 1980s before founding Image Comics in the 1990s, Jim Lee has enjoyed a career that's brought him to the upper echelons of DC Comics, where he now works as co-publisher. His creative zenith, however, is the bestselling 2002–03 Batman story arc "Hush."

Written by Jeph Loeb with inks by Lee's frequent collaborator Scott Williams, the 12-issue "Hush" (running from December 2002's *Batman* #608 through 619) gives the Dark Knight a new enemy with ties to Bruce Wayne's past, setting him apart from most members of Batman's rogues gallery, used here as pawns in an effort to destroy their common foe. (Spoilers! The mystery man turns out to be Bruce's childhood friend, Thomas Elliot, working in cahoots with the Riddler.)

Like Loeb's previous work *The Long Halloween*, "Hush" is a whodunit that serves first and foremost as a showcase for the work of its superstar artist, giving Lee an opportunity to draw Gotham's most popular supervillains, as well as Batman's frenemy Superman. Along the way, Loeb and Lee heat up Batman's relationship with Catwoman, revitalize the Riddler and Killer Croc, and anticipate the late second Robin Jason Todd's later return.

Lee is sometimes criticized for his impossibly wasp-waisted, torpedo-breasted women and the ornate costumes of his characters. He's a comics creator unafraid of showing readers how hard he's working. But there's an undeniable energy to his images, a respect for the grit of early Frank Miller, and a commitment to his vision that suits the fan-favorite's visit to Gotham City.

Gotham Gazette Exclusive

Jim Lee

Before becoming DC Comics' co-publisher, fan-favorite artist Jim Lee illustrated the smash hit 2002–03 Batman storyline "Hush." He followed it with a run on *All Star Batman & Robin*.

Who do you think is the most underrated Batman creator?
I'm gonna throw out Steve Englehart and Marshall Rogers. They did this awesome Batman-Joker storyline which kind of redefined Batman for me. It was superheroic, but had a lot of detective elements to it. It was just dazzling.

Why has the character lasted so many years?
I think one of the reasons is that the art form of comics is all about letting creators and the talent come in and do their definitive versions of these characters. We're not trying to say, "Hey, this is Batman. This is the style guide. This is the length of his ears. This is the length of his cape. Draw it just like this. You can only do *these* kinds of stories..." We fortunately work in a form, a creative field, where people are encouraged to do new things, add to the mythology—the Court of Owls, new costumes, new Batmobiles. That's how you keep it fresh and modern and contemporary. Everyone who comes to Batman, and every generation of fans, they go, "That's *my* Batman." It's slightly different from the one before, but at its core, its essence, it's the same character that we all know and love.

What do you think you brought to Batman with your work?
Apparently treads on his boots. A lot of people bring that up for some reason. [Laughs.] You never know as you're doing the work what you're gonna be remembered for. Frank Miller's work is what got me into comics. So anytime I take on a new character I try to blend the things I loved about the work that came before me. Neal Adams was probably the other twin tower. Those were the two big influences. It's just trying to take that and kind of modernize it and add something new to it. And kind of expand the Batcave a little bit, and try to make some sense out of where he keeps all his cars. Just try to apply some logic to this whole crazy concept of "I've got a cave. I'm just gonna fill it with computers and cars. I'll figure out a way to get that stuff out later." [Laughs.]

71 Batman: War on Crime

The live-action Batman movies are box-office behemoths. But none of them have captured the character as he's been presented for most of his career in comic books—in a skintight mask (in which he's able to turn his head) and a costume made of fabric. Fans, however, can get a glimpse of just what such a movie might look like in the graphic novel *Batman: War on Crime.*

Released in December of 1999, *War on Crime* is the second in a series of 64-page graphic novels written by Paul Dini and illustrated by Alex Ross—and published in the oversized format of DC Comics' "treasury edition" titles of the 1970s and 1980s—that pair DC heroes with real-world issues. Ross had won praise beforehand for his rendering of Batman in the apocalyptic 1996 "Elseworlds" limited series *Kingdom Come*. But Ross' Dark Knight takes center stage here, and Ross' painted, photorealistic art makes him as imposing as any yet seen, even as it presents a view of Gotham City sadly reflective of our world.

One of the biggest criticisms leveled against Bruce Wayne is that he uses his wealth and genius to fight costumed criminals far more often than he targets the root of corruption—poverty—and the people it most frequently affects—minorities. In *War on Crime,* Bruce is courted by a corrupt real estate developer intent on gentrifying an especially impoverished area of Gotham. Over the course of several nights, Batman visits the area and encounters Marcus, a small boy whose parents were killed in a holdup. When he sees Marcus become a part of the city's crime, Batman is horrified, and realizes his best chance for helping him lies with his alter ego.

Though Marcus' story mirrors that of the young Bruce Wayne, Dini and Ross, to their credit, refuse to focus their tale on the Dark Knight and his origin. Instead, they use it to spotlight an issue with which many comic book readers may be unfamiliar. There's an argument sometimes put forth that superhero stories should avoid such concerns, that the cape-and-tights crowd wasn't designed for matters of import, and that any attempt to pair the two is at best naive and at worst pretentious. Yet there's another argument: that characters who've inspired children can do the same for all ages, and help build a positive force for change. In the hands of Dini and Ross, the latter argument wins.

"When they showed an understanding of how the real world of crime was something that existed in Batman's universe in Christopher Nolan's *Batman Begins*—when they showed he's got a city with a lot of suffering in it and that that's what's causing a lot of the crime—I felt a validation," says Ross, whose work on the book won him the 2000 Eisner Award for Best Painter/Multimedia Artist (in addition to a Harvey Award for Best Graphic Album of Original Work). "That film came out after *War on Crime*, and I saw Christian Bale, at a press conference for the film, call out my work as one of the influences. There were many influences on *Batman Begins*, but I thought, 'That feels satisfying, to think that we were on the same page.'"

Gotham Gazette Exclusive

Alex Ross

Writer-artist Alex Ross brought the tradition of fine art to his painted comics *Marvels* and *Kingdom Come*, as well as the treasury-sized DC graphic novels he created with Paul Dini—among them the Eisner Award–winning *Batman: War on Crime.*

How do you view today's dichotomy between Superman and Batman?

Here's the root of what's behind a lot of my thinking…What Mark Waid and I did with *Kingdom Come* was to both work with the common theory that these guys are kind of at odds because that became popular in the last 40 years—to set them up as polar opposites. So therefore they should be somewhat ideologically contrary. To Mark's credit, he turned a story that I had a rough idea for, that put them on opposite ends of two different armies, and twisted it—where we thought things were going in one direction and they didn't go that way at all. If anything, Batman kind of came to Superman's rescue. I appreciate that, because as a fan I remember they were friends for decades, from their inception. They were not created to be friends, but they became fast friends, on covers before stories were set up. They were basically these guys who had visually different methods. One was gadgets and one was physical power, and they arrived at the same result. The same selfless acts of heroism, to look after people and do everything they could for the world they lived in.

Because of the needs of drama and the sake of the way we tell and craft stories, we've all embraced this modern ethic of "Well, they're just so angry at each other." Why? When I grew up as a kid, all the toys I had, all the comics I was absorbing…There was a visual distinctiveness that made them different people—just like we have friends who are not exactly like us, who don't all think the same as us. So if anything, the time that I put into it works within the new reality but tries to offer up the idea that at their core they're both frail human beings of failings.

Particularly Batman, who seems unquestioned in the modern mindset—he's the guy who's right about everything. Well, nobody's right about everything, and Batman can fail too. I appreciate seeing that understood. That he's somebody who can be humbled and should be humbled now and again.

Why has each of them survived the many metamorphoses they've gone through?

Part of it is just simply that everything that needed to be there visually was dynamic from the get-go. It was baked in from inception. When they were both designed, around '38, '39—they had the best stuff that could be added. I mean, Batman grabbed a hold of the visual uniqueness of his horns or ears, depending on how you see them, and the scalloped cape. They're such unique graphic symbols that Batman would be the best of all dark characters for all time to come. We've seen countless deviations of the archetypes they represent, and of course you have the pulp characters that preceded them. But none of them created the kind of simple, graphic symbolism that was honed to perfection with their creation. Over the years we may have seen that played with, but for the most part the characters that came out in the '30s are what worked and what still work now. They are the ultimate prototypes for everything in the creation of superhero characters. Those two archetypes. Everything else bounces from them. You could find anybody that you like from them—Iron Man has aspects that deviate from Batman, Spider-Man has aspects that deviate from Batman and Superman. Every character that's been created since owes to their precedent.

As a young fan, which version of Batman resonated most with you?

I always thought of Batman as being Neal Adams' archetypal style, because even if he wasn't drawing the books they were recrafted in his style after his impact in the field. But I saw reprints of Dick Sprang–era '40s and '50s stories, and that wide-bodied look for Batman that was very much stolen from the hand of Chester Gould was so interesting and engaging. So I was always a hybrid of loving Neal Adams and Dick Sprang equally.

With Batman, I would have loved to have just embraced Neal Adams' style and that longer, leaner kind of thing. But instead, opting for the darkness of his rendering, the long ears, but with this wider head, this thicker body...If people wonder, "Why does Alex Ross' Batman always look so fat?" it's because I thought I was trying to approximate a realistic version of the art style of Dick Sprang. As absurd as that is, that's what I thought I was doing. [Laughs.]

One of the distinct elements of your Batman is his eyes. You've always chosen to show them.

[Laughs.] It rests on the idea of "What looks visually engaging in a real person that you take seriously when trying to render realistically?" So I try to approach it with this practical sense that was way overthought on my part. I'm guilty of really taking it way too seriously and taking it to an extreme that's really unnecessary. But it's just what seemed visually dynamic to me. Like, if I treat the mask like it's a layer of makeup that just goes right up to the edge of the eyelid, where you don't know where skin ends and mask begins, that has a whole different kind of impression to it. He feels more real. Hopefully.

Honestly, with all the movies that have been made, they still use mainly rubber masks or latex masks, but they've never tried this effect fully. They put makeup around the actor's eyes to darken that area, but they still have this separation of a big rubber thing and where the eyes are. I'd love to see somebody try it with the idea of it being like makeup.

What sparked *War on Crime*?

Well, there was a lot of thought toward how comic book crime was a poor representation of what real crime was. That it was always fanciful, and becoming a more and more removed metaphor from what the real thing is. Which has a lot to do with urban blight and the difference between those that have and those that have not. Nobody really focuses on that, because it doesn't make for entertainment when you see Batman going and punching poor people in the face. So, wanting to represent that with some gravity and show that Batman understood it and saw that reality around him, that that is something that he did face and contend with...I wanted to bury down the issue of his flamboyant villains. All of whom are kind of acknowledged in subtle ways throughout the book. You see different aspects of showing them, but not colorfully and not flamboyantly. Yeah, they're there and that's part of his world, that he has to fight these particular lunatics. But there's a very real, hard world that he also engages with, that is crime that happens to people in inner city areas, that features Batman in situations you don't necessarily want to see illustrated all the time. Because it does bring in issues of race that are part of the climate of crime. Wanting to touch upon it sensitively but also show an understanding of the privilege he comes from and the despair that's around him in the city he lives in...There's no perfect way to have done that.

(Alex Ross)

Your art wound up informing Christopher Nolan's Dark Knight trilogy.
Well, I got a copy of the [*Batman Begins*] screenplay before the movie came out. Paul Dini got it to me. I really loved it. I was just enthralled at the idea that this was gonna be the way we were finally gonna deal with a much more grounded world. So I was a big supporter of those movies and how they would depict this fantastic world. I felt like, "Ah, this is finally it. It broke through. We actually are gonna see something that's more truthful."

Christian Bale's Batman has got really nothing in common with my style of drawing the characters. Nothing that I brought to it really translates over to him. But I would love any correlation there could have been between that series of films and my work because I was such a fan. So it doesn't always have to match up for me to like it. I'm a real stickler, because I'm a hardcore fan. I love certain versions of things and I hate others. You get really passionate about this stuff, and luckily I don't go online to share any of my opinions. Because plenty of other people are doing that. They don't need me in the mix. [Laughs.]

Your Batman comic covers have embraced most eras of the character's history.
There's a fun and frivolity to the character's history that shouldn't be forgotten. But we've had a sort of dark, serious version be the dominant way of making all comics these days. That does start to wear thin after a while, and you start to wonder, "God, is there any other way we can go back to a somewhat lighthearted or not as super-serious or deadly version as we make today?" Various creators try it, but for the most part the companies bank on trying to sell comics to an older, aggressive, mostly male audience.

Your covers have also captured the essence of the Joker.
[Laughs.] I don't know if that's true. Ultimately the only version of the Joker I've done is me doing this exaggerated expression that I can do. I was always trying to translate the original influence on the character's design, which was the Conrad Veidt movie from the 1930s called *The Man Who Laughs*. That black-and-white film is what established the Joker's face, and pretty much just combining that with

the name of the playing card they made a brand-new character out of it. They interpreted his black-and-white image as just a white face, and then added the lipstick and hair color and then, *boom*, he was off. My only deviation from that is to assume, looking at the old comic book coloring, that he may never have actually been intended to be illustrated like he was wearing a colorful clown-like outfit. In fact, he was dressed up in sort of the zoot suit era with long coats and big lapels. If anything, he might have been dressed up like he was going out for a fancy night on the town, and that clothing was tinted with colors. Just like Batman was tinted blue, even though he was supposed to be wearing black, Joker may himself have just been wearing a fine suit. That purple tone became embedded in the character over time, but it may never have been anything other than shading for black.

You mentioned your appreciation for the Dark Knight trilogy. Is that your favorite screen version of the character?

No, I'm not sure if I even have one, really, that is the perfect porridge of not too cold, not too hot. Batman has always been a character in conflict. Since they've put him in movies, they've been reinterpreting him from what he was. There's part of me that still wants to see a guy wearing fabric. Somebody who's actually built like the character, who's got that giant jawline and big physique. We've never really seen that. We probably never will see that. But worrying about how you bring something to life through Hollywood's reasons for using latex and padding and whatnot is always gonna leave the character somewhat unfulfilled. Unless you're talking about *LEGO Batman*. [Laughs.]

There's part of me that wants to go into that alternate reality where David Bowie and Pierce Brosnan accepted the job offers of being in 1989's *Batman*, and have David Bowie be the Joker and Pierce Brosnan be Bruce Wayne/Batman. Because that would have been casting type that matched the way that the characters looked in the comics at that time. I, like everybody else, wanted to see Jack Nicholson play the Joker, of course. Everybody wanted that for years. But imagine if Bowie had said yes. It would have been very appropriate for the character, his look and everything. It could have been magnificent, and I'm sure he would have done a phenomenal job. I would love to visit that reality and see what happened instead.

72 The Scarecrow

Fear. It's Batman's greatest weapon in his war against crime. But it's an emotion he himself has wrestled with since he was a child. That's what makes Professor Jonathan Crane such a formidable member of the Dark Knight's rogues gallery—for no one has mastered fear like the Scarecrow.

This "fantastic figure of burlap and straw, with a brain—cunning and distorted!" first appeared two years after Ray Bolger portrayed a more genial straw man in *The Wizard of Oz.* He debuted in September 1941's *World Finest* #3 ("The Riddle of the Human Scarecrow," by Batman creators Bill Finger and Bob Kane, with penciling assistance from Jerry Robinson). With a face, form, and name resembling another figure of Halloween—Washington Irving's Ichabod Crane—Jonathan Crane was introduced to readers as "a teacher of psychology in a university" who, as a small boy, "liked to frighten birds."

Shabbily dressed in old clothes, Crane is denied an invitation to a party his colleagues are attending. Alone in his home, he cries, "The fools! Do they think I would give up my precious books just to buy clothes? Bah! They think I'm strange and I look like a scarecrow—a scarecrow!...They judge human values by money—if I had money they'd respect me—and I could buy more books! Yes—if only I had money—lots of money—"

Crane is soon fired for his bizarre lectures—which involve firing guns in the classroom—but he finds a new career, dressed as "a symbol of poverty and fear combined! The perfect symbol—the scarecrow!" Crane takes his cue from protection racketeers and targets a businessman sued by his partner for embezzling. For a

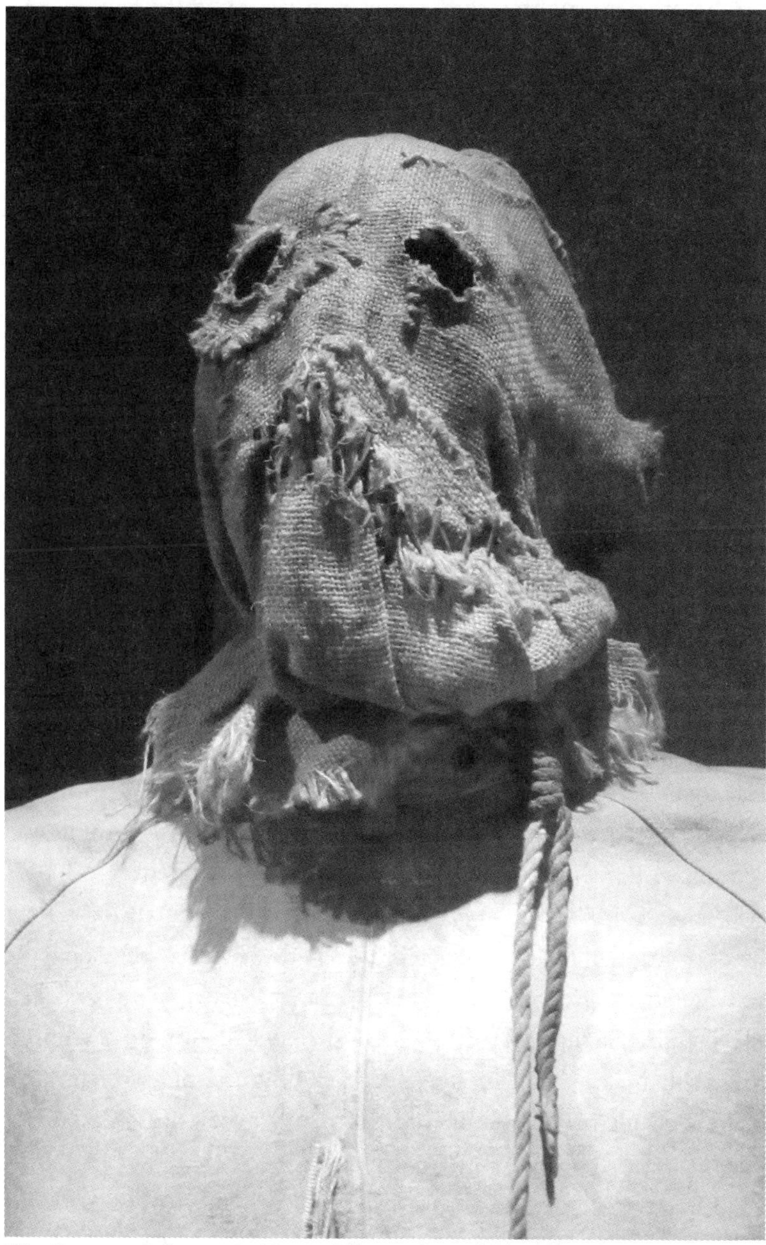

The Scarecrow's fear toxin has made him a formidable villain in Batman's rogues gallery. Pictured here is the mask worn by Cillian Murphy in Christopher Nolan's cinematic trilogy. (Sophia Quach McCabe)

fee, he offers to frighten the partner into dropping the lawsuit, but catches the attention of Batman and Robin.

In his first appearance, the Dynamic Duo's "sawdust friend" relied on smoke bombs, his natural agility (including "queer grasshopper leaps"), and surprisingly keen fighting skills. But after just one more Golden Age appearance (*Detective Comics* #73), the character vanished. When he reappeared in the Silver Age 23 years later, in February 1967's *Batman* #189, he acquired his trademark fear toxin. With it, he terrorized his opponents; first with phobias he projected into their minds, then by summoning up their own worst fears. The following year, he made his screen debut, in *The Batman/Superman Hour* episode "The Great Scarecrow Scare."

"The Prince of Panic" appeared frequently throughout the 1970s. His reputation grew when he joined the Injustice Gang, as well as the Legion of Doom in 1978's *Challenge of the Super Friends* animated series. Among his more noteworthy Bronze Age comic book stories was "The Autobiography of Bruce Wayne" in April 1983's *The Brave and the Bold* #197 (by writer Alan Brennert and penciler Joe Staton), which saw the Batman and Catwoman join forces to overcome his fear toxin, leading the two to fall in love and marry.

In 1995's *Batman Annual* #19, the Scarecrow's origin was refined so that his classroom gunplay injures a student. In 2005's two-issue *Year One: Batman/Scarecrow* it was explained that Crane was born to parents who rejected him, and was raised by his fanatically religious great-grandmother in an old mansion in Georgia. He acquired a fear of birds when she locked him in a church full of them, but won his revenge by killing the old woman, and channeled his phobia—much like Bruce Wayne—into a frightful persona.

On screen, the Scarecrow has the distinction of starring in "The Fear," the 1985 episode of *The Super Powers Team: Galactic Guardians* (a continuation of *Super Friends*) that marked the first time the Dark Knight's origin story was told outside of comic books. He appeared as a recurring villain in *Batman: The Animated Series*, voiced by Henry Polic II, and was chillingly redesigned for its continuation *The New Batman Adventures*, in which he was voiced by *Re-Animator* star Jeffrey Combs and Jeff Bennett. In Christopher Nolan's Dark Knight trilogy, Cillian Murphy plays a Crane who, on the surface, is more handsome than his predecessors, but whose face masks his insanity. Even more horrifying is the Scarecrow of the *Batman: Arkham* video games, who injects his fear toxin from syringes mounted on the fingers of his gloved hand. The fourth such game, *Arkham Knight*, features Crane as its principal antagonist, creepily voiced by John Noble.

In any form, the Scarecrow maintains his reputation as one of Batman's deadliest enemies by, time and again, giving the Dark Knight a taste of his own terrifying medicine.

73 The Top Five Batman Christmas Stories

Why are there so many great Christmas stories about a grim avenger of the night? Perhaps it's because night is never so sharply defined as when contrasted against the brightness of day—and few holidays shine as brightly as the one celebrated on December 25. Here are five standouts from the Batman's plethora of yuletide tales. Each demonstrates that, when it comes to Christmas, the Dark Knight's as welcome as old Saint Nick himself.

"A Christmas Peril!"

The first Batman Christmas story (titled "Christmas") debuted way back in 1942's *Batman* #9, but the first truly great Batman Christmas story was February 1945's "A Christmas Peril!" (in

Batman #27, written by Don Cameron and illustrated by Joker and Robin co-creator Jerry Robinson). Taking its cue from Dickens' *A Christmas Carol*, it tells the story of "Young Scrooge"—a rich, miserly orphan manipulated by his advisers into partnering with the mob in a crooked Christmas tree sales racket. Fortunately, he learns the spirit of giving from Batman and Robin.

"The Silent Night of the Batman"
Master artist Neal Adams draws one of his best Batman stories (written by Mike Friedrich for February 1970's *Batman* #219). This short tale finds the Dark Knight reluctant to stand down and enjoy Christmas Eve. But the people of Gotham, inspired by his example, have things under control, giving him a chance to sip eggnog and sing carols with the city's police force. Adams and writer Paul Dini later reworked the story into "The Not So Silent Night of the Harley Quinn," in January 2017's *Batman Annual* #1.

"Merry Christmas"
Caught in a blizzard on Christmas Eve, the Dark Knight runs afoul of a hoodlum prepared to rub out a snowbound family in order to cover his tracks. In this tale penciled by Irv Novick from February 1973's *Batman* #247, the Christmas miracle that saves the day works thanks to the storytelling of fabled Bat-scribe Denny O'Neil.

"The Night the Mob Stole Xmas"
Batman: The Brave and the Bold writer Bob Haney was known for outrageous stories that paired Batman with a multitude of DC heroes. Few were as zany as this one, from March 1979's issue #148 (penciled by Joe Staton), which sees the Dark Knight helping pliable sleuth Plastic Man out of his holiday blues by busting a band of cigarette smugglers.

"Wanted: Santa Claus—Dead or Alive"
The Dark Knight Returns creator Frank Miller cut his Bat-teeth on this story, his first Batman work, from 1980's *DC's Super-Star Holiday Special* (aka *DC Special Series* #21). Here, a crook posing as a department store Santa sees the light, and Batman intervenes before the reformed criminal can be murdered by his ex-cohorts.

Honorable Mention: All of the tales in the 1995 anthology *The Batman Adventures Holiday Special*—by the creative team behind *Batman: The Animated Series*—are worthwhile. Most of them were adapted in the "Holiday Knights" episode of 1997's animated *The New Batman Adventures*.

74 The Batplane

Though they're essential tools in his war on crime, the Batrope and Bat-Glider can only take Batman so high. In order to soar above and beyond his winged namesake, nothing less than a Batplane will do.

The Batplane was the Dark Knight's first official Bat vehicle, preceding the Batmobile by almost two years when it debuted. In September 1939's *Detective Comics* #31 ("Batman Versus the Vampire, Part 1," written by Gardner Fox and penciled by Bob Kane and Sheldon Moldoff), Bruce Wayne's fiancée Julie Madison is hypnotized by the evil Monk, and the young woman takes an ocean voyage to recuperate, prompting Batman to follow her in a rotor-equipped gyroplane he calls "the Batgyro." When the aircraft first takes to the skies, pedestrians cower below. "Look!" cries one onlooker. "A Bat!" yells another. "The end of the world! We are attacked by Martians!" says a third, apparently still convinced that Orson Welles' *War of the Worlds* radio broadcast from the year before was real. By the end of the story, when he rescues Julie from the Monk's clutches in Paris, the Batman's vehicle is referred to as "the Bat-plane." In the following issue, the hyphen is dropped, and he follows the Monk to Hungary in "the Batplane."

In the decade that followed, the Batplane evolved into a monoplane, often with its propeller replaced by an enormous bat head, much like the one mounted on the front of the 1940s Batmobile. (It was unexplained how the plane generated thrust.) With the jet age in full swing by the late 1940s, the Batplane was retrofitted with jet engines in February 1946's *Detective Comics* #108 in order to combat sky bandits.

When the 1950s arrived, they brought an entirely new Batplane. In October 1950's *Batman* #61 ("The Birth of Batplane II!"), after their cherished vessel falls into the hands of smuggling racketeers, the Dynamic Duo design and construct a replacement, inspired by the Navy's F9F Panther, that can convert into a helicopter or submarine. Batplane II came tricked out with a magnesium-fired Bat-Beam, human ejector tubes, a super ramjet power plant, a complete crime lab, and a "vacuum blanket" capable of conking out other plane's engines. "Wow! A Batmarine!" says Robin.

The Caped Crusaders acquired a Bat-copter in May 1951's *Detective Comics* #171 and one-man "Whirly-Bat" helicopters in July 1958's *Detective Comics* #257, yet the Batmarine continued to fly throughout the 1950s and 1960s. Artists would occasionally depict a Batplane based on the Air Force's needle-nosed F-104 or McDonnell F-101 Voodoo, before settling on a McDonnell Douglas F-4 Phantom II in the 1970s. Other inconsistent depictions followed in the 1980s, with the Batplane wavering back and forth between its F-101 design and one based on the F-15 Eagle.

As loosely adapted from real military aircraft as most Batplanes were, reality was completely replaced by fantasy with the introduction of the Batwing in Tim Burton's 1989 *Batman* film. Designed to resemble a flying Bat symbol, the Batwing proved so popular that versions of it were incorporated into 1992's *Batman: The Animated Series*, 1995's *Batman Forever*, and the comic books of the new millennium.

The most unique Batplane to date, however, was introduced in Christopher Nolan's *The Dark Knight Rises*. This prototype vehicle developed for the Department of Defense as a tool for "urban pacification" employs massive propellers for lift and propulsion, and to create cyclonic winds as a means of defense. Of all Batman's aircraft, in both appearance and maneuverability, "The Bat" most resembles an animal—a big, black, flying lobster.

75 See the Batcycle and Batcopter

Batman: The Movie—based on 1966's hit *Batman* TV show—gave several new vehicles to Adam West's Batman, including the Batboat, Batcycle, and Batcopter. The latter two are available for the public to see, and, in the case of the Batcopter, ride.

Almost as famous as the fabled Batmobile is its compact counterpart, the Batcycle (which first appeared, driven by Batwoman, in July 1956's *Detective Comics* #233). Though it was first seen on screen in the show's first-season episode "Not Yet, He Ain't" (in which it was a Harley-Davidson, rented by the production), the better-known version of the cycle made its debut in the film.

Designed by Tom Daniel and built by Richard "Korky" Korkes and Daniel Dempski (known collectively as Kustomotive), the Batcycle was a customized Yamaha Catalina (YDS-3) 250, with a modified sidecar that Robin occupied. Four Batcycles were built, the "hero" model (from which three rocket tubes protruded on the back of the sidecar) and three copies. On the hero bike, the sidecar held a detachable, self-propelled, gasoline-fueled go-kart with a 55cc Yamaha engine.

The 1966 Batcycle (with a replica sidecar) is on permanent display at the Petersen Automotive Museum in Los Angeles (which also houses the Batmobile from 1992's *Batman Returns*). The cycles seen in later Batman films, including *Batman & Robin*'s Redbird (driven by Robin) and Batblade (driven by Batgirl), as well as *The Dark Knight*'s Bat-pod, are on display in the Picture Car Vault, a stop on the Warner Bros. Studio Tour Hollywood.

The Batcopter (which first appeared in print in May 1951's *Detective Comics* #171) is now owned and operated by Captain Eugene Nock. Every summer, this one-of-a-kind Bell Helicopter—officially named "The Original Batcopter N3079G" (its on-screen serial number)—appears at comic conventions, state fairs, and air shows along the East Coast and throughout the Midwest. Though it no longer sports the Bat wings it had in the film (for which the federally chartered vehicle was leased), the Batcopter remains airworthy. So at many events fans can, for a fee, ride in it and experience what it's like to *be* Batman (sans exploding shark). Appearances are announced on the Batcopter's official Facebook page (www.facebook.com/N3079gBatcopter). From December to May, the Batcopter can be seen at Florida Suncoast Helicopters in Sarasota.

76 Mr. Freeze

Though often grim in his determination to rid Gotham City of crime, the Dark Knight doesn't close himself off to emotions. Would that the same were true of Dr. Victor Fries.

Mr. Freeze began his criminal career as "Mr. Zero" in February 1959's *Batman* #121 ("The Ice Crimes of Mr. Zero," by writer Dave Wood and penciler Sheldon Moldoff). The basis for two episodes of the 1966 *Batman* TV series ("Instant Freeze" and "Rats Like Cheese"), the story explained that Freeze was once a criminal scientist who, while experimenting with an ice gun he'd invented, saturated himself with a freezing solution that required he keep his body at a constant subzero temperature in order to survive. "Golly, Boss," says one of his minions, "you've become a—a human icicle!"

After perfecting an "air-conditioned costume" and building a refrigerated lair in a mountain outside of Gotham, the archvillain commits a series of robberies with his ice gun, eventually trapping Batman and Robin in giant ice cubes. But the Dynamic Duo break free by cracking their blocks together and cure Freeze of his condition.

Following his appearance in the first season of *Batman*—in which he was played by George Sanders—the character returned for two more two-parters in the show's second year; in each of which he was played by a different actor, Otto Preminger and Eli Wallach. He returned to comics, his physical impairment intact, in March 1968's *Detective Comics* #373 ("Mr. Freeze's Chilling Death Trap!")—in which he traded the name Mr. Zero for Mr. Freeze—then vanished for the better part of a decade before reappearing in September 1977's *Batman* #291 ("Where Were You on the Night Batman Was Killed?").

February 1979's *Batman* #308 ("There'll Be a Cold Time in the Old Town Tonight!") marked the first time a tragic motivation was given to Freeze's crimes. Suffering from loneliness as a result of his affliction, he seeks to share his life with a woman by causing her to have the same condition, only to have her betray him.

On September 7, 1992, an episode of *Batman: The Animated Series* aired that presented Freeze in a much more sympathetic light, redefining the character forever. Written by Paul Dini, the Emmy Award–winning "Heart of Ice" gave viewers a Freeze whose emotions were chilled by tragedy. A once-good man, this Victor Fries learned his wife, Nora, was terminally ill, and cryogenically froze her until he could discover a means of saving her. But his employer terminated the experiment—and the life of his beloved. In the ensuing struggle, Fries was doused with chemicals and reborn as Freeze—a villain consumed by revenge.

Hypnotically voiced by Michael Ansara, Freeze returned for several follow-up episodes of *Batman: The Animated Series*, the spinoff film *Batman & Mr. Freeze: SubZero*, and the spinoff series *Batman Beyond*, in which a new body is built for him, resulting in a heartbreakingly brief period of rehabilitation. Dini introduced his version of Freeze to comics in the excellent 1997 prestige-format one-shot *Batman: Mr. Freeze* (penciled by Mark Buckingham). Its release coincided with the box-office release of *Batman & Robin*, which reduced the villain to an unfunny punster played by a miscast Arnold Schwarzenegger.

But Freeze proved resilient enough to survive the Joel Schumacher–directed film. With his comic book history revamped to match that of his animated incarnation, he became one of Batman's greatest enemies, as well as a constant reminder of what could happen should the Dark Knight ever succumb to his own grief.

77 Arkham Asylum

The dark heart of Gotham City is the Elizabeth Arkham Asylum for the Criminally Insane—housing those citizens who lack Bruce Wayne's mental fortitude, and moral compass, for more than 40 years.

The most iconic piece of architecture in Batman's world aside from Wayne Manor itself, the asylum was introduced in October 1974's *Batman* #258 ("Threat of the Two-Headed Coin!" by writer Denny O'Neil and penciler Irv Novick), though references to an unnamed insane asylum had been made as far back as *Batman* #1. Initially located in New England and named "Arkham Hospital" (though the story's narration points out this is "a polite name for an asylum"), the facility took its name and location from the fictional Arkham, Massachusetts—the setting of many of author H.P. Lovecraft's horror stories.

In August 1980's *Batman* #326 ("This Way Lies Madness"), the structure is said to be located within the suburbs of Gotham by writer Len Wein, who gave the building a backstory when he penned its entry in March 1985's *Who's Who: The Definitive Directory of the DC Universe* #1. Wein's background was expanded upon by writer Grant Morrison and artist Dave McKean in their dreamlike 1989 graphic novel *Arkham Asylum: A Serious House on Serious Earth*.

Arkham Asylum was founded by Amadeus Arkham and named after his mother, who suffered from dementia, his solution to which was cutting her throat (the death was reported as a suicide). Amadeus then converted his family's mansion into an asylum, and went on to marry and have a daughter. But when one of his patients escaped and murdered his wife and child, Amadeus' madness was unleashed. He killed the man, and became an inmate of his own asylum.

Amadeus' nephew Jeremiah continued his uncle's work and, unfortunately, his legacy of insanity. In the 1992 *Batman: Shadow of the Bat* storyline "The Last Arkham," Jeremiah trapped Batman within the walls of Arkham in an effort to study him. The Dark Knight, however, faced a far greater challenge the following year, when part of the asylum was demolished by Bane and its residents set free. Shortly thereafter, Jeremiah opened a new asylum—modeled on the one depicted in *Batman: The Animated Series*—using the gothic castle located on Mercey Island, north of Gotham.

Arkham Asylum has since appeared in most screen incarnations of Batman's world, including Christopher Nolan's trilogy. Its biggest on-screen role is in Rocksteady Studios' *Batman: Arkham Asylum* video game—the first of the company's *Batman: Arkham* games—in which its patients take control of it.

Those brave enough to explore the real Arkham (or a reasonable facsimile thereof) can do so in the United Kingdom. In *Batman Begins*, North London's National Institute for Medical Research (the Ridgeway at Burtonhole Lane, Mill Hill, NW7) served as the building's exterior; its large interior stairwell is that of the city's St. Pancras Chambers, a restored 19th century luxury hotel connected to St. Pancras Station (on Euston Road, NW1). Dr. Jonathan Crane's industrial lab, located deep within the asylum, is in reality London's Abbey Mills Pumping Station (located on Abbey Lane, E15).

78 Danny Elfman's "The Batman Theme"

Some music screams. Some sighs. Danny Elfman's theme for director Tim Burton's 1989 *Batman* does both.

Elfman had worked with Burton on his two prior movies—*Pee-wee's Big Adventure* and *Beetlejuice*—both of which featured rambunctious compositions by the Oingo Boingo frontman turned film composer. Of Warner Brothers' interest in those scores, Elfman says, "No one cared. With *Batman, a lot* of people cared."

When executive producer Jon Peters expressed reservations about Elfman, Burton had the musician play "The Batman Theme" for Peters, resulting not only in Elfman scoring the film, but in his score getting its own release, separate from that of Prince's *Batman* album (which compiled the artist's soundtrack songs).

Recording with the London Symphony Orchestra, Elfman composed that rarest of movie themes—one that not only comments on the story's action, but appears to drive it. It starts slow, like the turning pages of a fairy tale, like rainwater running down the spires of a cathedral. But it builds quickly, culminating in a thundering climax of organ and gong. Then it's a march of fire, as singled-minded in its determination as Bruce Wayne. It finds room for reflection, even for a trace of humor, before settling on a note of stone-cold resolution.

Cheers erupted in theaters across the globe when audiences first heard "The Batman Theme" over the film's opening titles. Before production designer Anton Furst's Gotham City appeared, before Burton's imagery arrived, one could *see* the Dark Knight swooping, dodging, and lunging as it played.

"The Batman Theme" proved so popular it was used as the original opening theme for 1992's *Batman: The Animated Series*, in the LEGO Batman video games, and at Six Flags theme parks, where thrill-seekers would hear it as they waited to climb aboard the Batman rides.

As much as any illustration of the Dark Knight, or any actor, Elfman's theme *is* Batman.

79 Dark Night: A True Batman Story

As superheroes become an ever greater part of mainstream pop culture, stories appear almost daily of fans drawing inspiration from Batman—from the reports of a man in Cumbria, England, who donned a Batsuit in order to safeguard his town from those terrorizing it in clown suits to the chronicle of cancer survivor Miles Scott, detailed in the 2015 documentary *Batkid Begins*, to the many moving tales told in the 2013 documentary *Legends of the Knight*. One particularly affecting true story comes from a Batman creator. A man who's crafted a multitude of tales of the Dark Knight: Paul Dini.

While a writer and producer on *Batman: The Animated Series*, Dini was mugged and beaten by two men who were never identified or captured. With parts of his skull described by his doctor as "powdered," Dini began a long, slow road to physical and psychological recovery, spurred on by the very fictional characters whose stories he'd fashioned.

In June 2016, Dini's account of the incident and its aftermath was published by DC/Vertigo as *Dark Night: A True Batman Story*. Lushly illustrated by *100 Bullets* artist Eduardo Risso, the graphic novel offers an unflinching account of the kind of scenario the Dark Knight has prevented countless times. But in the absence of such a hero in real life, Dini internalizes Batman's strength, as well as that of his enemies, and ultimately rises above his anguish, closing the door on despair. Given that it's Dini himself who breathed life into these characters, it's a fascinating, inspiring meditation on self-healing.

What's especially impressive about *Dark Night* is that in telling his most personal story, Dini has created his most universal. One that speaks to every human heart in turmoil.

"The incident forced me to evaluate my life," says Dini, "and to say, 'When things happen, whether personally or professionally, when there is a setback, you'll persevere. You'll find a way to go on.'

"It's all we can do, really."

Gotham Gazette Exclusive

Paul Dini

Paul Dini won Emmys for writing the groundbreaking *Tiny Toon Adventures* before creating Harley Quinn and reinventing the Dark Knight's rogues gallery in *Batman: The Animated Series*. A producer on *Superman: The Animated Series* and *Batman Beyond*, he also wrote *Batman: Mask of the Phantasm*, *Batman Beyond: Return of the Joker*, and the *Batman: Arkham* video games, as well as the Eisner Award–winning *Mad Love* and his autobiographical *Dark Night: A True Batman Story*.

In *Dark Night: A True Batman Story*, you overcome a harrowing experience by using Batman as inspiration. Has he always served that role for you?
I've always responded to inspirational figures that are foremost in my brain. When I was a kid there were any number of characters from books or movies that I found inspirational at a tough time. Because I'd been so firmly entrenched in Batman's world for a few years prior to the attack, and certainly after it, he was one of the major characters that I looked at as a symbol of strength.

Which version of Batman first appealed to you?
I guess it was the Neal Adams / Irv Novick / Dick Giordano Batman. I would very much gravitate to Batman stories because of the strong covers, largely by Neal Adams around that time. The big one was [December 1969's] *Batman* #217, with him sweeping away from the Batcave with his cloak around him and Alfred crying as he says, "Take a last look, Alfred—then seal up the Batcave…Forever!" I thought, "Wow, this is big. Because he's not just making jokes with Robin and fighting the Riddler anymore. What's going on?" It was that one where Dick went away to college and Bruce closes the Batcave and moves into town. I thought, "That's a big story." Then there was a mystery on top of that, which I liked a lot. I just loved the way he was drawn. I loved the way that Adams and Giordano and Novick really redid the character and redid the world. So it was that story, it was "The Joker's Five-Way Revenge!," it was the Ra's al Ghul stories that were showing up around that time, and it was the Batman Christmas story, "The Silent Night of the Batman" that I really liked.

Another thing about the stories of that time—they seemed effortless, like they were just tossed off by geniuses who knew instinctively how to entertain us each month. "Oh yeah, here's this great Ra's al Ghul story"—they just dashed it off. "Here's a Two-Face story"—they just dashed it off. It was a sort of ongoing pleasure you'd get every month. Then of course Denny O'Neil's writing was a big part of that, the rethinking of Batman. That was really when I thought the character had some heft to him, and I really began to like him in the comic books.

Your work on *Batman: The Animated Series* was unique in that it operated in so many different modes—comedy, mystery, action, romance…
We were given a chance to tell the stories that we wanted to tell as long as they fit in that world. As long as they complemented Batman. And we all had a basic understanding of who he was and what his world was and the fun we could have there. I give a lot of credit to Jean MacCurdy, who started Warner Animation, and to Alan Burnett, who was very good at working with writers and figuring out where their strengths lay and with which characters. He created an

atmosphere that made it fun to work on those stories. I don't mean there were birthday cakes every day or conga lines in the hall. There was just a freedom of thinking that he brought in, that infused all the writers and story editors. We wanted to tell the best stories we could and the most interesting stories that we could. Fox Kids at the time was a very agreeable participant in that. They liked that we were challenging ourselves with the stories.

Over time I would say that changed, as they said, "The shows have to be more kid-friendly. We want to see more Robin." We bristled at that sometimes. But often it challenged us to come up with stories that really shone within those parameters. So it might never be 100 percent what a writer or director wanted their artistic vision to be. But it was pretty darn close for the type of show that we were doing.

That spirit just infused the *Batman* crew for many, many years. It also made the writers want to try different types of stories. Not everything had to be a Batman kind of story. It made the artists want to change the look of the way things were being done. A lot of the artists were looking over each other's shoulders at different interpretations. They would bring in different comic books and different art books and look at how different artists had solved a problem, like Jack Kirby or Frank Robbins or Wally Wood or Frank Miller or, in a couple of cases, Will Eisner. To study those creators' storytelling techniques and learn from their design sense. I'd see some Shane Glines model sheets and I'd say, "Those girls at the Wayne party, they're right out of a Dan DeCarlo comic, right?" And he'd go, "A little bit!" The artists would bring in little influences like that.

Bruce Timm would bring in a lot of Kirby. He really figured out how to use Kirby's dynamic storytelling sense in episodes that had nothing really to do with traditional Jack Kirby imagery. But there is a way that Kirby would lay out panels for maximum storytelling impact, and to see Bruce and Kevin Altieri and the other directors looking at things like that was incredible. Because they were breaking the mold of the way action-adventure shows had been done—which were very much standard left-to-right shows: close-up, pan out, a character runs through a scene. There was not a lot of that.

You became the show's villain expert, taking, for example, a somewhat two-dimensional comic book villain in Mr. Freeze and making him a tragic, sympathetic figure in your Emmy-winning "Heart of Ice."
Many of the classic Batman villains are about the loss of humanity, where they just feel forced to become somebody else, because that's the only way they can be functional. By taking on that darker, in some cases, more powerful other persona.

That also helped Batman identify with them, outsmart them, and even try to redeem them instead of simply punching them.
Batman, I think, looks at a lot of the villains and says, "There but for the grace of God go I. Because I had the resources and I had the drive and maybe I had a little something in my heart or in my mind beyond what they had, I am not what they are. But I certainly understand how they became what they became." Because he's also gone through a metamorphosis to become Batman.

The only way he stays sane is by adopting this personality. And the only way the Joker stays sane is by being who he is. So Batman does understand that he's a lot closer to these villains than people would think. That's why underneath he's got a bit of compassion for them. If they can be rehabilitated, he would like to see that rather than see them defeated or locked away or executed. There may be a way back, to some degree, for all of them.

Your Joker episodes took what many would perceive as a handicap—the limitations on violence in children's television—and used it to your advantage.
Well, Joker's interesting. Because what do you do with him? He's at his worst when he's just a guy making puns and doing silly stuff. You have to rethink him a bit to see, even though he's crazy, what his motivations are. I've always likened the Joker to a rock star—to have this high opinion of himself, to crave attention, to crave generating a response in people. When I was thinking about Harley, I was thinking about the women who write to guys like Charles Manson in prison, people who gravitate toward that charismatic but ultimately destructive personality. We couldn't really explore it to the great degree that people do in real life, but we were able to kind of wave

at it with their relationship. It also humanized him in a way that we couldn't humanize Two-Face or Poison Ivy.

If you see too much of the human side of the Joker, if you actually go and embrace for real the injured comedian that he is in *The Killing Joke*, he becomes too human, and the temptation is to go back and do more of that. Then you lose him as the murderous clown who's so unpredictable. Alan Moore did a very astute thing when he said *The Killing Joke* was a *possible* origin of the Joker. A piece of his origin story. Because if you go back and try and mine that for more story material, it's just gonna fall apart. It's better to put him in a human situation where he's got this up-and-down relationship with Harley, where he's got the obsession with Batman. That's when you see him at his most human. You may not have much pathos or sympathy for him but perhaps you can relate to him a bit.

Which of your scripts for *Batman: The Animated Series* are you proudest of?
"Heart of Ice" is one that I'm very fond of. "Almost Got 'Im," because I felt like we hit all the heights with that one. "Over the Edge" was a good later script. And "Harley and Ivy."

How did you come to pair Poison Ivy and Harley Quinn in "Harley and Ivy"?
I love writing female characters. I was sitting in my office and thinking, "Harley's kind of the doormat and Ivy doesn't take any shit from anybody. Pair the two of them up and see how they do." I felt they were different enough personalities that if you put them together they would find some common ground.

They both needed a friend. Ivy doesn't have very many human connections, if any. Harley is just looking to be loved and accepted by someone, and to have a pal. So they became friends for that reason. That's why they've remained friends, and sometimes a bit more.

How did Harley Quinn begin?
Rocketed to Earth from the doomed planet Harletron. [Laughs.] That's Harley's origin—"I came from a place like the Bizarro World. Everybody looked like me and acted like me! It was wonderful!"

I came up with the idea for "Joker's Favor," thinking about a guy who just happens to lose his temper, make a blunder, and then find out the guy he was yelling at was the Joker. "Oh my god, this is what happens when I am cruel, when I lose it. Suddenly I'm in deeper than I ever intended." So with my victim in place, I wanted characters around the Joker who could play off him and bring out different aspects of him.

I thought of a girl character. I was thinking of what type she could be, maybe a henchman type. Then I started writing scenes where the Joker is making jokes and his henchman didn't laugh, and the girl said something funny and they laughed at her, and the Joker gave them all a nasty look. I thought, "That's kind of cool." So the character became lighter than I was originally planning. I was thinking of her as a rank-and-file henchgirl. Then I thought, "What's a fun name? Harley's a fun name Harley Quinn, that's cute!" It seemed natural since so many of the villains' names are puns or have double meanings. I ran it by Bruce and Alan and they went for it, so Harley Quinn it was.

I made the character very wisecracky and very snappy. Arleen Sorkin is a good friend of mine, and at the time she was doing a lot of TV stuff, and that was sort of her character persona. The bubbly blonde. I'd seen her playing a jester type on *Days of Our Lives* when I was home sick one day and thought, "That fits." So I went to Andrea Romano, our voice director, and I said, "What about Arleen? She can do this kind of thing. The character can probably sound like Judy Holliday or Ellen Greene in *Little Shop of Horrors*."

I told Arleen that Harley Quinn was sort of a cross between the wayward girls that would follow around the Riddler and the Joker and the Penguin in the 1960s series—the henchwomen—and a little bit of the gum-cracking wiseguy-type henchgirls like Miss Adelaide in *Guys and Dolls*.

She put the voice together out of that. It sounds very close to her actual voice, but she kicked it over a little bit into the Judy Holliday range. She did the part really well, and the voice really worked with Bruce's model and the writing to create this character who was a little different from the tone of the show.

Batman is dark and serious, and most of the elements of his world have to be that way. The Joker represents a lightness but he's not really funny. Catwoman is the forbidden love. Poison Ivy is the seductress. Talia is more of his equal. But Harley Quinn is just an imp, just a screwball who enters and introduces a unique comic/tragic element into that world. Funny certainly, but also somebody who's buried who she is in order to be with a madman whom she sees as a misunderstood genius. As Harley's got this thing with the Joker, Batman sometimes thinks, "Maybe I can use that to my advantage." So there's no love between Batman and Harley, there's no heat between them, but they can certainly be a big part of each other's lives as adversaries or occasional frenemies or allies out of necessity.

In *Mad Love* you and Bruce Timm gave her a proper origin story.
I was very grateful the book got the response it did. Because a comic book was something that Bruce and I thought about doing just to see if we could do it. I think that it was really a great debut shot for us both. Because I'd done one or two little things in comics prior to that, and I think Bruce had done a few more. But it was the first big thing we did for DC, and to really score on that was great. It was not a straightforward comic book story the way that a lot people do comics. As we were right down the hall from each other, we could pop into each other's office with sketches for new ideas or changes to the script. Any business Bruce felt bogged down the story he could cut out and I would tighten up the dialogue so it all fit. It brought a lot of the emotion from the show onto the comic book page. Bruce draws in a very engaging way. Even when the Joker is a total maniac, in Bruce's hands there's an undeniable charisma and appeal to him. There's a sweetness to Harley—even when she's got tears dripping down her face and a manic grin while talking about how Batman's gonna die, you like her. I think that emotional connection between Harley and the readers took a lot of people by surprise, and I guess that's why it won an Eisner and a Harvey [Award]. It was unique at the time.

***Batman: The Animated Series'* continuity leaped forward 50 years with *Batman Beyond*.**
We were really thrown a curve with that one. At first we didn't want to do it. We thought, "Why make a new show? The one we're doing

now is great." What happened was there were new executives who came in on the network level. A show like the original animated *Batman*, that largely featured adults and had attracted an audience beyond eight-year-old boys, was anathema to them. It was not "kiddie show normal" to their rather traditional way of thinking. They said, "*Batman*'s run its course." Although we could have easily done another three seasons and not run out of story ideas. In fact, we had a bunch more that we wanted to do. They said, "Give us a kid in the Batman suit." They wanted a tween, I think. "We want to start all over again and make Batman a kid."

We were able to work that to our favor—the fact that that's all they wanted to deal with—after rebelling initially. After protesting, we started to figure it out. We realized it didn't have to be a kid in the Batman suit. That we could actually take some chances with it and create something kind of interesting. We had new people on the crew, including Glen Murakami and Darwyn Cooke, and there was a new energy to it. The writers started working on it, and we came up with the idea, "If we can put a kid in the suit, maybe we can make him high-school age rather than middle-school age. What if it's in the future and this is a protégé? Somebody new who encounters an older Bruce Wayne."

The idea of doing old Bruce Wayne was very appealing, to show that he was a guy who kept the battle up all throughout his life and had not really won the war. He had defeated certain adversaries. He had saved a lot of lives. But Gotham is always gonna be Gotham, it's always gonna be a magnet for villains. I felt like we were saying something kind of depressingly true about modern society in that the idea of the Joker was much more attractive to the youth of Gotham than Batman. The Joker had been this outlaw, he had been defeated and disposed of long ago, but his reputation had really appealed to the young criminal element of Gotham City. So he became more of a hero to them than Batman would have been. The Jokerz gang was sort of like the ultimate joke on Batman—"My colorful reputation will spawn years of imitators. It'll never be perceived as a bad thing." So people who had forgotten the horror that a certain type of evil could inflict were attracted to its more exciting, seductive elements. Sometimes that's history, unfortunately.

It made Bruce's existence a bit sad to see that this was continuing, and by bringing Terry into his life it revitalized and again empowered him. It made him want to take up the mantle, at least as far as being a mentor to Terry. So we made it a very interesting world to play in, and certainly the villains were a lot of fun.

***Batman Beyond: Return of the Joker* answered the question of what happened to Tim Drake's Robin. Its uncut edition was the first PG-13 DC animated film.**
I look back at the uncut version of that as one of the things I'm most proud of. It was a very frustrating process to undergo. Originally we were told to do a movie and really push the boundaries with it. We had about a year to make the movie. Bruce and Glen and I worked out the story, we ran it by Alan, he liked it, and then I went off and wrote the script.

We wound up showing it to some of the TV executives and they said, "We'll need a new cut of this. We will not promote this in our kids TV block because of the violence." That threw a big wrench into it. So we had to go back in and rework bits of the story and redo the animation. The initial release date went by the wayside, and we had to deliver a cut that they would approve of.

In the end it gave you the opportunity to give *Batman: The Animated Series* some closure.
It was sort of an ending. And it wasn't. Because these larger-than-life characters go on. But that was the death of the Joker—this time. I've killed that character I don't know how many times. I killed him there, I killed him in the "World's Finest" episode, I killed him in the *Arkham* games. The guy's got more lives than a cat. [Laughs.]

"World's Finest" remains the most satisfying on-screen pairing of Batman and Superman.
Ultimately I think it worked out to be a very good meeting between the two of them. That story took an awful lot of time to write. It was always in the back of our head that we would do Superman and Batman, and I remember working with Alan on and off for months on the story. I think the care we put in it shows, because it plays so

effortlessly on TV. Like, "Oh, it's very natural that we would do this Joker-Luthor pairing, and Lois Lane being interested in both guys, and Clark not being able to do anything about it." It just worked out very well all the way around. It took a lot of labor for it to get there story-wise, but I was happy with the way it worked out, and I think it was one of the high points of *Superman: The Animated Series.*

In *Superman* you had the perfect voice for Mr. Mxyzptlk, Gilbert Gottfried, and in *Batman: The Brave and the Bold* you had the perfect voice for Bat-Mite, Paul Reubens.
Oh yeah. Paul Reubens is great. But we never got to pair him and Gilbert up in an episode! Or we haven't yet. When I wrote the Bat-Mite episode I went in to talk to producers Michael Jelenic and James Tucker and their team about it, they said, "Bat-Mite's not gonna be as goofy as he was in other interpretations. But let's make sure that he's got a little bit of a threat to him, because he is an unworldly thing." Then it was just having fun with it. The first one where Batman talks him into becoming Batman and subjecting him to all the villains is a callback to Bob Clampett's "The Great Piggy Bank Robbery," as well as the *Tiny Toons* "Batduck" episode. But it worked. The Lord Death Man one, that was fun adapting the Batmanga story, and of course, the team-up with Scooby-Doo.

***The Brave and the Bold* series finale—"Mitefall!"—isn't just a strong animated series finale, but a particularly strong TV series finale in general.**
Oh, man. That was James and Michael. I wrote it, but they're the ones who masterminded it. I loved the party scene at the end. I had just put the character Gaggy, the Joker's old henchman from the 1960s comics, into *Gotham City Sirens*. He had a big rivalry going with Harley and kept trying to kill her. Turns out they were using Gaggy in *The Brave and the Bold* as well. They had Harley kick Gaggy out of the party scene at the end. [Laughs.] Just having everybody in there, from Krypto to Bat-Hound. And the final scene where he says, "Good night." It's like [wistfully], "Good-bye, this version of Batman. We'll see you again." And the opening, with Batman and Abe Lincoln and

John Wilkes Boom. I don't know, man. Hard to get crazier than that. [Laughs.]

Diedrich [Bader] was such a great Batman. It just goes to show you can have fun with Batman as long as you don't ridicule him. If you ridicule him, then you lose what's compelling about him. As long as you preserve the integrity of who Batman is and what he stands for, you can have all sorts of fun in his world.

I felt the same thing about *The LEGO Batman Movie.* I loved it. Jenny Slate and Zach Galifianakis were very good as Harley and the Joker. I love that version of Batman. I thought, "You could do this in live-action. Or elements of it. He doesn't have to be so goddamned serious." [Laughs.] I mean, there's the Fairy Princess Batman LEGO minifig. I don't have it yet, but I probably will get it. Because it's Fairy Princess Batman. You gotta get it.

Was it tricky writing the *Arkham* video games? Was it difficult coming up with a narrative for something interactive?

It was a big challenge for me. My first brush with writing them was when I wrote the cut scenes for a Sega Batman game based on *The Animated Series.* The game came out, and within two weeks the technology was obsolete. So it was never a big seller. It was like the lost episode of *Batman*, as it had some really nicely animated story sequences. So that wasn't really much of an introduction to game design.

When I did the *Arkham* games, it was a learning experience. I picked up fairly quickly the idea that you're designing a game experience for somebody who might not really know who Batman is. That's what the game designers told me. The mindset of a gamer in a lot of cases is about the game experience and much less about who the character is and what their world is. The team at Rocksteady, which includes Sefton Hill as the director and Paul Crocker, who was the head of story, did a very good job of educating me very early on about what you do and what you don't do as far as writing goes. You can't convey too much of the ongoing story within the action. Batman goes into a part of the asylum that's guarded by the hoods and he's gotta get through them to get to Poison Ivy, for instance. That has to be about the game, about how he takes down the guys, how he advances, what he finds within the game. I had a little bit of a learning experience figuring out not to put story elements in the fight scenes, because you're distracting from the game experience. And you can't put too much in the cut scenes because the gamer will feel like he's lost out on something if a key point is discovered during a cut scene. So it's a balance. You have to juggle those. But I learned pretty well in the first game how to do that.

Rocksteady has a tremendous design sense. It was something that I felt worked very well for Gotham and very well for Arkham. Maybe it's a benefit from the game team being located in London. The artists had a lot of London landmarks to draw on which gave a kind of old-world, European look to some of the touches of Gotham City. It worked very well for creating the Arkhamverse. It looks a little different from any version of Gotham I'd seen in the movies or in the comics or other games. It really established it as its own thing. Those games were a lot of fun to do. The first two in particular were very true to the world that they created within *Arkham Asylum*, and the extension of *Arkham City*.

What did you think of Margot Robbie's Harley Quinn in 2016's *Suicide Squad*?
I thought Margot was really good. In addition to having a lot of fun with the role, she showed the conflict and complexity in Harley. A lot of the movie worked very well for me. I loved seeing Batman on top of the car, and Joker and Harley inside laughing. When the preview came out I made Alan Burnett look at it online and said, "How often have we done that scene? Five times that I can think of." The scene with Batman rescuing Harley underwater and her trying to kill him, all good stuff.

Have you received a lot of feedback from fans who were inspired by *Dark Night: A True Batman Story*?
Fans have been very generous in sharing their own stories and their own experiences of things that either parallel my story or in some way echo that situation I went through. I thank them for their generosity and their compassion and their bravery in wanting to trust me with those stories, and their ongoing bravery to deal with that in their own life. I'm very grateful about that. One of the most touching things

was I heard from a police officer back east who said he was very much inspired, not by *Dark Night*, but by Batman, specifically the idea of Batman. *The Animated Series* was a big influence on him when he was growing up. He realized, "I can't be a superhero in real life. But I can be a policeman, and I can do really good things and I can be a really good cop." I checked the officer out online and we write back and forth. He really is an excellent person and an excellent officer and someone who inspires that heroic spirit in all the kids he works with. That extends far beyond me into the idea of Batman in general. I'm happy to see that the character means so much to so many people who use him as a positive force in their lives.

80 The *Batman: Arkham* Video Games

There are plenty of ways fans can experience Batman's adventures. But to actually feel what it's like to *be* the Dark Knight, there's no better way than the *Batman: Arkham* video games.

Developed by Britain's Rocksteady Studios, 2009's third-person action game *Batman: Arkham Asylum* sees the Dark Knight return the Joker to the titular island institution, and the Clown Prince of Crime break free with the help of Harley Quinn. Seizing control of Arkham, he frees all the inmates, sics them on Batman, and threatens Gotham with the deadly chemical Titan, derived from Bane's Venom compound. As Batman, the player must fight his or her way through six buildings filled with his greatest enemies, from Killer Croc to Poison Ivy.

Featuring a satisfying strike-and-counter combat system, strategy-enabling stealth gameplay, and 240 challenges courtesy of the Riddler, *Arkham Asylum* puts players inside the Batman's cape and cowl, giving them plenty of freedom to decide how they want to battle the bad guys. Written by *Batman: The Animated Series'* writer-producer Paul Dini, the game employs series stars Kevin Conroy, Mark Hamill, and Arleen Sorkin as Batman, the Joker, and Harley Quinn, respectively. The game is considerably more adult-oriented than the all-ages show, with a dirty, grimy aesthetic, occasional profanity, and a much higher body count. The needle-fingered Scarecrow alone—whose fear-gas-induced hallucinations are one of the highlights—is the stuff of nightmares.

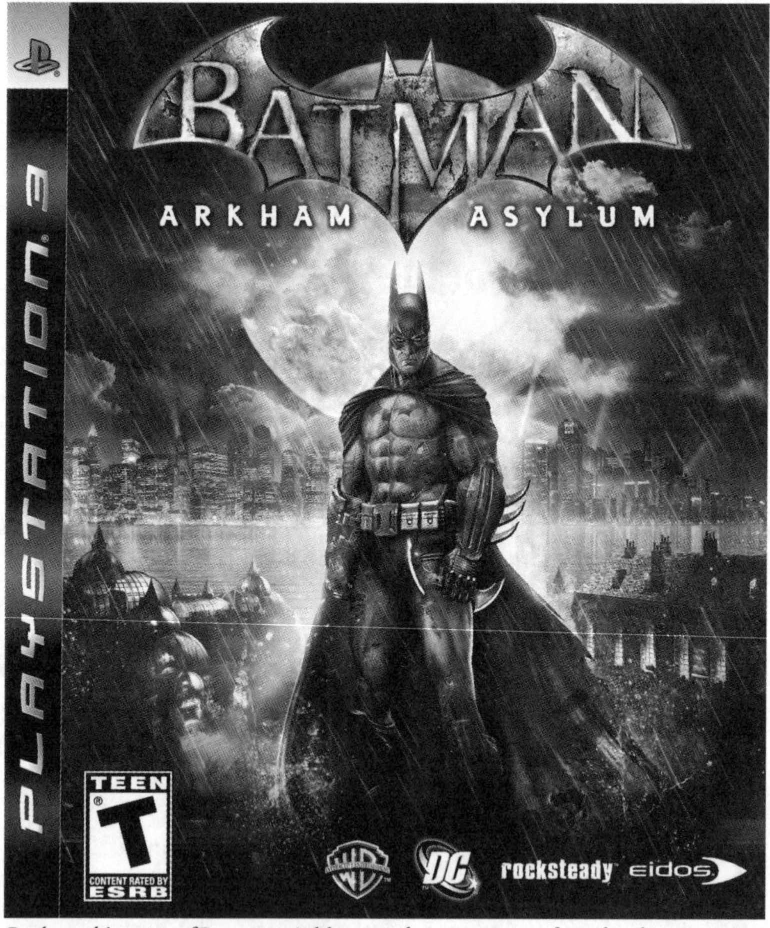

Rocksteady's series of Batman: Arkham *video games gives fans the chance to step into Batman's boots.*

The Arkhamverse expanded in 2011 with the release of the first follow-up game. Set one year after *Arkham Asylum*, *Arkham City* places Batman among the inmates of Arkham and the prisoners of Blackgate, when they're moved into Gotham's slum district under the governance of Hugo Strange. Dying of Titan, the Joker injects Batman with the chemical, forcing him to obtain a cure for them both. Again written by Dini, with the voices of Conroy and Hamill, *Arkham City* offers a host of new villains, and allows for open-world adventuring as players cape-glide through Gotham.

The 2013 prequel *Batman: Arkham Origins* is set five years prior to *Arkham Asylum*. With Roger Craig Smith and Troy Baker voicing Batman and Joker, it depicts their first battle, as mobster Black Mask places a $50 million bounty on Batman's head, giving the Dark Knight the worst Christmas Eve of his life.

Conroy and Hamill return for the fourth game, *Batman: Arkham Knight*, which allows for team-ups with Robin, Nightwing, and Catwoman, and features a drivable Batmobile that can transform into a heavily armed tank. Here, the city's three islands are threatened by the Scarecrow and the new title enemy, whose mask hides a familiar face. (Spoilers! It's the previously-believed-to-be-deceased Jason Todd.)

Most licensed video games fail to deliver the enjoyment of the stories from which they're adapted. But by empowering players to move, think, and fight like the Dark Knight, the *Batman: Arkham* games very often transcend their source material.

"We had to come in and make a statement," says Dini of *Batman: Arkham Asylum*. "'This is not a movie. This is not a tie-in with a movie. This is its own thing, and more than that it's an immersive and interesting gaming experience that just happens to be about Batman.'"

81 Poison Ivy

They say the weed of crime bears bitter fruit, and few weeds are as deadly as Poison Ivy. But she didn't grow overnight. Like any perennial vine, it took time before Ivy's persona took root.

She was introduced in June 1966's *Batman* #181 ("Beware of—Poison Ivy!" by writer Robert Kanigher and penciler Sheldon Moldoff), possibly inspired by Beatrice Rappaccini—the doomed title character in Nathaniel Hawthorne's tragic short story "Rappaccini's Daughter," about a girl who develops an immunity to poisonous plants but finds that she in turn has become poisonous.

Artist Carmine Infantino designed her leaf-covered leotard, and green, leaf-bedecked tights, necklace, bracelets, and crown, responding to the success of Julie Newmar's Catwoman on the 1966 *Batman* TV show.

"The only reason she came about," says Infantino, in an interview with Jamie Coville on JamieCoville.com, "was because of Catwoman on the *Batman* show. They wanted more female villains."

In her first appearance, she announced herself as "World Public Enemy No. 1" upon arriving in Gotham City, staking her claim on the title via her ability to manipulate men. Fixated on Batman, she tried to subdue him through her "lipstick with a chloroform base," but was prevented from doing so by the nose filter he wore. Jailed by the Dynamic Duo, she warned them, "Once you've caught Poison Ivy—you'll never get rid of it!"

True to her word, Ivy, still obsessed with making Batman her love slave, returned time and again to threaten him, and—as a charter member of the Injustice Gang—his Justice League teammates as well. Her origin was fully revealed when she battled Wonder Woman in September 1978's *World's Finest* #252 ("A Poison of the Heart," written by Gerry Conway and penciled by Jack Abel). It's explained that one Lillian "Lilly" Rose, a college student from Seattle, was seduced by Marc LeGrand, her French botany instructor, into stealing an urn full of ancient Egyptian herbs from their university's museum. Poisoned by LeGrand and left for dead, her body absorbed the toxins, and she wound up immune to all poisons, natural or man-made.

Her name was soon reestablished as Pamela Isley, first given to her by writer Len Wein in the earlier *Justice League of America* #111 (June 1974). But a rose—or, rather, a thorn—by any other name would prove just as deadly. Her bracelets now came loaded with poison thorn darts, though her principal tool remained her lipstick, eventually said to contain a hypnotic agent through which she could make any man do her bidding. No longer interested in making Batman her lover, she instead focused on financing her plant research through a series of criminal activities.

Following the events of DC's 1985 *Crisis on Infinite Earths* limited series, Ivy was given a new origin in January 1989's *Secret Origins* #36 ("Pavane," written by Neil Gaiman with art by Mark Buckingham). Here it was revealed that her established backstory was one she'd fabricated, and that while in college she'd instead studied biochemistry under Jason Woodrue (who later became the supervillain known as the Floronic Man). Mutated by Woodrue's botany experiments, her touch grew toxic, catalyzing mood alterations in anyone who made physical contact with her. She also acquired the ability to communicate with plants, which did her bidding while she fought to make them the dominant life form on the planet.

"What am I?" she asked in *Secret Origins* #36. "I am the Queen of the May, crowned in leaves, and blossom, and thorns. I am hope and beauty and truth. A symbol of growth in the dark times that are upon us..."

Ivy's popularity blossomed when she appeared in 1992's *Batman: The Animated Series.* Hypnotically voiced by Diane Pershing, this incarnation's visual design, by artist Lynne Naylor, was inspired by Red, the scarlet-tressed Tex Avery character who appeared in 1940s animated shorts such as *Red Hot Riding Hood* and *Swing Shift Cinderella.* She was introduced in the September 14, 1992, episode "Pretty Poison," one of the show's finest. *The Animated Series,* and its successor *The New Batman Adventures,* popularized the tragic side of Ivy's story: since her body rejects all contaminants, she cannot have children. This leads her to create humanlike plant creatures, one of whom, in the episode "Chemistry," briefly convinces Bruce Wayne to give up the mantle of the Bat and marry her.

Less successful was Ivy's appearance in 1997's *Batman & Robin* film, though Uma Thurman's injection of Mae West sass into the character made her performance the film's most watchable. Ivy has returned to TV several times, most notably in *Gotham,* in which she's renamed "Ivy Pepper" and portrayed by two actresses—as a child by Clare Foley and as a young woman by Maggie Geha. She returned to the big screen in 2017's *The LEGO Batman Movie* (voiced by Riki Lindhome) and is set to appear again in *Gotham City Sirens.*

Like much of Batman's universe, Ivy grew steadily darker in the 21st century (and greener, as her pale skin took on an emerald hue). Following her appearance in the *Batman: Arkham* video games, she was reintroduced to comics in DC's "New 52" Universe. In *Detective Comics* #231 ("The Green Kingdom," written by Derek Fridolfs with art by Javier Pina), her backstory was again rewritten. As a child, the new Ivy had an unusual skin condition, limiting the amount of time she could spend outdoors. Her father murdered her mother and buried her in their garden—an act for which Ivy later exacted revenge by planting a lethal kiss on his cheek. In college, she pushed experimental pheromone pills to other students before interning at Wayne Enterprises' Bio-Chem division. But she was fired by Bruce Wayne when she proposed using her research to brainwash his clients. As she was escorted out, she acquired meta-human powers when she accidentally spilled chemicals on herself.

Some sunshine, however, has entered Ivy's life in the form of Harley Quinn. Her teammate in the *Gotham Girls*, *Batman: Harley and Ivy*, *Gotham City Sirens*, and *Harley Quinn* comics (as well as the *Gotham Girls* web series), Harley has grown to become Ivy's best friend and romantic partner, after Ivy helped her escape her abusive relationship with the Joker. Issue #42 of *DC Comics Bombshells* depicts the couple's first kiss, signaling that while Ivy was once defined by her own abusive relationships with men, she's now taken root in a garden of her own.

82 Visit Gotham City Police Headquarters

So you've answered the Batphone, slid down the Batpole, and raced out of the Batcave in the Batmobile. What's next? Head to Gotham City to meet with Commissioner Gordon!

Most episodes of the 1966 *Batman* TV series feature a scene in which the Caped Crusaders park in front of a courthouse, hop out of the Batmobile, and bound up a flight of steps on their way to Gotham City Police Headquarters. While most of the show was shot at Desilu Productions (now RED Studios) in Hollywood and at 20th Century Fox Studios in Century City, this scene was filmed at Warner Bros. Studios in Burbank. There, the building (built in 1928 and known as the Embassy Courthouse, aka Building 61)—with its Corinthian-style columns, iron latticework, and massive front doors—is still located on Embassy Court, toward the front of

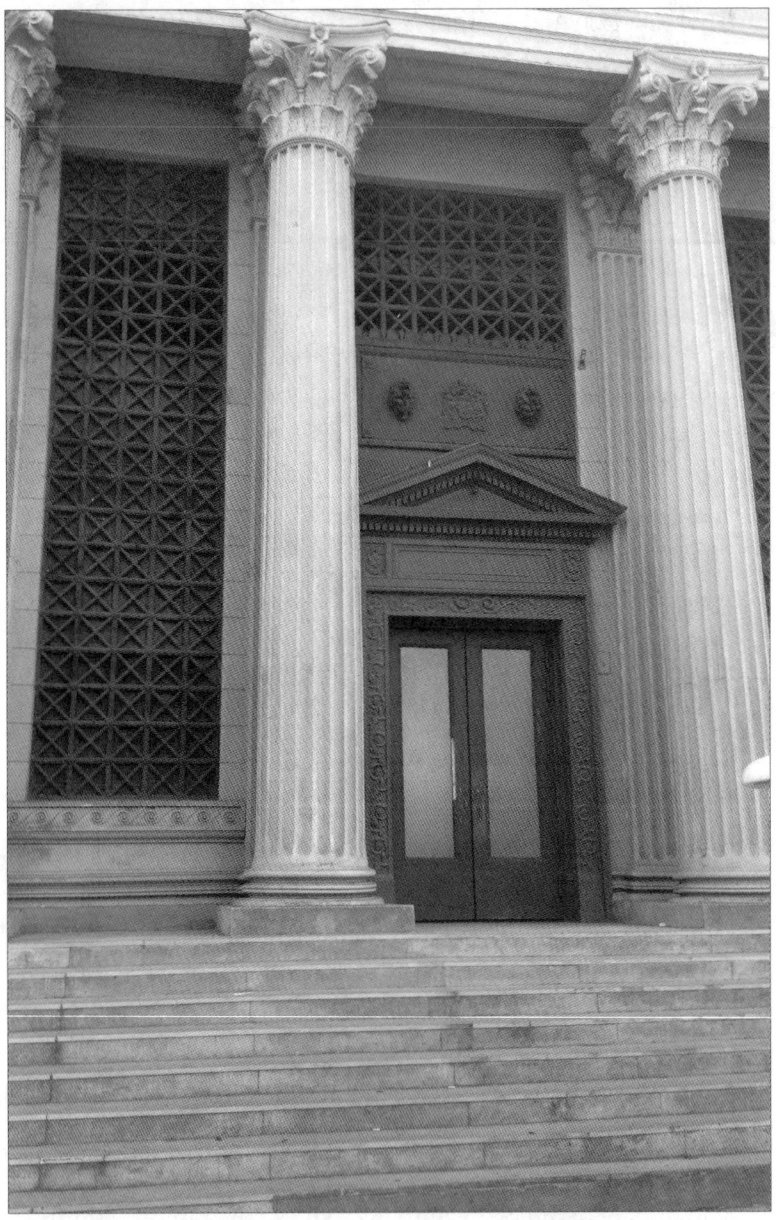

Gotham City's courthouse as it stands today at Warner Bros. Studios, in Burbank, California. (Joseph McCabe)

the backlot. Additional street scenes were shot on nearby Hennesy Street.

The courthouse isn't always a scheduled stop on the Warner Bros. Studio Tour. But fans who take the tour can ask their guide to make a brief stop at the building, and the guide will usually comply. Just be sure to have your camera ready. Then suck in your gut, puff out your chest, and strike a heroic pose in front of one of Gotham's most famous landmarks.

You can also visit the building used for the exterior of the Gotham Police Department in *The Dark Knight*. It's the United States Post Office, located in Chicago at 404 W. Harrison Street. In *Batman Begins*, *The Dark Knight*, and *The Dark Knight Rises*, the offices on the first floor of the Farmiloe Building—located at 28-36 St. John Street in Clerkenwell, London—served as the interior of the Gotham City Police Station.

83 The Outsiders

Batman has held membership in such venerable superhero teams as the Justice Society of America, the Batmen of All Nations (later renamed the Club of Heroes), the Mystery Analysts of Gotham City, and, of course, the Justice League. Yet he hasn't always seen eye to eye with his teammates, which is what led to the formation of the Outsiders.

With sales slumping on *The Brave and the Bold*, DC decided to cancel the long-running Batman team-up book, concluding it with its 200th issue. An agreement with one of the company's foreign publishers required DC to produce a fourth monthly Batman title (after *Batman*, *Detective Comics*, and *World's Finest*). And so July

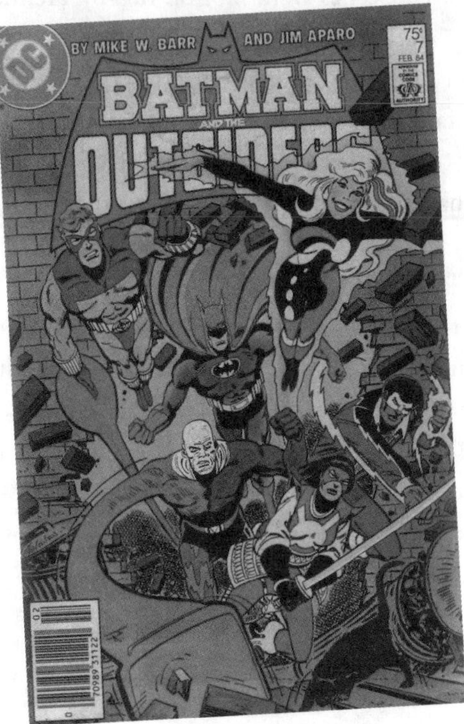

Though most famously a member of the Justice League, Batman formed his own team of heroes, the Outsiders, in 1983.
(Cover art by Jim Aparo)

1983's *The Brave and the Bold* #200 introduced the Outsiders in a 16-page insert comic. The group's adventures continued in the following month's *Batman and the Outsiders* #1.

Written by Mike W. Barr and penciled by longtime *Brave and the Bold* artist Jim Aparo, "Wars Ended…Wars Begun" begins when Bruce Wayne's friend Lucius Fox is abducted while on a business trip in the European nation of Markovia. Superman tells Batman he's assured the State Department that no Justice League member will enter Markovia, lest their actions instigate a war. So Batman resigns from the League, and recruits the electrical-bolt-throwing Black Lightning—who once rejected the League's invitation to join—to help him retrieve Lucius. Along the way, they encounter the shape-changing "Element Man" Metamorpho, who also refused to join the League, and three new heroes, each a creation of Barr and Aparo.

The first is Halo, a teenage woman who gives off an aura of light when using her energy powers. (Later in the series, she's revealed to be an ages-old energy being inhabiting the reanimated body of a dead murderer.) The second is Geo-Force, Markovia's own Prince Brion Markov, granted the power to manipulate Earth's gravity in order to stop the insurrectionist Baron Bedlam. The third is Katana, a samurai warrior who lost her husband and children and wields a sword that holds the souls of those it slays.

The Outsiders make their home in Gotham City, and fight such menaces as Bedlam, Batman's old enemy Kobra, the Masters of Disaster, and even a clone of Adolf Hitler, in tales illustrated by Aparo and, for a time, Alan Davis. Since *Batman and the Outsiders* was then DC's third-highest-selling book (after *The New Teen Titans* and *The Legion of Super-Heroes*)—and the only Batman title in the company's top 10—a spinoff title printed on higher-quality paper and sold through the direct market, was launched. August 1985's *The Outsiders* #1 introduces a new member, Looker; also created by Barr and Aparo, she was heir to the throne of the underground kingdom Abyssia, and as such possesses an array of psychokinetic powers.

Batman would leave the team and the title in April 1986's *Batman and the Outsiders* #32, after which it was renamed *Adventures of the Outsiders* (since DC's overseas publishing requirements had by then changed). The Dark Knight returned, however, in March 1987's *The Outsiders* #17 and the team relocated to Los Angeles. Alas, their book was canceled shortly thereafter, and the team disbanded in the wake of DC's 1988 crossover event "Millennium."

Revivals have occurred several times in the years since, including one in which the Outsiders served as the black-ops division of Batman Incorporated. The team also appeared in two episodes of

TV's *Batman: The Brave and the Bold*. Katana received her own short-lived monthly book in 2013, and became the Dark Knight's partner (and Alfred's goddaughter) in that same year's *Beware the Batman* animated series. She also made live-action appearances as a recurring character in the third season of TV's *Arrow* and in 2016's *Suicide Squad* movie. Her teammate Black Lightning earns his own television series in 2018.

"It's hard to believe nowadays," says Barr in July 2014's *Back Issue* #73 (in an interview with Philip Youngman), "but despite Batman's status as a fan favorite there was a time when his books didn't sell well—but not when he appeared in *Batman and the Outsiders*..."

84 The Top Five Batman Spoofs

As the 1966 *Batman* TV series, 2008's *Batman: The Brave and the Bold*, and *The LEGO Batman Movie* all demonstrate, the Dark Knight is often at his best when he isn't all that dark. And he can be downright sublime when spoofed. Here are five examples, guaranteed to make Batfans' smiles wider than the Joker's.

Bat Boy

The definitive comic parody of the Golden Age Batman, "Batboy and Rubin!" appeared in the eighth issue of *MAD* magazine (December 1953–January 1954). Written by *MAD* creator Harvey Kurtzman with art by the impeccable Wally Wood, the story's heroes battle the Fleagle and Flurgle gangs, while a mysterious villain preys on the good citizens of Cosmopolis. Faithfully adapted in the *Batman: The Brave and the Bold* episode "Bat-Mite Presents: Batman's Strangest Cases!" it's typical of the go-for-broke lunacy that made Kurtzman a comedy legend.

Bat-Bat

The hand of *The Ren & Stimpy Show* creator John Kricfalusi is evident in his work on producer Ralph Bakshi's 1987 animated series *Mighty Mouse: The New Adventures*, never moreso than with Bat-Bat. Introduced in the first-season episode "Night of the Bat-Bat" are "millionaire playbat Bruce Vein and his youthful ward Tick," who descend into their Batpit, become the bat-themed bat and his sidekick Bug Wonder, and take to the streets in their Man-Mobile.

Die Fledermaus

The Tick from 1994 is perhaps the definitive superhero spoof series, thanks in part to its resident Dark Knight—Die Fledermaus. A lazy, would-be lothario, Die Fledermaus wears a costume even more Bat-like than Bruce Wayne's and owns just as many gadgets. But he's too busy running from danger to use any of them. In the 2001 live-action *Tick* series, Die Fledermaus became Batmanuel, played by the future mayor of Gotham City in Christopher Nolan's films, Nestor Carbonell.

Big Daddy

Nicolas Cage brought his love of comic books to the *Ghost Rider* movies and Tim Burton's ill-fated *Superman Lives* with mixed results. But his impersonation of Adam West's Batman in his role as Big Daddy, the highlight of 2010's hyperviolent superhero satire *Kick-Ass*, is a thing of beauty. Never has poor parenting been so hilarious.

Badman

Christopher Nolan's cinematic trilogy inspired no end of "Badman" viral videos from Collegehumor.com, with Pete Holmes nailing Christian Bale's marble-mouthed delivery. The best of them, 2013's *Batman Vs. The Penguin* (aka "Batman Disturbs the Penguin"), features comedian Patton Oswalt in the role he was born to play, Oswald Cobblepot, in a short skewering the cinematic Batman's frequently ignored use of lethal force.

Honorable Mention: *Darkwing Duck*—Disney's 1991 animated action-adventure series charmed a generation of kids with its affectionate sendup of 1930s adventurers such as the Shadow, the Green Hornet, and, of course, Batman.

85 Gotham Central

Justice wears many faces in Gotham, and not all of them are swathed in a cowl. The men and women of the Gotham City Police Department have long protected and served their city. And in *Gotham Central*, they had a comic book of their own in which to do it.

Running 40 issues, from 2003 to 2006, *Gotham Central* was the brainchild of Ed Brubaker and Greg Rucka. Each had written Batman comics, and had collaborated on 2001's "Officer Down" storyline, in which Commissioner Gordon was shot and retired. Without Gordon or Harvey Bullock (who resigned from the GCPD after stepping outside the law to take down Gordon's shooter), *Gotham Central* focuses on a group of largely unknown officers under Commissioner Michael Akins. Some are honest, some corrupt, but all struggle with operating in Batman's shadow as they face the supervillains who threaten their home.

Brubaker and Rucka divided their GCPD into two shifts: day (its cases chronicled by Rucka) and night (written by Brubaker). Michael Lark was the book's first and primary artist, followed by Stefano Gaudiano, Kano, and Steve Lieber, all of whom were well suited for a character-based procedural. Though *Gotham Central*'s focus is on the Major Crimes Unit, it features appearances by Batman, and villains such as the Joker, the Mad Hatter, Two-Face, and Mr. Freeze.

Most noteworthy is *Gotham Central*'s development of police detective Renee Montoya (introduced in 1992's *Batman: The Animated Series*). Outed as a lesbian and slapped with a murder charge in the Harvey and Eisner Award–winning "Half a Life" storyline, she becomes, under Rucka, the book's heart and soul.

The success of TV's *Gotham* was predicated in part on *Gotham Central*, which demonstrated how the GCPD could carry serialized stories without the steady presence of the Dark Knight. But *Gotham Central* is far more adroit in its storytelling, its Gotham more real, more visceral than that of any monthly comic. Consequently, its Batman is more menacing.

"The biggest problem when you're writing Batman is you're Batman *all the time*," says Brubaker. "Often the book is first-person narrated. You're *hearing* about how awful Gotham is, but you're seeing Batman just running around on rooftops—and it looks cool—and you're in the Batcave with him. But nothing is less scary than Batman when you've been hanging out in the Batcave with him and Alfred. Batman is scary when you have to go up the stairs and turn on the Bat-Signal and the Joker starts shooting at you. That world becomes scary when you knock on the wrong door, like a lot of cops will do. But in this version Mr. Freeze is behind it."

Gotham Gazette Exclusive

Ed Brubaker

In his time at DC Comics, writer Ed Brubaker crafted a much-praised modern retelling of the Joker's origin in the graphic novel *Batman: The Man Who Laughs* and revamped Catwoman with artist Darwyn Cooke. His finest DC achievement, however, is his uncompromising look at the GCPD in *Gotham Central*, co-written by Greg Rucka.

What's the secret to doing a Batman story without Batman?
Well, when you do a Batman story where Batman is seen from other people's perspectives, Batman can be scary. He can feel like an urban legend or he can feel like something you would be angry about if you were a cop, that Batman exists. That was a situation where Greg Rucka and I were each writing a Batman book—he was writing *Detective Comics* and I was writing *Batman*—and we were becoming really good friends and we wanted to write something together. DC was pushing us to do *Batman and the Outsiders*, to relaunch that. We had a two-hour conversation, and by the end of the two-hour conversation we decided we wanted to do the book that we had jokingly talked about doing that would be more interesting. Which would be like *Homicide*, but in Gotham City. We had been joking around about that and Brian Bendis was doing *Powers* around the same time we started talking about it, and *Powers* had become a huge hit. So we were just like, "Look, here's a book that's pretty similar to that. That's the same kind of idea. But ours would be in a world where there are DC characters and supervillains, and it's about what it feels like to be a cop in a world where Batman can come in and wreck your case. Or solve it for you, after you've worked on it for months. What does that feel like?"

Miraculously, everybody just suddenly was into it. I certainly credit *Powers*' success for giving us the leg up. Then Greg and I were just such fans of David Simon's book *Homicide: A Year on the Killing Streets*. When we were working on Batman we used to call each other up and read sections of the book to each other. So it just kind of evolved. I think that pitching the Mr. Freeze thing, the opening scene, was the thing that made [editor] Bob Schreck go sell the book to [DC president] Jenette Kahn.

In some ways *Gotham Central* is reminiscent of Will Eisner's *The Spirit*. Some of the best *Spirit* stories didn't focus on the title hero.
Yeah, it was about the world that he created really, and it all existed around that. But yeah, I just think that world is so much more interesting when you're viewing it from someone else's point of view.

Up until the show *Gotham* was announced as *Gotham*, I had been hearing for a year that they were gonna do *Gotham Central* instead. To the point where I was shocked when they announced *Gotham*. Then I was like, "Oh, they're gonna do *Smallville*, but with Batman." So I was a little bit bummed, because I love the cast on that show, which looks great, and I was like, "It would have been great if it was *Gotham Central*." Now they'll probably never do *Gotham Central*...Never say never. But maybe not in my lifetime, or not while I'm young enough to appreciate it. [Laughs.]

On *Gotham Central*, you wrote the characters' evening shift and Greg Rucka scripted their daytime shift. It was a very different way of writing a comic book.
We're both control freaks, and it's fun to work together, but we knew that we wouldn't want to do it constantly. And we were both so busy that we each wanted to do our own shift, and then the idea was always that we would team up once a year for a big case, like on *Homicide*. So we would each do a storyline, and then we would team up and do a storyline. Then we would alternate who did the next storyline. It gave us a lot of freedom to create something together and also separately at the same time. I think that helped make it what it was. That and Michael Lark and Stefano Gaudiano's art and Matt Hollingsworth's colors. It's amazing to me, I hear more about *Gotham Central* now than I did when I was writing it.

Michael Lark was a particularly well-suited for the book.
I had worked with him on *Scene of the Crime*. We were looking for someone who was really grounded, who wanted to draw people in clothes. A lot of superhero artists are great, but when you get

a scene where it's people standing around in suits, everybody's busting loose like a Rob Liefeld drawing. So we needed someone who was more from the David Mazzucchelli school, where the people look like real people and the superheroes and supervillains look bizarre and stand out in a world where everyone else looks normal, and their costumes look a little ridiculous. I feel like it made it a darker, more fun story.

86 Man-Bat

Since the start of his storied career, Batman has adopted the appearance of his totem animal without surrendering his identity to it. The same cannot be said of the lycanthropic Man-Bat.

Man-Bat's tale began in June 1970's *Detective Comics* #400 ("Challenge of the Man-Bat!"), written by Frank Robbins and based on a story by Neal Adams, who penciled the issue. The tale centers on Kirk Langstrom, a nocturnal-mammal expert at the Gotham Museum of Natural History who idolizes Batman, and develops a serum from the glandular extractions of bats, with which he hopes to develop a bat-like sonar ability.

"It all began with good intentions," explains Adams. "He wanted to make Batman better than he already was."

But Langstrom gets more than he bargained for when he takes the solution. His eyes become hypersensitive to light, while his hands grow hairy and clawlike. Upon seeing his reflection, he's horrified to discover his ears have become enormous.

"I'm...gahrrr...becoming a...Man-Bat!" he cries.

In his mutated form, Langstrom winds up aiding Batman when a gang of thieves breaks into the museum. But the alliance is

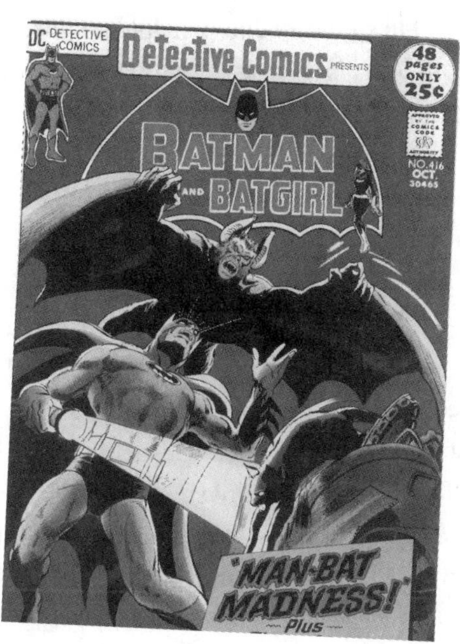

Kirk Langstrom's lab experiments transformed him into Man-Bat, a pitiful creature who became Batman's very own Dr. Jekyll / Mr. Hyde.
(Cover art by Neal Adams)

short-lived. In his next appearance—*Detective Comics* #402's "Man or Bat?"—he butts bat-heads with the Caped Crusader while trying to steal a rare biochemical to reverse his mutation process. Batman, as well as Langstrom's fiancée, Francine Lee, try reasoning with him, but the scientist loses himself to the creature inside. He completes his physical transformation and grows batwings. In the third issue of the Man-Bat trilogy, *Detective Comics* #407 ("Marriage: Impossible!"), Langstrom convinces Francine to take his serum, become a She-Bat, and marry him so they can mate and create an entire race of were-bats. But Batman administers an antidote before they can carry out their plans, restoring their humanity and their sanity.

Or so it seemed. Robbins both wrote and drew—in his wonderfully idiosyncratic scratchy style—Man-Bat's next two appearances, in *Detective* #416 ("Man-Bat Madness!") and #429 ("Man-Bat Over Vegas!"). These issues saw Kirk and Francine finally marry, but remain plagued by the serum they'd ingested.

"He's kind of like a helpless Jekyll and Hyde," says Adams of Man-Bat. "He's discovered his Hyde part and he likes it. But he's not doing anything terrible until he stays that way too long, and then he starts doing bad things."

In time, Man-Bat conquered his dark side and allied himself with Batman in catching criminals. He proved popular enough to appear in the *Batman* newspaper strip in 1970, in a book (written by Robbins and penciled by Adams) and 45 rpm vinyl record set from Power Records in 1974, and earn his own solo title. December 1975's *Man-Bat* #1 was buoyed by the monster-comic craze of the 1970s, but it lasted just two issues. It was immediately followed by an equally short-lived incarnation as a backup feature in *Detective Comics* #458 and 459. The Langstroms found greater success in 1977 as a part of the bimonthly Batman anthology title *Batman Family*. Here, Man-Bat garnered a rogues gallery of his own, and Kirk and Francine had a daughter named Rebecca. By the time the book finished its run the following year, Kirk had found a productive outlet for his skills, as a private eye.

Man-Bat again appeared semi-regularly in *Detective Comics* when *Batman Family* was folded into its pages. The Langstroms' daughter was shown to have inherited some of their mutated DNA in August 1980's *The Brave and the Bold* #165, though she was soon cured. Sadly, the same cannot be said of their son, Aaron, introduced in the 1996 *Man-Bat* limited series. Born with a form of cancer, his mother injected him with his father's serum to save his life, giving him Man-Bat's physical features.

Francine was threatened by Talia al Ghul when Batman's former lover coerced Kirk into giving her his formula, in order to transform members of her father Ra's al Ghul's League of Assassins into Man-Bat commandos. She employs them in a mad scheme for revenge carried out against the Dark Knight in Grant Morrison's 2006 *Batman* story arc "Batman & Son."

An even more monstrous version of Kirk Langstrom is introduced in the 1995 *Batman: Manbat* limited series, an "Elseworlds" alternate-universe tale written by Jamie Delano with painted art by John Bolton. He also appears in "On Leather Wings," the very first episode of 1992's *Batman: The Animated Series*, in which Langstrom is a zoologist at the Gotham City Zoo, fittingly voiced by *Beastmaster* star Marc Singer. Peter MacNicol provides the character's voice in 2004's *The Batman*, in which he's an employee of Wayne Enterprises who seeks to instill fear in others.

Neither steady friend nor constant foe, Man-Bat remains a compelling, tragic figure whose feral nature mirrors Batman's own.

Gotham Gazette Exclusive

Neal Adams

More often than any other living artist, Neal Adams is described as the Definitive Batman Artist. It's a title the wildly influential dynamic realism he brought to the character makes hard to dispute. He also co-created two of the Dark Knight's most popular opponents—Man-Bat and Ra's al Ghul.

You've had a long association with Batman. Why do you think he's the most popular character in pop culture today?
Because Sherlock Holmes was previously the most popular character in pop culture, and is still popular. I mean, Batman *is* Sherlock Holmes. People don't realize that Sherlock Holmes was also tremendously athletic for his time. He knew different styles of jujitsu, boxing. Bad guys would come to his place and bend his andiron and he'd just bend it back. [Laughs.] It's one of those little secrets that the Conan Doyle fans know, and that is that he's tremendously strong. We don't know how he got that strong, but very clearly in his off time he does stuff that we don't know about. Well, isn't that what Batman

is? Pretty much. He's the World's Greatest Detective, a chemist...He does all that stuff *and* he's a tremendous athlete.

That's what we want to be ourselves. At our best, we are Batman, aren't we? And we don't need to be bitten by radioactive spiders to do it. In fact, Superman comes from another planet. For all we know he's got three assholes. I'm just saying... [Laughs.] He's an alien as far as we know. Batman is not. Batman's a brother. Batman's down the block. He just happens to have a little more money. But maybe he's pretty good at keeping it. Donald Trump excused from that, we have to be realistic and say that if we got that money we'd try to very much not lose it. That's what Bruce Wayne is doing. So what is it about Batman that isn't admirable from our point of view? I can't think of anything.

Most of the DC superheroes accidentally got their powers, and an awful lot of the Marvel superheroes accidentally got their powers. Name a character and tell me how he *earned* his powers. The only character that did that is Batman. So yeah, he's our type of superhero. Because he's not a superhero at all—he's a hero. We want to be Batman. We don't want to be anybody else. Even Captain America, who's terrific, he got the Super-Soldier Serum. So even he is not as good as Batman. Batman made himself.

How would you describe your vision of Batman?

Batman is 29 years old. He's lithe. He's 6-foot-2 and a half, maybe three. He's handsome. He's got a chiseled jaw. He's got a father who was probably about 6-foot-1. He himself is taller. He's slimmer. He's got broader shoulders and a deeper chest...There's a thing that people don't know. If you're a gymnast, one of the things that happens is you get this deeper chest. You go out in the front and you go out in the back. That gives you great upper body strength, but you don't try to do your midsection and make it bulky. You keep your midsection trim and athletic. Then they have strong thighs and strong legs. But you do that because you're running. Not because you're building them up with heavy muscles, like bodybuilder muscles. So there's a standard for a person to be able to do those things. They're athlete standards. They're swimmer standards. They're gymnast standards. Take a gymnast and a swimmer and a general athlete and put them all together and make a man who can run a decathlon, then you have Batman. I know that because I study this stuff. If I do it right, then other people look at it and they go, "Wow." Maybe they didn't study it, but they automatically look at it and go, "That's gotta be right."

Tarzan is very similar, except that his arms seem to be longer, his chest seems to be deeper, and his feet seem to be more curved and his legs seem to be stronger. So if Batman went up against Tarzan, then probably Batman would have to take his licks for about a half hour and then he'd finally come back and scientifically beat the hell out of Tarzan. But he'd have to be conscious to do it. And the question would have to be, could he be? I mean, people talk about the Hulk and Superman fighting. I think of Batman and Tarzan fighting. That's the standard for me.

How did you go about designing Ra's al Ghul?
The idea of Ra's al Ghul was to create a character that was to Batman what Moriarty was to Sherlock Holmes. To think that Moriarty would have made it just as a math professor against the physically powerful Sherlock Holmes is silly. He clearly was a person who went and worked out. He clearly was a person who was physically very active, and knew jujitsu and all the rest of it just like Sherlock Holmes. So we miss on Moriarty an awful lot of the time. You have a Moriarty who doesn't quite live up to the Moriarty that we want to see. If he did, he would be Ra's al Ghul! [Laughs.] I said, "Okay, why don't I make the ideal Moriarty and make him Ra's al Ghul?" It was [editor] Julie Schwartz who came up with the name. So clearly he needed to be a little bit mixed racially, but that actually was good. I felt very comfortable with that.

I mean, who identifies with Ra's al Ghul? He's the bad guy of every culture. He's Asian, he's Arabic. He's a tremendously powerful man, and tremendously skilled. I don't look to design characters that are less than what they ought to be. I always look to design the characters so that when they do the things that they do, you go, "Yeah! They can do that." When you design a character, you have to design his life—how he got to here, and therefore what he is when he got here. Because you can't just say, "Oh yeah, and he went to a gym for a week and he's fine." That's not the way it works. You have to design him from childhood. So when you look at Ra's al Ghul you're

(Sophia Quach McCabe)

looking at somebody whose life you've somehow seen, and now he is what he is and that's what he looks like. Then you go, "Wow, that guy must have had quite a life." That's what I put into the characters that I do, that I get to play with.

You also created Man-Bat, the ultimate expression of Batman's feral side.

He's a little nuts. Because he's potentially a drug addict. He obviously is smarter than he seems to be. But he's a curator in a museum. He should be a full professor in a college. But he's not, and he gets pushed around by people. So he's not living up to his potential. But he's brilliant. He's brilliant but he doesn't know which choice to make, and he makes bad choices. So he's a misfit.

That's the simplest kind of character to do. It's a poor, sad character who you wish was five degrees smarter and he would pull himself out of it. But he just can't make that jump. So he's stuck in that terrible thing where, under the least provocation, he'll take that damn drug and turn into a bat. I love that character. With Batman essentially dealing with clowns, we need more of a greater variety of characters. People don't quite realize that Man-Bat is not a clown.

Batman and his coterie of villains come from *Dick Tracy*, who had these strange villains like Pruneface, all these strangely drawn villains. Since Dick Tracy's a detective, obviously Bill Finger and Bob Kane looked to that as the library of characters that they would draw from. They didn't notice that they were just collecting clowns. So Ra's al Ghul and Man-Bat are the better versions of who we want to see with Batman. We could use a few more. But they're not that easy to come by.

Your first Batman stories were with writer Bob Haney in *The Brave and the Bold*.

The Bob Haney stories are where the change really happened with Batman, with Bob Haney and me. *The Brave and the Bold* was my excuse to do a Batman book. The only one that was available was *The Brave and the Bold*. Bob Haney was writing it and I didn't realize what a good writer he was. Every book that he tackled was beautifully done, expertly done. It was rich in story. No offense to [editor] Murray Boltinoff, but Murray Boltinoff didn't tell Bob Haney what to write. Bob Haney was pretty much on his own and I was pretty much on my own. Murray Boltinoff was an expediter. He wasn't a heavy-handed editor like Julie Schwartz. So Bob and I got to really kick out. I don't want to say those stories are better than what I did with Denny O'Neil. They were further reaching, broader, bigger stories. Each one was a movie. Whereas each one of the things with Denny was kind of a short story. More intimate, tighter. But Haney's traveled all over the place. We did Bruce Wayne and Sgt. Rock during World War II. It was like, "Really?" [Laughs.] Bruce Wayne is a 19-year-old guy who was Batman at that time. It just pulled him into the edge of that time and managed to make it work. Sgt. Rock of course was made famous by Joe Kubert. So now we had to live up to Joe Kubert's book, which was probably the best comic book out at that time. Putting the two together, that was kick-ass, and a long, involved story. That story feels like it's about 40 pages long. Every one of Haney's stories was like that. Whereas, again, Denny's seemed like they were short stories. Good short stories, but not very long. So it was a very interesting and different thing.

What made your collaboration with Denny work so well?
Denny picked it up and took it forward. I think Denny was smart and I was smart. We were a new generation of comic book people. I don't mean to cut on other people, but a lot of people who wrote comic books felt that they were writing down. I've heard comments like, "Are we gonna keep on doing this the rest of our lives? I'm just gonna blow my brains out." If you write comic books downward then they're okay, but they're really *not* okay. So we didn't write down. Denny didn't write down. I didn't draw down or write down.

If you go back and look at the Bob Kane stuff, yeah, you can make fun of it because it was kind of stupid. But when Denny and I were doing it, it stopped being stupid. Then other people followed us very, very quickly. Denny and I were smart, but we expressed our smartness. We were smart and we wrote up...Well, maybe we weren't that damn smart to begin with, but we at least tried to do better comics. So there's nothing about us that was unique and wonderful. We just wrote in the upward direction rather than downward.

87 The Huntress

"She stalks the night like a sleek jungle cat...But hers is a concrete jungle, and her prey the deadliest of men. For she is... *The Huntress.*"

So began a typical story of the crossbow-wielding avenger Helena Wayne, the Huntress, when the character's adventures were chronicled in the back pages of *Wonder Woman* in the 1970s and 1980s.

Though a villain by the same name had stalked the DC Universe in the 1940s, Helena was unique—the daughter of the Golden Age Batman and Catwoman, aka the Bruce Wayne and Selina Kyle of Earth-Two.

She was created by writer Paul Levitz and artist Joe Staton, then teamed together on *Justice Society*, along with inker Bob Layton. "Layton argued for an Earth-Two Batgirl," recalls Levitz in the introduction to 2006's *The Huntress: Darknight Daughter* (collecting her early adventures). "Staton supported adding another woman to the team."

The Huntress' first appearance, in December 1977's *DC Super Stars* #17 ("From Each Ending...A Beginning!"), detailed her origin. When criminals blackmail a reformed, happily married Selina Kyle Wayne into once more becoming the Catwoman, she's accidentally killed during a robbery attempt, prompting a grief-stricken Batman to retire from crimefighting forever. Unbeknownst to him, however, his daughter, trained to the peak of physical and mental perfection by her parents, dons a purple—her late mother's color—mask and bodysuit, and a scalloped cape identical to her father's. She also takes an oath similar to Batman's, by her mom's grave: "I swear I'll dedicate my life and inheritance to bringing your killer to justice...and to fighting all criminals!"

By night, Helena continued Bruce Wayne's war on crime after his death (in both *Batman Family* and *Wonder Woman*), while by day working as an attorney in the law firm of Cranston, Grayson, and Wayne. Eventually, she joined the Justice Society along with her friend Power Girl (the Supergirl of Earth-Two), crossed paths with the Justice League and Batman of Earth-One (her "Uncle Bruce"), and even battled her father's archnemesis, the Joker. Sadly, Helena (along with Earth-Two's Robin) died in March 1986's *Crisis on Infinite Earths* #12 while saving a group of children from the Anti-Monitor. But she was reborn following the events of DC's "New 52" relaunch in 2011.

Another Huntress joined the DC Universe in 1989—Helena Bertinelli, the daughter of a mafia crime lord. This more aggressive version of the character, who looked much like Helena Wayne, first appeared in April 1989's *The Huntress* #1 (written by Joey Cavalieri with art by Staton), and eventually became field leader of the Birds of Prey, in which she fought alongside Oracle (former Batgirl Barbara Gordon) and Black Canary. A TV adaptation of the super team starred Ashley Scott as the Helena Wayne Huntress. The Bertinelli Huntress made memorable appearances in the animated *Justice League Unlimited* (voiced by Amy Acker) and the live-action *Arrow* (played by Jessica De Gouw). The Huntress' first screen appearance, however, came just two years after she first appeared in comics—in the two January 1979 *Legends of the Superheroes* TV special cheesefests (in which she was played by Barbara Joyce).

88 Killer Croc

"You get one warning, chumps—don't mess with Killer Croc!"

So Mr. Waylon Jones introduced himself in April 1983's *Batman* #358 ("Don't Mess with Killer Croc!" by writer Gerry Conway and penciler Curt Swan). Determined to replace the late Rupert Thorne as Gotham City's top mob boss, Jones suffered from a genetic disorder that left his skin hard and scaly. He was born in a Tampa slum to a mother who died giving birth to him. His father already gone, Jones was left in the care of his deadbeat alcoholic aunt, and ruthlessly tormented by his childhood peers, who called him "Croc." After viciously beating one of them, he was sent to juvenile hall, after which he took to a life of crime. At 16, he killed a fellow prison inmate and spent 18 years behind bars. Upon parole, he joined a carnival sideshow and got a job wrestling alligators before making his way to Gotham and running afoul of Batman.

Unlike most of the Dark Knight's best-known enemies, Croc was presented with some degree of sympathy in his first story, which spanned *Batman* #359 and *Detective Comics* #525 and 526. "I've spent my life in law enforcement," says Commissioner Gordon in *Batman* #359. "When I started, I had nothing but contempt for Croc's kind. I still despise that sort of human scum. Even so, I know nothing's ever so simple as we'd like to believe... Not even evil..."

Croc's bid for power resulted in the deaths of Trina and Joseph Todd, two aerialists recruited by Dick Grayson to help capture him when he extorted protection money from their circus. Their deaths led to their son, Jason, succeeding Grayson as Robin.

Eventually Croc wound up in Arkham Asylum, but escaped and fled to the city's underground tunnels, where he found a home among Gotham's homeless, whom he presumably died saving in *Batman* #471 when the tunnels were flooded.

But Croc survived, lifted to safety by the rising flood waters, though his condition worsened. A form of atavism, it saw him devolve. He grew increasingly dimwitted, and stronger and more reptilian, his claws and teeth bigger and sharper with each reappearance. The situation accelerated when Croc contracted the "Hush" virus, after which he developed the ability to regenerate his limbs, and a taste for human flesh. He made another bid for mob power when he escaped from Arkham in 2010's *Joker's Asylum II: Killer Croc* one-shot, but was betrayed by the very people he thought were his new friends. "They're the monsters...not me," he tells Batman. "Put me back."

Recently, however, Croc may have finally begun to find the acceptance he's long sought, in the company of Task Force X. He replaced long-standing member King Shark in the 2016 *Suicide Squad* movie—in which he's played by Adewale Akinnuoye-Agbaje—and the team's concurrent "Rebirth" comic book.

Killer Croc made his animation debut in the first-season episode of *Batman: The Animated Series* "Vendetta." Voiced by 1960s beach-movie star Aron Kincaid, this iteration of the character has gray skin, as opposed to his traditional green, and is a former professional wrestler called "Killer Croc" Morgan. Redesigned to more closely resemble his comic book counterpart in the subsequent *The New Batman Adventures*, Croc is voiced by Brooks Gardner. A more bestial-looking Croc is portrayed in 2004's *The Batman* (voiced by *The Animated Series*' Clayface, Ron Perlman), but one more articulate than his on-screen predecessor. In 2013's computer-animated *Beware the Batman*, he's voiced by Wade Williams, who, ironically, played Blackgate Prison's warden in *The Dark Knight Rises*.

The *Batman: Arkham Origins* video game, released in 2013, marked the first time an African American actor portrayed Batman's most famous African American antagonist—Khary Payton, of *Teen Titans*, *Young Justice*, and *The Walking Dead* fame.

Gotham Gazette Exclusive

Gerry Conway

Gerry Conway chronicled the Dark Knight's Bronze Age adventures in *Batman* from #337 to 359 (July 1981 to May 1983) and *Detective Comics* from #497 to 526 (December 1980 to May 1983). Working with the late great artists Don Newton and Doug Moench, he created Jason Todd, who would become the second Robin, and added a new member to Batman's rogues gallery in Killer Croc.

You created Jason Todd around the same time as Killer Croc...
Both of them were co-created with Don Newton. I was on a roll at that time working on Batman. I was doing both *Batman* and *Detective Comics*. So I had the freedom to really explore the character in a way that some other writers might not have had, and I tried answering some questions that I as a reader had. While I really enjoyed the later Dark Knight direction and the direction in which Denny O'Neil had previously taken the character, I kind of missed the Batman of the '60s and '50s, with Batman and Robin as a team; and also the kind of villains that Batman had had back in the day, in the '40s and the '50s, which were more influenced by the Dick Tracy–type crime villain. The weird, odd-looking characters that created situations for Batman that challenged him in unique ways. I felt we had gotten away from that to a degree with characters like Ra's al Ghul, who's a terrific character but isn't in the mold of the classic Batman villain.

I wanted to reinvent the Batman-Robin relationship. But since Robin was very much tied into the Teen Titans I couldn't really do that. It just didn't feel right. Dick Grayson was too old. His relationship with Batman was less student/mentor than equals, and the kinds of characters we had to work with for villains were more like the Ra's al Ghul mastermind than the down-and-dirty crime king variety. Killer Croc was an answer to that, because he was more of a street-level villain.

Or below street level.
Yeah. I also had this feeling that since Batman is in effect a creature of the skies, putting him underground would create some interesting

visuals and stories, with a villain that's literally an underworld villain. [Laughs.]

What type of partner did you intend Jason to be?
Dick Grayson was always portrayed as a good kid. Just a perfectly good kid who had a tragic past. I wanted to give Jason a little more of an edge, so that there was potentially some conflict between him and Batman about the moral gray area. That was one aspect of it. Ultimately, he became too much of a Dick Grayson clone. Which is why it was palatable to readers to have him killed off. Because he didn't differentiate enough, as it turned out.

Killer Croc has undergone very different interpretations in different media.
When you look at those early stories, he was intended to be a fairly physically threatening, violent villain. He was more of a crime boss character, but he was physically intimidating. He had a presence underground in the sewers. That was all part of his mystique. When he was brought into *Batman: The Animated Series*, I think part of the reason they brought him in was because they wanted a physically threatening character, which would be good for animation. As a result they enhanced him visually. Then when he was brought back into the comics, that was the influence. It sort of multiplied from there. Now you've got this 12-foot-tall, semi-human creature. That's just taking a character and expanding on the original concept. Because the original concept always was that he was a physically frightening character. How you execute that is really up to the artist who's doing the execution.

Croc might be the only major villain in Batman's rogues gallery who was created as an African American.
Yeah. I always tried to invoke diversity in my characters, back in the late '70s / early '80s. That really wasn't necessarily a priority, but I really tried to do that. I'm really happy that he has that role.

What did you think of Croc's appearance in the *Suicide Squad* movie?

I was glad to see it. I liked it a lot. It's a pretty good interpretation. It's actually closer in a lot of ways to the original conception—a human-scale, non-monosyllabic monster. A tortured man. So it's kind of appropriate.

One of your other Batman creations was mayor Hamilton Hill, who also resurfaced in *The Animated Series*.

Yeah, I felt so much of Gotham politics was being sidestepped, that there wasn't enough real political background to this material. You had Commissioner Gordon, but he's simply the police commissioner. You had people above him who also influence the police. I think Hamilton Hill to some degree was influenced by the mayor in *Jaws*. The idea of the callow political figure who doesn't really have the city's best interests at heart and is influenced by his own political interests. It was a fairly prevalent notion at the time. So creating a character like Hamilton Hill just allowed me to address that. And I always had an affection for alliterative names. So Hamilton Hill just seemed like the right name for that kind of a guy, partly because the character in *Jaws* was played by Murray Hamilton. It was probably subconscious as much as anything. Much of what I do is subconscious. Or unconscious. [Laughs.]

Which of your Batman stories are you fondest of?

Generally speaking I don't write individual stories. I write a series of stories around a particular character. I like the Hugo Strange storyline. That was fun. I thought that went well...I was proud of the fact that we ended up doing what amounted to a biweekly Batman, by starting stories in *Detective Comics* and finishing them in *Batman*. I liked doing that. I loved the range of stories I did with Gene Colan, just because of seeing Gene Colan's art on *Batman*. I thought it was a terrific look for the book. Next to people like Neal Adams and Frank Miller, and of course the original Jerry Robinson and Dick Sprang Batman comics, he was probably the best person to do that character. Because his visual style was just perfect for Batman. All those shadows and darkness. The way that Batman would move in and out of panels. It was terrific. I loved working with Gene on that book.

And I really liked *Detective Comics* #526, with all the villains in one story, that Don Newton and I did. He was kind of in the shadow of Gene at that point, because Gene's stuff was so overwhelming. But Don had this really great combination of draftsmanship and storytelling that you really rarely see in comics from that period, when there was much more of an emphasis on big visuals and less on character. He could make a scene of pathos really intense. I really enjoyed Don's work, and you can see the development of Don's work over the two or three years that he worked on that book. It gets dramatically better. Then he unfortunately passed away. But he was a terrific artist.

With both Gene and Don, I was writing full scripts. So my actual collaboration with them was less than it would have been if I'd been working Marvel style, where I was working off an artist's own style. Both of those guys didn't have as much free range in their storytelling as they would have if they were breaking the pages down themselves. But they both did terrific jobs.

89 Ace the Bat-Hound

In the Sherlock Holmes story "The Sign of the Four," the great consulting detective says of his canine companion, Toby, "I would rather have Toby's help than that of the whole detective force of London." Since the Batman has emulated Holmes in so many respects, it's fitting that he too should have a dog to call on for help in his criminal casework: Ace the Bat-Hound.

Created by Batman co-creator Bill Finger and artist Sheldon Moldoff—who drew inspiration from Superman's dog, Krypto (who'd debuted just a few months before Ace), and film star canines such as Rin Tin Tin and Ace the Wonder Dog—Ace was introduced in June 1955's *Batman* #92 ("Ace, the Bat-Hound!"). A German Shepherd watchdog rescued from drowning in a river by Batman and Robin, Ace repaid the Dynamic Duo by helping them nab escaped convict Bert Bowers; the criminal gave the dog a new name when he cried, "Leggo, you—you bat-hound!" Ace was later returned to his owner, the engraver John Wilker, after Batman rescued him from a gang of would-be counterfeiters. But Ace returned to aid Gotham's guardians on several occasions, wearing a black mask first given to him by Robin (to conceal a distinct diamond-shaped mark on his forehead that would reveal his identity), along with a Bat symbol on his dog collar.

Eventually, Wilker's job required him to travel so much he was unable to care for Ace, and the dog was given to Bruce Wayne. A small receiver hidden inside his collar brought him to the Dark Knight's side via a high-pitched noise triggered by a radio transmitter in the hollow of Batman's boot heel. Ace fought crime alongside his master during the Silver Age of Comics, but disappeared when editor Julius Schwartz assumed control of the Batman titles in the 1960s.

A new incarnation of Ace was introduced following the events of DC's 1985 *Crisis on Infinite Earths* limited series, one who originally belonged to the Native American shaman Black Wolf. After his master's death, following a case in which he and the Dark Knight stopped corruption within Black Wolf's tribe, Ace came to live with Bruce Wayne at Wayne Manor.

Since the events of 2005's *Infinite Crisis*, Ace has appeared less frequently in comics, though another incarnation of the cunning canine surfaced during DC's "Rebirth" relaunch. This version of Ace originally belonged to the Joker and was trained to kill Batman, before being rescued and retrained by Alfred Pennyworth.

Ace also served as a constant companion and guard dog for the elderly Bruce Wayne in the 1999 TV series *Batman Beyond*, and made regular appearances in two other animated series—2005's *Krypto the Superdog* (in which he was voiced by Scott McNeil) and 2008's *Batman: The Brave and the Bold.* Both of them saw him continue to take a bite out of crime.

90 Visit Wayne Manor

Want to see where Bruce Wayne lives? You have several locations to choose from.

The first structure to stand in for the "stately Wayne Manor" is the 1928 10-bedroom Tudor-style mansion used in the 1966 *Batman* TV series. It's located near Los Angeles, on the west side of Pasadena, at 380 S. San Rafael Avenue in South Arroyo. Unfortunately, the building isn't visible from the street, so the most you'll be able to see is its front gate.

Since Tim Burton's 1989 *Batman* movie was filmed at London's Pinewood Studios, it made sense for the production to utilize an English edifice for its manor. Knebworth House, located north of the city in Hertfordshire, was chosen for its gothic exterior (which the 15th century structure acquired in the Victorian era). Unlike the 1960s Wayne Manor, this one is open to visitors for special events and throughout the spring and summer months, with family-friendly gardens, a park, and a dinosaur trail. You can learn more at www.knebworthhouse.com. The interiors of the 1989 film's mansion were lensed at nearby Hatfield House, also in Hertfordshire. It was constructed in 1611 on the site of Queen Elizabeth I's childhood home, and it too is open to visitors during the tourist season. For more, visit www.hatfield-house.co.uk.

The exterior of the gloomy Wayne Manor seen in Burton's sequel, 1992's *Batman Returns*, was a miniature, and its interiors were Hollywood sets. But director Joel Schumacher brought some simple colonial charm to the following film in the series, 1995's *Batman Forever*, when the Webb Institute of Naval Architecture became the manor. The Webb Institute is at 298 Crescent Beach Road in Glen Cove, New York, on the north shore of Long Island. Though it's not open to visitors, it again became a part of the Dark Knight's world when it appeared on TV's *Gotham* in 2014. Schumacher's much criticized follow-up, 1997's *Batman & Robin*, found another manor home in Greystone Mansion. This 1928 Tudor Revival–style building is situated in Beverly Hills. Though the mansion itself is only open to the public for special events, its surrounding grounds are open free of charge year-round. To plan a visit, go to www.beverlyhills.org/exploring/greystonemansiongardens.

When Christopher Nolan rebooted the Dark Knight on the big screen, the franchise moved back to Britain for its Wayne Manor. *Batman Begins* utilized stately Mentmore Towers, a 19th century country house in the village of Mentmore in Buckinghamshire. Sadly, the building is currently closed, as is the Mentmore Golf and Country Club located on its grounds. Since Bruce Wayne's mansion burned to the ground at the end of *Batman Begins*, the billionaire moved into a downtown Gotham penthouse for its sequel *The Dark Knight*, in reality the Wyndham Grand Chicago Riverfront hotel, at 71 E. Wacker Drive in the Windy City. The complex's One Illinois Center was used for the interior of Bruce Wayne's penthouse.

The traditional route was taken once more in 2012's *The Dark Knight Rises*, with Wollaton Hall in Nottingham—the very same 16th century Tudor building on which *Batman Begins*' Mentmore Towers was based—providing the new Wayne Manor's exterior.

West London's Georgian country estate Osterley Park House served as its interior. Both can be visited via www.wollatonhall.org.uk/ and www.nationaltrust.org.uk/osterley-park-and-house.

In the new continuity established in 2016's *Batman v Superman: Dawn of Justice*, Wayne Manor has again burned down, and Bruce Wayne resides in a lakeside glass house on its grounds. A private building located 40 miles north of Detroit, in Michigan's Orion Township, was used.

91 *The LEGO Batman Movie*

There are almost as many Batman spoofs as there are straight iterations, going as far back as writer Harvey Kurtzman and artist Wally Wood's "Bat Boy and Rubin!" in December 1953's *MAD* #8. Few, however, balance satire with affection the way *The LEGO Batman Movie* does.

Batman first became a LEGO minifigure in 2006, and spawned a number of product lines based on versions as disparate as those of the 1966 *Batman* TV series and 2008's *The Dark Knight.* LEGO Batman video games and direct-to-video animated movies followed, leading to the Brick Knight's inclusion in the first LEGO theatrical film, writer-directors Phil Lord and Christopher Miller's 2014 *The LEGO Movie.* Voiced by Will Arnett, this version of the character parodied the obsessed Batman introduced in 1986's *The Dark Knight Returns* and continued through Christian Bale's gravel-voiced interpretation in Christopher Nolan's trilogy. But *The LEGO Movie* gave it a twist—by making Batman an overly confident dude-bro.

It's a version that makes sense. If someone is good at everything, why *wouldn't* they be an egomaniac? LEGO Batman's attitude is captured in the lyrics to his "Untitled Self Portrait":

Darkness
No parents
Continued darkness
The opposite of light
Black hole
Curtains drawn
In the basement
Middle of the night
Blacked-out windows
Other places that are dark
Black suit
Black coffee
Darkness
No parents
Super rich
Kinda makes it better

In *The LEGO Batman Movie*, the character returned. This time around, it's made clear his bravado masks a lifetime of sorrow, and a loneliness from his reluctance to accept family. There are, however, two principal conceits: first, that Batman's crimefighting career includes his adventures in *all* media and really did begin in 1939; and second, that he's operated until now without a Batgirl or Robin. Rosario Dawson and Michael Cera voice the two characters, while Ralph Fiennes and Zach Galifianakis lend support as Alfred and the Joker, respectively.

But it remains Batman's show, whether munching on Lobster Thermidor atop a jet ski in the Batcave's marina or extolling the virtues of sick pecs to anyone within earshot. Directed by *Robot*

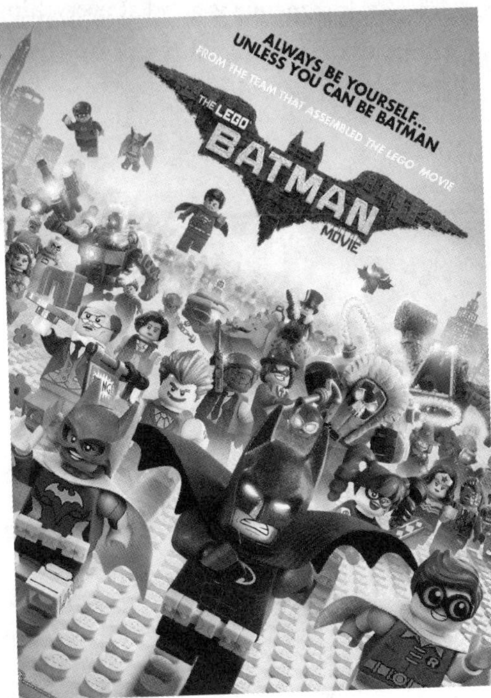

The LEGO Batman Movie *features the voice of Will Arnett as a pompous, egomaniacal version of the Dark Knight.*

Chicken veteran Chris McKay, *The LEGO Batman Movie* pokes fun at almost 80 years of Batmania, but does so with as much respect for its hero's mythology as any live-action film in which he's appeared.

"I can really buy the version of Batman as a total dick," laughs *LEGO Batman* fan Paul Dini, whose own scripts have often explored the Dark Knight's lighter side. "A wannabe rapper/Batbro type laying down mad tracks…I thought it was refreshing. He's kind of a goof, but they don't make him a figure of out-and-out ridicule. There's a moment toward the end of the movie when Batman decides to go it alone, and you buy it. He would do that. In any identity he would sacrifice himself over anybody else."

Gotham Gazette Exclusive

Will Arnett

Comedy star Will Arnett has won acclaim for his roles in *Arrested Development* and *BoJack Horseman*. But he's earned a special place in the hearts of Batfans for his turn as the Brick Knight in *The LEGO Movie* and *The LEGO Batman Movie*.

Have you had a deep voice your whole life?

Ever since I hit puberty it just started to drop, along with everything else...It's just always been kind of raspy and deep. When we were kids, just for vitamins and stuff, we always had a steaming cup of crushed glass in the morning.

Did you amuse your family with it?

Not really. My dad has it too but not as badly as I do—or as well, depending on how you look at it. So he's always claimed that if anything happened to me he could take over my career. I'm like, "Thanks a lot. I'm your son! Your son is dead! Are you not worried about that?"

Did you have a definitive Batman growing up?

I like Michael Keaton a lot because he was kind of funny. His Bruce Wayne to Batman was very different; they were very distinctive characters. His growl wasn't so deep or as dark perhaps as Christian Bale's—which is great—but it was very fresh. Keaton and Tim Burton came up with that conceit. They started it. That's Michael Keaton, man! And that's what we've come to take for granted as *the* Batman. He came up with it. At the same time, while he was Bruce Wayne, he was kind of a playful bon vivant/playboy. Michael Keaton is obviously an amazing actor and doesn't get enough credit. Just because there have been so many other good Batmen, I guess.

For *The LEGO Batman Movie*, how much improvising did you do with Zach Galifianakis as the Joker?
A lot of it was improvised. Zach and I had a day when we were in a room and [director] Chris McKay cleared everyone out and miked us up and had boom operators like on a movie set. We knew the area we were going to play in and we just started improvising, and we dug out that relationship and basically turned it into a rom-com between two enemies. It really drove the narrative of the film all the way to the end.

Which of your *LEGO Batman Movie* lines cracks you up the most?
There's a line when Bruce Wayne first meets Dick Grayson/Robin at an event and Dick says, "Hi, I'm Richard Grayson, I'm in the orphanage. But the kids call me Dick." And Batman says, almost under his breath, "Kids can be so cruel."

Somebody online said, "I like the movie but my only complaint was there's too many jokes." He said something along the lines of, "I laughed too much, I needed a break." Oh I'm sorry—you needed a break? Then go home! It's our job to put as many jokes in there as possible. [Laughs.]

Amidst all the comedy, *The LEGO Batman Movie* has a timely message...
One of the great messages about this film is that you can't do it all by yourself, and you're really only as strong as your weakest link. There's a message of inclusiveness, and I think that's a really good message. I think, by and large, most Americans understand that. I hope they respond to that in the movie and I hope that message gets through.

Do you like Lobster Thermidor as much as LEGO Batman does?
Oh yeah. I've had it millions of times. I don't ever remember a time when I've *not* had it.

92 The Top Five Contemporary Batman Collectibles

Unlike the merchandise released at the height of 1960s Batmania, today's collectibles are intended and priced as just that: collectibles. Here are five for the Batfan with the heart of a child and the income of an adult.

Corgi Batmobiles

UK toy company Corgi has been producing Batmobiles since 1966. The best of them were released between 2005 and 2007, representing most every era of the Dark Knight's comic history in 1⁄43 scale, with die-cast bodies, rubber tires, and working features. Many were produced as limited-edition variants packaged with exclusive painted metal figurines, and can still be found reasonably priced on eBay.

Batman: Black and White Statues

Since 2005, DC Direct has released almost 100 high-quality Batman: Black and White statues. Based on the work of seminal Batman comic artists, including Carmine Infantino, Neal Adams, Frank Miller, and Bruce Timm, the line also makes room for such idiosyncratic creators as Mike Mignola, Paul Pope, and Sergio Aragones.

Hot Toys Figures

Hong Kong–based Hot Toys has won high marks from fans for its film and television figures manufactured in 1⁄6 scale. Screen superheroes from Christopher Reeve's Superman to Marvel's Avengers have been rendered in startlingly lifelike detail, as have Adam West, Michael Keaton, and Christian Bale's Batmen, along with Burt Ward's Robin and Jack Nicholson and Heath Ledger's Jokers.

Tweeterhead Statues

Plenty of pricey Batman statues have appeared in recent years, but San Francisco specialty studio Tweeterhead has managed to keep costs within reason while producing a series as desirable as that of any company. *Batman Returns*' Catwoman and the heroes and villains of the 1966 *Batman* series have all received the Tweeterhead treatment, though the company's most appealing statues are those based on artist Dick Sprang's Golden Age Batman and Robin and their rogues gallery.

Custom-Made Batmobile

If you're shopping for the Batman fan who has everything and money's no object, why not splurge on a replica of the 1966 *Batman*'s Batmobile? Indiana's Fiberglass Freaks holds the official manufacturing license, producing the car originally designed by George Barris, priced from $125,000 to $250,000. For those with less coin, the $20 T-shirt available on its website (www.buybatparts.com) is also pretty nice.

93 Beware the Batman

Starting with 1992's *Batman: The Animated Series*, each of the Dark Knight's animated TV shows was spurred by the production of a live-action Batman movie: 2004's *The Batman* was motivated by *Batman Begins*, 2008's *Batman: The Brave and the Bold* followed the release of *The Dark Knight*, and 2012's *The Dark Knight Rises* birthed *Beware the Batman*—the character's first computer-animated series.

Premiering on Cartoon Network on July 13, 2013, *Beware the Batman* was developed by Warner Bros. Animation veterans Glen Murakami (*Batman Beyond*), Sam Register (*Teen Titans*), Mitch Watson (*Scooby-Doo! Mystery Incorporated*), and Butch Lukic (*Batman: The Animated Series*). It featured the voices of Anthony Ruivivar as Batman, J.B. Blanc as Alfred Pennyworth (a version that draws from the Bronze Age Alfred's background as an intelligence agent and *Batman: Earth One*'s gruff man of action), and Kurtwood Smith as Lieutenant James Gordon. The big addition came in the form of Tatsu Yamashiro (voiced by Sumalee Montano). Best known as Katana of the Outsiders and Suicide Squad, here the character is Alfred's goddaughter, a CIA operative turned avenging swordswoman who supplants Robin as the Dark Knight's partner.

The show's rogues gallery featured many faces new to the Dark Knight's animated adventures. Anarky (voiced by Wallace Langham) served as *Beware the Batman*'s chief criminal mastermind and king of chaos; other foes included Lady Shiva (Finola Hughes), Professor Pyg (Brian George), Mister Toad (Udo Kier), and Magpie (Grey DeLisle). Among the returning A-list characters were Barbara Gordon (again voiced by *Batman: The Animated Series*' Tara Strong), Harvey Dent (Christopher McDonald), Killer Croc (Wade Williams), Kirk Langstrom (Peter MacNicol), and Ra's al Ghul (Lance Reddick).

The most heavily serialized of the animated Batman shows, *Beware the Batman* is also the darkest, its Masked Manhunter looking more Bat-like than any other screen incarnation. But it's never a dour experience. The theme music by the Dum Dum Girls captures its tone—mysterious, fast-paced, and fun. It finds its footing a handful of episodes into its first and, unfortunately, only season, the front half of which ("Shadows of Gotham") climaxes with a gripping Ra's al Ghul / League of Assassins story arc. The even better back half ("Dark Justice") ends with a three-part story detailing the birth of Two-Face.

Several months after it debuted, *Beware the Batman* was put on hiatus by Cartoon Network, and eventually broadcast as part of the network's late-night Adult Swim programming. The lack of a toy line didn't help the show's visibility, and the design of its weaponry was made less threatening in the wake of the tragic July 2012 Century 16 movie theater shooting in Aurora, Colorado. Despite the alterations, *Beware the Batman* is second only to *Batman: The Animated Series* as TV's most suspenseful, cinematic take on the Dark Knight. Nominated for four Daytime Emmy Awards, as well as an Annie Award for Best Animated TV/Broadcast Production for Children's Audience, it's well worth the attention of every Batfan.

94 The Court of Owls

The League of Assassins, the Cult of Kobra, the Sacred Order of Saint Dumas—Batman has fought secret societies and shadowy terrorist organizations for decades. But no such group has hit the Dark Knight as hard as the Court of Owls.

When the DC Universe was rebooted in 2011's "New 52," Batman was permitted to keep most of his preexisting continuity, though his long-running eponymous comic book series had, after 71 years, come to an end. A second volume began with November 2011's *Batman* #1. Rather than reintroduce one of the members of the Dark Knight's rogues gallery, writer Scott Snyder and penciler Greg Capullo created a new enemy for their hero—the Court of Owls, an underground group of elites who've menaced and manipulated Gotham since colonial days. The Court adopted as its symbol the natural predator of bats.

Believing them a mere folk tale told to generations of Gothamites as a nursery rhyme, Bruce Wayne is targeted by the Court's undead knife-throwing Talons after he unveils a plan to improve Gotham by reshaping it. Convinced he's the only legend his city needs, Batman battles the group, and uncovers its plan to assume control of Gotham by killing off the city's leaders, as well as the Dark Knight's allies. He also discovers that Dick Grayson was once groomed to be a Talon, and that one of the Court's most prominent members, a Gotham mayoral candidate, could be the younger brother Bruce Wayne never knew he had.

The first Court of Owls storyline ran in *Batman* #1 to 11, and was collected in two volumes: *Batman Volume 1: The Court of Owls* and *Volume 2: The City of Owls*. As intended, it's an excellent entry point for new Batman readers (one that crossed over into DC's related titles as the "Night of the Owls" event). Veteran Batfans will also find it offers plenty of suspense. Snyder draws on his background as a horror scribe (he created DC/Vertigo's Eisner-winning *American Vampire*) to concoct a believably chilling conspiracy; Capullo, with the help of inker Danny Miki, delivers thrilling breakneck action sequences and makes the owl-masked Court among the creepiest villains to attack Gotham.

One of the finest writer-artist teams to chronicle the Dark Knight's adventures, Snyder and Capullo's collaboration continued through *Batman* #51; generating equally epic storylines like "Death of the Family" (featuring the Joker), "Zero Year" (retelling Batman's early days), "Endgame," and "Superheavy" (in which Commissioner Gordon takes on the mantle of the Bat). All of them emphasize the enduring relationship between Batman and his city, under constant threat from without and within.

"I love how Batman is always sort of at odds with himself," says Snyder. "On the one hand, he's out to inspire people. But he's also out to terrify certain people. On the one hand, he puts himself out there and sacrifices himself every night. On the other, that also leads to incredibly self-destructive behavior. He's mortal, he's immortal—all of those things at once. He exists at this intersection of heroism and self-destruction. There's something deeply and richly interesting there I think."

The Court also appeared on screen as a chief antagonist to a young Bruce Wayne and Jim Gordon in TV's *Gotham*.

Gotham Gazette Exclusive

Scott Synder

Scott Snyder reintroduced James Gordon Jr. as a villain for Dick Grayson's Robin in 2011's "The Black Mirror" storyline, and created the diabolical Court of Owls with penciler Greg Capullo. He followed his acclaimed "New 52" run on Batman with a new title, *All-Star Batman*.

What was your favorite Batman comic when you were growing up?
I still have my original issues of *The Dark Knight Returns* at my parents' house. Growing up in New York, the thing that was so incredibly affecting about it was, suddenly Batman existed in the city around us. You saw him facing problems in an actual landscape that looked like the city that we were living in, where you couldn't necessarily go to Central Park, and there was crime and there was graffiti. To see Batman saving people and being an inspiration in a city that was immediately my own was just a tremendous influence on me. It made me want to write, honestly. To see that you could make a superhero so relevant and personal and immediate was definitely the transformative moment for me in comics.

What's the most underrated version of Batman?
The work on *The Animated Series* was really seminal, with producers Bruce Timm and Alan Burnett. The reason I think it's underrated is

because I feel a lot of the origins of the villains and a lot of the things we assume are the modern interpretations of the characters that come from the comics, a lot of them filtered in from that animated stuff, like Nora from the Mr. Freeze episode.

What do you think you've brought to Batman with your work?
That's a hard question...We added a few owls? [Laughs.] For me and the team on the book right now it really is trying to live up to the examples of Frank [Miller] and other writers on the book. They were always trying to tell stories that were fun and modern and immediate, and did revolutionary things with the character in a colorful, bombastic, muscular way on the page. But ultimately when you peel those layers back they're tremendously personal stories. You see Frank's interests across his Batman books. For me, that's what it's about...In a way that makes the stories about your demons, your fantasies.

Why has the character endured?
Because at the core, the money doesn't matter, the gadgets...All that stuff is fun, but ultimately it's a story about somebody who faces tremendous challenges. Someone who faces this incredible adversity in childhood. The worst thing that could happen to a kid happens to him, and instead of giving up or seeing the meaninglessness in life, he turns it around and creates this engine for himself to become the greatest hero of all time, and create meaning for other people in the world. He takes something that's a random, meaningless act of violence and turns it into this fuel for himself to become someone who inspires other people to matter and to do things that matter. The folk hero is forever a powerful emblem. Especially in American folklore. The figure that overcomes his greatest fear and becomes this hero and tells us not to be afraid is everlasting. What interests me about the character is that primarily, but also where that starts to become pathological.

95 Clayface

Among his many skills, Batman is a master of disguise, capable of blending into most any environment. Yet even his mutability pales in comparison to that of the archcriminal Clayface, who's worn more masks than any member of the Dark Knight's rogues gallery.

The first Clayface, Basil Karlo, was introduced in June 1940's *Detective Comics* #40 ("The Murders of Clayface," by Batman creators Bill Finger and Bob Kane). His name a play on those of film stars Boris Karloff and Basil Rathbone (both of whom had appeared in the previous year's *Son of Frankenstein*), Karlo too is an actor; he goes mad upon learning his film *The Terror* is being remade. Like silent film star Lon Chaney, the "Man of a Thousand Faces," Karlo is a makeup artist, and he's hired as a consultant on the film, which stars Bruce Wayne's ex Julie Madison. After Madison's boyfriend is attacked by Karlo, he identifies him to Batman before he dies, and the Dynamic Duo nabs Clayface.

Clayface II was Matt Hagen, who first appeared in December 1961's *Detective Comics* #298 ("The Challenge of Clay-Face," again written by Finger with pencils by Sheldon Moldoff). As befitting a story from the atomic age, in which many of Batman and Robin's cases were far-out science fiction, Hagen turns supervillain after he's exposed to a radioactive pool in an underwater cave during a treasure-hunting expedition. With the power to change his shape into anything he desires, Hagen becomes a thief, and is only stopped by Batman when he fails to refresh his powers in his radioactive pool.

July-August 1978's *Detective Comics* #478 heralded "The Coming of...Clayface III!" (written by Len Wein and penciled by Marshall Rogers). S.T.A.R. Labs employee Preston Payne, suffering from hyperpituitarism, injects himself with an enzyme taken from Matt Hagen's mutated blood in an attempt to cure his condition. But his experiment goes awry and he becomes a formless monster with a toxic touch that depends on an exoskeleton to survive; his only friend is a mannequin he names Helena.

Proving that the role of Clayface knows no gender boundaries, the fourth character to bear the name was a woman, Sondra Fuller, arriving in July 1987's *Outsiders* #21 ("Strike Force Kobra," by writer Mike W. Barr and artist Jim Aparo). When the terrorist leader Kobra attempts to create his own evil superteam, Fuller, insecure about her appearance, allows him to turn her into a shapeshifter (referred to as "Lady Clay") with the ability to duplicate the powers of metahumans.

When Fuller visited the original Clayface and Clayface III at Arkham Asylum, a new criminal group was born—the Mud Pack, which first appeared in *Detective Comics* #604's "The Mud Pack—Part One: Men of Clay." In this storyline, Karlo injects himself with DNA from his fellow Clayfaces to become the short-lived Ultimate Clayface.

"Looking back on it," says artist Norm Breyfogle, who illustrated the supervillain team's debut, "Clayface was perfect for me because he was so malleable, literally and figuratively. You could really go overboard in depicting the elements. That was something I always tried to inject into Batman—to make his lunging positions and his lunges and every action exaggerated. But Clayface really gave me that opportunity as well."

By this point, Fuller and Payne had fallen in love, and their son Cassius—the fifth Clayface, who inherits both of his parents' abilities—was born in May 1994's *Shadow of the Bat* #27 ("Creatures of Clay: Child's Clay," written by Alan Grant and penciled by Bret Blevins). When DEO scientist Peter Malley attempts to study a sample of Cassius' skin, it fuses to his own. This results in the creature known as Claything, the sixth Clayface, in January 1998's

Batman #550 ("Chasing Clay," by writer Doug Moench and pencilers Kelley Jones and J.H. Williams III).

Little is known about the background of the seventh Clayface, Todd Russell, introduced in January 2002's *Catwoman* #1 ("Anodyne, Part One of Four," by writer Ed Brubaker and penciler Darwyn Cooke). An Army veteran on whom experiments were performed, Russell loses his memory and gains shapeshifting powers, with which he attacks Gotham's prostitutes before being stopped by Catwoman.

The eighth Clayface, Johnny Williams, first appeared in October 2003's *Batman* #618 during writer Jeph Loeb and penciler Jim Lee's "Hush" storyline. A firefighter caught in a chemical fire that mutates him into a shapeshifter, Williams is manipulated by the villainous Hush, who holds Williams' family hostage to compel his cooperation in an elaborate revenge plot against Batman. But Williams turns the tables on the criminal and assists Batman in bringing Hush to justice, though at the cost of his own life.

The ninth Clayface, the most recent as of this writing, is the unnamed samurai who briefly confronts Batman Japan in June 2011's *Batman Incorporated* #6 ("Nyktomorph," by writer Grant Morrison and artist Chris Burnham).

The first Clayface to appear on screen was Matt Hagen, Clayface II, in the "Dead Ringers" episode of Filmation's 1977 animated series *The New Adventures of Batman*, in which he was voiced by Filmation founder Lou Scheimer. Hagen's Clayface is also featured in *Batman: The Animated Series*, incorporating elements of Basil Karlo's Clayface. Here, Hagen is an actor disfigured in an auto accident and granted a chance to recover his career by a corrupt businessman, who turns him into the most recognized version of Clayface (as evidenced by the amount of merchandise bearing his visage). Introduced in the episode "Feat of Clay," this Clayface—superbly voiced by *Hellboy* star Ron Perlman—returned several times throughout the acclaimed series' run.

The Batman brought a new version of Clayface to the screen in 2004, that of Batman's friend and ally Detective Ethan Bennett (*The Practice*'s Steve Harris), who's tragically transformed by the Joker's Joker Putty into a shapeshifter. The Karlo version of Clayface also makes its first screen appearance in this series (voiced by *CSI: Crime Scene Investigation*'s Wallace Langham and Lex Lang).

Two versions of Clayface appeared when the character made his live-action debut in the 2003 "Feat of Clay" episode of TV's *Birds of Prey*: a shapeshifting sculptor (Kirk Baltz) who gets his powers via special formula—and is recruited by the Joker to kill Catwoman—and his son Chris Cassius (Ian Reed Kesler), who takes his father's formula and gains the ability to turn people into clay. A version of Basil Karlo's Clayface (played by Brian McManamon) was introduced in the "Wrath of the Villains: A Legion of Horribles" episode of TV's *Gotham*, with a morphable face he uses to impersonate James Gordon.

Given the limits of the era's special effects, it's easy to see why Clayface never appeared on the 1966 *Batman* TV series, which opted for another master of disguise in the villain False Face. But an issue of the *Batman '66* comic book, July 2015's #23 ("The Quagmire of Clayface," by writer Jeff Parker and penciler Giancarlo Caracuzzo), at long last rectified the situation—by revealing that False Face's real name is Basil Karlo and transforming him into Clayface.

96 The Mad Hatter

Given the number of psychopaths who comprise the Dark Knight's rogues gallery, it stands to reason that one of them took his cue from one of literature's most famous madmen.

When the Mad Hatter first appeared in October 1948's *Batman* #49 ("The Scoop of the Century!" by Batman co-creator Bill Finger and artist Jim Mooney) he was introduced as a mere throwaway character in a story focused on introducing Bruce Wayne's on-again, off-again girlfriend Vicki Vale. A photographer at *Picture Magazine* who comes to suspect Bruce is Batman, Vale's first meeting with Bruce at his yacht club is interrupted by a man "who might have stepped from an illustration of *Alice in Wonderland*." Indeed the Hatter bears a close resemblance to his namesake, right down to his overbite (as rendered by artist John Tenniel in the 1865 novel). He steals a gold cup from the club, and the next day leaves a clue for the Dynamic Duo in the form of a hat. Perhaps anticipating readers' criticisms, writer Bill Finger has Robin point out the similarities of the Hatter to their other enemies: "This Mad Hatter character is trying to imitate the Joker and the Penguin by sending a clue in advance!"

By story's end, the Hatter's hideout is revealed as an abandoned theater decorated with *Alice in Wonderland* sets. When Batman and Robin arrive, he mimics *Alice*'s Red Queen and attempts to remove Batman's head with an axe. Fortunately he's distracted by Vicki, who appeals to his vanity by asking him to pose for a picture, letting Batman land an uppercut.

An altogether different Mad Hatter appeared eight years later, in April 1956's *Detective Comics* #230 ("The Mad Hatter of Gotham City!" again written by Bill Finger, with pencils by Sheldon Moldoff). This version of the character, who went by the name Jervis Tetch, was a red-haired, mustachioed "fanatical hobby-robber" obsessed with adding Batman's cowl to his collection of stolen headwear. Depicted as a kind of big-game hunter (complete with neckerchief and riding pants), this Hatter inspired the character's first screen appearances—the 1966 *Batman* TV series episodes "The Thirteenth Hat"/"Batman Stands Pat" and "The Contaminated Cowl"/"The Mad Hatter Runs Afoul." Here, the character was played by Broadway star David

Wayne, in a top hat equipped with a mind-control device, with which he tried to steal Batman's cowl.

The Mad Hatter first appeared in animated form in an episode of Filmation's 1968 *The Batman/Superman Hour* ("A Mad, Mad Tea Party") in which he's voiced, like most of the show's characters, by Ted Knight.

The original Mad Hatter returned decades later (in January 1982's *Detective Comics* #510), and disposed of his cowl-fixated successor, whom he revealed as an impostor. In his next appearance, in *Detective Comics* #526, the Hatter uses his TV counterpart's mind-control gimmick.

Since then, the Hatter's unusually large head has been explained as the result of macrocephaly, and his modus operandi has reflected his obsession with *Alice in Wonderland*, wonderfully realized on screen in the 1992 *Batman: The Animated Series* episode "Mad as a Hatter." Written by Paul Dini, the episode features a sublime Roddy McDowall (who played the 1966 series' villainous Bookworm) as the voice of Tetch. In this incarnation, the character is a Wayne Industries scientist obsessed with a co-worker named Alice. When she rejects his advances, he kidnaps her with his mind-control technology. "I've waited my whole lonely life for her!" he tells the Dark Knight. "Then all you've waited for is a puppet," says Batman. "A soulless little doll."

Peter MacNicol and Benedict Samuel play Tetch in, respectively, the *Batman: Arkham* video game and TV's *Gotham*.

"Will you, won't you, will you, won't you, will you join the dance?" asks *The Animated Series*' Mad Hatter, quoting his favorite author. For almost 70 years, he's made the invitation a tempting one for Batfans.

97 TV's *The Batman*

As magnificent as 1992's *Batman: The Animated Series* and the DC Animated Universe it spawned were, there was a downside to their success—they cast a long shadow on whatever animated series would follow them. Few fans would hold 2004's *The Batman* in higher regard than its predecessors, but there's enough of interest in creators Michael Goguen and Duane Capizzi's interpretation of the Bat mythos to please devotees.

Designed by Jeff Matsuda, who'd previously worked on TV's *Jackie Chan Adventures*, *The Batman*'s characters are the most off-model of any screen version of Gotham's heroes and villains—with its Joker sporting dreadlocks, its Riddler a lanky Goth, and its Penguin an orange-haired martial arts master. The anime-influenced look may have been just a bit too outrageous for some. But folks were also irked by the fact that the DCAU's beloved *Justice League Unlimited*, still in production when *The Batman* debuted, was forbidden from using most of the Dark Knight's rogues gallery, since a "Bat-embargo" reserved them for the new series, while *Batman Begins* made the Scarecrow and Ra's Al Ghul unavailable to either show.

The quality of *The Batman*'s animation, however, is consistently excellent, the result of a single studio, Korea's Dong-Woo, handling all five seasons of the show. Its action sequences benefit most from the consistency, punctuated by the Dark Knight's liquid-like cape, as expressive here as in the comics of artists Norm Breyfogle or Kelley Jones.

The show sounds great, too, with Seasons 1 and 2 offering moody theme music composed by U2's The Edge. In these early seasons, Batman (voiced by Rino Romano) is hunted by and then

Launched in 2004, the animated series The Batman *was initially dismissed as merely a vehicle for creating merchandise. Over time, however, the episodes featured many imaginative takes on the Dark Knight's adventures.*

allied with two original characters—Gotham City police detectives Ellen Yin (voiced by *Agents of S.H.I.E.L.D.*'s Ming-Na Wen) and Ethan Bennett (Steven Harris). Bennett's also a friend of Bruce Wayne's, which leads to complications, particularly when he becomes the series' first Clayface (in a story arc reminiscent of Harvey Dent's transition to Two-Face). Rounding out the cast are Alfred Pennyworth (Alastair Duncan) and, in Season 2, Commissioner Gordon (*The X-Files*' Mitch Pileggi), as well as another original creation, gruff Chief of Police Angel Rojas (Jesse Corti). That the three newcomers are each of a different ethnicity—the first regular minority characters in a Batman TV show—shows the progress American television had made in representation, even if the series' adrenaline-fueled stories aimed at younger audiences left limited room for the kind of rich characterizations that distinguished *Batman: The Animated Series. The Batman*'s villains were defined more by their costumes and abilities than their psychology.

The Edge's music was replaced in Season 3 by Andy Sturmer's jazz theme, reminiscent of the 1966 *Batman* series, and Yin and Rojas left. But the show improved with the addition of Batgirl (voiced by Danielle Judovits). A replacement for Robin—then appearing in TV's *Teen Titans*—Barbara Gordon is given an arc in which she must prove herself worthy of being Batman's partner. Her eventual triumph, and Hugo Strange's emergence as Gotham's top villain, leads to the show's best season, its fourth, which saw *BTAS*' Alan Burnett sign on as producer.

Season 4 at last introduced Dick Grayson's Robin (Evan Sabara), in a fun rivalry with Barbara. It also yielded the fan-favorite, far-future episode "Artifacts" (which references *The Dark Knight Returns*) and the excellent "Strange New World," in which everyone in Gotham is seemingly turned into a zombie. Best of all was Season 4's redesigned Bruce Wayne, finally given the lantern jaw the Dark Knight deserves. The season finale brought on the Justice League, the members of which reappeared throughout Season 5, by which time Batgirl and Commissioner Gordon's roles were reduced.

The Batman was successful enough to generate a direct-to-DVD animated movie, 2005's *The Batman vs. Dracula*, along with a monthly spinoff comic book, *The Batman Strikes!*, which ran for 50 issues. The show received six Daytime Emmy Awards, and was nominated for six more, including two for Kevin Michael Richardson's performance as the Joker (the first time an African American actor had played the role).

Jarring at first in its departures (and initially accused by critics of existing primarily to sell toys), *The Batman* nonetheless emerged as an intriguing alternative take on the Dark Knight's world, one that further demonstrated its visual potential on screen.

98 Answer the Batphone

When Commissioner Gordon calls, the best place to answer is at Geppi's Entertainment Museum. Located at 301 W. Camden Street in Baltimore, Maryland (in Camden Station, on the second floor of Camden Yards), the museum houses approximately 60,000 pop culture artifacts from comic books, newspaper strips, radio, film, and television. All of which have chronicled the adventures of the Batman.

Start your Bat-centric visit in the standing gallery "A Story in Four Colors." There you'll find on display a near-mint copy of the Caped Crusader's very first appearance, in May 1939's *Detective Comics* #27. Numerous other key Batman comics can be found in this gallery, as well as titles featuring DC Comics' other heroes, and those of Marvel Comics.

The Dark Knight dominates another gallery down the hall—"Revolution." This room is devoted to the 1960s, when Batmania first swept the nation, and the 1970s. Here, you'll see a massive statue of Batman watching over his city atop a rooftop, the Gotham skyline behind him. In front of this statue sits the bright red Batphone, the receiver of which you can lift to hear the commissioner's voice. Next to the phone you'll see a familiar bust of William Shakespeare, the head of which you can tilt back as you prepare to slide down the Batpole. The Bat-Signal projects the Bat symbol across this room to complete the effect. It makes for a great photo.

On both sides of the statue are display cases filled with vintage Batman merchandise, including card games, masks, night-lights, napkins, pencil boxes, puppets, and, of course, plenty of toy

Batmobiles. Additional Batman items can be found in neighboring display cases devoted to a variety of superheroes.

Before leaving the museum, be sure to scan the walls for Batman movie posters and original art. And don't forget to hit the museum's gift shop for a variety of contemporary Batman items.

Tip: planning a trip to Baltimore to visit Geppi's Entertainment Museum? Consider going during the city's annual Baltimore Comic-Con. It's held every autumn at the Baltimore Convention Center, just across the street from the museum.

99 TV's *Gotham*

Could a Batman TV show work *without* Batman? Is the spirit of the Bat so strong it could infuse an entire series sans Dark Knight? Those questions are answered by *Gotham*.

After *Smallville* ended its 10-season run in 2011, Warner Brothers returned to an idea from which the Superman prequel show had evolved—a series centered around Bruce Wayne in the years before he became Batman. Bruno Heller, the creator of *Rome* and *The Mentalist*, discussed with the studio the idea of focusing such a show on young police detective James Gordon's investigations, starting with the murders of Thomas and Martha Wayne. From that sprung a one-hour drama that incorporated most of the Batman's nascent rogues gallery.

Gotham's first season, which premiered September 22, 2014, pairs Gordon (played by *The O.C.*'s Ben McKenzie) with an initially corrupt Harvey Bullock (Donal Logue) at a GCPD under the thumb of mob boss Carmine Falcone (John Doman). It offers viewers a piece of Batman history seldom seen, as young Bruce

The television series Gotham, *which premiered in 2014, features a young Jim Gordon and an even younger Bruce Wayne.*

(David Mazouz) wrestles with his parents' deaths with the help of his legal guardian and manservant Alfred Pennyworth (Sean Pertwee). Complicating their lives are burgeoning crime lord Oswald Cobblepot (aka the Penguin, played by scene-stealing Robin Lord Taylor), teen street urchin Selina "Cat" Kyle (Camren Bicondova), disturbed forensic scientist Edward Nygma (Cory Michael Smith), and a new character, club owner and mobster Fish Mooney (Jada Pinkett Smith). Breaking from tradition, Gordon's lady love Barbara Kean (Erin Richards) goes gleefully insane by season's end, opening the door for another romantic partner, Arkham Asylum physician Leslie Thompkins (*Deadpool*'s Morena Baccarin).

An overreliance on criminal-of-the-week procedural stories and a tone that veers erratically—between the 1966 *Batman* show's camp and the urban operatics of Christopher Nolan's film trilogy—hampers that first season. But the Penguin's rise to power as he manipulates the police, Mooney, Falcone, and rival mob boss Salvatore Maroni

(David Zayas) is compelling stuff. *Gotham* has found more consistent footing over time. The sprightlier second season is divided into two halves. "Rise of the Villains" brings in fan-favorite comic characters Silver St. Cloud (Natalie Alyn Lind) and the Order of St. Dumas, while expanding the role of Wayne Enterprises' Lucius Fox (Chris Chalk), as our heroes confront a crooked mayoral campaign. The second half, "Wrath of the Villains," introduces Victor Fries (Nathan Darrow), a new take on antihero Azrael (James Frain), and the nefarious Hugo Strange (BD Wong).

In Season 3's first half, the show hit its stride as a macabre soap opera, played out against the machinations of the Court of Owls. "Mad City" introduces Jervis Tetch (Benedict Samuel) and finds Cobblepot falling in love with Nygma. And *Gotham*'s potential Joker, the psychopathic Jerome Valeska (Cameron Monaghan), emerges as a key player, leading to Bruce beating him senseless. Fortunately, Bruce stops himself from killing Jerome. Gordon hasn't always exhibited such restraint, with *Gotham*'s greatest point of controversy his execution of a criminal.

It might be disillusioning for longtime Batfans to watch the city's bastion of virtue learn his lessons the hard way, but *Gotham* is a world without heroes. A world that, with each episode, cries louder for a Dark Knight.

"We're telling the story of the education of a young boy and the story of the education of a young policeman," says Heller. "Everything else that happens, it happens to support that…For the real DC fans we try to put in little indications that we know where we're going and what we're doing; and we do love that world and we'll always pay attention to that mythology. If we start drifting too far away from it and thinking that we know better than the great history of DC, we'd be making a mistake. We've got to try and be fresh and original, but we have to always remember that we're dealing with *the* great American myth."

100 Batman v Superman: Dawn of Justice

However one feels about *Batman v Superman: Dawn of Justice*—and to say the film polarized superhero fans upon its release is putting it mildly—it's remarkable that the big-screen's first pairing of the world's two most iconic superheroes took so long to arrive. In print, Batman first met Superman in 1952's *Superman* #76, and on radio they'd shared adventures since 1945. So when director Zack Snyder's $250 million team-up arrived in theaters in March of 2016, it was past due in every regard.

Not that audiences resented the wait. The film took in almost $900 million in worldwide box office, buoyed not only by the Dark Knight, played for the first time by Ben Affleck, and the Big Blue Boy Scout (returning *Man of Steel* star Henry Cavill), but by the first feature-film appearance of their longtime teammate Wonder Woman, gamely portrayed by Gal Gadot. Intended as the cornerstone of the DC Extended Universe, the film also offered teasing glimpses of the Flash, Aquaman, and Cyborg—and served as a lead-in to 2017's *Justice League*, which unites all six heroes.

Many fans, however, were put off by what they saw as an overeager attempt at creating a shared cinematic universe like that carefully developed by Marvel over the course of numerous films; others found the movie's relentlessly dour tone uninviting. *Batman v Superman* incorporates elements from two of the most successful stories in DC Comics history—1986's *The Dark Knight Returns* (including the comic's armored Batsuit in its title bout) and 1992's *The Death of Superman* (in the Man of Steel's fatal battle with Doomsday)—but its seismic events are curiously unmoving, the result of a convoluted script (by Chris Terrio and David S. Goyer) and, in its original theatrical version, disjointed editing and direction by Snyder. Prior to helming 2013's *Man of Steel*, Snyder had admitted to disliking traditional superhero comics in favor of the sex and violence portrayed in *Heavy Metal* magazine. In a July 17, 2008, interview with *Entertainment Weekly* promoting his *Watchmen* movie, the filmmaker had said of Christopher Nolan's *Batman Begins* that Batman "gets to go to a Tibetan monastery and be trained by ninjas. Okay? I want to do that. But he doesn't, like, get raped in prison. That could happen in my movie. If you want to talk about dark, that's how that would go."

There's plenty of darkness in *Dawn of Justice*. But none of it is presented with the humor writer-artist Frank Miller brought to *The Dark Knight Returns* or the intelligence Nolan brought to his trilogy. Much of it goes against the core character of Batman as established over 77 years of comics. Here, Bruce Wayne not only wields guns but brands the criminals he catches (leading to their murder in prison). The lesson he ultimately learns—that, however frightened he might be of the power he wields, he shouldn't kill Superman—is one fans have understood since they were small children.

Few children would see *Batman v Superman* in its more coherently edited "Ultimate Edition" on home video, the first film featuring either character to earn an R rating. Yet in both its theatrical and home video releases, their actions are so motivated by fear, anger, and sadness that there's little trace of the nobility that makes them icons. A smarter, more satisfying take on their first meeting, one suitable for all ages, can be found in the 1997 three-part "World's Finest" episode of *Superman: The Animated Series*.

Story, characterization, and tonal problems aside, the beefy, lantern-jawed Affleck looks more like Batman than any actor who's played him on screen. His performance is an earnest one (even if he can't match the range of his predecessor Christian Bale). So there's no reason to think Affleck *can't* anchor a solid film about the Dark Knight, provided he has the chance to do so. As Bruce Wayne tells Diana Prince at the end of *Batman v Superman*, "We can do better. We have to."

Acknowledgments

Triumph Books' Adam Motin, Josh Williams, Sam Ofman, Andrea Baird, and Michelle Green are the best team in the business. They deserve all the credit in the world for making this book possible.

My additional thanks to stalwart Bat supporters Ed Burns, Patrick Killoran, Rich Rissmiller, David Angwin, Eric Cheung, Jeremy Meyer, Rebecca Compton, Matthew Budman, Cristina Beltran, Darrell Schweitzer, Jon B. Cooke, Yvonne Jones, Jeff Victor, Jami Philbrick, Heather Newgen, Scott Huver, Tony and Melinda Ruben Liberatore, James White, Silas Lesnick, Adam and Erin Sorensen, Jennifer Heddle, Charlotte Martyn, Brian Walton, Sandy and Tony Darin, Mark and Carol Wheatley, Marc Hempel, Mark Buckingham, Irma Page, Dave Stannard, Tatjana Babić, Dave Bradley, Ade Hill, Will Salmon, Rachel Heine, Dan Casey, Jane Wilson, Dave Severine, Katrin Biemann, Dominic Corry, Tammy Smithers, Jenni Frazer, Heidi Petre, Alex and Jason Schultz, Lin Workman, Eddy Zeno, Phil Pirrello, Jess Nevins, Neil Gaiman, Lesley Aletter, Marjorie Kase, Mark Waid, Bob Ficarra, Gary Miereanu, Brandy Phillips, Patty Medina, Jessica Tseang, Brianna Bricker, Chrysafis Andreou, Mac and Dinah Larson McLean, Gill Pringle, Phil Pirrello, Morgan Jeffery, and Marc Tyler Nobleman.

Further gratitude to the Santa Barbara Bat bunch: Ted White, Ashleigh Lynch, Erin Travers, Seth Meeker, J.V. and Suzanne Decemvirale, Aleesa Alexander, Gavin Hartnett, Diva Zumaya, Sam Frankeberger, Maggie Bell, James Brugger, Faye Fong, Amit Vainsencher, Laura and Gere DiZerega, Rachel Johnson, Jeff Baker, Ana Mitrovici, Justin Carey, Marta Faust, Thomas DePasquale, Teresiana Matarrese, Miguel Lastras, and Anylú Pérez Tapia.

To the old friends who lent support via social media: Meredith McGinn, Lynne Curry Einbinder, Kristin Suess Donaldson, Stephanie Farrelly, Stephanie Mullen, and Gina Maria.

To my Future Publishing family: Rich Edwards, Nick Setchfield, Ian Berriman, Jonathan Coates, Catherine Kirkpatrick, Jane Crowther, Matt Maytum, Matthew Leyland, Jordan Farley, Rosie Fletcher, Jen Neal, and Lauren O'Callaghan.

And to my family: Joan Marie McCabe (née Maguire) and Joseph Francis McCabe; and Jeanne, Jim, and John McCabe. As well as the entire Quach family.

My deepest thanks to the love of my life, my wife, Sophia Quach McCabe, who makes all things possible. And to everyone in this book who allowed me to interview them, most especially Paul Dini, as great a gentleman as he is a writer.

Finally…thanks to Bill Finger and Bob Kane, for brightening the world with their Dark Knight.

Bibliography

Augustyn, Brian, and Michael Mignola. *Batman: Gotham by Gaslight*. New York: DC Comics, 2013.

Barr, Mike, et al. *Batman and the Outsiders*. Burbank, CA: DC Comics, 2017.

Batgirl: A Celebration of 50 Years. Burbank, CA: DC Comics, 2017.

Batman & Superman in World's Finest, The Silver Age Omnibus. Volume 1. Burbank, CA: DC Comics, 2016.

Batman: Archives, Volume 1. New York: DC Comics, 1997.

Batman: Archives, Volume 2. New York: DC Comics, 1997.

Batman: Archives, Volume 3. New York: DC Comics, 1997.

Batman: Archives, Volume 4. New York: DC Comics, 1998.

Batman: Archives, Volume 5. New York: DC Comics, 2001.

Batman Arkham: Killer Croc. New York: DC Comics, 2016.

Batman Arkham: Man-Bat. Burbank, CA: DC Comics, 2017.

Batman Arkham: Mister Freeze. Burbank, CA: DC Comics, 2017.

Batman Arkham: Poison Ivy. New York: DC Comics, 2016.

Batman Arkham: Scarecrow. New York: DC Comics, 2016.

Batman Arkham: The Riddler. New York: DC Comics, 2015.

Batman Arkham: Two-Face. New York: DC Comics, 2015.

Batman: Featuring Two-Face and the Riddler. New York: DC Comics, 1995.

Batman: Knightfall Omnibus Volume 1. Burbank, CA: DC Comics, 2017.

Batman: Knightfall Omnibus Volume 2: Knightquest. Burbank, CA: DC Comics, 2017.

Batman: The Brave and the Bold: The Bronze Age Omnibus Volume 1. Burbank, CA: DC Comics, 2017.

Batman: The Dailies, 1943–1946. New York: Sterling Publishing, 2007.

Batman: The Dark Knight Archives, Volume 1. New York: DC Comics, 1992.

Batman: The Dark Knight Archives, Volume 2. New York: DC Comics, 1997.

Batman: The Dark Knight Archives, Volume 3. New York: DC Comics, 2000.

Batman: The Dark Knight Archives, Volume 4. New York: DC Comics, 2003.

Batman: The Dark Knight Archives, Volume 5. New York: DC Comics, 2006.

Batman: The Sunday Classics, 1943–1946. New York: Sterling Publishing, 2007.

Bigley, Al. *Big Glee! The Albert Bryan Bigley Archives*. bigglee.blogspot.co.uk.

Brennert, Alan. *Tales of the Batman: Alan Brennert*. Burbank, CA: DC Comics, 2016.

Brubaker, Ed, and Greg Rucka. *Gotham Central Omnibus*. New York: DC Comics, 2016.

Carlin, Mike, ed. *Batman in the Seventies*. New York: DC Comics, 1999.

Catwoman: Nine Lives of a Feline Fatale. New York: DC Comics, 2004.

Clarke, Frederick S, ed. *Cinefantastique* 24/25 (February 1994).

Colan, Gene. *Tales of the Batman: Gene Colan, Volume One*. New York: DC Comics, 2011.

Comic Vine. CBS Interactive Inc., comicvine.com.

Daniels, Les. *Batman: The Complete History*. San Francisco: Chronicle Books, 1999.

_____. *DC Comics: Sixty Years of the World's Favorite Super Heroes*. Boston: Little, Brown, 1995.

Davis, Alan. *Legends of the Dark Knight: Alan Davis*. New York: DC Comics, 2013.

DC Comics Database. Fandom by Wikia, dc.wikia.com/wiki/DC_Comics_Database.

Didio, Dan, ed. *Batman in the Sixties*. New York: DC Comics, 1999.

_____. *Batman in the Forties*. New York: DC Comics, 2004.

_____. *Batman in the Fifties*. New York: DC Comics, 2004.

_____. *Batman in the Eighties*. New York: DC Comics, 2004.

Dini, Paul, and Chip Kidd. *Batman Animated*. New York: HarperCollins, 1998.

Dini, Paul, and Alex Ross. *Batman: War on Crime*. New York: DC Comics, 1999.

Dini, Paul, and Eduardo Risso. *Dark Night: A True Batman Story*. New York: Vertigo, 2016.

Dini, Paul, and Bruce Timm. *The Batman Adventures: Mad Love Deluxe Edition*. New York: DC Comics, 2015.

Englehart, Steve, et al. *Batman: Strange Apparitions*. New York: DC Comics, 1999.

Eury, Michael, and Michael Kronenberg. *The Batcave Companion*. Raleigh, NC: TwoMorrows Publishing, 2009.

Fleisher, Michael L. *The Encyclopedia of Comic Book Heroes, Volume 1: Batman*. New York: Macmillan, 1976.

Garcia, Robert T., and Joe Desris. *Batman: A Celebration of the Classic TV Series*. First edition. London: Titan Books, 2016.

Giordano, Dick, ed. *The Greatest Batman Stories Ever Told*. New York: DC Comics, 1988.

_____. *The Greatest Batman Stories Ever Told. Volume 2*. New York: DC Comics, 1992.

Goodwin, Archie. *Tales of the Batman: Archie Goodwin*. New York: DC Comics, 2013.

Breyfogle, Norm. *Legends of the Dark Knight: Norm Breyfogle Vol. 1*. New York: DC Comics, 2015.

Greenberger, Robert. *The Essential Batman Encyclopedia*. New York: Del Rey/DC/Ballantine Books, 2012.

Greenfield, Dan and Cliff Galbraith. *13th Dimension*. 13thdimension.com.

Infantino, Carmine. *Tales of the Batman: Carmine Infantino*. New York: DC Comics, 2014.

Jesser, Jody Duncan, and Janine Pourroy. *The Art and Making of the Dark Knight Trilogy*. New York: Abrams, 2012.

Kraft, David Anthony, ed. *Batman: Comics Interview Super Special*. New York: Fictioneer Books Ltd., 1989.

Levitz, Paul and Joe Staton. *Huntress: Dark Knight Daughter*. New York: DC Comics, 2006.

Levitz, Paul. *The Little Book of Batman*. Cologne, Germany: Taschen, 2015.

Loeb, Jeph, and Jim Lee. *Batman: Hush*. New York: DC Comics, 2012.

Loeb, Jeph, and Tim Sale. *Batman: The Long Halloween*. New York: DC Comics, 2011.

Miller, Frank, and David Mazzucchelli. *Batman: Year One*. New York: DC Comics, 1987.

Miller, Frank. *Batman, The Dark Knight Returns: 30th Anniversary Edition*. Burbank, CA: DC Comics, 2016.

Moore, Alan, and Brian Bolland. *Batman: The Killing Joke*. New York: DC Comics, 2012.

Morrison, Grant, Chris Burnham, and Yanick Paquette. *Absolute Batman, Incorporated*. New York: DC Comics, 2015.

Morrison, Grant, et al. *Absolute Batman & Robin: Batman Reborn*. New York: DC Comics, 2012.

Morrison, Grant and Andy Kubert. *Batman and Son*. New York: DC Comics, 2008.

Morrison, Grant, and Tony S. Daniel. *Batman R.I.P.* New York: DC Comics, 2010.

Morrison, Grant, et al. *Batman: The Return of Bruce Wayne*. New York: DC Comics, 2011.

_____. *Batman: Time and the Batman*. New York: DC Comics, 2012.

Nobleman, Marc Tyler, and Ty Templeton. *Bill the Boy Wonder: The Secret Co-Creator of Batman*. Watertown, MA: Charlesbridge, 2012.

O'Neil, Dennis, et al. *Batman: Tales of the Demon*. New York, NY: DC Comics, 1991.

Reed, Robby. *Dial B for Blog*. dialbforblog.com.

Smith, Kevin, and Marc Bernardin. *Fat Man on Batman*. SModcast Podcast Network, soundcloud.com/fatmanonbatman.

Snider, Brandon T. *The Dark Knight Manual: Tools, Weapons, Vehicles & Documents from the Batcave*. San Rafael, CA: Insight Editions, 2012.

Snyder, Scott, and Greg Capullo. *Batman. Volume 1, The Court of Owls*. New York: DC Comics, 2012.

_____. *Batman. Volume 2, The City of Owls*. New York: DC Comics, 2013.

Snyder, Scott, Jock, and Francesco Francavilla. *Batman: The Black Mirror*. New York: DC Comics, 2013.

Batman Collected. First edition. Boston: Bulfinch, 1996.

Spear, Geoff and Chip Kidd. *Stacked Deck: The Greatest Joker Stories Ever Told*. Stamford, CT: Longmeadow Press, 1990.

Starlin, Jim, and Jim Aparo. *Batman: A Death in the Family*. New York: DC Comics, 1988.

Rucka, Greg, and J. H. Williams. *Batwoman: Elegy*. New York: DC Comics, 2010.

Thomas, Roy, ed. "The Bat-Spotlight Falls on Dick Sprang." *Altar Ego* 19 (December 2002).

The Worldwide Guide to Movie Locations. movie-locations.com.

Wein, Len and José Luis García-López. "Batman vs. The Incredible Hulk." *DC Special Series* 27. New York: DC Comics/Marvel, 1981.

Wein, Len. *Tales of the Batman: Len Wein*. New York: DC Comics, 2014.

Williams, J. H, and W. Haden Blackman. *Batwoman: Hydrology Volume 1*. New York: DC Comics, 2012.